Chaucer's England

LITERATURE IN HISTORICAL CONTEXT

Barbara A. Hanawalt, editor

Medieval Studies at Minnesota, Volume 4

University of Minnesota Press
Minneapolis

The University of Minnesota Press gratefully acknowledges assistance provided for the publication of this book by the Carl D. Sheppard Fund.

Published by the University of Minnesota Press
2037 University Avenue Southeast, Minneapolis, MN 55414

Printed in the United States of America on acid-free paper

Library of Congress Cataloging-in-Publication Data

Chaucer's England: literature in historical context/ [compiled by] Barbara A.
    Hanawalt
        p. cm.—(Medieval studies at Minnesota; v. 4)
        Includes index.
        ISBN 0-8166-2019-9 (hc)
        ISBN 0-8166-2020-2 (pb)
1. Chaucer, Geoffrey, d. 1400—Contemporary England. 2. English
literature—Middle English, 1100-1500—History and criticism.
3. England—Civilization—Medieval period, 1066-1485. 4. Great
Britain—History—14th century. 5. Literature and society—England.
I. Hanawalt, Barbara. II. Series.
PR1906.5.C48   1992
820.9'001—dc20
                                                                91-12381
                                                                CIP

Chaucer's England

Medieval Studies at Minnesota

Published in cooperation with the Center for Medieval Studies,
University of Minnesota

Volume 4   Edited by Barbara A. Hanawalt
Chaucer's England: Literature in Historical Context

Volume 3   Edited by Marilyn J. Chiat and Kathryn L. Reyerson
The Medieval Mediterranean: Cross-Cultural Contacts

Volume 2   Edited by Andrew MacLeish
The Medieval Monastery

Volume 1   Edited by Kathryn Reyerson and Faye Powe
The Medieval Castle

Contents

✣

Part III. Literature of the Countryside

Abbreviations
✥

Anonimalle	*Anonimalle Chronicle* ed. V. H. Galbraith (Manchester, 1970)
BIHR	*Bulletin of the Institute for Historical Research*
CLR	*Chaucer Life-Records* ed. M. Crowe and C. Olson (Austin, Tex., 1966)
Cotton Julius B II (in Kingsford)	MS Cotton Julius B II in *Chronicles of London* ed. C. L. Kingsford (Oxford, 1905)
EETS	Early English Text Society
EngHR	*English Historical Review*
Eulogium	*Eulogium Historium sive Temporis* ed. F. S. Haydon 3 vols., Rolls Series (London, 1858-63)
Hardyng, *Chronicle*	John Hardyng *Chronicle* ed. Henry Ellis (1812, rpt. 1974)
Knighton, *Chronicon*	Henry Knighton *Chronicon* ed. J. R. Lumby 2 vols., Rolls Series (London, 1889-95)

Letter Books	*Calendar of Letter Books A-L, 1275-1498* ed. Reginald R. Sharpe 11 vols. (London, 1899-1912)
Malory, *Works*	Sir Thomas Malory *The Works* ed. Eugéne Vinaver 2nd ed., 3 vols. (Oxford, 1973)
MED	*Middle English Dictionary* ed. Hans Kurath et al. (Ann Arbor, Mich., 1965–)
PMLA	*Publications of the Modern Language Association*
RS	Rolls Series
Rymes, ed. Dobson and Taylor	*Rymes of Robyn Hoode* ed. R. B. Dobson and J. Taylor (London, 1976)
TRHS	*Transactions of the Royal Historical Society*

Preface

✛

M uch of the pleasure one derives from scholarly pursuits comes from the serendipity of events. The genesis of this volume grew out of an invitation from Lee Patterson to give a talk at *Duke* for a special issue of the *Journal of Medieval and Renaissance Studies*. In the course of my visit, during which I spoke on poaching and included literary evidence, I came to know about the "new historicism." It was exciting. My former colleagues at Indiana University, Lawrence Clopper and Paul Strohm, had been valued intellectual companions, and we had often discussed the problems of interpretation, particularly the overlap of literary and historical interpretation. Now Lee Patterson contributed a new dimension to our discussions. When the College of Liberal Arts at the University of Minnesota generously gave the Medieval Studies Center a fund to explore appointments in medieval English literature, Kathryn Reyerson asked if I would give some thought to an appropriate topic that would fit under a medieval studies rubric. I immediately thought about the possibilities of a colloquium series that would bring together literary scholars and historians who work on late medieval English literature and society. A second goal was to bring together in one volume the essays of both English and American scholars. Considering that we are united by a common language, the Atlantic has proved to be a surprising intellectual barrier. The lecture series was very exciting for the audience who heard all ten talks and especially for me. During the course of several months medievalists, both faculty and students, on the University of Minnesota campus enjoyed the intensity of discussion that is central to the stimulation of university life. The regret for the speakers was that it had not been a workshop in which they too could have heard and discussed all of the papers. This volume brings to the participants and the wider intellectual community the excitement that we at the University of Minnesota shared in the winter of our great content in 1990. We are all grateful to the College of Liberal Arts and to Kathryn Reyerson, Director of the Medieval Studies Center at the University of Minnesota, for making the colloquium series and now the volume possible. The editorial assistance of Elizabeth Dachowski and Alice Klingener greatly facilitated the grace of the volume.

B.A.H.

Introduction

✤

Barbara A. Hanawalt

The intersection of history and literature is hardly a new endeavor for scholars of the historical and literary fields, but independent developments in both has made possible a fruitful, new interdisciplinary approach. In the past, scholars ventured into each other's territory as primitive raiders. Langland and Chaucer experts poached from standard historical works or collections of printed documents and gleefully incorporated their trophies in biographies of Chaucer or books about Chaucer's London. No less unprincipled were the historical savages who purported to write social history on the basis of "facts" raided from the fiction of Chaucer and Langland. I will not attempt to chronicle this past period of tribal infringements on the hunting ground of the other discipline, for that has already been done with thoroughness and wit (Lee Patterson, *Negotiating the Past: The Historical Understanding of Medieval Literature* [Madison, Wis., 1987]). Rather, I will seek to demonstrate, through discussing the essays in this volume, the change in interpretation that has resulted from the development of serious social history inquiry in my tribe and the application of techniques of literary analysis to historical materials in the literary tribe.

The branching out of historical inquiry into previously unused archival records has permitted historians to begin a reconstruction of late medieval social history that provides a richer understanding of the context in which authors wrote. Thanks to the work of the historians in this volume, among others, we now know a great deal about the peasantry, the gentry and their country culture, education, urban life, and crime. As we know more about these and other aspects of late medieval life, the literature that the society produced takes on richer meaning. Rather than the circular arguments of the past in which Chaucer was used to inform social historians about the society of his day, the historians in this volume have developed their perception of society based on historical inquiry. Knowing the historical situation intimately, they have then looked again at the literature to find echoes of social realities in the texts. Thus Nicholas Orme has analyzed the manuals on hunting and then looked at the role that hunting scenes play in the literature.

On the side of the specialists in English literature there has also been a major change, sometimes bearing the label of the "new historicism" or the "new philology." I will not emphasize either term here, partly because I do not feel competent to discuss the theoretical implications of the terms and partly because the contributors tended, when asked, to say that they were doing what good scholars had always done or should have been doing. Whatever the label, this new endeavor includes both a careful textual reading of the literature combined with an equally careful textual reading of historical sources. In trying to gain a greater understanding of the traditional great literary pieces, the authors also read literature outside the canon as well as some of the same sorts of record sources that social historians have been reading. The result is a greater appreciation for the subtleties of all the texts. Susan Crane's analysis of the Peasants' Revolt of 1381, for instance, leads her to a greater understanding of the raucous voice of the Wife of Bath.

The enrichment of interpretation for both disciplines comes across in the reading of these essays. In this introduction I will pull out some of the interpretational strategies that make this volume such an exciting contribution to the study of literature in the historical context. While all of the essays combine literary and historical materials to demonstrate how the historical context influenced the development of literary work, many of them also make use of various methodologies to bring out a richer understanding of the material. Crane uses anthropology very effectively to investigate the meaning of writing itself. Wallace borrows from the discipline of geography to compare spatial relations in London and Florence. Hanawalt and Bennett borrow methodologies from sociology. Hanawalt uses a model of organized crime developed by criminologists to investigate the Robin Hood ballads, while Bennett uses prosopographical techniques to study both patrons and audience. Both Strohm and Green add reflective discussions on the limitations of disciplinary crossover. And Wallace reminds us of the value of comparative study. Thus many of the essays in this volume move interdisciplinarity beyond merely linking historical and literary approaches to texts.

The essays fall naturally into three groups. The first set provides the reader with the political context of that great flourishing of vernacular literature in the latter part of the fourteenth century. The second moves the action into the capital, London, with its own particular politics. Finally, the events and literature of the rather violent countryside occupy the third section.

The Political Context

One could have no better essay than Michael Bennett's on "The Court of Richard II and the Promotion of Literature" to set the stage for this volume. It was during the reign of Richard II that English vernacular literature came into prominence, and the eloquence reached then did not linger after that monarch's death into the fifteenth century. While recent scholarship has tended to shift the focus away from Richard and his court and look at urban and rural contexts for the revolution in literature, Bennett makes a strong argument for the impact of Richard. It is an argument of circumstantial evidence, since the chamber accounts, which would record patronage, are missing and Bolingbroke's coup produced such an anxiety about instability that much writing and many physical objects that would have left testimony to Richard's tastes and influence were destroyed. The case, therefore, rests on the type of court that Richard, in his mature years, put together and on an analysis of Richard's cultural preferences. The court was one in which great poets apparently found audiences (of women as well as men), made contact with other authors, and perhaps even received some patronage from Richard. His personal tastes ran to an interest in his lineage, saints, illustrated books, and beautiful objects. But even Richard destroyed evidence of his cultural consumption, for, in grief over the loss of his queen, he destroyed their residence in Sheen.

Bennett is able to make a convincing case because of his own detailed study of the social and cultural milieu of the northwest Midlands. This area, which produced *Sir Gawain and the Green Knight* and *The Pearl*, was also one in which Richard spent time in 1387 and 1398-99 in an effort to find support among its people. The Cheshire notables all had close ties with the court in these last years of the reign. Richard was vacillating in his political patronage and may also have been in his literary support, but it seems unlikely, Bennett concludes, that he had nothing to do with establishing the tradition of English vernacular literature.

Paul Strohm's essay, "Saving the Appearances: Chaucer's *Purse* and the Fabrication of the Lancastrian Claim," takes us naturally to a transition from the reign of Richard to that of Henry. It shows us, along the way, what a consummate courtier Chaucer had become during his years around Richard's court and thereby lends credence to Bennett's arguments. Strohm builds his textual analysis with subtlety, looking at the various arguments and rationalizations that Henry or his supporters put forth to justify his own ascendancy and the overthrow of Richard. In modern parlance, the advisers floated a number of trial balloons to see which would work best. The story, as it unfolds, also has a modern ring, with forged chronicles trying to make Henry's right by descent stronger. Henry argued for right by conquest or "I stole it fair and square," and pushed the idea that Richard preferred grace and the support of the clergy and people (*collaudatio*). Strohm then goes on to look at the textualization of Henry's claim, pointing out that the Lancastrians apparently comprehended that "a text can be powerful without being true."

In his plea for patronage, Chaucer distills three of the Lancastrian arguments into just over two lines. He makes the conquest more glorious by alluding to "Brutus Albyon" and also gives prominence to royal lineage and free election. Strohm's careful reading not only of Chaucer's text but also of the Lancastrian claims as texts gives us a clearer picture of the way in which medieval writers framed arguments in a style that convinced their audiences.

In an amusing and revealing postscript, Strohm shows how the trail of forgeries continued with a supposed "proclamation" that Chaucer was said to have used as a model. This "document" appeared in Robert Bell's 1854 edition of Chaucer and was perpetuated in Skeat even though the "proclamation" does not exist.

The court and country milieu that Bennett discussed in relationship to the northwest Midlands also plays a role in Nigel Saul's "Chaucer and Gentility." Few scholars could speak with such assurance on the topic of gentility as Nigel Saul, for he has written two remarkable, richly documented books on the gentry. As Saul points out, most "practitioners" of the gentle status in England gave little thought to a concept of gentility. Lineage and virtue were important for definition, but these categories, which appear to be so self-explanatory, needed further explanation. Lineage meant "ancient" family ties, but could a person be gentle by cultivating the fine manners and behavior that went with gentility? In Saul's essay, as in Wallace's, we see that the Italian influence is already becoming strong in late-fourteenth-century England. International trade, diplomacy, and travel were making Englishmen aware of an Italian grandeur that did not stem from noble blood running in the veins of long-established families but was evident in men of business with cultivated tastes. England was also beginning to see families in this category, so that a shift of definition was valuable.

Since Chaucer himself knew Italy and its authors, it is not surprising to find his concept of gentility tinged with the attributes of *virtu* and the qualities one expects of "gentle" behavior. The *Wife of Bath's Tale*, he finds, contains some of the most succinct definitions of gentle behavior, including the usual prescription of old wealth and lineage, but also a considerable discourse on "gentle behavior." The emphasis Chaucer places on behavior as the definer of gentility gives his outlook, as Saul argues, an "individualist quality." Saul is careful to point out that Chaucer's view is hardly original, and, bringing this section of the book to closure, he notes that the other writers in and around Richard's court were also writing on gentility with much the same concepts that Chaucer was using. Thus the collection of writers in the orbit of the court, with or without Richard's personal patronage, found a milieu and an audience for their work.

London as a Literary Setting

No city in England could approach London in size (probably 50,000 to 60,000 in the 1380s), in administrative importance as the seat of government, and in the wealth and magnificence of its citizens. One would expect London to play a major role in supplying material and even patrons for the poets who collected at the royal court. London drew men from all over the country as servants, apprentices, lawyers, administrators, guildsmen, clergy, beggars, and poets. It was a home for Chaucer and for Langland for a time. But when one comes to question the importance of London as a subject of literature or as a cultural center for the meeting of poets, the city is, as David Wallace points out, surprisingly absent.

In "Chaucer and the Absent City," Wallace explores the rich theater played out in the London streets and Guildhall, as it is recorded in the city's Letter Books. Those who cheated their customers by plying false wares or prostitutes who sold themselves were made public spectacles; rough music accompanied them to the pillory. Executions were public, as were the arbitrated settlements pledged before witnesses with wine. Charlatans duped the public and were caught. Apprentices broke their vows to their masters by rioting and visiting harlots. Chaucer's *Cook's Tale* and the *Canon's Yeoman's Tale* capture the flavor of this London low life, but the vision of a unified city is missing from *The Canterbury Tales*. The action even begins outside London, in Southwark, rather than in the city.

Wallace contrasts Chaucer's "plurality of discourses" about London with the concise view of city politics and society that Boccaccio presents in the story of Cisti the baker in *Decameron* (VI. 2). Cisti, while also a figure of humble status, is very aware of the politics of the city and the limitations that a man of his status has in influencing the course of events. But he uses this understanding, not in drunkenness and a world turned upside down, as the Cook and Yeoman do, but by turning drink into a sophisticated bridge for communication between social ranks. No such unified picture of London's society and politics appears in Chaucer or, for that matter, in Langland.

Wallace's essay makes a double contribution to the intersection of history and literature. Using the historical context and materials from the Letter Books, he brings greater meaning to Chaucer's characters and his language. He also challenges the historian to question whether or not there was a unified concept of a civic entity in London. London, based on its records, appears to be a collection of wards, guilds, parishes, masters and apprentices, conjugal families, and inns under the control of taverners such as Harry Bailey. If Harry Bailey has a hard time holding together and arbitrating the disputes among his company, the mayor of the City has an equally difficult time with his citizens. Wallace has effectively used the concept of absence rather than presence to enhance scholarly inquiry.

The London that Langland inhabited also shows us the low life of the city, but, as Caroline Barron has shown in "William Langland: A London Poet," it is a picture painted with poignancy and compassion rather than with humor. To Langland, who apparently lived on Cornhill in London, the monarch was a distant figure, but the mayor of London—as Barron points out, he is the only historical character to appear by name—has specific obligations that he should fulfill to make the lot of the London poor easier. He speaks of those same offenses that Wallace cites from the Letter Books, saying that if the mayor controlled such dishonesty the poor could cope better and the rich would not live in tall timbered houses that they built with their ill-gotten gains. But Langland also had sympathy for the merchants and guildsmen. They listened to his poems and perhaps gave him meals. He certainly knew among them many devout people who lived Christian lives. They were people who could be saved, although the poor would not have to work as hard as they for salvation.

The intimate view that Langland provides of London, in contrast to that of Chaucer, raises the question of who formed Langland's audience. One of the most common intersections of history and literature has been exactly this question of determining the audience for whom medieval authors wrote, be it the alliterative poets or the balladeers relating the exploits of Robin Hood. If we know more about the people that the writer had in mind as his readers or listeners, then it is easier to catch the nuances of the poems.

In the case of Langland's audience, Barron provides new information and reinterpretations of the evidence we have from wills and manuscript copies of *Piers Plowman*. We know that some of the manuscripts were in the hands of members of the higher clergy and merchant class, but a will and a manuscript reference indicate that his circle of readers and perhaps his gossips also came from a lower rank of Londoners. William Palmere, who left a copy of *Piers Plowman* in his will, was a learned clerk who owned other books as well, but he was not an exceedingly wealthy man. Barron has pursued the evidence that John But, who wrote a continuation of one Passus, making sure that Will got credit for his poem, was a king's messenger. His will indicates a man of modest means from the same region of the country as Langland. Langland's audience, therefore, was drawn from a range of literate Londoners.

Lawrence Clopper's many years of work on Langland and on the historical context of *Piers Plowman* has led him, in "Need Men and Women Labor? Langland's Wanderer and the Labor Ordinances," to raise the issue once again about the identity of Langland. Working with the "autobiographical" passage in which Langland has his Wanderer, Will, confront Reason and Conscience, he shows how the two personifications question him about the major provisions of the Statute of Laborers. The Statute of Laborers, passed in 1351 in an effort to keep prices and wages to the pre–Black Death level, was well known and well hated by the laborers of England. Although the statute called for punishment of the lords and employers who gave excess wages, in fact, only the laborers were prosecuted. It had a further provision that one should not give alms to the able-bodied poor who could work for their living. The questioning of Will takes place on Cornhill and follows the questions that justices enforcing the statute were to ask of offenders.

The Dreamer is quite willing to explore his occupation and his conscience with the two interrogators, and in doing so, Clopper argues, the author gives us insight into his own concern about the way he spends his life compared with those laboring poor he sees around him. Is his poetry a legitimate labor, is his wandering only idleness? Should he be compared with the "lollares and lewede ermytes"? He answers that he lives humbly and takes alms only to feed himself, not to accumulate wealth. As a cleric, he must keep to his calling even if it means taking alms. He has his niche in a hierarchical society and cannot betray it by ordinary labor.

Clopper's sagacious use of the text of the Statute of Laborers to elucidate this section of *Piers Plowman* takes us back to the London that the poets give us. Nineteenth-century novelists might recognize these descriptions of London as the sort of areas in which Bohemian artists lived and the sort of scenes they made a part of their novels. But this is not a Marxian working-class London that the poets portray; the society is a hierarchical one with traditional, feudal values. The apprentices and yeomen might rebel against the hierarchy, but they are not factory workers. Will may, likewise, live in the poverty of London and not be a Salvation Army worker, a Fabian socialist, or an artist. Langland may not have received patronage from the merchant class, but he was not, so far as we know, in the same hierarchy as Chaucer, that is, not at the royal court. Although Langland and Chaucer moved in different echelons of the hierarchy, for both of them the most forceful view of London was not the wealth or power of the city, but the poverty and pathos, deceit and low life of the city. The pervasiveness of the lower-status groups in literary sources for the urban context suggests further study for both historians and literary scholars.

Literature of the Countryside

As we work our way down from the glitter of the court through the low-life of London, we must remember that 90 percent of the population lived in the countryside and made their living on the land. In Ricardian England, the countryside was not necessarily a benign pastoral. While Langland and his audience found in *Piers Plowman* simple, honest, laudable virtues, the violence of the Peasants' Revolt in 1381 alarmed people about the potential disorder that this large population might cause. The lavishly illustrated books of hours that became so popular during this period and later could sanitize and tame the peasants, but contemporary accounts of their behavior and of the risks to life and limb involved in venturing into the countryside predominate in the literature. There is an edge of violence to field and forest in the late fourteenth century.

Nicholas Orme's contribution, "Medieval Hunting: Fact and Fancy," serves as a transition from the high culture of the court to the violence of the countryside. Hunting was basic to male identity in all classes with legal or illegal access to the forests. The imagery entered into kingship, with Richard himself taking as his symbol the white hart, a beautiful and pathetically chained image of a hart. Hunting treatises were among those books that nobles either authored themselves or commissioned. The sport, in their hands, was an elaborate ritual with the correct dress, hounds, horn calls, and ceremonies at killing and butchering. The ritual was well known among all classes of medieval England, since clergy as well as wealthy Londoners joined nobles and gentry in hunting, and peasants had many occasions to observe their betters at a hunt. Orme, therefore, finds that the hunting scenes in *Sir Gawain and the Green Knight* reflect both the love of hunting and the ritual one finds in the manuals.

The knowledge of hunting is pervasive as a metaphor in the literature of the period and is one that is likely to escape a modern reader far removed from the sport. It is an area deserving more attention from historians and literary scholars. To our modern tastes, for instance, the sheer number of animals taken in the three scenes in *Sir Gawain and the Green Knight* suggests a slaughter. But this carnage is also true to life. Orme can find in the literature no contemporary sensibility of "animal rights" akin to modern feelings.

Hunting took place in forests and could lead to sinister or mysterious experiences. Specters could appear out of the mists, and darkness or mysterious chapels could appear. On the less fanciful side was the ever-present element of poaching. *The Parlement of the Thre Ages*, which resolves into a dream poem on the three ages of man, begins with a description of the beauties of nature and a successful poaching expedition. The Robin Hood poems and other outlaw ballads center their drama around illegal hunting. Not only did outlaws poach, action that might actually please their audiences, but they also used their skill with weaponry on travelers.

Barbara Hanawalt, in "Ballads and Bandits: Fourteenth-Century Outlaws and the Robin Hood Poems," has measured the ballad bandits against the real bandits that appear in criminal court records. She finds that the depiction of bandit life is very similar to that of real groups of bandits in terms of membership, rules of conduct, and daring exploits such as jail escapes and attacks on corrupt officials. Where the ballad bandits differ from the real bandits is in their choice of goods to steal and of victims.

For Robin Hood and his band, life in the forest was an idyll: the weather was always good; it was always summer; their meals were shared with good companions and unwilling guests; venison accompanied by red wine, brown ale, and white bread was the invariable fare. Money was easily plucked from their corrupt "guests." When they needed to lie low, Sir Richard at the Lee's castle was at their disposal. Real bandits also poached and feasted in the forest, robbed the corrupt and wealthy, and took shelter in lords' castles. They also found ready employment as thugs acting in a lord's interest in extortion and intimidation. But for real bandits winter descended. A lord might not need their services or might evict them from the castle when the sheriff pursued them. The majority of the victims, therefore, were peasants, because it was the peasant households that could provide blankets, cooking utensils, bread, grain, and the other items one would need for winter. It was also the peasants who received the bandits, usually in exchange for part of the loot. Thus, while Robin Hood would not attack yeomen and plowmen, real bandits did. Robin Hood would not steal from women, but the real bandits made no such courteous distinctions.

If real bandits were such an ever-present threat, why then were the Robin Hood stories so enjoyed, and why did some bandits, like the Folvilles, win such esteem that they appeared in *Piers Plowman*? When real bandits attacked hated justices, the public approved because a common oppressor had been humbled, just as Robin Hood could get the best of the Sheriff of Nottingham. The Robin Hood of the legend, however, has universal characteristics that make him generally appealing. He is also not an outlaw without controls—he honors the king and the Virgin Mary, and will not seduce the wives and daughters of yeomen and plowmen or steal their goods. The real outlaws could turn out to be as oppressive for the peasantry as the corrupt officials were, which is why they were indicted and why they appear in great numbers in the court records.

The peasantry, of course, had a number of oppressors. Richard Firth Green in "John Ball's Letters: Literary History and Historical Literature" applies a close reading of the texts of letters attributed to that revolutionary orator of 1381. When the peasants revolted against the Statute of Laborers, the poll tax, and a number of other local grievances, they did so without a sophisticated ideology or a firm idea of what they wanted to replace the current system. Such ideology as they had seems to have been formulated largely by John Ball, and, as Green argues, the letters preserved in the chroniclers Knighton and Walsingham probably are of his authorship. Green's explication de texte shows that the messages of revolution were very traditional ones with analogues in sermons and carols. Much is traceable to Franciscan preaching manuals. The seven deadly sins appear prominently (although Wrath is left out, perhaps because it appeared too apt a description of the revolt). Discussions of law also appear in several guises. On the one hand, the rebels are anxious to maintain that they have truth on their side and that they are not a lawless rabble. Hobbe the Robber, Ball says, will not be tolerated, and indeed the rebels punished plunderers. On the other hand, they resented the ubiquitous presence of lawyers, who, they claimed, abused the laws and burdened the poor.

While the material and tradition that Ball drew upon was conventional, Green distinguishes an individual voice in leaving out Wrath and in chastising Hobbe the Robber. His message may have been conservative, but then, too, the rebels might have been, as well. The peasants were, perhaps, less revolutionaries than reactionaries. In any case, Green concludes, they were Lollards, as Walsingham and Knighton charged. More jarring than Ball's letters was *Pierce the Ploughmans Crede*, which is genuinely radical.

John Ball's letters also play a part in Susan Crane's "The Writing Lesson of 1381." Like David Wallace, she asks us to explore "absence" as a tool of interpretation. One lesson she draws from the revolt of 1381 and the letters is that literacy and articulation are fundamental to understanding the peasant response to these tools of dominance. She sees the attack of peasants against written records and the lawyers who transcribe them as an attack of the powerless illiterate against those who use literacy as an oppressive tool. She convincingly supports her point with a discussion of both historical destruction of writing and Lévi-Strauss's exploration of the prestige of literacy in his essay "A Writing Lesson." Not only did King Richard and the Parliament repudiate the charters of manumission granted at Mile End, but Walsingham's version has the king also say that the message of their slavery will be written on their bodies for all to read. Even as illiterates, therefore, their very bodies could serve as messages.

She suggests that we explore the alternative explanation of Derrida that literateness is not everything and that articulateness can also empower. But the writing she investigates indicates that the peasants were also denied the power to speak coherently. The chroniclers of the revolt deny articulateness to the crowd by comparing them to wild animals and jackdaws. Other chroniclers speak of the "great noise" of the rebels. Ball's letters, which, we have seen, are conservative in nature, might have been more important as written objects than for their message. As she explores other literature, she finds that alterations from the B-text to the C-text of *Piers Plowman* render the plowman less articulate, placing greater emphasis on the plow. In Langland's scene describing the coronation of Richard II, the commons can give assent only by a "great cry and noise." In Chaucer, as well, inarticulateness and illiteracy are the province of the powerless. The Wife of Bath, for instance, finds her adversaries in literate clerks and says that there are no comparable female texts. Crane draws a delightful parallel between the Wife of Bath, who burned her clerical husband's book, and an old woman in Cambridge who participated in the burning of books during the revolt there. The old woman summed up the frustration of the illiterate as she prodded the ashes: "Away with the knowledge of clerks, away with it."

The countryside, then, looking at it through both historical and literary lenses, may be the residence of honest plowmen, but the possibility of meeting mysterious threats, strong armed robbers, and wild, insubordinate peasants loomed large in people's imaginations.

It is fitting to end with Green's and Crane's essays, for they are the authors who make the most reflective comments about the process of putting literature into a historical context. Green raises the question of how we, either historians or literary scholars, are to use literary sources. Are they artifacts of a purely literary tradition? Can they, as Keith Thomas says, serve only to illustrate what we already know? And how do we interpret the texts? Historians are likely to take them at face value, while literary scholars will try to look behind the text itself. On the other hand, Green argues, the skills of textual analysis are not reserved to literary scholars, for historians working with legal records have the critical tools to see fiction in their materials. He makes the perceptive point that the differences in approaching texts may be one of temperament rather than training. The literary scholar will take a text and refer the historical context back to it. The historian will take a text as a stepping-stone to understanding society.

Green's observation reminds me of my first serious experiences in reading extensively in Middle English texts at the Newberry Library. Like a historian going through legal cases, I would order up volumes of carols and poetry and blaze through them looking for information on family. My colleague, Gordon Wattley, was surprised (probably appalled, as well, but too polite to say so) at how much I covered. Finally, I've come to appreciate how much more a careful reading informs scholarship. For instance, 1981 brought commemorative volumes on the Peasants' Revolt of 1381. For the most part, historians had little new to add to what was already known. The sources are limited and worked over, although local revolts are now better documented. But none of the essays produced the fresh insights that come out in both Green's and Crane's essays on John Ball's letters, a source that historians have looked at repeatedly.

In the new intersection between history and literature, then, one of the lessons that historians are learning is how to read a text: the care needed, the search for analogues, the absence as well as the presence of materials. It would now be primitive, indeed, to snatch a quote from Langland to fill in a hole in historical evidence. In addition, scholars in literature have forced us to look more closely at our own texts for the elements of narrative and fiction in them. We are asked to call into question the language, ordering of events, and motives of the authors to a larger extent than we have before. Court cases can be unpolished folk tales, and chronicles can be read as literary texts as well as history.

On the literature side, the new social and cultural history has provided a richer context in which to analyze texts. While the first attempts in this direction were to identify audiences for literary works, we now have examples in this volume of how historical context can elucidate text. In providing this new material, the analysis of medieval literary texts is moving away from exclusive scrutiny of the great literary texts and is looking at the lesser ones, along with chronicles and legal materials.

One of the greatest values of this volume for both historians and literary scholars is that it provides working examples of strategies and methodologies available for expanding our interpretations of historical and literary texts. In doing so the authors have revealed the wide possibilities available in new approaches to literary texts. In making the boundaries between what have traditionally been regarded as literary texts and historical texts more porous, the essays permit the reader to understand better the environment in which literature arises. Probing the textual matrix of late-fourteenth-century literature shows how close historical and literary events can be.

PART I

✢

The Political Context

CHAPTER 1

The Court Of Richard II and the Promotion of Literature

Michael J. Bennett

The circumstances of the great flowering of English verse in the late fourteenth century represent a major problem for the social and cultural historian. It is at once exhilarating and humbling to reflect on the England of Richard II, a country of only two million inhabitants, but with Chaucer, Gower, Langland, and the *Gawain*-poet all at the height of their literary powers. Needless to say, the achievement of this remarkable generation of poets presents major problems of interpretation. It is not simply that what John Burrow has termed "Ricardian poetry" includes such varied, complex, and subtle work, though that is still enough for most people.[1] It is also that the poets of this time were responsible for a cultural revolution, so enlarging the capacities and enhancing the status of the English language as to accomplish a vital breakthrough or, perhaps even more remarkable, a number of parallel breakthroughs to vernacular eloquence. To underline the magnitude of the achievement, it is enough to point to what Paul Strohm has termed "the narrowing of the Chaucer tradition" in the period after 1400.[2] This attenuation is even more striking if one notes the sudden collapse at about the same time of the formal alliterative school.[3] By comparison with the literary torrent of the 1370s to 1390s, the fifteenth century is a desert, scarcely able to keep a single channel flowing.

For several centuries scholars have sought to understand the historical context of the age of Chaucer and the "triumph of English." Even a generation ago, the range of factors, from the political to the philological, adduced to help explain the literary achievement made for a heady brew. Over the last decade or so, however, a positive avalanche of studies relevant to the question has appeared. Literary scholars have made most of the running in this new wave, and their works have grown impressively in historical sense.[4] More tardily, a few historians, who previously contented themselves with ransacking Chaucer and Langland for illustrative detail, have begun to wake up to a larger agenda of cultural history. Nevertheless the welter of recent scholarship is far from providing a clear or coherent picture. Much of the work has had to be destructive, dissolving old assumptions and making plain the massive gaps in the evidence. Even the best studies, by highlighting the complexity of English society and its literary culture, and the subtlety of the interrelation between them, have tended merely to underline the magnitude of the problems.

What has been achieved is a fuller documentation of the social conditions of literary production in the late Middle Ages. The close analysis of literary texts and the manuscripts in which they survived has focused attention on the "middle classes" of town and countryside. To understand the early sponsorship of Middle English literature, it is necessary to look, with Janet Coleman, at the city of London and, with Thorlac Turville-Petre, at the manor houses of the provincial gentry.[5] There has been a corresponding deflection of attention away from the royal court and the aristocracy to the "middle classes" of town and country. The idea of the court of Richard II as the nucleus of cultural activity, in particular, has received some hard knocks. The scholars who assembled at the Colston Research Society symposium at Bristol in 1981 came close to staging a second deposition of the king. V. J. Scattergood, speaking for the "estate" of literary scholars, implied that the picture of Richard II "presiding at the center of a literary court culture based on the English language" could not stand close scrutiny. J. W. Sherborne, speaking for the historians, declared that the view that the royal court was a "'notable center of the arts' . . . no longer commands respect."[6]

The problem is how far the democratizing and rusticating push can validly go. In the hands of some literary scholars and historians it seems to have gone rather too far. In an iconoclastic paper on cultural diffusion in the later Middle Ages, for example, Peter Coss sought to overturn traditional assumptions about cultural relations between court and country. Basically, he does a valuable service by drawing attention to the cultural vigor of the emerging country gentry class. Where he fails to carry conviction is in his presentation of the manor house as an adequate milieu for all levels of literary output, from the Robin Hood ballads, through the whole gamut of English romance, to the finer alliterative works.[7] Whatever the importance of the "middle classes" as sponsors of the basic groundswell of English literature, when it comes to setting the conditions for the sudden scaling of the heights of vernacular eloquence, the gentry and the bourgeoisie seem unlikely heroes. In late medieval England, as Elizabeth Salter has observed, social contexts imposed definite ceilings on literary quality.[8]

Needless to say, English verse of sorts was composed in the homeliest of milieus. Richard Newton, a Cheshire gentleman, penned a piece of doggerel, modestly alliterative and with the makings of a "bob and wheel," about his son's shrewish wife in the 1390s. It was doubtless written at Newton Hall, little more than a farmhouse, entirely for family consumption.[9] There are many more accomplished versifiers whose work still does not assume an audience of any sophistication. John Audley, a Shropshire priest, composed a series of religious poems, mostly dreary and commonplace, in the early fifteenth century. He regarded the compilation of his anthology as an act of penance, and doubtless the reading of it should be seen in the same light. He wrote his verse at Haughmond Abbey, where he served a chantry in the patronage of Lord Strange of Knockin.[10] Yet it is perhaps instructive that both men knew far larger worlds than would at first be supposed. Richard Newton was a soldier, who like so many of his fellow Cheshire men was recruited into Richard II's retinue in the late 1390s.[11] In one of his poems John Audley appears to offer a portrait of himself as a worldly young man, "gentle Sir John," well regarded among his fellows for song and merriment. Striking documentation of this other world, and indeed of the dramatic episode that transformed the young gallant into the morbid poet of the anthology, can be found in the records of King's Bench. Prior to his retirement to Haughmond, John Audley was in the retinue of Lord Strange of Knockin and more often to be found in London and the Home Counties than in Shropshire. In 1417 at Easter Sunday high mass in the church of St. Dunstan in the East, London, he aided and abetted Lord Strange in his sacrilegious assault on Sir John Trussell.[12]

It is clearly inappropriate to underestimate the geographical mobility and social horizons of that small minority of Englishmen in the late fourteenth century who had the education and inclination to write verse. It might well be that some works were produced wholly in the confines of a single knightly household, as presumably was the case with *The Lame for Sir John Berkeley* or apparently *The Destruction of Troy*.[13] Yet in both cases there is reason to suppose that the poet had traveled with his patron in the king's wars on the continent. It is harder still to localize works produced by men in the service of the aristocracy, like the author of *William of Palerne*, who served the earl of Hereford, or William Paris, the author of *St. Christina*, who was in the service of the earl of Warwick. Both men must have moved around England: the former was from Gloucestershire, but his lord was mainly resident in Essex; the latter was from Warwickshire but wrote his poem while in exile with his lord on the Isle of Man.[14] When it comes to works of greater literary quality, the evidence of more complex social milieus becomes even more striking. All that is known about the world of William Langland is that it straddled the Malvern Hills and the streets of London. The author of *St. Erkenwald* appears even more torn: he demands that his audience both appreciate highly wrought verse in Cheshire dialect and take an informed interest in a London cult. The authors of the *Morte Arthure* and several other alliterative works appear as thoughtful observers of, if not actual participants in, the great military enterprises of Edward III's reign. The alliterative dialogue, *Winner and Waster*, not only makes wry reference to the movement of westerners to the southeast but also seems to address itself directly to the concerns of careerist audiences.[15]

It is often claimed that the role of the middling classes of town and country as sponsors of vernacular literature is supported by "hard" evidence from the manuscripts themselves. The bulk of Chaucerian verse, after all, survives in compilations for gentlemen, lawyers, and merchants, while important alliterative works survive as unique copies made for modest landed families. Yet it must be borne in mind that many key works from the late fourteenth century survive only in later copies. It is thus vital to distinguish between the primary audience for which a poem was composed and the secondary audience that a successful work itself created, between the charmed circle in the late fourteenth century who heard rather than read Chaucer and the people in subsequent generations who bought or made copies of his work. In any event, detailed investigation of individuals and families involved in the transmission of literary texts, as of the poets themselves, tends to reveal more central and complex social locations than was initially assumed. In the early sixteenth century, for example, the unique manuscript of *St. Erkenwald* survived in the circle of the Booths of Barton and Dunham Massey, while other alliterative text were being copied in the neighborhood of Eccles, the Booths' native parish.[16] Since the poems were certainly composed some time earlier, it is worth tracing back the Booth family generation by generation. The lineage first achieved national eminence in the late fifteenth century, when William Booth and his half-brother Lawrence Booth capped off distinguished careers in the church as archbishops of York. Given that *St. Erkenwald* is a poem associated with London and Saint Paul's cathedral, it is noteworthy that Lawrence Booth was dean of St. Paul's around the time that the surviving text was being copied by a Cheshire scribe.[17] The Booth brothers owed their ecclesiastical advancement in large measure to prior success in administration and politics, and connections with London and the court went back some way. William Booth was treasurer of the household of Humphrey, duke of Gloucester, in 1425, and held the living of Putney. His uncle, Henry Booth, was a successful lawyer, and the early tradition that William was trained at the Inns of Court seems well based. In the reign of Henry V, John Booth of Barton, the archbishops' father, and Henry Booth, their lawyer uncle, were active in the London property market. Perhaps John Booth amassed some wealth in the French wars; he certainly acquired a French mistress, Lawrence's mother. In the 1390s he was a retainer of first John of Gaunt and then Richard II himself. The roots of careerism in this lineage stretch back at least one more generation. Thomas Booth of Barton, the grandsire of the archbishops, was almost certainly literate and certainly highly mobile. He was keeper of the king's horses north of the Trent.[18]

The groundswell of literary achievement in late fourteenth-century England certainly needs to be set against a backcloth of unprecedented mobility and careerism. The Black Death and subsequent epidemics opened up new opportunities at all levels. More specifically, the Hundred Years' War encouraged the mobilization of the manpower of the nation on an unprecedented scale. Traditions of education and careerism became entrenched in some of the remotest regions. It is the congregation of talent in and around London, the intersection of networks of soldiers, clerks, lawyers, and merchants, that would appear to be the social context of what Anne Middleton terms "public poetry," with its concern with the promotion of the "common weal," in the reign of Richard II.[19] Though it could embrace the court, and indeed the court might be its epicenter, it is certainly the case that this sort of literary culture is wholly conceivable on the fringes of rather than within the court itself.

Nonetheless it is a little perverse to come so close to the royal court, and then to remain so obdurately on its threshold. It is worth pondering, at the outset, the name of one poet, a master of Arthurian romance, whose reputation lived on in Scotland: "Huchown of the Awle Ryale," or Hugh of the royal household. The man is an enigma, but it is reasonable to suppose that he was an Englishman of the late fourteenth century.[20] Geoffrey Chaucer was most assuredly "of the royal household." He spent his formative years and much of his adult life in the service of kings, queens, and princes, and his development as a poet was shaped by the influences opening up to him through royal service in England and overseas. His earliest known work, *The Book of the Duchess*, was written to commemorate John of Gaunt's first wife some time between 1368 and 1371. Even if textual references and literary tradition did not directly attest the court connections of many of Chaucer's mature works and Gower's *Confessio Amantis*, the poems themselves bespeak a courtly ambience. The verse of Chaucer and Gower, as J. W. Nicholls observes, "reflects the ease of reference to the habits, aspirations and short-comings of polite society," but, he goes on, in none of their work is to be found the "same kind of rigorous analysis of courtesy that . . . lies at the heart of *Sir Gawain and the Green Knight*."[21] Though working in a regional dialect, in alliterative meter, and under rather different influences, the *Gawain*-poet was no less a courtier than Chaucer.

In seeking to explain the "rise of English" as a literary language, therefore, it would be most unwise to leave the royal court out of the account. Of course, larger social and cultural forces were at work. William Langland's *Piers Plowman* and a range of other works attest to an important breakthrough by the 1370s. The dating and the context of "formal" alliterative poetry, from *Winner and Waster* to *Pearl* and *Sir Gawain and the Green Knight* remain uncertain, but some of the works, at least, were presumably written by then.[22] It is by no means farfetched, however, to link this early progress with possible encouragement from the crown. In the late 1360s there are a number of signs of a more aggressively nationalistic ethos at the court of Edward III. In the case of the next major breakthrough, that of the mid-1380s, the grounds for attributing a role to the court are even stronger. The condemnation of Wycliffism in 1382 had created a less favorable climate for English works, and even in 1386 John Trevisa was conscious of the need to justify his translations of Latin works for his patron, Lord Berkeley.[23] Yet at this very time Chaucer was addressing his first masterpiece, *Troilus and Criseyde*, to a courtly audience. At this time, too, John Gower, who had previously written only in French and Latin, was encouraged to undertake his most ambitious project in English by Richard II himself. When considering Chaucer, Gower, and the *Gawain*-poet, their forging of a language and style capable of high literary expression, and their rapid scaling of the heights of vernacular eloquence, it is tempting to see the sort of assurance that could only come from the highest sponsorship.

To assess the role of the court in English culture, it is necessary first to grapple with the term *court*. In the last two decades scholars have shown themselves ever more wary of the term, especially in relation to cultural patronage. The court of Richard II, not least Gervase Mathew's rather romanticized view of it, seems to have all but dissolved in the face of scholarly investigation. Yet writers in all three languages in fourteenth-century England used the term court in a fashion that should give skeptics pause. To say that contemporaries acknowledged the existence of the king's court, of course, does not mean that it had institutional existence. The concept is somewhat nebulous: though it centers on the king's person, it can range out to embrace the king's chamber, the royal household, the council, the offices of state, and, of course, the chief law courts and Parliament itself. Even if the latter institutions had long since gone "out of court," and even if the household and perhaps the chamber itself could function independently, it remains the case that the king could by personal intervention symbolically reappropriate such offshoots of the *curia regis* and temporarily transform their functionaries into courtiers. Needless to say, the natural focus must be on the immediate entourage of the king, often defined, in the case of Richard II, as the knights and squires of his chamber. Yet the king's companions always included men and women whose positions were wholly informal: members of the royal family; his "favorites," high-born and low-born; his confessor and chaplains; his hosts on his perambulations; foreign visitors; and so on. There were times, too, when his company was so lacking in structure and decorum, as in certain exercises of devotion or debauchery, that the term *court* is wholly inappropriate. There is a definite sense in which the court could exist without the king, and that the king himself could "go out of court."

What is important to bear in mind is that the court was more a cultural construct than an institution. Its essence, in fact, defies institutionalization. That is not to say that it is mere improvisation. A courtly ambience, still less a court culture, could not be conjured out of thin air by a charismatic prince or an inspired poet. Perhaps it can best be likened to a theater. Material and organizational props are vital, but what is required to bring together the means and the inspiration are shared expectations about what constituted a princely court and shared conventions about how courtly life is to be enacted. In late fourteenth-century England it seems likely that such expectations and conventions, albeit of a basic sort, were becoming more widely diffused. The romance and the lyric certainly introduced the world of courts to more people than could ever hope to have their lives conform to art. Kings, princes, and nobles were well able to see the value of presenting themselves as patrons and exemplars of chivalry and courtesy. Meanwhile their servants were becoming ever more experienced and adept in stagecraft.

In this sense the "court" of Richard II was a cultural force from the moment of his accession. It would certainly be inappropriate to hail the ten-year-old monarch as a patron in his own right. More than most kings, he had at first to play a role cast for him, and if he did not measure up to the ideals of kingship it was not for the want of prompters. Indeed a great deal of the cultural energy of the first half of his reign can be attributed to the desire to shape a still malleable mind. Richard certainly grew up in palaces built and furnished by his predecessors, attended and guided by men and women chosen on his behalf. Edward III, his grandfather, was a great builder, a promoter of pageantry and spectacle, and an inspiration for chivalric and courtly literature, some perhaps in English. Just as Richard inherited the splendor of Windsor and the amenities of Eltham, he also inherited men like Geoffrey Chaucer and, quite conceivably, the *Gawain*-poet. Still, if the boy-king can take no credit for this courtly ambience, there is evidence of an early determination to build on his legacy. The extension and renovation of the palaces of Eltham, King's Langley, and Sheen in the mid-1380s must testify to Richard's interest in providing a congenial setting for courtly dalliance.[24] The "courtly" verse produced at this time presumably also reflected in some measure the tastes of the king and his entourage.

The personality of Richard II defies easy categorization. His temperament was somewhat mercurial, and in any case it must have changed over time. The evidence, a great deal of which is hostile and retrospective, must be handled with some caution. As regards the quality of his character and the company he kept, for example, there are indications of an unruly temper and a boisterous entourage. Yet the weight of the evidence is otherwise. As he grew to maturity in the 1380s, there are increasing signs of sensitivity and refinement. His court, in the meantime, assumed a rather precious, even effete, character. Thomas Walsingham dismissed his courtiers as more knights of Venus than of Bellona, more of the bedchamber than of the battlefield.[25] Ladies certainly figured prominently in court circles, and it is significant that his improvements at Eltham and Clarendon included dancing rooms.[26] After his declaration of his majority in 1389, there are signs of higher cultivation. By the mid-1390s Richard's "court of love" had evolved into a court promoting universal peace. There is certainly growing evidence of a lively and cultivated mind.[27] Richard had wide interests, ranging from hunting and haute cuisine to geomancy and astrology. His piety was thoughtful rather than reflexive: he enjoyed sermons, was assiduous in the observance of favored saints' days, actively promoted new cults, and took an informed interest in ecclesiological and theological issues. His kingship was no less self-conscious: he had a sense of history, an antiquarian as well as a pragmatic fascination with his regalia, a keen awareness of the ideological and legal dimensions of his monarchy. In all his endeavors, personal and political, he showed a concern for self-dramatization. He was sentimental and romantic: after the death of Queen Anne he had their palace at the Sheen razed to the ground. Even if there were no evidence at all for Richard's encouragement of letters, his personal style and the general ambience of his court could not but have been a stimulus to literary activity.

If a man can be known by the company he kept, Richard can certainly be regarded as a man of literary tastes. He not only took over a court establishment that included Geoffrey Chaucer, but seems to have been especially close to a number of younger courtiers with known literary interests, most notably Sir John Montagu, earl of Salisbury, and Sir John Clanvowe. In the 1390s litterateurs like Jean Froissart, Eustace Deschamps, Otho de Grandson, Philippe de Mézières, Christine de Pisan, and Jean Creton did not share the contempt for the English court evident in some modern scholarship. There is evidence that Richard had a taste for books. There is the unusually grand and exquisitely illustrated *Book of Statutes* compiled for him around 1389.[28] There is the handsome *Book of Divinations* presented to him around 1391.[29] As a wedding present Charles VI gave him the exquisite Belleville breviary.[30] Pietro da Verona, literary agent of the duke of Berry, was in the process of selling him a splendid Bible in 1399 and was mortified when, on his arrival in London, he learned of Richard's deposition.[31] Of course, it can be countered that the only books apparently made for his private use are objets d'art or treatises rather than literary items, though it must be borne in mind that what survives is not necessarily representative of what once existed. It might be argued, too, that insofar as Richard had a taste for poetry, it would have been French.[32] It is certainly indisputable that Richard had wide cultural interests, and no man of literary taste could be other than a Francophile. Yet neither his broad cultural interests nor his French connections preclude a role in the promotion of English literary works.

In fact the status of the English language at the court of Richard II was certainly not as modest as is sometimes implied. Perhaps the king was most at home speaking French, but it is doubtful. His first wife, Anne of Bohemia, after all, was apparently fully conversant in English, even to the point perhaps of basing her devotions on the gospels in English. His uncles, John of Gaunt and Thomas of Woodstock, certainly showed a commitment to the English Bible. According to an early tradition, John of Gaunt led the lords and gentry in Parliament in blocking an attempt by the bishops to ban English translations of the scriptures, while Thomas of Woodstock owned a Lollard Bible.[33] At the same time, as is evident from even the most cursory survey of Chaucer and his circle, quite a number of courtiers and bureaucrats had English literary tastes. Sir Simon Burley, the king's governor and counselor until his execution in 1388, is worthy of attention in this context. Though his book collection was mainly French, he did own an English work of sufficient rarity as to indicate a specific commission.[34] All in all, Froissart had good reason in 1395 not to take it for granted that the king read French with any facility. In the last years of his reign Richard had a young French wife, but one of his closest friends was his cousin Edward, duke of Albemarle, who showed his commitment to his native tongue by translating Gaston Febus's *Book of Hunting*. When the Kenilworth chronicler expressed his outrage that Richard allowed his Cheshire retainers to address him familiarly *"in materna lingua,"* he was probably referring not simply to the use of English but to the use of regional brogue.[35]

There are grounds for supposing that Richard II played a more positive role in the promotion of English letters than has been recently allowed. It is true enough that important progress had occurred by the 1370s: William Langland had written the first version of *Piers Plowman* and Geoffrey Chaucer had started to develop an English poetic inspired by and bearing comparison with recent French and Italian models. Nonetheless there is evidence of a further breakthrough in the mid-1380s, the very time when it becomes meaningful to talk about the impact of the king's personality and the role of the court. Occupying pride of place in the progress of English verse in the 1380s, of course, are Chaucer's mature works, *Troilus and Criseyde*, *The Legend of Good Women*, and some of *The Canterbury Tales*, and their association with the court of Richard II is thus instructive. Three other writers who aspired to vernacular eloquence around this time had connections with the royal household. Thomas Usk, a clerk of the city of London, who wrote *Testament of Love* around 1387, seems an improbable candidate. What needs to be remembered, however, was that he was the intermediary between the king and the court party in London, and a sufficiently notorious royalist to warrant execution in 1388. It is interesting to speculate as to his responsibility for Nicholas Brembre's alleged design to rename the city "New Troy."[36] Sir John Clanvowe, a knight of the king's chamber since the beginning of the reign, was another man who seems to have set himself to writing English poetry around this time. His *Book of Cupid* was clearly a work associated with court festivities on St. Valentine's day.[37] A more important and certainly more striking illustration of the connection between the royal court and the "rise of English" is John Gower's *Confessio Amantis*. Since Gower had previously written only in Latin and French, his decision to write his most ambitious work in English is highly significant. The evidence linking Gower's new enterprise with Richard II has been too readily dismissed. According to the original prologue to *Confessio Amantis*, the king and Gower were traveling on the Thames in the royal barge when the king asked for a poem on the theme of love. [38] The fact that the prologue was subsequently altered surely enhances rather than diminishes its credibility. Even if Gower's royal commission were a total invention, which seems most unlikely, his attempt to invoke the king's name is clear evidence that Richard was regarded in his own time as a king who took poets on boat trips and discussed their work with them.

There is certainly much that is obscure about Richard II's relations with the London poets, especially in the 1390s. John Gower rapidly repented of his association with the court, and perhaps from the early 1390s was looking to Henry of Bolingbroke as England's savior. Chaucer doubtless shared many of his old friend's reservations about Richard's style of kingship. Though he remained close to many courtiers, including John of Gaunt, who finally married Chaucer's sister-in-law in 1396, and Philip de la Vache, steward of the new queen's household, he seems not to have frequented the court. He remained on the king's payroll, as he had been for as long as the king himself controlled the flow of patronage. Some of the evidence, not least the rebukes that he occasionally administered the king, suggests that he had a wholly special status, as a living national treasure. It seems wholly fitting that both the king and the poet made special efforts, carefully documented by S. Ferris, to have the grant to him of an annual tun of wine dated on the feast of St. Edward the Confessor.[39]

It might well be that in the 1390s the London poets found themselves having to make space for men from the provinces. After all, the king's uneasy relations with London and the southeast generally are a matter of record. Beginning with his expedition to Scotland in 1385, he began to broaden his horizons dramatically and started to cultivate the provinces. In 1386-87 he "gyrated" round the north and west Midlands, recruiting into his household the gentry of those parts, most especially Cheshire. His attempt to use these royalist forces to take back the reins of power led to the "Merciless Parliament" in which his friends and counselors were condemned to death. From 1389, however, the king began quietly to reconstruct a royalist party in the country. After a row with the city of London, he set about the transferral of the main offices of government to York. During the second half of 1392 the northern city became the capital of England.[40] In 1394-95 he conducted his first expedition to Ireland, spending Christmas at Dublin. In 1396 he again made York his headquarters for weeks on end. In his last two years he spent a great deal of time at centers in the west Midlands, most notably at Chester, Shrewsbury, Lichfield, Coventry, and Bath. During the same period he raised the earldom of Chester to the status of a principality and retained seven hundred knights, gentlemen, and yeomen from Cheshire with fees ranging from £40 per annum to 6*d*. a day. An elite corps of two hundred Cheshire men acted as his bodyguard, familiarly conversed with him in their mother tongue, and addressed him as "Dycoun." Prior to embarkation for Ireland, he held court at Cardiff and other castles in south Wales. By this stage he had had all the crown jewels and regalia brought from the Tower of London to Windsor castle and to other fortresses on the Welsh border. With some justification, the people feared that he would never again look on the rest of England with favor, but would seek to exploit its resources from bases on the periphery.[41]

Even if it is a little hard to document, the king's involvement with the provinces had a cultural dimension. In his travels in the late 1380s and the 1390s he often took up residence in the large monasteries of the west Midlands, the very places, like Evesham, Lilleshall, Gloucester, to which Derek Pearsall has drawn attention as places where regional poets might have found not only Latin histories and French romances but also old models of alliterative verse.[42] He spent time, too, with "courtier" bishops: Robert Waldby at York and Richard Scrope and John Burghill at Lichfield. Presumably unencumbered by his household, he was entertained in house parties, as by Thomas, Lord Berkeley, at Berkeley castle in Gloucestershire, Lord Beaumont at Beaumanoir in Leicestershire, Nicholas Audley at Heighley castle, and John Macclesfield at Macclesfield in Cheshire.[43] The recreation afforded by his hosts can only be surmised. The king certainly enjoyed listening to the preaching of friars. He attended the mystery plays at York in 1396 and might well have been similarly entertained at Coventry or Chester in 1398. It is interesting to speculate as to what he made of Lord Berkeley's sponsorship of John Trevisa, who in 1386, when the king was a guest at Berkeley, was hard at work on a translation of *Polychronicon*. The king was interested in history. He commissioned a hagiography of his great-grandfather, Edward II, who, of course, had been murdered in Berkeley castle.[44] The general impression is that Richard had a special interest in the history of his crown and his people from their putative Trojan origins through the Arthurian glories and the Anglo-Saxon martyr-kings to his own immediate forebears.[45]

The serious historical concerns of the more "formal" alliterative works, so different from the Chaucerian tradition, would certainly have appealed to him, even if the dialect and meter did not. Of course, the bulk of the extant alliterative works are no more than workmanlike translations from Latin or French sources. Some of the more interesting works, like *Winner and Waster*, *Parliament of the Three Ages*, and *St. Erkenwald*, clearly draw on the experiences of social and geographical mobility that were the lot of so many from the northwest Midlands in the second half of the fourteenth century. Nonetheless, with works like *Sir Gawain and the Green Knight* and *Pearl*, it is necessary to envisage a poet and a primary audience who knew Cheshire and its dialect but who were interested in the subtle analysis of courtly values and behavior.[46] The tendency has been to concentrate on some magnate allegedly resident in the area, whether a grandee like John of Gaunt, duke of Lancaster, or a prominent knight like Sir John Stanley. The problem is that there was no aristocratic lineage based in Cheshire, and it seems perverse to focus on Stanley without acknowledging his connections with the royal household. If ever there was a "court" in the northwest it was when Richard II spent time there in 1387 and 1398-99. Conversely, a number of Cheshire men were acquiring prominence in court circles in the 1380s. In the last years of the reign, it is hard to find a single Cheshire family of note who did not have a member in the royal retinue.[7]

Whatever the date of *Sir Gawain*, it was copied by a Cheshire scribe at the very end of the fourteenth century. It thus seems inconceivable that it was not given an airing at some level in the king's household as it moved around the west and northwest Midlands. Though he was talking about "a magnate on his travels," Derek Pearsall has observed that the poem "would have made an excellent entertainment, in every respect, for a Christmas and New Year 'house party' in such an environment."[48] An occasion of this sort was Richard II's sojourn at Lichfield over Christmas and New Year 1398–99. It was a great state occasion, with a brother or cousin of the Byzantine emperor and a papal nuncio among the foreign visitors at the court.[49] The king's Cheshire retainers and guardsmen were all in attendance, and many of them, like Sir John Stanley, controller of the wardrobe, appear in the bishop's register seeking licenses for marriages and domestic chapels.[50] The bishop's palace at Lichfield was a magnificent building, but time would have been spent, too, at the bishop's country retreat, "Beaudesert," set high above the moors on the site of an Iron Age hill fort. Of course, it is tempting to believe that *Sir Gawain* was actually being composed at or shortly after this time. After the breakup of the king's household on his return from Ireland in June 1399, several hundred of his Cheshire retainers made their way home across Wales along a route and in a state of mind not unlike Sir Gawain's. For the Ricardian loyalists, trekking through Snowdonia, taking their bearings from Anglesey, and crossing into Cheshire not by way of the city of Chester, not in Bolingbroke's hands, but across the shoals to "the wyldrenesse of Wyrale," the lines "wonde ther bot lyte / That auther God other gome wyth goud hert lovied" (lines 701-2) would have had a special significance. Sir John Stanley, a native of Wirral and the most powerful man in the northwest, had betrayed Richard II and come to terms with the usurper.[51]

Needless to say, the evidence for a connection between the court of Richard II and the *Gawain*-poet is highly circumstantial. The lack of documentation of the king's patronage to Chaucer in his capacity as a poet is likewise a problem. What needs to be stressed, though, is that the records of Richard's personal expenditure, the chamber accounts, do not survive. As R. F. Green has stressed, it is there where "details of the king's spontaneous gifts and rewards to those who had pleased or diverted him" would be found, and there "that the nature and extent of any royal interest in literature would be clearly revealed."[52] The point has the greater force in that increasingly large sums were paid into the chamber in the 1390s.[53] An entry on the issue rolls of the Exchequer for Easter 1399, however, does offer a glimpse of what is otherwise a closed book. In addition to bulk payments of 1,000 marks, £106 13s. 4d. and £113 6s. 8d. to chamber officials, it includes a number of smaller disbursements, clearly representing gifts authorized by the king in chamber. There were ten marks for William Byngeley and his companions, minstrels, and £10 for Hugh Coton and Nicholas Wodham, "masters of the baron of Kinderton." Even more tantalizing for afficionados of the hunt for the *Gawain*-poet is the gift of £20 to "Massy."[54]

It is not just the records of Richard's expenditure on entertainment and the arts that are missing. Precious few artifacts survive as evidence of his interests and tastes. Still, it is necessary to bear in mind both the general ephemerality of a great deal of court culture and some particular factors working against the survival of Ricardian works. Without doubt the king spent vast sums on feasts and tournaments and "live" entertainments. For him and his court, *Troilus and Criseyde* and *Sir Gawain and the Green Knight* would have been viva voce performances, not books in a library. Richard, in any case, has all the appearance of being as fickle in his tastes as he was restless and impulsive. The flow of patronage in any particular direction was probably short-lived. His career is full of false starts, shifts of tack, and aborted initiatives, and there is evidence of considerable loss of material during his own lifetime. His first attempts at princely munificence were nullified by the political upheavals of 1386-88. His happiest years, 1390-94, in which he and his queen presided over a charming courtly society at palaces like Eltham and Sheen, leave little record at all, save Chaucer's own envoi in *The Legend of Good Women.* After the death of the queen, the grief-stricken king ordered the razing of Sheen lock, stock, and barrel. Around 1395-96 there is a great deal of cultural patronage associated with negotiations for peace with France and the union of Christendom in a crusade. This phase came to a head in a veritable "field of cloth of gold" near Calais, when the courts of England and France came together to celebrate Richard's marriage to Isabel of France. Unfortunately the ships carrying home the pavilions and their rich contents went down in an unprecedentedly violent storm in the Channel. The king's perambulations in the years 1397-99 further served to disperse his possessions. The issue rolls in 1398 are full of references to the cost of transporting the king's jewels and other valuables, while the circumstances of his return to England in 1399 left royal treasure dispersed in Dublin and a whole series of western seaports.[55]

In the wake of the Lancastrian usurpation, many items associated with Richard II and his court must have been destroyed. Two recently discovered references to the cultural activities of the king's kinsmen, Thomas Holland, duke of Surrey, and John Holland, duke of Exeter, are suggestive. A chance reference in a property dispute, for example, reveals that Surrey had set on the gates of Warwick Castle stone images of a white hart and a white hind, the cognizances of the king and the Hollands, and that Bolingbroke had them pulled down in 1399.[56] Another odd survival in the Public Record Office is a label for the key to a chest of books that Exeter had buried at Dadlington in Devon.[57] As regards Richard II himself, it is chastening to note that the splendid portrait at Westminster Abbey was covered over, while for a time it must have seemed that the splendid effigy of himself and his wife would be melted back down. Even such textual references as survive to his literary interests came close to being totally expunged, as in the original envoi to *The Legend of Good Women* and the original prologue to *Confessio Amantis.* The version of his *Book of Divinations* that has survived in the Royal Library omitted the preface dedicating the work to Richard II, and in Bodley MS. 581 his portrait has been deliberately effaced.[58] Even the epitaph in which the king wished to have himself likened to Homer survived only by grace of Henry V's decision to rebury him in Westminster Abbey.[59]

It is hard to know what Richard II or his panegyrist intended to convey by likening him to Homer, "*animo prudens ut Homerus.*" There is no doubt that "prudence" was a virtue to which Richard would have laid claim. The dedications of the tracts contained in Bodley MS. 381 make this plain. The author of the compilation of the *Liber Judicorum* wrote, "I have compiled this present book of geomancy, in as brief a form I was able, at the special request of our most excellent lord Richard, the most noble king of the realms of England and France, who governs in sublime fashion not so much by the force of arms as of philosophy and the two laws; and indeed he has not declined to taste the sweetness of the fruit of the subtle sciences for the prudent government of himself and his people."[60] Of course, there remains the problem of Homer. Gervase Mathew thought it not impossible that the king wrote poetry himself. A more general reading would be that the king regarded himself as a man who, like Homer, understood the past and foresaw the future, drawing on the traditions of his people, securing their transmission, and shaping them for visionary ends. If the king felt that he had played some role in the promotion of English literature, especially the more historically minded literature of the alliterative tradition, the identification with Homer would be the more apt. Richard II, after all, presided over a court in which a remarkable cluster of poets found inspiration, and his sponsorship beginning in the mid-1380s might well have been crucial in firmly establishing the status of English as a language of high literary endeavor. If the deposition and death of Richard II were responsible for the final breakup of the remarkable coterie of courtiers that had been the primary audience for Chaucer's verse, and for the ending of that eccentric flow of patronage that was probably the frame for the finest works in the alliterative revival, it would explain a great deal about the sudden ending of England's first "golden age" of literature and about the patterns of literary activity and sponsorship in the fifteenth century. The Lancastrian kings should perhaps be seen as maintaining, in a less eclectic and generous spirit, a tradition of royal patronage first properly established in the reign of Richard II.

Notes

1. J. A. Burrow, *Ricardian Poetry: Chaucer, Gower, Langland and the "Gawain Poet"* (London, 1971).

2. P. Strohm, "Chaucer's Fifteenth-Century Audience and the Narrowing of the 'Chaucer Tradition,'" *Studies in the Age of Chaucer* 4 (1982), 3-32.

3. T. Turville-Petre, *The Alliterative Revival* (Cambridge, Eng., 1977), p. 122.

4. E. Salter, "The Alliterative Revival," *Modern Philology* 64 (1966), 146-50, 233-37; G. Mathew, *The Court of Richard II* (London, 1968); D. Pearsall, *Old English and Middle English Poetry* (London, 1977); Turville-Petre, *Alliterative Revival*; R. F. Green, *Poets and Princepleasers: Literature and the English Court in the Late Middle Ages* (Toronto, 1980); J. Coleman, *English Literature in History, 1350-1400: Medieval Readers and Writers* (London, 1981); E. Salter, *Fourteenth-Century English Poetry: Context and Readings* (Oxford, 1983); P. Strohm, *Social Chaucer* (Cambridge, Mass., 1989).

5. Turville-Petre, *Alliterative Revival*; Coleman, *English Literature in History, 1350-1400*.

6. V. J. Scattergood, "Literary Culture at the Court of Richard II," in *English Court Culture in the Later Middle Ages*, ed. V. J. Scattergood and J. W. Sherborne (London, 1983), p. 30; J. W. Sherborne, "Aspects of English Court Culture in the Later Fourteenth Century" in *English Court Culture*, ed. Scattergood and Sherborne, p. 6.

7. P. R. Coss, "Aspects of Cultural Diffusion in Medieval England," *Past and Present* 108 (1985), 35-79.

8. E. Salter, "Chaucer and Internationalism," *Studies in the Age of Chaucer* 2 (1980), 73.

9. British Library, Additional MS. 42134, fol. 20; M. J. Bennett, "*Sir Gawain and the Green Knight* and the Literary Achievement of the North-West Midlands: The Historical Background," *Journal of Medieval History* 5 (1979), 67-69.

10. *The Poems of John Audelay*, ed. E. K. Whiting; EETS, OS 184 (1931); M. J. Bennett, "John Audley: Some New Evidence on His Life and Work," *Chaucer Review* 16 (1982), 344-55.

11. Bennett, "*Sir Gawain and the Green Knight*: The Historical Background," pp. 69-71.

12. Bennett, "John Audley," pp. 346-48.

13. T. Turville-Petre, "The Lament for Sir John Berkeley," *Speculum* 57 (1982), 332-39; T. Turville-Petre, "The Author of *The Destruction of Troy*," *Medium Aevum* 57 (1988), 264-69

14. T. Turville-Petre, "Humphrey de Bohun and *William of Palerne*," *Neuphilologische Mitteilungen* 75 (1974), 250-52; Pearsall, *Old English and Middle English Poetry*, p. 251.

15. In general see D. Pearsall, "The Alliterative Revival: Origins and Social Backgrounds" in *Middle English Alliterative Poetry and Its Literary Background*, ed. D. Lawton (Cambridge, Eng., 1982), pp. 38-39.

16. R. Morse, ed., *St. Erkenwald* (Cambridge, Eng., 1975); C. A. Luttrell, "Three North-West Midlands Manuscripts," *Neophilologus* 42 (1958), 38-50.

17. E. Axon, "The Family of Bothe (Booth) and the Church in the Fifteenth and Sixteenth Centuries," *Transactions of the Lancashire and Chesire Antiquarian Society* 53 (1938), 32-82. Lawrence Booth was a prebendary at St. Paul's, 1453-56, and dean, 1456-57 (A. B. Emden, *A Biographical Register of the University of Cambridge to 1500* [Cambridge, Eng., 1963], pp. 78-79).

18. The present writer and Compton Reeves are currently preparing a joint paper on the early history of the Booths.

19. M. J. Bennett, "Careerism in Late Medieval England" in *People, Politics and Community in the Later Middle Ages,* ed. J. Rosenthal and C. Richmond (Gloucester, 1987), pp. 19-39, esp. p. 36; A. Middleton, "The Idea of Public Poetry in the Reign of Richard II," *Speculum* 53 (1978), 94-114.

20. F. J. Amours, ed., *The Original Chronicle of Andrew of Wyntoun,* vol. 4, Scottish Text Society 54 (Edinborough, 1906), pp. 18-27, where "Huchoun that cunnande was in littratur" is credited with a great "Gest of Arthure," the "Awntyr of Gawain," and the "Pistill of Susan." Early speculation associated a Scots "Huchoun" with all the major alliterative works (H. N. MacCracken, "Concerning Huchown," *PMLA* 25 [1910], 507-34). Since English poets were known and emulated in Scotland, and since his works would seem to have been English, it is odd that there has been no sustained "Huchoun" hunt south of the border, not least now that William Dunbar's "Master John Clerk" has come to life as an English alliterative poet (Turville-Petre, "The Author of *The Destruction of Troy,*" p. 266). The name "Hugo de," of course, appears at the head of MS Cotton Nero A x in the same near contemporary hand as "Hony soyt qui mal pence" at the end.

21. J. W. Nicholls, *The Matter of Courtesy: A Study of Medieval Courtesy Books and the Gawain-Poet* (Woodbridge, 1985), p. 142.

22. W. G. Cooke, "*Sir Gawain and the Green Knight*: A Restored Dating," *Medium Aevum* 58 (1989), 34-48, shows that Gawain's armor and the architecture of Hautdesert would not have been out of place as early as the 1340s. The *terminus ante quem,* however, remains 1400, and in view of the whole tone of the work, most scholars will doubtless continue to prefer a late fourteenth-century dating.

23. R. Waldron, "John Trevisa and the Use of English," *Proceedings of the British Academy* 74 (1988), 171-202.

24. Mathew, *Court of Richard II,* pp. 32-34; C. Given-Wilson, *The Royal Household and the King's Affinity: Service, Politics and Finance in England, 1360-1413* (New Haven, Conn., 1986), pp. 30-32.

25. Thomas Walsingham, *Historia Anglicana,* ed. H. T. Riley, 2 vols., Rolls Series (London, 1863-64), 2:156.

26. R. A. Brown, H. M. Colvin, and A. J. Taylor, *The History of the King's Works,* vol. 2 (London, 1963), p. 934; T. B. James and A. M. Robinson, *Clarendon Palace: The History and Archaeology of a Medieval Palace and Hunting Lodge near Salisbury, Wiltshire,* Reports of the Research Committee of the Society of Antiquaries, no. 45 (1988), pp. 40-41.

27. Mathew, *Court of Richard II,* esp. chs. 3-5; Scattergood and Sherborne, eds., *English Court Culture,* passim.

28. St. John's College, Cambridge, MS. A. 7.

29. Bodleian Library, Oxford, MS. 581; Scattergood, "Literary Culture at the Court of Richard II," in *English Court Culture,* ed. Scattergood and Sherborne, pp. 41-42; H. Carey, "Astrology and Divination in England in the Late Middle Ages," unpublished D. Phil. thesis, Oxford, 1984, ch. 5.

30. Bibliothèque Nationale, Lat. 10483-84; J. J. G. Alexander, "Painting and Manuscript Illumination for Royal Patrons in the Later Middle Ages," in *English Court Culture,* ed. Scattergood and Sherborne, p. 147

31. M. Meiss, *French Painting in the Time of Jean de Berry,* 2 vols. (London, 1967), 1: 64-65.

32. There is a list of Richard II's books, mainly old-fashioned romances in French, in an Exchequer memoranda roll of 1385, but a recent study has shown them to be old works, recently pawned, and revealing nothing of the king's own tastes (R. F. Green, "Richard II's Books Revisited," *Library* 31 [1976], 235-39).

33. M. Deanesly, *The Lollard Bible and Other Medieval Biblical Versions* (Cambridge, Eng., 1920); C. Buhler, "A Lollard Tract: On Translating the Bible into English," *Medium Aevum* 7 (1938), 167-83, esp. 178.

34. S. H. Cavanaugh, "The Identification of a Lost English Analogue of the 'Death of Begon' Episode from the Old French Epic *Garin le Loherain,*" *Medium Aevum* 57 (1988), 64-67.

35. British Library, Additional MS. 35295, fol. 260r-v.

36. Mathew, *Court of Richard II,* pp. 54-55.

37. The poem includes a compliment "to the Queen at Woodstock" and was probably composed between 1386 and 1391 (*The Works of Sir John Clanvowe,* ed. V. J. Scattergood [Totowa, N.J., 1975], pp. 9-10, 14).

38. *Confessio Amantis,* Prologue, 1.24-92 (*The English Works of John Gower,* ed. G. C. Macaulay, EETS, ES 81 and 82 [1900, 1901]).

39. S. Ferris, "Chaucer, Richard II, Henry IV and October 13," in *Chaucer and Middle English Studies in Honour of Rossell Hope Robbins,* ed. B. Rowland (London, 1974), pp. 210-17.

40. C. M. Barron, "The Quarrel of Richard II with London, 1392-7," in *The Reign of Richard II: Essays in Honour of May McKisack,* ed. F. R. H. Du Boulay and C. M. Barron (London, 1971), pp. 173-201.

41. A. Tuck, *Richard II and the English Nobility* (London, 1973), chs. 6 and 7; R. R. Davies, "Richard II and the Principality of Chester," in *Reign of Richard II,* ed. Du Boulay and Barron, pp. 256-79; Bennett, *"Sir Gawain and the Green Knight*: The Historical Background," pp. 81-84.

42. D. Pearsall, "The Origins of the Alliterative Revival," in *The Alliterative Tradition in the Fourteenth Century,* ed. B. S. Levy and P. E. Szarmach (Kent, Ohio, 1981), pp. 1-24.

43. Tuck, *Richard II and the English Nobility,* p. 227; P. Morgan, *War and Society in Medieval Cheshire, 1277-1403* (Manchester, 1987), p. 187; Public Record Office C1/69/ 281.

44. F. Devon, ed., *Issues of the Exchequer from Henry III to Henry VI* (London, 1837), p. 259.

45. Richard was described as a great searcher out of antiquities relating to his royal ancestors (*Chronica Monasteri Sancti Albani,* ed. H. T. Riley [London: Rolls Series, 1866], 3:29). He was able to recite the histories and names of kings from the earliest habitation of the kingdom (E. M. Thompson, ed., *Chronicon Adae de Usk* [London, 1876], pp. 29, 142).

46. M. J. Bennett, "Courtly Literature and Northwest England in the Later Middle Ages," in *Court and Poet,* ed. G. S. Burgess (Liverpool, 1980), pp. 69-79.

47. M. J. Bennett, *Community, Class and Careerism: Cheshire and Lancashire Society in the Age of "Sir Gawain and the Green Knight"* (Cambridge, Eng., 1983); J. L. Gillespie, "Richard II's Cheshire Archers," *Transactions of the Historic Society of Lancashire and Cheshire* 125 (1975), 1-39.

48. Pearsall, "Origins and Social Backgrounds," p. 51.

49. G. B. Stow, ed., *Historia Vitae et Regni Ricardi Secundi* (Philadelphia, 1977), p. 151. The chronicle noted that over the Christmas season at Lichfield there were great tournaments each day, and such was the concourse of people that 28 or 26 cows, 300 sheep, and innumerable poultry were consumed daily.

50. Lichfield Joint Record Office, B/A/1/7, fols. 122-26.

51. Bennett, *Community, Class and Careerism,* pp. 234-35.

52. Green, *Poets and Princepleasers,* pp. 5-6.

53. An average of £2,000 per annum in the early 1380s, rising to £3,400 between 1386 and 1392, had become £7,000 in the late 1390s (Given-Wilson, *Royal Household and King's Affinity,* p. 87).

54. Public Record Office, E403/562, m. 8. That the author of *Sir Gawain and the Green Knight* and, more especially, *Pearl* was a member of the prolific Mascy or Massey clan in Cheshire is argued from wordplay, acrostics, and cryptography in B. Nolan and D. Farley-Hills, "The Authorship of *Pearl*: Two Notes," *Review of English Studies,* n.s. 22 (1971), 295-302; C. J. Peterson, "The Pearl-Poet and John Massey of Cotton Cheshire,"

Review of English Studies, n.s. 25 (1974), 257-66; E. Kooper, "The Case of the Encoded Author: John Massey in *Sir Gawain and the Green Knight*," *Neuphilologische Mitteilungen* 83 (1982), 158-68.

55. *Calender of Inquisitions Miscellaneous*, vol. 7, 1399-1422 (London, 1968), p. 70.

56. J. B. Post, "Courts, Councils, and Arbitrators in the Ladbroke Manor Dispute, 1382-1400," in *Medieval Legal Records Edited in Memory of C. A. F. Meekings*, ed. R. F. Hunnisett and J. B. Post (London, 1978), p. 323.

57. Public Record Office, E 101/699/25. Many of the books were apparently French (*Calendar of Inquisitions Miscellaneous*, 1399-1422, pp. 70, 75-76).

58. Carey, "Astrology and Divination in England in the Late Middle Ages," p. 175.

59. *The Chronicle of Fabian, Which He Nameth the Concordaunce of Histories* (London, 1559), p. 378.

60. J.-P. Genet, ed., *Four English Political Tracts of the Later Middle Ages*, Camden Society, 4th series 18 (1977), p. 23; Carey, "Astrology and Divination in England in the Late Ages," p. 182.

CHAPTER 2

Saving the Appearances
Chaucer's *Purse* and the Fabrication of the Lancastrian Claim

Paul Strohm

The Argumentative Environment

The particular logic and sequence of Henry of Derby's actions upon his return to England in July 1399 remain concealed behind the discrepant and unreliable chronicle accounts through which we attempt to know them. Nevertheless a general pattern does emerge: a pattern mixed, whether through uncertainty or deviousness, but moving by its own logic ever closer to a claim on the throne. Swearing to the northern lords at Doncaster that he aimed only to secure his heritage and to put Richard "in gouernaunce,"[1] and through his emissaries to Richard at Conway that he wished only to be hereditary steward or "Anglie senescallo iure hereditario,"[2] he is described by Creton as assuring Richard at their first meeting at Flint Castle that his goal was to aid in governing the people, "sil plaist a nre seigneur ie le vous aideray a gouverner mieulx quil na este gouverne le temps passe."[3] But from that moment in mid-August when he took the king under control, no doubt remained that Henry would be king. Only to be determined were the procedure and the argumentative rationale by which Richard's deposition and his own advancement would occur.

Numerous indications suggest that Henry and his allies spent much of the period from mid-August to the very eve of his climactic 30 September meeting with the estates in Westminster Hall generating and canvassing different routes and rationalizations leading to his elevation. On 19 August, writs were issued, in Richard's name but presumably under Henry's direction, summoning the relevant estates of the realm to Parliament, in order to conduct "ardua regni negotia."[4] The fact that Henry summoned the estates does not necessarily mean that he possessed a final plan. Whatever steps were to be taken—whether to secure Richard's abdication, or to seek his deposition, or to argue for Henry's legitimate descent, or to argue for divine anointment, or to seek some combination of election or acclaim—his parliamentary summons would assure the presence of an appropriate body to witness and to weigh their impact. That Henry meant to furnish the assembled estates with a yet-to-be-determined argumentative avenue to the crown is signaled by a nearly simultaneous letter to abbots and major ecclesiasts, asking them to examine "cunctas Chronicas regni Angliae statum tangentes, et gubernationem," and inviting persons competent to expound the chronicles, together with the relevant texts, to come to the site of Parliament.[5] The aims of this inquiry become clearer in the light of Henry's creation, early in September, of a committee of *doctores, episcopi,* and others to consider the matter of deposing Richard and choosing Henry in his place, of how it was to be done and for what reasons—"et qualiter et ex quibus causis."[6]

This committee provided a focal point for the political and argumentative pressures that were generating a rich variety of rationales or *causae* for Henry's advancement. Because none of the existing accounts of the events surrounding Henry's usurpation predates the climactic 30 September gathering at which he claimed the vacant throne, the reconstruction of these *causae* involves a good deal of guesswork. Nevertheless, an environment of partially realized preaccession dynastic theory can be derived from among those arguments finally instated as official Lancastrian explanation, from rejected alternatives and other evidences of contradiction embedded within Lancastrian chronicles, and from those few surviving sources—belated and mostly French, together with some cobbled-together fifteenth-century Yorkist texts—located outside the scope of the Lancastrian propaganda machine.

Descent

The fifteenth-century chronicler Hardyng claims that attempts to have Henry of Derby designated Richard's heir predated the actual usurpation:

> I herde the . . . erle of Northumberlonde saie divers tymes, that he herde duke Iohn of Lancastre, amonge the lordes in counsels and in parlementes, and in the common house, amonge the knyghtes chosyn for the comons, aske be bille forto beene admytte heire apparaunte to kyng Richarde, considerynge howe the kynge wase like to haue no issue of his bodie.

Finding the lords and commons adamant on behalf of the earl of March,

> when the duke of Lancastre wase so putt bie, he and his counsell feyned and forgied the seide Cronycle that Edmonde [Crouchback, son of Henry III] shuld be the elder brother [rather than Edward I] to make his sone Henry a title to the croune. . . . Whiche Cronycle, so forged, the duke dide put in divers abbaies and in freres . . . forto be kepte for the enheritaunce of his sonne to the croune. [7]

Edmund was great-grandfather of Blanche of Lancaster, Gaunt's first wife and mother of Henry of Derby. Had Gaunt's story about Edmund been accepted, Henry's claim would have been strengthened on the matrilineal side. This account of Gaunt's stratagem—written by a chronicler who was himself an inveterate forger[8] and was writing with clear purpose of undermining the Lancastrian claim—seems extremely dubious, but it receives some surprising corroborations. Gaunt is, for example, said by sources less partial to Richard to have carried his tale of Crouchback's seniority to Parliament. [9]

Farfetched as the idea of forged chronicles might be, Henry's own invitation to "certas personas instructas in Chronicis" to show up with relevant texts suggests that he had some hopes for their contents.[10] Finally, several sources suggest that Henry's most ardent or impatient supporters did resurrect the argument for his legitimate descent within the committee of *doctores* in the last days before his elevation. Hardyng says that "kyng Henry, vpon saynt Mathee daye afore he wase made kinge [that is, on 21 September], put forth that ilke cronycle claymynge his title to the crown be the seide Edmonde."[11] This suggestion is seconded by the more authoritative Adam of Usk, present among the *doctores*. Adam, struggling with the rest of them to find some justification for Henry's accession, nevertheless has his limits. He notes that the Crouchback story was raised by certain members of Henry's committee ("in concilio per dictos doctores habito, per quosdam . . . ").[12] But even this pliant group admitted that the evidence of authoritative chronicles argued against it, and Adam goes on to provide a lengthy list of contrary citations.[13] The argument basing Henry's title on birth had, in short, been repeatedly refuted throughout the decade, and no reputable person appears to have accepted it. Yet, the skepticism of Adam and the other pro-Lancastrian *doctores* notwithstanding, it was to resurface on 30 September and repeatedly throughout the period of Lancastrian rule.

Conquest

The Frenchman Creton, reaching England in July with Salisbury and Richard's vanguard, learned that Henry "avoit Ja conquis / Dangleterre la plus grant pt."[14] Richard's subsequent loss of two armies in two weeks through a combination of incompetence and treachery, and Henry's good fortune in tempting Richard out of Conway and into his power on 14-15 August, enabled Henry to enjoy nearly complete success without the necessity of a single real battle. Although this conquest would eventually be shown to be more precarious than anyone in September-October 1399 could have imagined, and although it would have to be periodically renewed, it nevertheless represented a stunning momentary success. Still to be determined from mid-August onward, however, was the role of this conquest in securing Henry's title. Everyone knew by mid-August that Henry would be king; the question was whether the blunt *fact* of conquest could be brought to bear argumentatively in order to rationalize Henry's accession.

Henry was a realist, and we cannot doubt that the fact of conquest was central to his perception of his claim. Yet his contemporaries—including those of his own party—remained committed to the development of a rationale that did not rely on the embarrassing fact of his seizure of power. A parenthetical passage in the impeccably Lancastrian *Annales* discloses the gulf that had opened (and would, in most cases, remain open) between Henry and his followers on this issue. All the documents based on the official Lancastrian "Record and Proces del Renunciation"—including the *Rolls of Parliament* (RP), Julius B II, and, in abbreviated form, Walsingham[15]—agree in citing Henry's assurance that conquest was a minor element of his argument for the throne and that no one need think that "be waye of Conquest I wold disherit any man of his heritage."[16] But the *Annales* supplement them by offering an explanation for Henry's disclaimer. According to the *Annales*, Justice Thirning and the community of opinion he represented refused to accept Henry's earlier proposal to claim the kingdom through conquest because of the legitimate fears it would engender among the populace.[17] Whether Thirning, the *doctores*, or other persons are to be thanked, Henry's argument for the consequences of conquest was moderated—though, as we will see, it was not to be withdrawn.

Resignation/Deposition

Henry could *chalange* or claim the realm only after its throne had been vacated; all parties agree to that. But some uncertainty seems to have existed throughout the fall of 1399 as to whether the Lancastrian party should seek Richard's abdication or his deposition. As embodied in the various after-the-fact textualizations upon which we must depend, a clear-cut decision between these two alternatives was never made; whether through thoroughness on the one hand or disorganization on the other, the Lancastrians simply pursued both at once.

With regard to abdication, not one but two stories were placed in circulation—neither having any apparent basis in fact. The first is that, meeting with Northumberland and others prior to vacating Conway castle, Richard had agreed to step down. The second is that, visited by the duke and the archbishop and their party at the tower on 29 September and presented by them with a written statement of resignation, he read it aloud and freely signed it. The two stories are conjoined in the "Record & Proces del Renunciation" composed and circulated by the Lancastrians after Henry's accession and embodied in the *Rolls of Parliament* and in Julius B II. In its account of the 29 September visit to the tower, the Julius B II translation has Northumberland and others reminding the king that

> *at Coneway in north Walys, beyng there at his luste and liberte* [RP: *in sua libertate existens*], *behiht . . . that he wold leve off and re-*

nounce to the crovne . . . in the beste manere and ffourme that he myht, as the counseyll off wyse men and lernyd wolde ordeyne.[18]

The fabricated nature of the "promise" may be indicated most simply by the fact that Creton, the best single authority for the discussions at Conway and Flint, reports nothing of it, confining his accounts to the suasions employed by Northumberland to induce the king to leave the security of the former castle. The "Record and Process" nevertheless represents the promise as fondly remembered by the king, who "louyngly [*RP: benigne*] answeryng seyd, that he wolde perfourme with effecte that he hadde byfore byhiht." [19] The king's voluntary compliance is emphasized throughout. Presented with a previously drafted instrument of resignation, we are told that he read it aloud "with a gladde chere [*RP: ac hillari vultu*]." So obviously fabricated are these assertions of Richard's good cheer that one must finally prefer the almost equally outrageous counterfabrication of the *Traïson*, in which a chivalric Richard is so angered as to accuse his visitors of treason and to challenge any four of their best to combat: "Je diz que vous faitez encontre moy come faulses gens. . . . Ce vueil je prouuer et combatre contre quatre des meilleurs de vous trestous et veez la mon gaige." [20] (This account concludes more characteristically, with Richard peevishly and pathetically throwing down his hat as gage.) Even discounting the historicity of the French accounts, common sense leads to the conclusion that Richard's signature was undoubtedly obtained, not with his cheerful concurrence, but under duress.[21] So, too, can we suppose that duress was involved in other purportedly voluntary gestures, as when Richard "toke off his ffyngir a Ryng off golde, his Signet, and putt hit on the ffyngir off the Duk."[22]

With this ring, and this resignation, Henry's supporters went to the meeting at Westminster Hall the next day, taking care to display the ring and to read the resignation to those gathered "ffirst in latyn as yt was wretyn, and affterward in Englyssh."[23] Those estates present accepted (*RP: admiserunt*) the resignation. At this point in the process, however, a new wrinkle was introduced. Adam of Usk, describing the activities of his committee of *doctores*, noted that, although Richard was ready to cede the crown, it was determined that the process would be more secure if he were deposed by the authority of the clergy and people: "licet cedere paratus fuerat . . . tamen . . . ipsum fore deponendum cleri et populi autoritate . . . pro majori securritate fuit determinatum."[24] In fact, the committee followed through; the "Record and Process" continues that, Richard's resignation having been accepted, "yt were nedefull and spedefull vnto the Rewme in voydyng off mys-conceytes and evyll suspecions, That dyuers Crymes and defautes by the same kyng . . . shulde be opynly redde and declared to the peple"[25]—after which a lengthy series of *gravamina* or crimes was read into the record, following the general form of an appeal, saving only that Richard himself was neither present nor permitted to respond. Having heard the *gravamina*, "alle the States, with oon accorde and wille, assentyd and consentyd, that it shulde be procedid fforth to the kyngis deposicion [*RP: ad Depositionem*]."[26]

Those gathered in Westminster Hall were probably not overly concerned with the nice issue of their parliamentary standing, which has mainly occupied modern commentators on the deposition.[27] They cannot, however, be considered a casual group, for they show an exceptional concern that no loophole be left unplugged, "that no thing shulde lak ne ffayle, that ouht to be done or requyred in the fforseyd thinges."[28] For the real concern of this primarily Lancastrian gathering was that the throne be found unquestionably void, opening the way to Henry's accession.

Collaudatio

Adam of Usk imagines the clergy and the people lending their *auctoritas* to the deposition; the "Record and Process" has the estates admitting or accepting the resignation; the same document claims their consent ("unanimiter consenserunt"[29] to Henry's claim. Yet, *prior to Henry's accession on 30 September,* the whole matter of election seems to have carried much less weight than modern, parliamentarily oriented historians like Stubbs have given it. The most that seems to have been imagined by the August-September theorists of succession is some form of ratification or *collaudatio*, in which assembled representatives of the estates accept or endorse proposals placed before them. Only after Henry's coronation was the idea of election to gain much currency, and then less among Henry's immediate circle than others.

Divine Grace

In a document that appears to have been considered for use by the Lancastrian propaganda machine and then withdrawn, Richard agreed to renounce the guidance of the realm or *regimen regni* as well as to designate Henry his successor, but sought in a separate *protestacio* to retain the distinctive, sacral qualities conferred upon him by divine unction: "noluit nec intendebat renunciare carecteribus anime sue impressis a sacra unccione."[30] That this passage, one of the few credible utterances produced by the Lancastrians in the months following Henry's accession, was soon withdrawn is no surprise; the puzzle is how or why it was produced in the first place. The answer is probably that members of the Lancastrian party other than Henry himself had relatively little concern about matters of unction; their concern was with the "regimen regni" rather than with sacral or thaumaturgic kingship, and some of them evidently found Richard's proposal reasonable enough. Henry's ambitions were, on the other hand, dynastic, and issues relating to God's grace were of the utmost importance to him—as the most cursory consideration of his coronation arrangements will reveal.[31] Even Henry's fervent supporters, however, appear to have been less than captivated by his various attempts to claim for himself and his heirs the perquisites of sacral kingship, and claims for divine unction move to the fore only at and around (rather than prior to) the actual accession and coronation, when Henry's direct personal involvement was most in evidence.

This, then, is the larger controversial environment in which Henry advanced to the throne. It is an environment embracing real facts (such as Henry's overwhelming political power), symbolic gestures (such as the transfer of Richard's signet), rumor and disputation (among, for example, the members of Henry's committee), and, eventually, texts. This environment would, in fact, provide a generative matrix within which a variety of texts representing a broad spectrum of approaches to Henry's kingship would be produced and consumed. Within these texts, particular *causae* could be embraced or excluded, new argumentative combinations could be devised according to the vantage points of their authors. Moving to a consideration of these texts, in all their recombinant variety, we will be reminded of things that the Lancastrians evidently knew all along: that an argument can accomplish its purpose without necessarily being plausible, that a text can be powerful without being true.

The Textualization of Henry's Claim

Whether or not John of Gaunt really tried to plant forged chronicles, the story captures at least one indisputable truth about the Lancastrians: their keen and precocious awareness of the value of textualization, of the sense in which a written account placed in the right kind of circulation can generate its own kind of historical truth. Who knows what words Henry spoke in laying his 30 September claim to the vacant English throne? The crucial point is that sometime in the several months after Henry became king, a written version of his claim was placed in circulation by the Lancastrians, to be subsequently incorporated in the *Rolls of Parliament*, in Walsingham, in the *Annales*, in Evesham chronicle, and in a host of derivative documents.[32]

At that meeting of 30 September, Richard's resignation having been accepted and the throne standing visibly vacant, Henry stepped forward to *chalange*—that is, to assert title to or to lay claim to—the realm of England.[33] Speaking, for broadest effect, "in Englyssh tunge,"[34] he is said to have pronounced the closest thing we will ever have to a "Lancastrian claim":

> *In the name of the Father, of the Sone and the Holy Gost I Henry of*
> *Lancastre chalange this reme of Inglond . . . as that I am descended*
> *be right line of the blod comyng fro the good lord kyng Henry thrid*
> *and thorowgh the rizt that God of His grace ath send me with the*
> *help of my kin and my frendes to recover it, the whych reme was in*
> *poynt to ben undoo for defaute of governance and undoying of the*
> *good lawes.*[35]

Were these "really" Henry's words? When Gertrude Stein objected to the likeness Picasso was painting of her, saying, "I don't look like that," the artist is reputed to have replied, "You will." To the question of whether or not this was really Henry's speech, one could reply that, from the standpoint of five hundred years of subsequent history, it might as well have been. Two considerations argue, however, for the fidelity of this widely circulated version. The first is the agreement by several authorities, including eyewitness Adam of Usk, that a written copy existed, that Henry *read* his remarks: "quandam protestacionem in scriptis redactam . . . legit,"[36] that they existed in the form of a *schedulum* or written document.[37] The second is that this claim shows a consistent tilt toward arguments more likely to have been appealing to Henry than to his advisers, that it reveals a stubborn tendency to walk over some of the very cliffs against which apologists like Adam of Usk had sought assiduously to warn him.

Contained within this *chalange* or *protestacio*[38] or *vendicatio*[39] are three arguments for Henry's kingship (though not, Chaucerians will note, the same three that tradition would encourage us to expect). In barest summary, the three arguments are founded upon descent, grace, and "recovery" or reclamation—although each appears in a highly distinctive form.

The first of Henry's arguments revives, though in modified terms, the discredited argument for descent through Henry III. ("Oh, no," one can imagine his advisers saying, "not that Edmund thing!") Henry's modification, undoubtedly adopted as a result of the cautions of his own committee, is to omit the specific contention that Edmund Crouchback, and not Edward I, was Henry's older son. Yet, that contention is still implied in Henry's claim of "right" or direct descent, for otherwise the mere fact of relationship to Henry III would do nothing to unsettle Richard's superior claim. What we have here is a rather obstinate reintroduction, by Henry, of a slightly blurred or cosmetized version of a *causa* that even his best friends could not believe.

So, too, would Henry's second argument, for divine grace, appear not to have held much attraction for his advisers. The "Record and Process" reports that, before speaking, Henry marked "hym mekely with the signe off the crosse in his ffor heede, and in his breste, nempnyng the name off Crist,"[40] and his challenge proceeded "in the name of" the Trinity. Beyond these routinely pious claims, however, lay a bolder assertion, that "God of His grace ath send me." Henry, according to this formulation, presents himself less as the active champion of good rule than as the passive agent of God's will. This is a point that, incidentally, Henry was to underscore repeatedly in his coronation ceremonials, of which a brief example may be given here. Around the time of the coronation the Lancastrians resurrected a hoary legend about the discovery of a vial of celestial unguent, originally given by the Virgin to St. Thomas of Canterbury, too late for the anointment of Richard and now available for Henry's prophetic use.[41] This brazen fabrication—accompanied in one manuscript by the marginal notation "unguentum fictitum"[42]—in turn set the stage for a particular emphasis on anointment within the coronation ceremony. As described in the "Record and Process,"

> *kyng Herry lay vpon a cloth off golde before the hyh awter in Westm' Chirche. And there in ffoure parties off his body his clothes were opyn, and there he was anoynted, with* Veni Creator Spiritus *y-songyn. And affter this anoyntyng his body was leffte vp into another place.*[43]

Henry, literally lifted and transported about, here presents himself not as conqueror but as passive vehicle of God's will.

Finally, the concept of recovery or reclamation of a kingdom about to be lost by bad governance and disrespect for law effects a reintroduction of Henry's discredited argument for conquest, in terms most likely to appeal to the assembled estates. The parliamentary estates were precisely those that had most to gain by due process and rule of law, and the articles drawn against Richard repeatedly emphasize his arbitrariness: "He seyd opynly, with a sterne chere and ouertwert, that his lawes weren in his mouthe, and other while in his breste, And that he allone myht chaunge the Lawes off his Rewme."[44] Here then is conquest, but in a form designed to allay the fears attributed to Thirning in the *Annales*. Henry would, in fact, allude to his "conquest" immediately after his advancement, but as part of a further reassurance, that no one should think that "be way of conquest I wald disherite any man of his heritage . . . ne put him out of that he hath and hath had be the good lawes and customes of the reme."[45] Only subsequent to the accession is the bare claim of conquest to gain independent force as one of the Lancastrian *causae*.

Even this cursory discussion reveals the eccentric and contradictory nature of Henry's three claims. Nobody seems to have believed the argument from descent, or to have cared much about the motions of God's grace; only the final, pragmatic argument—bearing on the *regimen regni* and a re-institution of respect for law—seems directly addressed to actual concerns of the parliamentary commons. Why then the trumped-up arguments for descent and unction? Rather evidently because Henry's concerns were more dynastic than those of his subjects. The predictable payoff of his argumentative exertions was to come early in his first Parliament, when the

29

archbishop of Canterbury spoke on Henry's behalf, reminding the estates "comment Dieu . . . ad envoiez le Roy" to recover the realm, how the estates of the realm "luy ont acceptez en leur droiturel Roy," and how precedents had been established by the king's *progenitours*, and asking for confirmation of the king's oldest son as Prince of Wales and as "droit heriter a les Roialme & Corone." [46] Accomplishment of this aim undoubtedly meant more to Henry than any consideration of argumentative consistency.[47]

Henry's *chalange* of the throne, developed into a narrative *proces* in the period between December 1399 and December 1400 and circulated broadly by the Lancastrians, enjoyed wide adoption, not only in the after-the-fact rolls of Henry's first Parliament, but in the *Annales*, Walsingham, Evesham, and other influential chronicles.[48] Other accounts were concurrently being generated as well. Chaucer's *Purse*, probably completed in winter 1399-1400, was among the earliest. [49] So, too, was Gower's *Cronica Tripertita*, probably completed fairly soon after Richard's death in February 1400.[50] Adam of Usk, a member of Henry's committee of *doctores* and an eyewitness of some of the events he describes, wrote from memory, perhaps as late as 1415.[51] Among the French chroniclers, Froissart treated the events of the deposition in his final redaction, after 1400. Creton wrote his *Metrical History*, partially from firsthand evidence of the events of August 1399, in the winter of 1401-2, and the derivative and less reliable *Traïson* was composed slightly later.[52] Of less interest here than chronology or genealogy, however, is the sheer range of narrative and explanatory materials generated around Henry's highly controversial assumption of the crown, and the variety of ways in which writers drew upon different elements of pre- and post-accession Lancastrian theory.

Henry's *chalange* (repeated practically verbatim in Walsingham and the *Annales*, as well as in other versions depending on the "Record and Process") hinged on direct descent and recovery by God's will; the archbishop of Canterbury speaking on his behalf at his first Parliament claimed recovery by God's will and the "acord & assent" of the estates of the realm. [53] Adam of Usk, writing after the fact, attributed to Henry an argument of which he personally disapproved, that of *successio* or descent.[54] The continuator/compiler of the *Eulogium* emphasized descent from Henry III, with the lords assenting and the commons acclaiming.[55]

Froissart, writing a year or two after the fact from "thin and garbled" information reaching him abroad,[56] comes up with a slightly different version, though a version still woven from argumentative strands we have already encountered, basing the *calenga* or challenge on three arguments. The first, in which Froissart strips away the rhetoric of "recovery," is conquest; the second is descent or heredity; the third consists of what Henry and the states would have considered a prior condition, the voidance of the throne through Richard's resignation and Richard's own (probably bogus) wish that Henry should succeed him: "premierement par conquest, secondement pour tant que ilse disoit estre droit hoir de la couronne, et tierchement par ce que le roy Richart de Bourdeaulx luy avoit resigne le royaulme en sa main."⁵⁷ Although none of the French chronicles was particularly authoritative for events after Creton's departure from England in late August 1399, an alternative interpretative line is advanced in both Creton and in the *Traïson*. Each, in its way, places a good deal of emphasis on election, not just after-the-fact acclamation, but as the vehicle of Henry's advancement. I am not, of course, suggesting that election originated with them. It was always lurking at the fringes of the different English explanations, with texts about after-the-fact acclamation or *collaudatio* inclining toward the concept of election, just as texts about recovery tended to incline toward the excluded admission of conquest.⁵⁸ But Creton, for example, has an extended account of the canvassing of popular will prior to Henry's elevation, climaxing with

> Se leverent tous deux ensemble
> Les archevesques, ce me semble,
> Et alerent au duc tout droit,
> Qui Ja roy eslu estoit
> De par tout le peuple commun . . .
> Apres tous les interroga
> Ly mesmes, et leur demanda
> Si cestoit ainsi leur vouloir:
> Ilz respondirent, ouil, voir,
> Si hault, que ce fut grant merveille.
> Ce ly mist la pusse en oreille
> Telement, que sans plus atendre,
> Il volt acepter et entendre
> A la couronne dengleterre.⁵⁹

[It seemed to me that the two archbishops rose together and went directly to the duke, who was now elected king by all the common people. . . . Afterward, he questioned them, and asked them if it was their will. They responded "yes" with a wondrously loud voice. This "put such a flea in his ear" (Webb) that, without waiting any longer, he accepted and took possession of the crown of England.]

The *Traïson* also emphasizes a process of assent leading to Henry's selection, with all the lords and prelates and commons of (England and) London crying, "Ouy ouy nous voulons que Henry duc de Lencastre soit nostre Roy et nul autre," prior to Henry's ascent to the throne and pronouncement of his reasons—that he had come to claim his "droit heritaige" and that Richard "auoit forfait sa vie et sa couronne" by his murder of Gloucester and Arundel.⁶⁰

What, in the light of these varied possibilities for rationalization or explanation of Henry's kingship, are we then to make of the particular Lan-

castrian argument offered by Chaucer in the last stanza of *To His Purse?*
With the economy of a poet, Chaucer weaves his argument into a bit over
two lines, shaped not as exposition at all but as discreetly elegant, vo-
catively couched address to his new monarch:

> O conquerour of Brutes Albyon,
> Which that by lyne and free eleccion
> Been verray kyng . . .

This passage contains nothing wholly original—that is, no single element
not otherwise available within the broad tradition of Lancastrian argu-
mentation. It is nevertheless distinctive, in that its selection and arrangement and weighting of arguments differ from any other rendering we have
seen.

With his reference to Henry as conqueror, Chaucer cuts through more
frequent and authorized reference to "recovery" with a starker formulation, but then mitigates any severity by displacing the conquest to the legendary Britain of the chronicles.[61] This subtle instatement of the idea of
conquest, transposed into a register that passes over local perturbation to
associate Henry with England's largest destinies, would undoubtedly have
been to the liking of a king who had himself, as we have noted, evidently
already proposed an argument based on conquest to his *doctores* and only
papered over this bold claim with talk of recovery after receiving cautionary advice. Henry's own reversion to the idea of conquest surfaced almost immediately in his postaccession assurance to his subjects that none
should "thynk that by wey off conquest I wolde disherite eny man,"[62] and
we would hardly expect any reference so pleasing to this martially inclined
king to remain perpetually at the margins of postcoronation texts.

Chaucer's references to "lyne" and to "verray" kingship seem a rough
equivalent to Henry's own "right line of the blod," though with the implied circumstances—that awkwardly concocted and inherently unper-
suasive business about Edmund Crouchback—tacitly pushed even farther
to the background than in Henry's own challenge.

Most surprising is probably Chaucer's reference to "free eleccion"—a notion present only at the margins of English commentary[63] and fully embraced only by the anti-Lancastrian Creton and his follower, the author of
the *Traïson*, as a way of showing the instability of claims resting on a
foundation as untrustworthy as that of general acclaim. Yet, if presentation of a garland of arguments supportive of Henry's claim may be supposed to be Chaucer's purpose, free election is certainly better suited to his
situation and temperament than other arguments made available to him
by tradition. Strong emphasis on Richard's crimes or on his voluntary resignation would, for one thing, have been of dubious propriety. For Chau-

cer, loyal Ricardian for some twenty-two years of his maturity, suddenly to embrace extensive accounts of malfeasance or outrageous fabrications about Richard's resignation *hillari vultu*, while his former monarch yet lived, would have demonstrated a degree of opportunism and inconsistency foreign to his nature as we otherwise know it.[64] Nor would strong iteration of the sacramental or thaumaturgic elements of Henry's kingship have been consistent with the emphases revealed generally in Chaucer's poetry.

I do not mean to suggest that Chaucer has forged a seamless argument. If Henry is of the right "lyne," why did he need to conquer the kingdom? If he conquered it, why did he require "free eleccion?" Still, in this threefold justification, Chaucer advances a line of argument that appropriately mediates his own position and Henry's rather urgent and continuing interest in bolstering his own legitimacy by asserting a series of accomplished and agreed-upon facts: whether or not Richard did resign, Henry *did* conquer the kingdom; whatever Henry's lineage, he *does* possess royal blood; the estates of the realm certainly *did* seem to want him.

Although lost alternatives can certainly be imagined, Chaucer's appears to be the first among extant texts to present this particular argumentative configuration. The same configuration will appear in the *Cronica Tripertita* of fellow poet John Gower—though, interestingly, as one of two different treatments of the subject, one close in spirit to the account of the "Record and Process" and the other close to Chaucer's own three-part formulation.

Close to the "Record and Process" is Gower's address to Henry in what may be his last poem, "In Praise of Peace." There, Gower closely tracks the "official" Lancastrian arguments for God's grace ("God hath the chose") and assistance in recovery of a kingdom in decline ("The worschipe of this lond . . . / Now stant upriht"), and of right descent ("Thi title is knowe upon thin ancestrie"), coupled with the after-the-fact endorsement of the estates of the realm ("The londes folk hath ek thy riht affermed"). Downplaying conquest, underscoring grace, deftly introducing practical considerations about the state of the realm, mentioning descent, and reminding his reader of *collaudatio* or affirmation by the estates, Gower would seem here to have woven together the different strands present in the parliamentary account, itself an uneasy amalgam of the Lancastrian apologies of Thirning and Arundel on the one hand and Henry's supposed words on the other.[65] Yet, in the *Cronica*, he takes a slightly different line, and one almost identical to Chaucer's own. The *Cronica* concludes with Henry's accession and consolidation of rule (and the death of Richard, supposedly by self-starvation), and includes a defense of Henry's threefold right or *trino de iure*:

> Regnum conquestat, que per hoc sibi ius manifestat;
> Regno succedit heres, nec ab inde recedit;
> Insuper eligitur a plebe que sic stabilitur.

> *[He conquered the realm, and because of this, right is clearly on his
> side; he succeeded as heir to the kingdom and thus has not abdicat-
> ed from it; in addition, he was chosen by the people and thus firmly
> established.]*[66]

Or, as he marginally summarizes even more succinctly, but in a different
order: "successione . . . eleccione . . . conquestu sine sanguinis effusione."
In a sense, it's a case of the less said the better; Gower's prose summary is
probably more persuasive than his metrical version, in which he gets into
argumentative absurdities like "succedit . . . nec . . . recedit."

Although both Chaucer's poem (October 1399-February 1400) and the
"Record and Process" (1400) were probably available when Gower wrote
the *Cronica* (post-February 1400) and "In Praise of Peace" (1401-4?), any attempt to construct a clear genealogy would probably be vain. The point is
that the rich environment of texts and theories surrounding Henry's accession permitted a variety of acceptably Lancastrian arguments and that
Gower employed them selectively, according to circumstance. In the heavily anti-Ricardian and almost jingoistic *Cronica* he had no reason, for example, to withhold mention of conquest; the more conciliatory "Praise of
Peace" aspires to surmount conflict and hence relies upon the blurred and
contradictory but ultimately reassuring formulations of the "Record and
Process."

Despite the inner variety of Gower's arguments and their subtle differences from those of Chaucer, the sentiments of all three texts may be con-
strued as broadly "Lancastrian." These texts in turn remind us that heg-
emonic interests—or in this case the interests of a Lancastrian proto-
hegemony—can be advanced by varied utterances that need not be strictly
consistent one with another, so long as all are produced and received within a matrix of generally consistent sentiments and ideas.

The Exchange-Value of Chaucer's Poem

Yet to be explored is the nature of Chaucer's contribution to the already
formidable Lancastrian propaganda effort.

Henry's assumption of control upon landing in England in July 1399 was
so rapid that one can easily forget how many unassimilated pockets of potential resistance remained.[67] As early as December 1399, Richard's disaffected former dukes, together with supporters like Thomas Merke, the
former bishop of Carlysle, and John Montagu, the earl of Salisbury, were
meeting to plot the murder of Henry and his sons, leading to their failed

uprising of January 1400. Intermittent struggles with the Welsh, and with Northumberland and Percy and other disaffected northern lords who claimed that Henry had broken the promise made to them at Doncaster not to seek the crown, began almost immediately and persisted through most of the first decade of the century. Principled resistance to the usurpation continued among the Franciscans, some of whom professed to believe Richard still alive.[68] This is not the place to attempt a summary of Henry's military and diplomatic counterstrategies, save in one regard: his apparent attempt to enlist litterateurs in his dynastic cause. One incident suggests the presence of programmatic elements behind Henry's relations with writers of the day.

Christine de Pisan, writing in her partly allegorical, quasi-autobiographical *Lavision*, narrates a surprising commingling of literary activity and personal and dynastic ambition, involving herself, the poet and Ricardian adherent John Montagu, and England's new king.[69] In 1397, John Montagu, formerly Ricardian chamber knight and now earl of Salisbury, came to France in connection with negotiations for Richard's marriage to the young Isabella. Although his writings, evidently in French, are now lost, Christine describes him as a lover of poetry and a "gracieux ditteur." After acquaintance with her poems, she tells us, he proposed an arrangement by which her son Jean would join the earl's household, to be raised with his son. No sooner, she laments, was this advantageous arrangement concluded, than the "pestilence" of rebellion broke out, leading to the deaths of Richard and Salisbury. At this point Henry, becoming acquainted with the "dittiez et livres" she had already sent in order to please the earl, took the boy into his own household and sent two "notables hommes" to gain her assent and to invite her to come to England herself. Not believing that such disloyalty could turn out well, she played along with the heralds, asked to see her son briefly in France, and then kept him in France once he had returned. Christine, understandably enough, portrays Henry as stirred to action by his admiration for her poems. Yet we may imagine another motive as well, springing from Henry's desire for legitimacy, for the adherence of established figures, for the celebration of poets.

If Christine, possessed at this early point in her career only of a modest reputation as an author of short lyric poems, seemed a suitable object of Henry's courtship, how much more was to be gained by Chaucer's adherence? Evidence of manuscript circulation and public reference suggests that Chaucer was relatively little known throughout most of his career, except among a circle of courtly civil servants and London intelligentsia. But his sudden emergence to prominence, with broadened circulation of his *Tales* and *Troilus* soon after his death in February 1400, would lead to his instatement as "the noble rethor Poete of breteine" during the first years of Henry's reign, and something of this imminent emergence must have been evident to his contemporaries in 1399-1400.[70] Furthermore, in his initial clemency even to those *duketti* and others who had profited most from Richard, Henry had shown his interest in solidifying his relations with known Ricardians while their former king yet lived, and Chaucer's own career in Richard's service would have added significance to his acceptance of Henry's claims.

Exploring the implications of Petrarch's acceptance of Visconti patronage, David Wallace has anatomized the senses in which each "exchange" with a tyrant typically magnifies the tyrant's worth.[71] Chaucer's poem, hailing Henry's accession even as it requests his assistance, invites a form of exchange with his sovereign. Although Henry's backdated confirmation and expansion of Chaucer's grants may have occurred without the incentive of the poem, we may reasonably assume them to result from the exchange Chaucer invites.[72] And, if so, we may say with confidence that Henry enjoyed the tyrant's prerogative, gaining far more from this exchange than the relative pittance of which Chaucer was belatedly assured.

Postscript: The Power of Theory and the Theory of the "Source"

Production of pseudo-Lancastrian documents has not, by the way, ceased—though the motives and circumstances have changed. A recent instance involves a document, the existence of which rests secure in the estimation of most Chaucerians: the "proclamation" to the people of England by which Henry is supposed to have claimed the throne by conquest, hereditary right, and election. This proclamation is believed, in turn, to have been Chaucer's "source." Yet this "proclamation" nowhere exists. The idea of such a proclamation may have originated with Henry's 30 September *chalange*. But, as we have already seen, that statement makes no mention whatever of election, and elides the idea of conquest in favor of a claim based on divine grace. The supposed "proclamation" was, effectively, devised by Robert Bell in his 1854 edition of Chaucer, in which he appended to *Purse* the comment that "in Henry IV's proclamation to the people of England he founds his title on *conquest, hereditary right*, and *election*; and from this inconsistent and absurd document Chaucer no doubt took his cue."[73] Bell's comment was quoted by Skeat in his 1894 edition, and from there it entered the mainstream of twentieth-century Chaucer criticism, where—supported by our own preference for secondary opinion over documentary evidence and by powerful critical presuppositions—it has persisted substantially unchallenged.[74]

The imagined "proclamation" may be seen as a by-product of a set of assumptions about authorship current between the mid-nineteenth and mid-twentieth centuries. These assumptions hold that the choices (or preoccupations) of a sovereign "author" can be traced in a firmly bounded oeuvre or body of work, and within individual components of that oeuvre. So much about the genesis of the literary work and its relation to tradition is, however, left unexplained by the idea of virtually unlimited authorial initiative that this idea necessitated a secondary, apparently contradictory formulation, involving the author's purposive selection and manipulation of a preexisting "source." The point of reconciliation between the sovereignty of the author and the source upon which he or she was required to depend, a reconciliation ultimately in the author's favor, is that his or her choices can be traced in the modifications of (or occasional decisions not to modify) a known original. According to this theory, Chaucer—as author—purposefully adopts the rationale of Henry's own proclamation—in this case, verbatim and slavishly or halfheartedly, as befits a begging poem.[75]

Not only does it encourage invention of a bogus source, but such source hunting actually devalues the very authorial role it sets out to defend. For Chaucer's poem is, in actuality, not passive or halfhearted at all. It is a fresh and conceptually energetic fabrication in its own right. Not that it is wholly "original" or solely author generated; I have sought to show that it is a product of complicated immersion within its textual environment. But the way to an appreciation of those qualities we summarize under the heading of "authorship" is by confronting, rather than avoiding, the complexities that attend the realization of a particular text within an array of competing alternatives.

Nineteenth-century and earlier twentieth-century scholarship drifted into this devotion to the bounded "source" out of a desire to professionalize humanistic inquiry—or at any rate out of a mistaken idea about how to professionalize it. Eager to establish literary discussion as an endeavor that can be learned, taught, defended, and verified, early scholars turned to the prestigious model of later nineteenth-century science, drawing from it a distaste for fuzzy boundaries and a wish for clear delineation of persons, interests, choices, texts, sources, oeuvres. But any approach to the problem of textual origins must accept facts of reliance on preexisting and often contradictory traditions, of multiple determinations, of limits to authorial control. I, too, wish to imagine an "author," but one less bounded and more open to the multiple voices of the time, to a number of sources rather than just one, to the inscription of a text within a matrix of diverse and sometimes contradictory pronouncements.

Notes

1. Hardyng, *Chronicle*, p. 350.
2. *Dieulacres Chronicle*, excerpted in M. V. Clarke and V. H. Galbraith, *The Deposition of Richard II* (Manchester, 1930), p. 51.
3. Jean Creton, *Histoire du Roy d'Angleterre Richard*, ed. and trans. J. Webb in *Ar-

chaeologia 20 (1824), 374. The tactical nature of Henry's oaths at Doncaster and Conway and the "unsystematic" but keenly opportunistic route by which Henry moved toward a claim on the throne are admirabley canvassed by J. W. Sherborne, "Charles VI and Richard II," in *Froissart: Historian*, ed. J. N. N. Palmer (Woodbridge, Suffolk, 1981). He observes that 10 September was the first date by which Henry may be said with certainty to have resolved upon kingship (as opposed to stewardship or other capacities), but that his strategy had been tending in this direction for several weeks (p. 240).

4. *Annales Ricardi Secundi, Regis Angliae*, ed. H. T. Riley, Rerum Britannicarum Medii Aevi Scriptorii (London, 1866), pp. 251-52.

5. *Annales*, ed. Riley, p. 252. *Annales* has both writs and monastic letters in early September, subsequent to Richard's arrival in London and incarceration in the Tower; Lapsley, relying on evidence dating the writs to the 19th, also thinks the letters were sent at an earlier date. See Gaillard Lapsley, "The Parliament Title of Henry IV," *EngHR* 49 (1934), 423-49, 577-606.

6. Adam of Usk, *Chronicon*, ed. Edward Maunde Thompson, 2nd ed. (London, 1904), p. 29.

7. Hardying, *Chronicle*, pp. 353-54.

8. C. L. Kingsford, "The First Version of Hardyng's *Chronicle*," *EngHR* 27 (1912), 468.

9. According to the continuation of the *Eulogium Historiarum*, "Dux dicebat quod Rex Henricus Tertius habuit duos filios, Edmundum seniorem et primogenitum, et Edwardum. Qui tamen Edmundus dorsum habuit fractum, et propter hoc judicavit seipsum indignum esse ad coronam; quare pater eorum eos sic componere facit, quod Edwardus regnaret." See *Eulogium* (including *Continuatio Eulogii*), 369-70.

10. *Annales*, ed. Riley, p. 252.

11. Hardyng, *Chronicle*, p. 353.

12. Adam of Usk, *Chronicon*, p. 30.

13. Ibid., pp. 30-31.

14. Creton, *Histoire*, p. 315.

15. *Rolls of Parliament* (*Rotuli Parliamentorum*) (London, 1783), 3 (1377-1411):415-24 (hereafter *RP*); Cotton Julius B II (in Kingsford), pp. 19-47; Walsingham, Historia 2:234-38.

16. *RP* 3:423.

17. "Sed hoc omnino prohibuit Dominus Willelmus Thernyng, Justiciarius; quia tali occasione commovisset bilem totius populi contra eum; eo quod visum fuisset populo, si sic vendicasset regnum, quot potuisset quemlibet exhaeredasse pro votis, leges mutasse, condidisse novas, et veteres annullasse" (*Annales*, ed. Riley, p. 282).

18. Cotton Julius B II (in Kingsford), p. 20.

19. Ibid.

20. *Chronique de la Traïson et Mort*, ed. Benjamin Williams (London, 1846), p. 67 (hereafter *Traïson*).

21. As John Hardyng claims to have learned at first hand from the earl of Northumberland: "I herde the seide erle saie, that . . . Henry made kynge Richarde vnder dures of prisoun in the Toure of London in fere of his life to make a resignatioun of his right to hym" (Hardyng, *Chronicle*, p. 353).

22. Cotton Julius B II (in Kingsford), p. 23.

23. Ibid.

24. Adam of Usk, *Chronicon*, p. 30.

25. Cotton Julius B II (in Kingsford), p. 24.

26. Ibid., p. 41.

27. William Stubbs, *The Constitutional History of England* (Oxford, 1880), 2:549, finds the gathering parliamentary. Lapsley, "Parliamentary Title," p. 431, finds those gathered deliberately nonparliamentary. B. Wilkenson, "The Deposition of Richard II and the Accession of Henry IV," *EngHR* 54 (1939), 230-39, with whom I would tend to agree, finds them simply a convenient gathering, the precise standing of which did not trouble the Lancastrians.

28. Cotton Julius B II (in Kingsford), p. 43.

29. *RP* 3:423.

30. Stowe MS. 66, excerpted in G. O. Sayles, "The Deposition of Richard II: Three Lancastrian Narratives," *BIHR* 54 (1981), 266.

31. H. G. Wright, "The Protestation of Richard II in the Tower in September 1399," *Bulletin of the John Rylands Library* 23 (1939), 151-65.

32. Lapsley, "Parliamentary Title," observes, "The new government seems to have taken great pains to circulate copies of the official documents recording the steps by which it came into being, and in consequence practically all writers had access to them either directly or indirectly" (pp. 432-33). See also Sayles, "Deposition of Richard II," and C. L. Kingsford, *English Historical Literature in the Fifteenth Century* (Oxford, 1913), p. 20. As James Sherborne, "Perjury and the Lancastrian Revolution of 1399," *Welsh History Review* 14 (1988), 218, just observes, "It is hard to think of another moment of comparable importance in medieval English history when the supply of information was so effectively manipulated as it was by Henry on this occasion."

33. *MED*: "the act of laying claim to something." See John A. Alford, *Piers Plowman: A Glossary of Legal Diction* (Cambridge, Eng., 1988), under *chalengen*, definition 2.

34. Cotton Julius B II (in Kingsford), p. 43.

35. Stowe, MS. 66, in Sayles, "Deposition of Richard II."

36. Adam of Usk, *Chronicon*, p. 33.

37. *Continuatio Euologii*, in *Eulogium*, p. 384.

38. Adam of Usk, *Chronicon*, p. 33.

39. *Continuatio Eulogii*, in *Eulogium*, p. 384.

40. Cotton Julius B II (in Kingsford), p. 43.

41. Walsingham, *Historia*, pp. 239-40; *Annales*, ed. Riley, pp. 297-300; Wright, "Protestation," pp. 151-65, especially pp. 159-62.

42. Walsingham, *Historia*, p. 239.

43. Cotton Julius B II (in Kingsford), p. 49. The traditional ceremony does not require the king to lie down, and imagines the anointing to occur away from view, behind a *pallium* or covering. See "Liber Regalis," in *English Coronation Records*, ed. L. G. W. Legg (Westminster, 1901), p. 92.

44. Cotton Julius B II (in Kingsford), p. 31.

45. Stowe MS. 66, in Sayles, "Deposition of Richard II."

46. *RP* 3:426.

47. On the quality of Henry's arguments, the final word might appropriately be given to Richard, duke of York. Speaking in this case against the title of Henry VI and challenging Henry IV's claim to have been "right enheriter to Kyng Herry the third," Richard commented that "his said saying was oonly to shadowe and colour fradulently his . . . unrightwise and violent usurpation" (*RP* 5:377).

48. Sayles, "Deposition of Richard II," pp. 257-64.

49. George B. Pace and Alfred David, *Geoffrey Chaucer: The Minor Poems*, The Variorum Chaucer 5.1 (Norman, Okla., 1982), pp. 121-22.

50. John H. Fisher, *John Gower: Moral Philosopher and Friend of Chaucer* (New York, 1964), p. 112.

51. Lapsley, "Parliamentary Title," p. 436.

52. J. N. N. Palmer, "The Authorship, Date and Historical Value of the French Chronicles on the Lancastrian Revolution," *Bulletin of the John Rylands Library* 61 (1978), 154, 170.

53. RP 3:426.

54. Adam of Usk, *Chronicon*, p. 33.

55. *Continuatio Eulogii*, in *Eulogium*, p. 384.

56. Sherborne, "Charles VI and Richard II," p. 63.

57. Jean Froissart, *Chroniques*, in *Oeuvres*, ed. Kervyn de Lettenhove (Brussels, 1867-77), 17:204.

58. Both tendencies are present in the first version of his challenge, when, "post eleccionem," he adds a speech of reassurance that his "conquest" will not lead to disrespect for laws and customs (Stowe, MS. 66, in Sayles, "Deposition of Richard II").

59. Creton, *Histoire*.

60. *Traïson*, pp. 68-69.

61. A point to me in conversation by Alfred David. M. Dominica Legge offers a similar observation in an article erroneous in almost every other particular. See M. Dominica Legge, "The Gracious Conqueror," *Modern Language Notes* 68 (1953), 18-21.

62. Cotton Julius B II (in Kingsford), p. 46.

63. Though see Lapsley's brilliant (and paritally convincing) attempt to construct a proelection party from hints in Adam of Usk and other texts (Lapsley, "Parliamentary Title," pp. 585-89).

64. Chaucer's response to critical episodes by modifying his Ricardian ties, without actually forswearing them, is discussed in my "Politics and Poetics: Usk and Chaucer in the 1380s," in *Literary Practice and Social Change in Britain, 1380-1530*, ed. Lee Patterson (Berkeley, Calif., and Los Angeles, 1990), especially pp. 90-97. See also S. Sanderlin, "Chaucer and Ricardian Politics," *Chaucer Rivew* 22 (1987-88), especially pp. 171-75.

65. John Gower, "In Praise of Peace," in *The Complete Works of John Gower*, ed. G. C. Macaulay, 4 vols. (Oxford, 1899-1902), 2:132.

66. *The Major Latin Works of John Gower*, trans. Eric W. Stockton (Seattle, 1962); John Gower, *Chronica*, in *Works*, ed. Macaulay, vol. 4.

67. Evidence against Richard's unpopularity (and for the continuing influence of Lancastrian propaganda) is adduced by Caroline Barron in "The Deposition of Richard II" in *Politics and Crisis in Fourteenth-Century England*, ed. J. Taylor and W. Childs (Gloucester, 1990).

68. See *Eulogium*, pp. 389-94.

69. Christine de Pisan, *Lavision-Christine*, ed. Sr. Mary Louis Towner (Washington, D.C., 1932), pp. 165-66.

70. The quotation is from Lydgate, "The Life of Our Lady," in Caroline Spurgeon, *Five Hundred Years of Chaucer Criticism and Allusion* (Cambridge, Eng., 1925), 1:19; for the flood of tributes after 1400, see pp. 14-19.

71. David Wallace, "'When She Translated Was': A Chaucerian Critique of the Petrarchan Academy," in *Literary Practice and Social Change*, ed. Patterson, pp. 156-215.

72. On the initial delay and eventual backdating of Henry's confirmation, see Sumner J. Ferris, "The Date of Chaucer's Final Annuity and of the 'Complaint to His Empty Purse,'" *Modern Philology* 65 (1967), 45-52.

73. Robert Bell, *Poetical Works of Geoffrey Chaucer* (London, 1846), 8:142.

74. See, for example, V. H. Galbraith, "A New Life of Richard II," *History* 26 (1942), 234; Legge, "Gracious Conqueror," p. 19; and Pace and David, *Geoffrey Chaucer*, p. 131.

75. V. J. Scattergood, *Politics and Poetry in the Fifteenth Century* (London, 1971), p. 116, describes Chaucer's poem as "not markedly enthusiastic."

CHAPTER 3

Chaucer and Gentility

Nigel Saul

Chaucer is a difficult poet for the historian to interpret. He rarely lays bare his conscience in the way that, for example, his contemporary Langland does. Nor does he ever make his poetry a medium for the expression of complaint. His manner is quiet and reflective, ironic and amused. He is in a sense a poet's poet. He is not one to don the mantle of prophet or legislator.[1]

Chaucer's concerns, moreover, are emphatically general, not particular, in character. They embrace the whole range of human experience—the pain and the joy of love, the conflict between Acceptance and Denial, the relationship between the transient and the eternal, even the power of alchemy and magic—anything, indeed, that appealed to his sensitive and inquiring mind. If there is a theme common to these concerns, it is an abiding interest in the ethical basis of behavior. How were men and women to act when confronted with difficult choices? And on what principles? How were they to choose between good and evil, truth and honor? These are questions constantly and variously explored in the canon. It was in the course of exploring them that Chaucer made his contribution to one of the most vigorous and long-running of medieval debates, that on the essence of gentility.

On the face of it, most writers in the Middle Ages had little trouble identifying the key attributes of gentility. In Oliver de la Marche's neat summation, they were lineage and virtue. Lineage was held to be the essential prerequisite for gentility. As Oliver put it, "The gentleman is he who of old springs from gentlemen and gentlewomen, and such men and their posterity by marriage are gentle." Nobility, "which is the beginning of gentility," could be acquired, he went on to say, either by service to a prince or by profession in arms. But *ancient* nobility could come "only from ancient riches; and happy is he, and the more esteemed, who commences his nobility in virtue than he who brings his to an end in vice."[2] This statement of Oliver's was for the most part but a refinement of those of earlier writers. The fourteenth-century Italian jurist, Bartolus, for example, had also highlighted the preeminence of lineage and virtue. He saw what he called "civil nobility," nobility conferred by a prince, as resting on princely recognition of the beneficiary's claim to ancient riches and fine manners, and its counterpart, "natural nobility," as denoting those marked out by their virtue (specifically by their capacity to rule). Bartolus's contemporary Beaumanoir had also concentrated on the same two qualities, but had posited a different relationship between them. Lineage in his view was a consequence of virtue. The *gentilshommes,* in other words, were to be seen as descendants of those sought out after the Fall as the wisest, strongest, and most handsome to rule over people and defend them against their enemies.[3] In the works of Lull and John of Salisbury, and in the comments of knights whose experience lay in the practice rather than the theory of arms, a broadly comparable line was taken: lineage and virtue were the essence of gentility; lineage raised it above nobility, but virtue made it a source of honor.[4]

Vitiating these arguments, however, was a problem that gnawed away at their logic: the claims of birth and of virtue were mutually incompatible. Virtue was an individual quality that a person might or might not possess, whereas birth was a hereditary attribute with which even those without virtue might be endowed. The point was driven home mercilessly from the twelfth century onward by a host of clerical writers whose own claim to authority rested on qualities other than lineage. Nobility of the body, they said, was a carnal thing: it was little better than "a sack full of filth," deriving from "an unclean and shameful act of the parents." It could not be respected or honored because it had not been "personally earned."[5] True nobility was only to be found in the mind. As the first line of one of the *Carmina Burana* put it, "man's nobility is mind, image of the deity." The mind, in other words, was the source of all reason, and reason in its turn was the source of all virtue. Virtue was therefore the property of those who cultivated their minds through reason—namely the clerics. It could not belong to those whose only interest was hunting and hawking and tending their "inherited dunghills," for such were the representatives of "carnal nobility." It had to belong to the more learned, the more educated, the "true nobility." Yet how were those people regarded by the "carnal nobility"? As Jean de Meung complained, they were prized "hardly so much as an apple."[6]

So different were these two approaches to the essence of gentility that any attempt to reconcile them might appear vain, but nevertheless attempts were made. One such invoked the power of example: an individual, it was argued, in particular by Dante, could ennoble his stock by his fine deeds; he could establish a tradition and manner of life that might stand the test of time and even pass into a second generation. Another involved an appeal to eugenics: descent from a virtuous ancestor, it was suggested, could infuse and legitimize a lineage; succeeding generations would feel bound to follow in his path. Lineage, in other words, was cast in the role of instructress of the stock.[7] Neither argument, it has to be said, was particularly convincing. The gap separating the two sides was altogether too wide to be bridged by verbal dexterity. Some writers never tried bridging it at all; they settled either for one side or the other.[8] Others, however, still kept on trying. One who did so was Geoffrey Chaucer.

Chaucer's attempts to wrestle with this problem form a constant if intermittent theme in his work, rarely uppermost in his concerns but surfacing periodically in the context of discussion of other issues. A brief and possibly early statement of his views is to be found in his lyric or "Moral Balade" called simply *Gentilesse*.[9] The line that he took there was heavily influenced by the thinking of such sources as Dante's *Convivio*, Boethius's *De Consolatione*, and to a lesser extent the *Roman de la Rose*.[10] Gentility—"gentilesse"—was seen as a personal, not a hereditary, quality. Its ultimate source was "the firste stok"—Christ, in other words, or just possibly Adam and Eve.[11] Anyone claiming to be gentle must follow in his footsteps, seeking virtue and eschewing evil—for virtue is the source of dignity, not dignity of virtue, whatever a man's station in life. The characteristics of this "firste stok" were righteousness, truth, and freedom, and unless his heirs were of like character, loving virtue as he did, they would never be gentle, even if they wore a crown or mitre or diadem. Vice might well be "heir to old richesse," concludes Chaucer,

> But ther may no man, as men may wel see,
> Bequethe his heir his vertuous noblesse
> (That is appropred unto no degree
> Put to the firste fader in magestee,
> That maketh hem his heyres that him queme),
> Al were he mytre, croune, or diademe.[12]

Though highly derivative in content and source material, the poem is thoroughly Chaucerian in style, and its argument forms a subtheme in more than one of the tales told by the pilgrims on the road to Canterbury. In the *Wife of Bath's Tale* it almost overshadows what is supposed to be the main theme, the proper relationship in marriage between a husband and wife. The story is of course a familiar one. A knight who has committed an act of rape has had his sentence of death commuted into a twelve months' quest to find the answer to a seemingly impossible question—what is it that women most desire? Just when his time is running out, and he is still without an answer, he alights upon a group of maidens near a wood. As he approaches them, however, they vanish, leaving only one wizened old hag, to whom the knight out of desperation decides to put his question. The answer she gives, elicited on condition that he agrees to grant her whatever she wants, turns out to be the correct one—womanly sovereignty in marriage—and when he returns to court he is granted his life. But at this very moment, when he thinks that his ordeal is over, the debt is called in. The old woman springs forth and reminds him of his promise to her. "Keep your promise," she cries, "and take me for your wife." There is no escape for the knight, and he bows to her will. The two then retreat to bed, and as the hapless groom edges further and further away from his repulsive partner, the latter reminds him of the ethical code of his order and of his duties as a husband:

> But, for ye speken of swich gentillesse
> As is descended out of old richesse,
> That therfore sholden ye be gentil men,
> Swich arrogance is nat worth an hen.
> Looke who that is moost vertuous alway,
> Pryvee and apert, and moost entendeth ay
> To do the gentil dedes that he kan;
> Taak hym for the grettest gentil man.
> Crist wole we clayme of hym oure gentillesse,
> Nat of oure eldres for hire old richesse.
> For thogh they yeve us al hir heritage,
> For which we clayme to been of heigh parage,
> Yet may they nat biquethe, for no thing,
> To noon of us hir vertuous lyvyng,
> That made hem gentil men ycalled be,
> And bad us folwen hem in swich degree.[13]

Later on she says, invoking the memory of ancient Rome:

> Thenketh hou noble, as seith Valerius,
> Was thilke Tullius Hostillius,
> That out of poverte roos to heigh noblesse,
> Reedeth Senek, and redeth eek Boece;
> Ther shul ye seen expres that it no drede is
> That he is gentil that dooth gentil dedis.[14]

Gentility, then, it is clear, has more to do with manner of life than with lineage or ancient riches. And just to press home the point she says:

> And he that wole han pris of his gentrye,
> For he was boren of a gentil hous,
> And hadde his eldres noble and vertuous,
> And nel hymselven do no gentil dedis,
> Ne folwen his gentil auncestre that deed is,
> He nys nat gentil, be he duc or erl;
> For vileyns synful dedes make a cherl.[15]

Having finished her homily, she then asks the knight to kiss her. This, once he has overcome his disgust, he agrees to do. He closes his eyes, and when he reopens them he finds that she is transformed into a beautiful maiden. By conceding mastery, and thus, according to the hag's terms, exhibiting virtue, he gains his eventual reward.

Although the *Wife of Bath's Tale*, like the lyric *Gentilesse*, draws on earlier material—the theme of the Loathly Lady is a familiar one in the literary and popular poetry of the day[16]—Chaucer's remodeling of that material is so substantial that the final poem may be considered an expression of his own views.[17] The hag's wedding-night homily can to that extent be read as a statement of his personal conception of gentility—namely, that it had nothing to do with birth or descent; it was purely a matter of individual virtue; and that only those could be accounted gentle who did gentle deeds. There can be no doubt that in the argument about the essence of gentility Chaucer sided with those like Dante who had emphasized the primacy of *virtus*; indeed, he even went so far as to cite such antique writers as Seneca and Boethius among his authorities. But how in that case did he resolve the dilemma that had confronted the earlier commentators—the dilemma that, however much gentility might be held to reside in the virtuous, in the real world it was the attribute of self-perpetuating aristocratic lineages. Did he address himself to the problem? Was he even aware of it? To be sure, he did not resort to the rhetorical pyrotechnics of his predecessors; he did not pray in aid either eugenics or the power of example. His solution was altogether more modest; it was to show how the two ideals were reconciled in the behavior of one of the most attractive of his pilgrim characters—the "verray parfit gentil knyght." Here was a man who united in his person the best of both these seemingly opposed worlds. He was a belted knight, very much a *strenuus miles*, and probably, too, the dependent of a lord (he had fought in "his lordes werre"); clearly, in other words, he was a man of good lineage and blood worth. But he was also a lover of "chivalrie, / Trouthe and honour, fredom and curteisie." "As wel in cristendom as in hethenesse," he was "honored for his worthynesse." Never once in his life did he offer a discourtesy to anyone.[18] He was living proof that those of knightly descent could espouse a code of virtuous behavior.[19] The two sets of values need not be opposed, Chaucer was saying; they could be reconciled. Those born to gentility could practice gentility.

The Knight, of course, like the Priest and the Plowman, is not a sharply defined figure. He is sketched in deliberately generalized terms because he is meant to be representative of one of the three orders into which society was divided. Probably for this reason there are no other people of knightly or noble rank among Chaucer's pilgrims.[20] As numerous commentators have pointed out, the great majority of their number come from the middle strata of society, whence of course Chaucer himself came.[21] The Sergeant-at-law, the Franklin, the Yeoman, the Merchant, the Prioress, the Shipman, the Clerk of Oxenford, the Physician, the Wife of Bath, the Monk, and perhaps even the Manciple can all be said to fall into this category. Of these, just a few would have been considered in status terms to be gentle. The Sergeant-at-law is an obvious case: medieval sergeants were generally of landed estate at the end of their careers, if not at the beginning, and were invariably knighted on admission to their order.22 The Monk might be considered another possible case, considering his fine array and the general convention in the Middle Ages that all who proceeded to major orders should be of free condition.23 But the great majority of the others, surely, would have been outside the fold. They would have been lumped with the "lewd churls" of whom Chaucer spoke—people like the Cook, the Reeve, and most obviously the Miller, whose tale Chaucer told his "gentil" readers to skip if they did not want to be subjected to a "churlish yarn."24 The one pilgrim whose position in the pecking order is open to question is the Franklin. To judge from the details afforded of his public career, it appears that he was a prominent member of the county officeholding elite:

> At sessiouns ther was he lord and sire;
> Ful often tyme he was knyght of the shire
> . . . .
> A shirreve hadde he been, and a countour.
> Was nowher swich a worthy vavasour.25

And the fact that he chose to make his pilgrimage in the company of the Sergeant-at-law tends to lend weight to this impression. But a glance at the lists of those actually appointed to the leading positions in shire administration in the later fourteenth century gives grounds for doubt. The great majority of sheriffs and J.P.s—justices at "sessiouns"—were not franklins but knights or very well-to-do esquires, and their preponderance became steadily greater as time went on. Only in the lesser stations of the officeholding hierarchy, notably in the commissions appointed to collect parliamentary subsidies, were these men and their like strongly represented.26 The Franklin's record of officeholding is thus a reflection more of his group's aspirations than of the reality of their achievement. A generation or two later the position would be different. Men of the Franklin's condition would indeed be appointed to the peace commissions and picked for the shrievalty, for by then they were being gathered within the fold of gentle society. But in the late fourteenth century this time was still some way off. The franklins were already feathering their nests, certainly: in the less crowded conditions that followed the Black Death they were enlarging and reorganizing their holdings, and on manors where lordship was weak they were able to assert a measure of ascendancy over the local peasantry. 27 But it was with their sons ultimately that their hopes would lie. Hence the Franklin's exaggerated concern for his own son. He is not behaving as he should as an aspirant to gentility. He does not take advice, and

> . . . for to plee at dees, and to despende
> And lese al that he hath, is his usage.
> And he hath levere talken with a page
> Than to comune with any gentil wight
> Where he myghte lerne gentillesse aright.[28]

Small wonder that the Franklin is so preoccupied with gentility. Doubtful of his own possession of it on grounds of rank or inherited wealth, he sees his son squandering any chance of acquiring it by manner of life.[29]

Not surprisingly, gentility figures prominently in the tale that the Franklin goes on to relate. It takes the form of a contribution to the debate initiated by the Wife of Bath on matrimony and relationships in love. At the outset the Franklin propounds his own view of the ideal marriage, and it is a very different one from that espoused by the Wife. Sovereignty should be exercised by neither partner, he argues; love and liberty should not be compromised; each partner should remain unconstrained despite the bonds created by marriage. The working of these counsels of perfection in practice he then examines through the medium of the story of Arveragus and his wife Dorigen. Dorigen, whose husband has gone to Britain to seek honor, has rashly ("in pley") promised that she will become the mistress of her lover, a squire Aurelius, if only he will remove the rocks on the Breton coast, which she fears will endanger her husband's return. Unexpectedly, with a magician's help, Aurelius is able to fulfill the charge. Dorigen is thus faced with a dilemma. Is she to remain faithful to her husband? Or is she to keep her word to the esquire? Rather than make the decision herself, she turns to Arveragus, whose advice to her is to keep her word to the esquire. "Trouthe"—that is, loyalty to a promise—he considers more important than the preservation of outward honor. The way is then open for Aurelius to respond to this act of "gentilesse" by showing that he too, though only an esquire, is capable of gentle behavior. He releases Dorigen from the ill-considered promise that she had made to him, and the tale ends in a manner satisfactory to all concerned—satisfactory obviously to the characters, but satisfactory, too, to the Franklin. For, as in the Wife's tale, though in a different way, the principle is asserted that gentility is dependent not on birth but on behavior and manners. If, as Arveragus says, "Trouthe is the hyeste thyng that man may kepe,"[30] then a humble esquire is as capable of keeping it as a knight.

The view that gentility was a quality distinguished by virtue rather than by birth is of course only to be expected of a man who was himself lacking in high birth. Little or no gentle blood flowed through Chaucer's veins. Born the son of a London vintner whose father had inherited a vintner's business in Ipswich, he was of solidly mercantile background.[31] What gentility he had rubbed off onto him from a career in service. Sometime before

1357 he was admitted as a page in the household of Elizabeth de Burgh, and from 1367 he was in regular receipt of wages as a member of the king's household. Increasingly thereafter it was in courtly circles that he moved. But all the while he took care to nourish his links with the London bourgeoisie. Between 1374 and 1386 he served as controller of the royal customs in the port of London, and between 1389 and 1391 he was clerk of the king's works at Westminster, London, and Windsor. He kept a house at Aldgate in the City, and among his acquaintances there were to be numbered John Philpot, a leading merchant-financier, and Nicholas Brembre, lord mayor in 1383 and a prominent supporter of the court. Even after he had set himself up as a country gentleman at Greenwich, as he probably had by 1385, it was to the environs of London that he returned to die. He took a lease on a house in the grounds of Westminster Abbey in December 1399, ten months before his death. His claim to gentility, then, owed very little to the advantage of birth. It was derived almost entirely from his record of service to the crown. The attitude to gentility evinced in his poetry is a reflection of that fact.

In this sense those who have seen Chaucer as an exponent of individualism are obviously right. Chaucer is very much his own man; he cannot easily be fitted into neat social or occupational categories. The gently ironic tone and the sense of ambivalence, even of detachment, that critics have detected in his work are explicable in terms of his delicate social equipoise. He was a townsman and yet a courtier, a Londoner and yet a country gentleman. Contradiction lay at the heart of his outlook. He fought in war, but was unwarlike himself.[32] He frequented court, but managed to distance himself from court politics. He lived at a time of religious ferment, but rarely let slip his own innermost thoughts on religion.[33] Given the range and number of influences to which he was subject, lack of conformity is only to be expected of him. In his outlook as in his career Chaucer was emphatically sui generis: a man on his own, a spectator rather than a participant.

It is the individualist quality of his outlook that has led one critic to suggest that he should be seen as an apostle for a market economy.[34] *Worth*, David Aers has argued, is defined in the *General Prologue* of *The Canterbury Tales* according to professional criteria; it withholds any sense of that benevolent and organic interaction central to traditional social ideologies. [35] In Chaucer's world traditional ideologies are dissolved by market mechanisms, and human relationships are reshaped "around the exchange of commodities."[36] The pilgrims become agents for whom traditional ideas of community and common profit are little more than anachronisms.

To the extent that the pilgrims are defined in the *General Prologue* largely by reference to their occupations or professions, this observation is certainly true. But in a wider sense it can be called into question. In the tales—as opposed to the *General Prologue*—Chaucer evinces little interest in the world of the market. While he retreats some way from the old aristocratic idea of an elite defined by birth, he advances hardly at all in the direction of embracing an ethic defined by success in economic terms. From his remarks on gentility it is clear that the winning of worldly wealth held little appeal for him. Like Dante he judges people according to their worth, and worth is defined not by economic criteria but by reference to values derived largely from classical antique and Christian sources, in particular virtue, fidelity, and above all "trouthe."[37] Possession of riches as a yardstick is indeed emphatically rejected by the old hag in the *Wife of Bath's Tale:*

> But, for ye speken of swich gentillesse
> As is descended out of old richesse,
> That therfore sholden ye be gentil men,
> Swich arrogance is nat worth an hen.[38]

Chaucer's avoidance of economic criteria to define gentility was wholly in accord with the contemporary outlook. Gentility was viewed at the time as a *quality,* and accordingly was assessed in qualitative terms. The heralds, when considering a man's eligibility to bear arms, never overtly addressed the matter of his income—any more than the courts did when deciding the status of those who appeared before them. What both groups looked for were such marks of status as possession of furred apparel, removal from menial employment, and—less tangibly—renown for martial valor.[39] Not until 1530, at the very end of the Middle Ages, is the information finally let slip that only those with an annual income of £10 per annum or movable goods worth £300 could be considered gentle.[40] The reason for this contemporary reticence is not hard to find. Gentility as a value system (for a value system is what it was) paid little regard to wealth per se; it merely took it for granted. Its object was to affirm and sustain the preeminence of the landed elite, and this it did by enveloping them in an aura of glamour and mystique. Their bloodworthiness was stressed, as was their reputation for prowess and martial virtue. Possession of wealth was naturally recognized as a prerequisite for living the gentle life-style, but it was never made its central defining characteristic. Priority was almost always accorded to a man's quality over a man's means, and this the prolonged debate over the essence of gentility served only to reaffirm.

For over half a millennium gentility was defined in these qualitative terms. The rise in the course of that period of new social elites did remarkably little to alter its character; certainly it did nothing to promote its redefinition according to more overtly economic criteria. In the twelfth century the ambitious clerical careerists remained happy to conduct the argument in qualitative terms, because their own claim to recognition was based on quality—the quality of one's mind, that is. Their aspirations could thus be satisfied by nuancing existing definitions of gentility; there was no need wholly to replace them. More surprisingly, the rising professional elites of the late Middle Ages seem also to have accepted the upper-class definitions as they found them. Hardly anywhere, at any rate, did they make an attempt to forge any of their own. In England this was probably because of the relative insignificance of the bourgeois and professional sector; its members formed too small a proportion of the total population to sustain an ethic that could challenge that of the landed aristocracy. [41] In the more heavily urbanized Low Countries it was probably because of the deeper interpenetration of rural and urban society; the urban patriciates partook of the same recreations and amusements as the local nobility and gentry; they even organized tournaments, for example—which their counterparts in the English cities never did. Only in the north Italian states, and in particular in Florence, does it seem that an exception was to be found to this broadly uniform state of affairs. There the relationship between rural and urban society was very nearly as close as in Flanders, if not closer. But the implications for cultural development were very different. In Florence the urban elite forged their own distinct set of values—ones that drew heavily on the legacy of ancient Rome. The chivalric values of the landed aristocracy were challenged and countered by the newer civic or humanist values of the Renaissance.

On the face of it this is an important and striking difference—made all the more so by Italy's subsequent cultural distinction. But in reality it was a difference of degree rather than of kind. To the north of the Alps as well as to the south, the character of the old aristocratic ethic was being redefined. Virtue was gradually being accorded primacy over lineage—at least by the theorists. The claims of hereditary wealth were being downplayed. Nobility, in other words, was being presented in such a way as to be more appealing to the administrative and professional elites. The arguments were propounded first, and at greatest length, in Italy, because it was there that the influence of the classical sources for the reinterpretation was most pervasive. But it was not long before the rest of Europe caught up. In England John Gower led the way. In Book 6 of his *Vox Clamantis*, written before 1381, he reminded the king of the common origin of all people and of the eligibility for nobility of anyone possessed of goodness of spirit; a wise king, he argued, would match the achievements of his ancestors with his own good behavior.[42] Chaucer took a similar line a decade or so later. In the "Moral Balade" *Gentilesse*, he followed Gower in stressing the common origin of people, and in *The Canterbury Tales* he argued consistently for the importance of virtue in any definition of gentility. His positions were followed in the fifteenth century by those of lesser writers working in the genre of courtesy literature.[43]

That these arguments, though conducted at a theoretical level, were not entirely divorced from contemporary reality is suggested by changes in the aristocratic life-style in the late Middle Ages. By the later fourteenth century the aristocracy, in England as elsewhere, were no longer, if they ever had been, an exclusively military elite. They were becoming a service nobility, valued by rulers for their administrative abilities as well as for their skills in arms. They were literate—literate in England probably in three languages, French, Latin, and the vernacular—and they were patrons of art and literature.[44] Lineage and pedigree still mattered to them, as they were to do for some time to come, but they were no longer so important in legitimizing their aspirations to rank and social position. These could be justified in the late fourteenth century by reference to possession of "virtue"—that is to say, of such qualities as "trouthe," "sagesse," and good manners. Sir William Montagu and Sir Thomas Hungerford, to name two of the most successful climbers of the century, owed their rise far more to their deployment of these skills than to purity of descent or prowess in arms. The former made his name as a diplomat and councillor, the latter as an administrator and general man of affairs.[45]

The changing character of the nobility would have been apparent to Chaucer because it was reflected in the changing character of his own immediate circle at court. The court for centuries had been little more than a glorified household—in time of war, a household-in-arms—but in the reign of Richard II it was beginning to turn into a court in the Renaissance sense. [46] Its membership was becoming more civilian in character. The chamber knights, for example, who made their first appearance in the 1360s, were men whose employments were mainly civilian rather than military—in Walsingham's words, they were knights of Venus rather than of Bellona.[47] They had about them some of the attributes of courtiers in the later sense: they were the principal executants of the royal will, they were in almost constant attendance on the royal person, and above all they stood at the center of a vigorous courtly culture. Sir John Clanvowe, a chamber knight from 1381, was a poet of considerable distinction: his *Boke of Cupide* was indeed until the nineteenth century thought to have been written by Chaucer.[48] His colleague Sir John Montagu, later earl of Salisbury, was also a poet, and, although none of his work has survived, he is known to have been complimented by no less an authority than Christine de Pisan. [49]

These are men who would have been known to Chaucer. They would have identified with him as he did with them. As Derek Pearsall has shown, they probably constituted the main audience for his work.[50] One of their number, Sir Philip la Vache, was directly addressed by Chaucer in the ballade *Truth*, while another, Sir Peter Bukton, who was to come into his own in Henry IV's reign, may well have been the Bukton who was addressed in one of the "Envois" of Chaucer's last years.[51] Is it too fanciful to suppose that their attitudes and aspirations are echoed in his writings? On the evidence of his discussion of gentility it is probably not. The emphasis that Chaucer placed on inner worth and on the superiority of "trouthe" to honor would have been wholly in accord with their outlook on the world. In the late fourteenth century there was a general trend toward the interiorization of values that affected all areas of belief. Its most obvious manifestation was in the area of religion. The hostility toward images, the rejection of transubstantiation, and the skepticism toward outward ceremony all indicated how the attribution of sacredness was being withheld from external objects and concentrated in the individual human mind. People were no longer accepting an automatic identity between inner and outer, between spirit and substance; the evidence of disharmony between the two was altogether too strong to be ignored.[52] When forced to make a choice, they almost invariably settled for "inner." That Chaucer should have done the same merely indicates the extent to which he was a child of his age.

From a historical standpoint Chaucer's views on gentility are therefore possibly less interesting in their own right than for the light that they shed on changing attitudes in his lifetime. What the poet had to say was after all fairly unoriginal; for the most part it was a restatement of the commonplaces of Stoic and early Christian philosophy. The significant thing is that he was writing in and for the court. The court in the late fourteenth century was in a state of flux. Its military role was weakening, while its civilian aspect was strengthening. There was a demand for a set of values that would reflect and do justice to that change. This was the significance of the appeal to virtue. Lineage and descent were, of course, to figure in conceptions of gentility for a long while to come, but after Chaucer's time they were never to figure alone. Virtue was to have a prominent place in all future definitions of the idea.

Notes

1. As G. Shepherd points out in "Religion and Philosophy in Chaucer," in *Geoffrey Chaucer*, ed. D. Brewer (London, 1974), p. 289.

2. Quoted by M. Keen, *Chivalry* (New Haven, Conn., and London, 1984), p. 150.

3. Keen, *Chivalry*, pp. 149, 151. Bartolus's views are also discussed by A. Wagner, *Heralds and Heraldry in the Middle Ages*, 2nd ed. (Oxford, 1956), pp. 68-69.

4. It is this subtle difference between nobility and gentility that is highlighted by the remark usually said to have been made by James II in reply to a petitioner pleading for her son to be made a gentleman: "Madam, I could make him a nobleman, but God almighty himself could not make him a gentleman," quoted in D. A. L. Morgan, "The Individual Style of the English Gentleman," in *Gentry and Lesser Nobility in Late Medieval Europe*, ed. M. Jones (Gloucester and New York, 1986), p. 17.

5. A. Murray, *Reason and Society in the Middle Ages* (Oxford, 1978), pp. 270-77, in particular, p. 275.

6. Ibid., p. 277.

7. This was Beaumanoir's view; see p. 42. The arguments are reviewed by Keen, *Chivalry*, pp. 157-61.

8. The heralds came down strongly in favor of lineage. The humanist writers came down equally strongly in favor of virtue.

9. *The Works of Geoffrey Chaucer*, ed. F. N. Robinson, 2nd ed. (London, 1957), p. 536. All citations are from this edition.

10. The sources are noted in *Works*, ed. Robinson, p. 861.

11. The problems of interpretation are discussed by Robinson in *Works*, p. 862, where the reading "stock-fader" is regarded as "very tempting." The idea that Christ was the

only source of gentility was a popular one at the time. It was repeated in that *omnium gatherum* of Christian common places, the *Parson's Tale*, lines 460-65.

12. Chaucer, *Gentilesse*, in *Works*, ed. Robinson, lines 16-21.

13. Chaucer, *The Wife of Bath's Tale*, in *Works*, ed. Robinson, lines 1009-1124.

14. Ibid., lines 1165-70.

15. Ibid., lines 1152-57.

16. *Works*, ed. Robinson, pp. 702-3. My discussion of the tale focuses specifically on its treatment of gentility. The marriage theme has been treated admirably by a number of scholars, notably Derek Pearsall, *The Canterbury Tales* (London, 1985), pp. 71-91.

17. Pearsall, *Canterbury Tales*, pp. 86-89, compares the tale in detail with its nearest English analogue, Gower's tale of Florent (*Confessio Amantis* 1, lines 1407-1861), and highlights the differences.

18. The literature on the Knight is voluminous. The most important recent contribution has been Maurice Keen, "Chaucer's Knight, the English Aristocracy and the Crusade," in *English Court Culture in the Later Middle Ages*, ed. V. J. Scattergood and J. W. Sherborne (London, 1983), pp. 45-62, which effectively rebuts the arguments of Terry Jones, *Chaucer's Knight: Portrait of a Medieval Mercenary* (London, 1980).

19. A similar point may be made in regard to the knight in *The Wife of Bath's Tale*. He, too, acted in accordance with the best traditions of his order and duly gained his reward. See pp. 43-45.

20. Unless one counts the Esquire, the Knight's son.

21. The point has been made most recently by Paul Strohm, *Social Chaucer* (Cambridge, Mass., and London, 1989), p. 67.

22. John H. Baker, *The Order of Serjeants at Law*, Selden Society, Supp. Ser. 5 (London, 1984), pp. 18-19.

23. There is a case for identifying him with no less exalted a figure than William Clown, abbot of the great Augustinian house of St. Mary-in-the-Fields, Leicester. See the balanced discussion of the evidence in David Knowles, *The Religious Orders in England*, 3 vols. (Cambridge, Eng., 1961), 2:365-66.

24. Chaucer, *The Miller's Prologue*, in *Works*, ed. Robinson, lines 3176-77. On Chaucer's use of the distinction between "gentils" and "churls," see Derek S. Brewer, "Class Distinction in Chaucer," *Speculum* 43 (1968), 299-301.

25. Chaucer, *General Prologue*, in *Works*, ed. Robinson, lines 355-56, 359-60.

26. Nigel Saul, *Knights and Esquires: The Gloucestershire Gentry in the Fourteenth Century* (Oxford, 1981), ch. 4, and idem, "The Social Status of Chaucer's Franklin: A Reconsideration," *Medium Aevum* 52 (1983), 16-18. The meaning of the term "vavassour" is discussed by Peter R. Coss, "Literature and Social Terminology: The Vavassour in England," in *Social Relations and Ideas: Essays in Honour of R. H. Hilton*, ed. T. H. Aston, P. R. Coss, C. Dyer, and J. Thirsk (Cambridge, Eng., 1983), pp. 109-50. There can be little doubt that a "countour" is a pleader—probably in this case a pleader in the county court. The origins of the term are discussed by Baker, *Order of Serjeants at Law*, pp. 8-9.

27. Saul, "The Social Status of Chaucer's Franklin," pp. 22-23, where the case of the Hyde family of Denchworth (Oxfordshire) is discussed.

28. The Franklin's words to the Squire, lines 690-94 (*Works*, ed. Robinson, p. 135).

29. The Franklin's exclamation, "Would that £20 of land dropped into my hands now," gives an idea of what he regarded as an estate of some value. It fell somewhat short of that needed to support a knight. Since the early fourteenth century, the threshhold for knighthood had been set at an annual income of at least £40. The size of franklins' holdings is discussed in my "Social Status of Chaucer's Franklin," pp. 15-16. For some useful observations on the relationship between the Franklin and his tale, see R. M. Lumiansky, *Of Sondry Folk: The Dramatic Principle in the Canterbury Tales* (Austin, Tex., 1955), pp. 180-93.

30. Chaucer, *The Franklin's Tale*, in *Works*, ed. Robinson, line 1479. Commentary on the *Franklin's Tale* abounds. In reaching my own interpretation, I have been particularly

influenced by R. B. Burlin, "The Art of Chaucer's Franklin," *Neophilologus* 51 (1967), 55-73, reprinted in *Chaucer, The Canterbury Tales: A Casebook*, ed. J. J. Anderson (London, 1974), pp. 183-208—though I by no means accept all of Burlin's arguments.

31. My brief summary of Chaucer's career is based on the materials in *CLR*. To deny Chaucer a hereditary claim to gentility is not to suggest that his origins were humble. Clearly they were not. The Chaucers were a well-to-do family, and Robert, the poet's grandfather, married into the still more prosperous Westhall family of Ipswich. Unlike many other families of their standing, however, the Chaucers do not appear either to have married into the gentry or to have consolidated a set of landholdings in the countryside near London or Ipswich. Although John, the poet's father, had seen active service in the Weardale campaign of 1327 (see A. Ayton, "John Chaucer and the Weardale Campaign, 1327," *Notes and Queries*, March 1989, 9-10), there is no evidence that the family made use of a coat of arms before the poet's own time.

32. He had seen active service in the campaign of 1359-60, when he was captured (*CLR*, pp. 23-28). For Chaucer's attitude to war, see John Barnie, *War in Medieval English Society: Social Values and the Hundred Years' War, 1337-1399* (London, 1974), pp. 131-35.

33. Chaucer's religious views are treated by Geoffrey Shepherd, "Religion and Philosophy in Chaucer," in *Geoffrey Chaucer*, ed. D. Brewer (London, 1974), ch. 10; and Basil Cottle, *The Triumph of English* (London, 1969), ch. 6. The statement of Christian doctrine in the *Parson's Tale* has its origin in the commonplaces of the age rather than in Chaucer's own views.

34. David Aers, *Chaucer* (Brighton, 1986), pp. 19-20.

35. Aers is here quoting Jill Mann. No reference is given, but the source is likely to be Mann's *Chaucer and Medieval Estates Satire* (Cambridge, Eng., 1973), p. 200.

36. Aers, *Chaucer*, p. 20.

37. For a useful discussion of the meaning of these words, see G. Mathew, "Ideas of Knighthood in Late-Fourteenth Century England," in *Studies in Medieval History Presented to F. M. Powicke*, ed. R. W. Hunt, W. A. Pantin, and R. W. Southern (Oxford, 1948), pp. 354-62.

38. Chaucer, *The Wife of Bath's Tale*, in *Works*, ed. Robinson, lines 1109-12.

39. To the justices, clothing and evidence of honorable employment, such as employment in service, were of particular importance; see Robin L. Storey, "Gentlemen-bureaucrats," in *Profession, Vocation and Culture in Later Medieval England*, ed. Cecil H. Clough (Liverpool, 1982), pp. 90-93. For the somewhat vaguer criteria employed by the heralds, see the grant of arms made by Garter to Edmund Mylle in 1450, quoted by Keen, *Chivalry*, p. 163.

40. Wagner, *Heralds and Heraldry in the Middle Ages*, p. 79. Contemporary vagueness in regard to monetary qualifications is highlighted by another document of the same time—an order of Charles Brandon, duke of Suffolk, the Earl Marshal. This laid down one set of fees to be paid by the possessors of "one hundreth poundes of land or fees" or "in moveable one thousand markes," and another for "all other beinge of substance under the same vallour." No threshold for the latter category was mentioned (ibid.).

41. For the cultural affinities between the London merchants and the landed gentry, see Sylvia L. Thrupp, *The Merchant Class of Medieval London (1300-1500)* (Chicago, 1948), ch. 6.

42. *The Major Latin Works of John Gower*, trans. Eric W. Stockton (Seattle, 1962), p. 243.

43. For aspects of this literature, see Morgan, "The Individual Style of the English Gentleman," and E. F. Jacob, "The Book of St. Albans," in his *Essays in Later Medieval History* (Manchester and New York, 1968), pp. 195-213.

44. The educational attainments of the nobility were stressed by K. B. McFarlane, *The Nobility of Later Medieval England* (Oxford, 1973), pp. 228-47. A recent study of the subject is Nicholas Orme, *From Childhood to Chivalry: The Education of the English Kings and Aristocracy, 1066-1530* (London, 1984). For the development of literacy, see Michael T. Clanchy, *From Memory to Written Record* (London, 1979), in particular, pp. 182-201.

45. For Montagu, see McFarlane, *Nobility of Later Medieval England*, pp. 159-61, and for Hungerford, see John S. Roskell, "Sir Thomas Hungerford," in his *Parliament and Politics in Late Medieval England*, 3 vols. (London, 1981-83), 2:15-43.

46. The process of evolution from household to court was, of course, a long-drawn-out one spanning a century or two. D. A. L. Morgan, "The House of Policy: The Political Role of the Late Plantagenet Household, 1422-1485," in *The English Court from the Wars of the Roses to the Civil War*, ed. David Starkey (London, 1987), pp. 25-70, sees it as beginning in the reign of Henry VI. But this may be too late. As Anthony Tuck points out in his review in *History Today* 58 (March 1988), 58, many of the shifts that Morgan identifies have their origin in the reign of Richard II. Certainly, by his reign the court was ceasing to wear the aspect of a "war-band."

47. *Chronicon Anglie, 1328-1388*, ed. Edward M. Thompson, RS (London, 1874), p. 375. For the rise of the "chamber knights," see Chris Given-Wilson, *The Royal Household and the King's Affinity: Service, Politics, and Finance in England, 1360-1413* (New Haven, Conn., and London, 1986), pp. 204-12, and idem, "The King and the Gentry in Fourteenth-Century England," *TRHS*, 5th series, 37 (1987), 87-102.

48. *The works of Sir John Clanvowe*, ed. V. J. Scattergood (Cambridge, Eng., and Ottawa, 1975).

49. Nigel Wilkins, "Music and Poetry at Court: England and France in the Late Middle Ages," in *English Court Culture in the Later Middle Ages*, ed. V. J. Scattergood and J. W. Sherborne (London, 1983), pp. 188-89.

50. Derek Pearsall, "The *Troilus* Frontispiece and Chaucer's Audience," *Yearbook of English Studies* 7 (1977), 68-74.

51. For *Truth*, see *Works*, ed. Robinson, p. 536, and for *Lenvoy de Chaucer a Bukton*, ibid., p. 539. For aspects of these men's careers, see Given-Wilson, *The Royal Household and the King's Affinity*, pp. 166, 191-92. Philip la Vache was son-in-law of Sir Lewis Clifford and a friend of Chaucer and possibly godfather to his son, the "little Lewis" for whom the treatise on the Astrolabe was written in 1391; see K. B. McFarlane, *Lancastrian Kings and Lollard Knights* (Oxford, 1972), pp. 182-83.

52. There are useful observations on this theme in D. Brewer, *Chaucer and His World* (London, 1978), pp. 175-76, and McFarlane, *Lancastrian Kings and Lollard Knights*, pp. 224-26.

PART II

✛

London as a Literary Setting

CHAPTER 4

Chaucer and the Absent City

David Wallace

C haucer's *Canterbury Tales* does not begin in London: it begins
south of the Thames in Southwark and moves us steadily away
from the city walls. Chaucer's solitary attempt at pure London fiction comes to an abrupt end after just fifty-eight lines: "Of this cokes
tale," writes the Hengwrt scribe, "maked Chaucer na moore."[1] The pro-
jected return journey from Canterbury is never made. In Chaucerian fiction, then, the City of London is chiefly remarkable for its absence. This
essay attempts to read that absence. I begin by establishing the relationship of London to Southwark; I then consider texts from fourteenth-
century London and Trecento Florence that offer precedents for the kinds
of urban narrative that Chaucer might have written. Having shown how
Boccaccio's story of Cisti the baker (*Decameron* VI. 2) succeeds in generating a unifying ideology of associational form, I proceed to a detailed reading of Chaucer's *Cook's Tale* as a London narrative. I end by observing
how, as a plurality of discourses, Chaucer's London continues to defy poetic and political representation as a single, unified site.

London and Southwark

The absence of London from *The Canterbury Tales* is rendered more striking when Chaucer's text is read against its Italian twin, Boccaccio's *Decameron*. Boccaccio's text begins and ends in Florence. The form of governance that orders its storytelling is established in the church of Santa Maria Novella, a key site in both the religious and political history of the city.
The rhetorical skills that the ten young Florentines take to the countryside
will prove indispensable for the governance of the city once the plague has
abated and civic life can be reestablished. Their tales feature dozens of historical Florentine protagonists and Florentine locales; the Sixth Day is entirely devoted to stories set in Florence. The only figures in Chaucer's text
that may be paired with historical personages are Chaucer himself and
"Herry Bailey" (I.4358), who is presumably to be associated with the "Hen-
ri Bayliff ostlyer" recorded by the Southwark Subsidy Rolls in 1380-81.
The "Cook of London" (I.4325), who names Harry Bailey, identifies himself as "Hogge of Ware" (I.4336). The Cook is himself addressed with face-
tious reverence by the Host as "gentil Roger" (I.4353); he may be associat-

ed with the "Roger of Ware of London, Cook," a convicted nightwalker who figures twice in pleas of debt.[2]

The choice of a Southwark tavern as the gathering place for Chaucer's pilgrimage is at once realistically plausible and arrestingly eccentric. Pilgrims from London to Canterbury often spent the night in Southwark so that they could begin their journey before the city gates were opened for the day: Chaucer's pilgrims, we should note, "made forward erly for to rise" (I.33). But there was nothing to prevent Chaucer from assembling his pilgrimage at a familiar London landmark, the cross at St. Paul's, for example. The effect of assembling at Southwark is to emphasize the randomness of this encounter between Chaucer and the "compaignie" (which is itself a random grouping, "by aventure yfalle, In felaweshipe," I.26). And the business of establishing a form of governance in Southwark under the tutelage of an innkeeper must have seemed (to a London readership) comically misguided. Southwark functioned as a dumping ground and exclusion zone for early modern London: messy or marginal trades such as lime burning, tanning, dying, brewing, innkeeping, and prostitution flourished there; criminals fleeing London courts and aliens working around London trade regulations found a home. Southwark was a suburb of London but also an independent parliamentary borough (albeit a borough lacking a charter of incorporation). The "tangled and disharmonious snarl of jurisdictions"[3] overlapping in Southwark is a historian's nightmare. Southwark recognized no single authority but was divided between five manorial jurisdictions (four in ecclesiastical hands; one owned first by the Crown and later by the City); each had its own set of courts. Southwark's parishes were only partially coterminous with these manorial jurisdictions, and the boundaries of the aggregate term "Southwark" vary from document to document. The Crown controlled the courts and prisons of the Marshalsea and King's Bench and exercised its authority through permanent county officers such as sheriffs, escheators, coroners, and justices. The City of London struggled tirelessly to swallow up (sometimes by legal tactics, sometimes by simple encroachment) the unchartered community on its south bank that continually undermined the monopolies and privileges of its trade and craft guilds: the charter of 1444 confirming the City's rights in the Guildable manor speaks of the "diverse doubts, opinions, differences, ambiguities, controversies, and dissensions"[4] that had characterized relations between London and Southwark since time immemorial. This is the site at which Chaucer's pilgrim body recognizes Harry Bailey as "oure governour" (I.813).

Chaucer's relationship to London at the opening of his *Canterbury Tales* is thus markedly different from the *Decameron's* relationship to Florence. Boccaccio establishes a form of associational governance within the city that is then carried to the countryside. Chaucer establishes no form of governance until his pilgrimage has left the city; his order of storytelling is then established at a place experienced by fourteenth-century London as a challenge to its own integrity, as "a perpetual jurisdictional affront."[5] Southwark defined itself against London politically but, economically, found London indispensable. The name of Southwark, in short, identifies governance as a problematic issue, takes this issue out of the city, and yet cannot quite leave the city behind.

Having emphasized the centrifugal impulse of Chaucer's Canterbury pilgrimage—its rapid distantiation from London as a point of origin—we should also recognize that there was much movement in the opposite direction in late-fourteenth-century England. Religious and secular magnates continued to maintain residences in the capital and to buy up and rent out properties. The royal household moved in a tighter circle around London and more of its administrative apparatus was permanently housed at Westminster.[6] Foreigners, *uplondish* and *outlandish* men, sought out the royal court, the law courts, the Inns of Court, and the international markets; young men and women from every part of Britain came to serve their time as apprentices, to find work, or to contract marriages. Both modern historians and medieval Londoners tend to speak of London as a fluid entity, a place to which people come and go, rather than as a permanent, sharply delimited site.[7] And yet, at the same time; London authorities were keen to represent London as "the capital city and the watch-tower of the whole realm," and to insist "that from the government thereof other cities and places do take example."[8]

Narrative and Governance in Fourteenth-Century London

Chaucer's London was, by postpandemic standards, a metropolis: the poll tax returns of 1377 indicate a population more than three times greater than that of York or Bristol, its nearest English rivals. And although Chaucer wrote little of the city he lived and worked in, there are many contemporary texts that give us a detailed sense of the specifically *urban* character of London life. Many of them feature the kind of tricksters and impersonators that flourish as the urban division of labor grows ever more complex. One such character, a Welshman called John Haslewode (alias John Harehull), goes on a tour of London breweries with a white staff in his hand, purporting to be "a taker of ale for our Lord the King."[9] Another, Roger Clerk of Wandlesworth (Wandsworth), offers to exercise his skill as a physician to cure the bodily infirmities of Johanna, wife of Roger atte Hacche. Having received a down payment of 12*d*., Roger Clerk hangs a scroll (*cedulam*) around Johanna's neck upon which, he says, "was written a good charm for fevers." Later, on being asked what the words of this charm of his were, Roger replies:

> "Anima Christi, sanctifica me; corpus Christi, salva me; in isanguis Christi, nebria me; cum bonus Christus tu, lava me." *And the parch-*

David Wallace

ment being then examined, not one of those words was found writ-
ten thereon. And he was then further told by the Court, that a straw
beneath his foot would be of just as much avail for fevers, as this
charm of his was; whereupon, he fully granted that it would be so.[10]

The court in question is that composed of the mayor and aldermen who
sat in the Chamber of the London Guildhall. The Letter Books that record
their proceedings usually employ Latin, but often switch to Anglo-Norman
or Middle English when noting proclamations and ordinances. Their narratives of crimes and misdemeanors often detail some quite spectacular examples of native wit and inventiveness. In 1380, for example, John Warde
and Richard Lyneham, two men considered "stout enough to work for
their food and raiment," came before the court accused of impersonating
mutes through an elaborate pantomime employing pincers, an iron hook,
two ell measures,

and a piece of leather, in shape like part of a tongue, edged with sil-
ver, and with writing around it, to this effect,— "This is the tongue
of John Warde"; with which instruments, and by means of diverse
signs, they gave many persons to understand that they were traders,
in token whereof they carried the said ell measures; and that they
had been plundered by robbers of their goods; and that their tongues
had been drawn out with the said hook, and then cut off with the
pincers; they making a horrible noise, like unto a roaring, and open-
ing their mouths; where it seemed to all who examined the same,
that their tongues had been cut off: to the defrauding of other poor
and infirm persons, and in manifest deceit of the whole of the peo-
ple, etc.[11]

This piece of street theater, which seems no great crime by modern standards, evidently shocked and scandalized the mayoral court. The "evil intent and falsity" of the malefactors are denounced at some length and the
punishment meted out to them is exceptionally severe: on the Monday,
Wednesday, and Friday before the Feast of St. Simon and St. Jude they are
to be placed upon the pillory, with their pincers, hook, leather tongue, and
ell measures hanging around their necks; they are then to be jailed in Newgate until further notice. The Guildhall was evidently determined to stage
some theater of its own (a one-week run) "to the end that other persons
might beware of such and the like evil intent, falsity, and deceit." What accounts for this severe reaction by the London authorities? The reference to
"other poor and infirm persons" offers one line of explanation: both secular and religious authorities in this period showed a new and determined
resolve to discriminate between "genuine" paupers (who had a right to beg
because of physical infirmity) and sturdy beggars (who could work but
were too idle to do so).[12] A second explanation, a complementary rather

than alternative one, concerns the false signifier of the text-inscribed severed tongue. City authorities needed to enforce a respect for the integrity of symbolic representation within the city, since the limits and partialities of their own power could only be disguised through the persuasive power of symbolic forms. When the tongue is isolated as the object of attention, the listener is invited to disassociate the tongue from what the tongue speaks of. Chaucer's Pardoner issues one such invitation in modeling his false preaching: "Myne handes and my tonge goon so yerne / That it is joye to se my bisynesse" (VI.398-99).

The City authorities could not allow the populace to see its tongue wagging as it spoke its judgments, sentences, and ordinances. And yet, at times, the limitations of the symbolic acts performed by and within the mayoral court were readily apparent. One such high point of symbolic drama came in 1387, when the right hand of William Hughlot was laid upon the block in the Guildhall Court, ready to be chopped off by an axe held by one of the sheriff's officers.[13] The right hand that Hughlot was about to lose had earlier stabbed a barber in his house in Fleet Street, assaulted an alderman, and wounded one of the Fleet Street constables. But Hughlot's hand was never amputated because at the last minute John Rote, the alderman he had attacked, asked "that execution of the judgment aforesaid might be remitted unto him." Hughlot was then sentenced to imprisonment for a year and a day and "condemned to suffer the disgraceful punishment of the pillory." But he never went to the pillory and was released from prison just nine days later. Such leniency is soon explained: it is exercised, the Letter Book tells us, "in reverence for our said Lord the King, whose servant the said William then was." The mayor and aldermen are at pains to emphasize, throughout the document, that they too are officers of the king. But even as officers of the king they were not bold enough to strike off the right hand of someone in royal service: they settled for a lesser drama, in which Hughlot was obliged, on the day of his release from prison, to carry a lighted wax candle from the Guildhall to the Church of St. Dunstan, the parish in which he had committed his crime.

The light sentencing of William Hughlot is in sharp contrast to the fate of two men convicted of breaking into the house of a "citizen and mercer of London" in 1390.[14] The brief entry devoted to their trial concludes as follows: "The said John Prentys and John Markyngtone are guilty of the felony aforesaid. Therefore they are to be hanged. Chattels of the same felons there are none etc." The fact that the two men have no possessions, that they are men of no substance, means that they have nothing with which to pay for their crimes except their miserable lives. This ideal of commutative justice is dramatized in the punishment of the pillory (which is generally reserved for people of lower degree): the malefactor is reunited with his crime as he stands with the symbols or instruments of his transgression around his neck. John Haselwode, the would-be ale-taker, stood with his white wand at his side; Roger Clerk, the quack physician, having been led through the City with trumpets and pipes on a saddleless horse, stood with his magic spell and a whetstone around his neck and urinals hanging before and behind him.[15] Such imaging of justice, which freezes malefactors in time at the moment of their crime, is most perfectly represented by Dante's *Inferno*: we think, for example, of the Florentine usurers sitting in the seventh circle with their purses hanging around their necks (each one decorated by their family coat of arms).[16] The lower reaches of the *Inferno* are encompassed by the walls of a city; Dante's Hell is a subterranean version of Dante's Florence.

But although the narratives in the London Letter Books terminate with a Dantean imaging of justice—an hour in the pillory warns of, prefigures, an eternity of punishment—the narrative energy that precedes such closure is more strongly reminiscent of Boccaccio. These texts do, after all, issue from a group of merchant capitalists that compares with the *Decameron*'s first audience and matches Boccaccio's mercantile origins. And they reflect a comparably detailed understanding of the urban milieu that they seek to control and regulate. In unraveling a fraud case in 1391, for example, *Letter Book H* takes us on a journey through the streets and suburbs of London almost as complicated as that of Andreuccio of Perugia through Naples: we follow a cloth merchant's servant through various wards, parishes, and hostelries inside and outside the city walls until he is finally locked into a room at "'Le Walssheman sur le Hoope,' in Fletestret, in the Parish of St. Martin without Ludgate, in the suburb of London": here he is finally parted from his master's merchandise by a con artist posing as a nobleman's servant.[17]

Such a detailed concern with the regulation and division of time and space in the city is a constant feature of the Letter Books; when we read their narratives in sequence we begin to see how the lines of power in the city run. On folio cxiii of *Letter Book H*, for example, we find the names of eleven women who have paid the sum of 13*s.* 4*d.* each for the privilege of maintaining market stalls at specific points around the High Cross of Cheapside for one year.[18] On the reverse side of the same folio (two pages later in Riley, who breaks up the sequence of the manuscript), we find that these fees are to be diverted to one John Charney by virtue of his office as *venator communitatis London*, "Common Hunt for the Commonalty of London." Common Hunt is responsible for overseeing the stables and kennels maintained for the use of the citizens of London. The art of city government here, then, consists in a masculine oligarchy selling city space to women traders so that London citizens can pursue their aristocratic pretensions outside the city walls through the art of hunting. Such models of expropriation were not, of course, made visible to the general public: the *Letter Book* keeps to Latin here and only turns to the vernacular when it wishes the citizens, foreigns, and aliens of London to take notice of its ordinances and proclamations.

I am not suggesting that Chaucer spent his evenings leafing through record books at the Guildhall.[19] But it is important to recognize that these records attest to a sophisticated understanding of the functioning and governance of urban space; they suggest, in short, an urban consciousness.[20]

Urban Narrative: Italian Precedents for Chaucer

So far we have simply established that Chaucer had ample opportunity to develop the kind of urban narrative we associate with the Italian Trecento. Why, then, does he refuse this possibility? We might begin our attempt at an answer by noting that the urban scenes of both Dante and Boccaccio are set within all-inclusive (hence all-explanatory) ideological frameworks. Dante deploys the greatest framework imaginable: his sunken city is reached only by the path that leads us beneath the Trinitarian inscription of *Inferno* III, which begins: "PER ME SI VA NE LA CITTÀ DOLENTE" (THROUGH ME YOU ENTER THE WOEFUL CITY). Here, beyond this inscription, the familiar mechanisms of urban justice are regulated with superhuman impartiality. Boccaccio, however, operates above ground within an ideological space that may be read in conjunction with, or as part of, a Florentine tradition of mercantile historiography.[21] This begins with Giovanni Villani, who assigns the moment of inspiration for his *Chronicle* to 1300, the year of Dante's imaginary journey through the afterlife, and makes a Dante-like attempt to square events in Florence with an all-encompassing, God-guided scheme of historical explanation. Matteo, who took up the *Chronicle* on Giovanni's death, is interested more in the city-state of Florence and less in any putative universal history it might form part of. By the time we get to Goro Dati at the turn of the next century, the Florentine state has become the transcendent subject of history: "the commune," says Dati, "cannot die."[22] The *Decameron* situates itself, in time of composition, revision, and ideological positioning, somewhere near the midpoint of this Trecento tradition of merchant-class chroniclers. The imaginative power of the afterlife makes itself felt, but the compelling confidence of Boccaccio's text is invested not in the interpretive power of religion, but rather in the city-state's ability to regulate itself through its own urban mechanisms and to identify and expel those who threaten its internal equilibrium.[23]

Chaucer, like Boccaccio, explicitly rejects the Dantean option of writing a text with pretensions to omniscience: "ther is noon dwellynge in this contree," he writes in opening his *Legend of Good Women*, "that eyther hath in hevene or helle ybe" (F, 5-6).[24] And yet he is also denied the Boccaccian option of associating with a vernacular tradition that is gradually adapting the religious universalism of monastic chronicling to the market-driven exigencies of urban society. London was the center of chronicle writing in Chaucer's time, but was not the *subject* of it; there was no tradition of merchant-class chronicling in fourteenth-century England.[25] We might make an exception here for *Letter Book H*, which suddenly turns into a chronicle of sorts in June 1381. On the same folio that records Ralph Strode's prosecution of a poulterer who had attempted to sell eighteen pigeons, "putrid and stinking, and an abomination to mankind," we hear of "the most wondrous and hitherto unheard-of prodigies that have ever happened in the City of London."[26] The hero of this narrative is Sir William Walworth, the then mayor; the climactic scene is played out at Smithfield, where Mayor Walworth rides at Watt Tyler with peasants to the one side of him and king, lords, knights, esquires, and citizens on the other. The narrative concludes, after the jousting mayor has unseated and slain the rebel captain, with the mayor and his accomplices being knighted in the field beneath the royal banner. When the Letter Book scribe turns historian, then, he sounds more like a chivalric chronicler than a mercantile one. The rebels are not analyzed as a class, as part of the social equation calculated so carefully elsewhere in the Letter Book, but are reported as a prodigy, a natural disaster. This strategy is shared by clerical authors in 1381 and by the poet who, meditating upon the earthquake of 21 May 1382, remembers the rebels only to fold them back into clerical discourse:

> The rysyng of the comuynes in londe,
> The pestilens, and the eorthe-qwake,
> Theose threo thinges, I understonde,
> Beoth tokenes the grete vengaunce and wrake
> That schulde falle for synnes sake,
> As this clerkes conne declare.[27]

This sense of being obliged to record every egregious act of nature and to interpret it as a message from the Almighty is shared by Giovanni Villani. But once Giovanni's *Chronicle* has been abruptly silenced by the plague of 1340, the most egregious act of all, the floods, fires, and falling chimney pots begin to fade from Florentine historiography; attention is now concentrated upon the inner workings of the city itself. But the later chroniclers never cut the cord that attaches them to the religious universalism of earlier generations; they tend, rather, to identify the workings of Providence more closely with the exigencies of Florentine polity. By the 1370s the citizenry has enough faith in its defining civic virtue of *libertas* to set it against the hierocratic authority of Rome: Florence goes to war against the papacy. In Boccaccio, too, we see a powerful commitment to what might be termed an ideology of associational form. In the next few pages we will consider how this ideology of association within a self-sufficient, self-regulating city is developed in one short novella. We will then move straight to a reading of the *Cook's Tale* and see how associational form plays in Chaucer.

The first thing to say about this ideology of associational form is that it is an ideology, not an ontology.[28] The Florentine Republican regime of 1343-78 certainly started out as one of the broadest-based regimes in the history of early modern Europe: shopkeepers, artisans, and tradesmen shared in the business of government with patrician merchants, bankers, and rentiers. But powerful class antagonisms did, of course, remain. The greater guilds controlling the major industries did not think that the principle of *libertas* should extend to include lower guildsmen; the shopkeepers and craftsmen of the lower guilds were keen to accentuate their own privileged status by keeping the lower classes out of office and by preventing them from forming guilds of their own. No single group was trusted to hold office for very long (the priors of the Signoria served two-month terms), and no citizens were trusted with the administration of justice: outsiders were hired on short, fixed-termed contracts to serve as *podestà* or *capitano del popolo*. This, then, was the fragile and intricate political structure that prevailed in Florence as Boccaccio wrote his *Decameron*. Republican regimes were keen to celebrate Ciceronian *aequitas*, an ideal that puts all members of a specific social group on level terms with one another.[29] But although this might be achieved within (or across) the lowest and highest political forms of a commune—from the parish guild to the Signoria—the space between such constituent forms was itself, of course, hierarchized. There was a need, then, for some form of cultural production that would both challenge ideologies that were hostile to associative polity and conceal the divisions within such polity by reconciling hierarchized relations along a single plane of *aequitas*, of *unitas civium*. Such complex ideological maneuvers, which defeat the strict logic of political theory, are most adeptly performed by imaginative texts that conceal their own ideological character through the techniques of novelistic realism. Let us consider just one such narrative: the second novella of the *Decameron*'s Sixth Day.

Cisti the Baker and the Ideology of Associational Form

The novella begins with the narrator, Pampinea, questioning the logic of Fortune and Nature (and hence of class-structured society): why do they sometimes assign a noble spirit to an inferior body or social calling? Pampinea insists that these powers show great wisdom in "burying their most precious possessions in the least imposing (and therefore least suspect) part of their houses, whence they bring them forth in the hour of greatest need" (p. 485; VI. 2. 5).[30] Here, then, is an attempt to develop the notion of an intelligence buried deep within the lower reaches of Florentine society that will make itself heard at times of danger. In Pampinea's novella this intelligence is embodied by the unlikely figure of "Cisti fornaio," Cisti the baker.

The novella is set in 1300, the year in which a papal delegation visited Florence to make peace between two feuding factions, the Black and White Guelfs. Pope Boniface's representatives, who assumed the role of peacemakers, were in fact working to bring the pro-papal Blacks to power by exterminating the Whites. This is precisely what was to happen in November 1301, when Boniface turned to Charles de Valois and his army: the Whites were massacred or (like Dante) exiled and the Blacks came to power. By beginning her novella with this papal delegation of 1300, then, Pampinea is indeed setting it at an "hour . . . of greatest need" for the citizenry of Florence.

According to Pampinea, the papal delegation was lodged during its visit to Florence under the roof of Messer Geri Spina, a prominent Florentine merchant and friend of the pope. Most mornings they would walk with their host past the Church of Santa Maria Ughi, beside which Cisti had his bakery. Cisti realizes that it would show "gran cortesia" (2.10) to offer Messer Geri and the papal envoys some of his delicious wine, but, being conscious of the difference in rank between himself and Messer Geri, he considered it would be presumptuous of him to issue an invitation (p. 486). So he resorts to the stratagem of sitting outside his door each day, dressed in a freshly laundered apron, with white wine cooled in a bucket and spotless wineglasses. He drinks his wine just as Messer Geri is passing with the ambassadors:

> e a seder postosi, come essi passavano, e egli, poi che una volta o due spurgato s'era, cominciava a ber sì saporitamente questo suo vino, che egli n'avrebbe fatta venir voglia a' morti. (VI. 2.12)

> [He then seated himself in the doorway, and just as they were passing, he cleared his throat a couple of times and began to drink this wine of his with so much relish that he would have brought a thirst to the lips of a corpse. (p. 486)]

Cisti dares not speak across the difference in social rank that divides him from Messer Geri and the papal envoys, but in clearing his throat to drink he both draws attention to his lowly status (plebeians customarily spat and freed their throats from catarrh before drinking) and inscribes his social superiors within this common human desire to drink cool wine in hot weather. By the second day, Messer Geri has been seduced: Cisti fetches a bench from his bakery and serves his guests from a small flagon of his best wine. This becomes a regular occurrence. When the diplomatic mission is concluded, Messer Geri holds a magnificent banquet, to which he invites some of the most distinguished citizens of Florence; he also invites Cisti, who cannot be persuaded to attend the "magnifico convito" (2.18). Messer Geri then orders one of his servants to take a flask to Cisti, so that each of his guests may be served with half a glass of the exquisite wine during the first course. The servant replaces the small flask with a huge one and presents it to Cisti. When Cisti sees this, he says: "Figliuolo, messer Geri non ti manda a me" (My son, Messer Geri has not sent you to me, VI. 2. 20).

Cisti, a man of noble qualities, can read this huge flask as a counterfeit sign; Messer Geri would not have sent it to him. The servant returns to Messer Geri, and reports Cisti's words. Messer Geri sends the servant back to Cisti, briefed to repeat that he is sending the servant to *him*; and if Cisti should give the same answer, he is to ask "to whom I am sending you" (p. 487). The servant, returning with the huge flask, does as he is told and asks the question he was sent with: "'Adunque,' disse il famigliare 'a cui mi manda?' Rispuose Cisti: 'A Arno'" ("So then," said the servant, "to whom is he sending me?" Cisti replied: "To the Arno," VI. 2. 23-24).

When these words are reported back to him, Messer Geri demands to see the flask that his servant had presented to Cisti. On seeing the huge flask, he immediately understands the force of Cisti's comment. Having scolded the servant, he sends him back to Cisti with the small flask. Cisti now acknowledges that the flask has been sent to him; he fills it up and sends it back. A few days later, he fills a small cask with wine of the same vintage and sends that along, too. He then, finally, visits Messer Geri and explains the rationale for his actions. His visit is not, strictly speaking, necessary: the only thing he now needs to explain is the significance of sending Messer Geri his wine. In an extraordinary closing sentence, Cisti takes the opportunity to inscribe himself in what can only be described as a relationship of feudal vassalage: "Ora, per ciò che io non intendo d'esservene più guardiano, tutto ve l'ho fatto venire: fatene per innanzi come vi piace" (Now, since I do not intend to be the guardian of the wine any longer, I have let it all be sent to you: do with it henceforth as you please, 2. 29).

Cisti suggests that as *guardiano* he has enjoyed *possessio* of the wine, and *usus fructi*: but now he returns it to the *dominium* of Messer Geri. Messer Geri, for his part, prizes Cisti's gift and thanks him "as profusely as the occasion seemed to warrant" (p. 488): he cannot, of course, appear to be in Cisti's debt, since this would disturb the dialectical mutuality of the feudal bond. But the bond can be acknowledged as a permanent one: "e sempre poi per da molto l'ebbe e per amico" (and from then on he held him as a man of worth and as a friend for life, 2. 30).

Boccaccio is not suggesting that Florence should resolve its political difficulties through a revival of the vassalic bond. There is, however, a kind of *eros* that grows between the two men as they come to recognize one another, one that is best expressed through the suggestive power of feudal relations. The language and structure of courtly love is, after all, deeply indebted to the founding metaphors of feudalism. The metaphors of postfeudal society, in which we speak not of bonds but of contracts, do not have the ideological force of feudal mutualities. But although he defers to the vertical plane of feudal hierarchizing, Boccaccio also insists upon the lateral, associative aspects of social relations: his novella sees a ceaseless movement back and forth across city space. It falls to Cisti, the Florentine baker, to alert Messer Geri to the importance of this lateral dimension. He initiates this process while Messer Geri is moving across Florence, in the company of papal envoys, between the headquarters of the White and Black Guelfs, the factions that have torn Florence apart for generations. Once these envoys have left the city, a new diplomatic mission is conducted across the face of Florentine society as the *famigliare* moves back and forth between the baker and the Black Guelf. Through this transfer of tokens and messages, which owes as much to the devices of courtly love as to the protocols of Florentine politics, Boccaccio suggests an ideal unity of the Florentine body politic in the face of external treachery.

Chaucer's Cook and the Limits of Associational Ideology

In moving from Florence to London, from Cisti the baker to Perkyn the apprentice, we should note that the teller of each tale is a representative figure; representative, that is, of the city they speak of. Pampinea, the oldest of Boccaccio's women, is the guiding intelligence of Boccaccio's *brigata*: she conceives of the plan for an organized flight from Florence, works out the ground rules for the *brigata*'s governance, and rules as queen for the first day. Chaucer's Cook, who speaks twice of "oure citee" (I.4343, 4365), is the only pilgrim to associate the pilgrimage collectively with London. He is also the only pilgrim to be explicitly identified as a Londoner: the five guildsmen he serves as cook are assumed to be from London only on the basis of their association with him. But although he is twice identified as a "Cook of London" and is said to be a connoisseur of "Londoun ale" (I.382), the Cook identifies himself as originating not from London but from Ware, a town in Hertfordshire thirty miles due north of the city. Ware had been a notorious trouble spot since the 1350s, when attempts to enforce the Statute of Laborers had led to rioting; the vicar of Ware and a local hermit were indicted for preaching that the statute was wicked. In 1381 a subsequent vicar of Ware led a good cross section of his townsmen on an attack against John of Gaunt's castle in Hertford; they then marched on to London and took a prominent part in sacking Gaunt's palace at the Savoy.[31]

The name of Ware, then, comes freighted with suggestions of unruliness or violence imported to the city from the provinces. And some of the details with which Chaucer's Cook is credentialized as a Londoner have disquieting or unsavory connotations. The Host's suggestion that many of the Cook's pasties have been doctored recalls an ordinance of 1379: no pastie maker in the City of London shall bake in pasties "rabbits, geese, and garbage, not befitting, and sometimes stinking, in deceit of the people"; no one shall purchase such garbage from the cooks of Bread Street or from the cooks of great lords.[32] And the Cook's familiarity with the language of

70

Flemings—"'sooth pley, quaad pley,' as the Flemyng seith"—reminds us of the wholesale slaughter of Flemings that went on in London in 1381. The Cook's incorporation of a Flemish proverb into his own discourse seems, on the face of it, benign, if not impressively cosmopolitan. But in 1381, according to one chronicle, such an awareness of linguistic difference became the mechanism that led to murder: on being asked to say "Breede and Chese" by the London mob, the Flemings would say "Case and Brode" (*kaas en brood*) and so seal their own fate.[33] The fact that the Cook knows some Flemish, then, does not mean that he is a friend of Flemings. He might, of course, have learned the language in a brothel, since many London prostitutes were of Flemish origin.[34]

The opening couplet of the *Cook's Tale* brings us directly to an intricate structure of social and political relationships set within "oure citee," the unifying term: "A prentys whilom dwelled in oure citee, / And of a craft of vitaillers was he" (I.4365-66). Two sets of political relationship are suggested here, one defined internally and the other externally. The first, that of the apprentice to his master (there can be no apprentices without masters) is one of strict subordination with some overtones of feudal mutuality. An apprentice is enjoined to respect his master as his lord, his "seigneur"; one young man, apprenticed to his uncle, is directed to hold the stirrup while his master mounts his horse as a mark of respect and obedience.[35] The apprentice, who is by definition a "foreign" or noncitizen, elects to work for his master for a specified number of years in the hope of learning his master's craft and of eventually being sponsored for citizenship by his master's guild. But this ideal of an orderly hierarchy within the guild structure is immediately brought up against the political hostility that sets one guild against the next: "And of a craft *of vitaillers* was he." It would hardly be possible, for a contemporary audience, to think of the London victualers without thinking of their binary pairing, the nonvictualers, and of the affrays, riots, and disputes between these rival parties that fill the London Letter Books in the 1380s. But our attention is soon distracted from such matters by some vigorous lines of physical description:

> Gaillard he was as goldfynch in the shawe,
> Broun as a berye, a propre shorte felawe,
> With lokkes blake, ykemb ful fetisly.
> (I.4367-69)

Such fruit, animal, and grooming imagery puts the *Riverside* annotator in mind of both Alison and Absolon from the *Miller's Tale*.[36] Interestingly, though, we are not invited to make comparisons between the apprentice and the *General Prologue*'s Squire, although certain points of description clearly overlap:

> So hot he loved, that by nyghtertale
> He sleep namoore than dooth a nyghtyngale.
> (I.98-99)
> He was as ful of love and paramour
> As is the hyve ful of hony sweete.
> (I.4372-73)

The squire and the apprentice are young men of comparable age and of comparable sexual energy living in the shadow of a powerful master. But whereas the squire's sexuality is seen as charming and innocuous (and is not associated with the energy of a professional killer),[37] that of the apprentice is at once ridiculous and dangerous. It is ridiculous in that any attempts to regulate it through the elegant, *fetys* decorums of courtly behavior only serve to remind us that the apprentice is a churl: he is dark in complexion; he is short in stature. And yet if this energy is left uncultivated it poses an immediate threat to civil society—or, more specifically, to "the shoppe":

> At every bridale wolde he synge and hoppe;
> He loved bet the taverne than the shoppe.
> For whan ther any ridyng was in Chepe,
> Out of the shoppe thider wolde he lepe—
> Til that he hadde al the sighte yseyn,
> And daunced wel, he wolde nat come ayeyn.
> (I.4375-80)

The chief threat to the sober world of commerce here would seem to be a restless personal energy that cuts across the threshold of "the shoppe." But as the passage continues, this reckless individualism suddenly shows associative tendencies and a capacity for planning and organization:

> And gadered hym a meynee of his sort
> To hoppe and synge and maken swich disport;
> And ther they setten stevene for to meete,
> To pleyen at the dys in swich a streete.
> (I.4381-84)

The term *meynee*, used over thirty times by Chaucer, is a slippery but indispensable term occupying that liminal space between the shop and the street: its primary meaning is "family, household"; its second, "a body of retainers, attendants, dependents, or followers; a retinue, suite, train"; its third, "a company of persons employed together or having a common object of association; an army, ship's crew, congregation, assembly, or the like."[38] *Meynee* is itself a neutral term, "deriving ultimately from the Latin *mansionem*," that is rarely employed in neutral contexts: specific *mey-*

nees are generally figured as a force for good or evil, as constructive or destructive of social and moral order. Chaucer speaks in one place of "the
ryght ordene hous of so mochel a fadir and an ordeynour of meyne"; at another of "he Jakke Strawe and his meynee": the same term covers both
God Almighty and the leader of the *Peasants' Revolt*.[39] The occasion of its
deployment in the *Cook's Tale* is particularly complex: it is applied to a
group of young men who come together to agree on a time and place in the
city so that they can reconstitute themselves as an organized body; they
will then engage in the random business of dice playing.[40] This, according
to the Cook, poses a direct and immediate threat to the master's business,
his "chaffare" (I.4389): the rolling dice soon lead to the "box ful bare"
(I.4390), a diminution of the master's capital. But we should note that it is
not so much the vice of gaming that the tale insists upon as the root of social evil, but rather the act of association that makes such evil possible.
This emphasis predominates again once the master has given the apprentice his walking papers:

> And for ther is no theef withoute a lowke,
> That helpeth hym to wasten and to sowke
> Of that he brybe kan or borwe may,
> Anon he sente his bed and his array
> Unto a compeer of his owene sort.
> (I.4415-19)

This new association of wasters makes capital from its own excesses: as
the tale breaks off a new shop arises to challenge that of the master; the
dangerous sexuality of Perkyn returns as the energy that spins the wheels
of commerce:

> . . . That lovede dys, and revel, and disport,
> And hadde a wyf that heeld for contenance
> A shoppe, and swyved for hir sustenance.
> (I.4420-22)

We have still not moved far from the world of the London Letter Books.
Many of the themes from Chaucer's tale are developed in a case heard before Mayor Brembre in 1385. This concerns a woman called Elizabeth, wife
of Henry Moring, who, "under colour of the craft of embroidery," retained
various female apprentices and ran a prostitution ring. Things went well
until one of the apprentices, under pressure from her mistress, stole a breviary from a chaplain she was sleeping with. [41] The comic potential of this
story was entirely lost on the mayoral court: Elizabeth is to be put upon
the *thewe*, the pillory for women, and then taken to "some Gate of the
City, and there be made to forswear the City, and the liberty thereof, to
the effect that she would never again enter the same." Through such dra-

73

mas of punishment and expulsion the City authorities were able to suggest that their political interventions were motivated by a concern for the City's moral welfare. And by associating prostitution with unruly gatherings they are able both to discredit such gatherings and to find a pretext for breaking them up:

> *Also,—whereas many and divers affrays, broils, and dissensions, have arisen in times past, and many men have been slain and murdered, by reason of the frequent resort of, and consorting with, common harlots, at taverns, brewhouses of huksters, and other places of ill-fame, within the said city, and the suburbs thereof; and more especially through Flemish women, who profess and follow such shameful and dolorous life.*[42]

This proclamation of 1393 goes on to restrict prostitutes to two sites outside the City walls, namely Cock Lane (Smithfield) and the Stews in Southwark. It also empowers City officers to remove the upper garment and hood of any prostitute they see outside these areas: if they bring these items of clothing to the Guildhall they "shall have the half thereof for their trouble." This drama of unveiling is, of course, consistent with what goes on in the final couplet of the *Cook's Tale*: the wife of the compeer of Perkyn, the riotous apprentice, pretends ("or contenance") to be a respectable businesswoman, but as the couplet completes itself she is revealed to be a whore. Her whoredom, of course, further delegitimizes the association of apprentice Perkyn with "his owene sort."

It seems that the more we attempt to contextualize Chaucer's *Cook's Tale*, the more strikingly it differentiates itself from the Boccaccian tale of Cisti the baker. In the Italian novella two men of differing class and culture meet, albeit fleetingly, at a common level of understanding. In the English tale, the differences between master and apprentice prove so intractable that the master cuts the cord that binds them together. Whereas Boccaccio's narrative generates an associational ideology that will unite the city against external dangers, the social divisions within Chaucer's city widen dramatically as the tale runs on. And two of the proverbs that frame and inform the Cook's narrative reflect an ideology not of association, but of its opposite. The first, spoken by the Cook himself, borrows the wisdom of Solomon: "'Ne brynge nat every man into thyn hous,' / For herberwynge by nyghte is perilous" (I.4331-32). The text from Ecclesiasticus with which the Cook glosses the *Reeve's Tale* itself forms an excellent introduction to the fragmented and mistrustful London milieu he is out to evoke: "Bring not every man into thine house, for many are the plots of the deceitful man" (11.29). And the nugget of popular wisdom that comes "mysteriously" to the master as he contemplates his wayward apprentice also counsels the wisdom of putting limits on forms of association: "nat every man"; not every apple "Wel bet is roten appul out of hoord / Than that it rotie al the remenaunt" (I.4406-7).

This antiassociational rhetoric is remarkably consonant with that which informs a mayoral proclamation of 1383. This proclamation, the earliest Middle English entry in the London Letter Books, begins by situating king, mayor, sheriffs, and aldermen on a single vertical axis of power; it then goes to extraordinary lengths by way of defining, or finding names for, the kind of political association that threatens this hierarchy:

> *The Mair, Shirreues, and Aldermen, and alle othere wyse wyth hem, that habbeth the gouernaille of the Citee, under oure lige Lord the Kyng, by vertue of the Chartre of oure franchise, comaundeth on the Kynges bihalf, and on hire owene also, that noman make none con-gregaciouns, conuenticules, ne assembles of poeple, in priue nen apert, ne no more than other men, with oute leue of the Mair; ne ouer more in none manere ne make alliances, confederacies, conspiracies, ne obligaciouns, forto bynde men to gidre, forto susteyne eny querelis in lyuingge and deyengge to gidre; upon peyne of en-presonement.*[43]

The proclamation goes on to give "euery fre man of the Citee" powers to arrest any such gathering "he may aspie": everything, in theory, at least, from a parish guild meeting to the dice game in the *Cook's Tale*. London and Crown authorities had good reason to be nervous of "swich con-gregaciouns or covynes"[44] in this period, of course. The proclamation above dates from the turbulent period of Northampton's mayoralty.[45] The experience of 1381, when laborers had employed the associational mechanism of the "commissions of array" to organize themselves for their march on London,[46] was still a recent memory. And in 1388 Richard II was to issue writs at the Cambridge parliament requiring all guilds, fraternities, mysteries, and crafts to give an account of themselves to the Royal Chancery.[47] Some London guilds, it seems, avoided making any kind of return; some London craft fraternities apparently tried to pass themselves off as parish guilds.[48] The parish guild of St. Bridget, Fleet Street, was anxious to point out that although it was called a fraternity, it was really not a fraternity, and that "theirs is no malicious gathering" even though they wear hoods on the Feast of St. Bridget's Translation. Besides, they have no money and no rents; some of the members named in the return are dead, others have moved away, and the rest, "since they heard the decision of the last parliament, have refused to pay anything towards keeping the premises made."[49] As the return runs on, this fraternity or guild of St. Bridget seems to evaporate before our eyes.

The mayors and aldermen of London, we have noted, were quick to claim that their authority descended directly from the king, especially when that authority was challenged or their dignity offended. A man who tells an alderman to kiss his arse (*culum*) is extending the same invitation to his mayor and his monarch.[50] A butcher who objects to aldermen who ride on the pavement is speaking "in disparagement of our Lord the King" and is hence obliged to walk barefoot through the Shambles (a horrible fate) with a candle to the Guildhall Chapel.[51] But in borrowing authority from the king, the City oligarchy was, of course, making itself vulnerable to it. In 1377 rumors spread that the City was about to be taken into the king's hands and the mayor replaced with a royally appointed captain. In 1392 Richard committed the mayor and sheriffs to prison and appointed his own warden. On 20 February 1388 Nicholas Brembre, mayor of London from 1383 to 1386, was hanged by the Lords Appellant.[52] Such episodes remind us that although the London Letter Books evoke an orderly, hierarchical vision of society, the class of merchant capitalists they (usually) represent was continuously engaged in political struggles with Crown, magnates, small masters, foreigns, aliens, and peasants. The signs of such struggles are visible not only in major political events of the kind noted above, but in the business of everyday life:

> *Whereas the foreign drapers bringing woollen cloths to the City of London for sale, do sell the same in divers hostelries in secret, where they make many disorderly and deceitful bargains, as well between foreigner and foreigner, as between foreigner and freeman, to the great scandal and damage of all the City.*[53]

The city is figured in this ordinance as an all-encompassing entity ("all the City") that is sensitive to acts of moral outrage; and yet this notion of a city is clearly predicated on acts of exclusion and disenfranchisement. Noncitizens were habitually referred to as "foreigns"; although a foreign might live in London he was not, in any meaningful political sense, a Londoner. So when foreigns got together within the walls of London this could only be interpreted, by the City authorities, as a threat to the City. In 1387, for example, an attempt by journeymen cordwainers to form a fraternity was taken as "a deed which notoriously redounds to the weakening of the liberties of the . . . city."[54] At such moments the mayoral oligarchy reveals itself as just one more associational form that is anxious to discourage attempts at association lower down the political scale. At other moments it acts to preserve one form of association by banning another. In 1396, for example, the mayoral court heard that "there had arisen no small dissension and strife between the masters of the trade of Saddlers, of London, and the serving men, called *yomen*, of that trade." This dispute centered on the right of the *yomen* to dress themselves in livery and meet as a fraternity. The *yomen* insist that they have been meeting like this since "time out of mind," and that their objects are religious. Their masters argue that this tradition is no more than thirteen years old,

> *and that under a certain feigned colour of sanctity, many of the serving-men* (servientes) *in the trade had influenced the journeymen*

among them, and had formed covins thereon, with the object of rais-
ing their wages greatly in excess; to such an extent, namely, that
whereas a master in the said trade could before have had a serving
man or journey-man for 40 shillings or 5 marks yearly, and his
board, now such a man would not agree with his master for less
than 10 or 12 marks, or even 10 pounds, yearly; to the great-
deterioration of the trade.[55]

Here, once again, the decisive rhetorical gesture consists of ripping away
a veil of apparent respectability, or piety, to reveal corruption and rascality
beneath. This time, however, the unveiling process is credentialized not by
a moral vocabulary or by the language of the church, but by the language
of the shop: an unadorned economic language that, in the mayoral court,
carries the force of moral argument. This whole dispute, of course, is
pitched very close to the ideological terrain of the *Cook's Tale*; further cor-
respondences suggest themselves as the case progresses. Whereas apprentice Perkyn would leave the shop for street processions and weddings,
these journeymen leave for funerals:

And further . . . the serving-men aforesaid, according to an or-
dinance made among themselves, would oftentimes cause the jour-
neymen of the said masters to be summoned by a bedel, thereunto
appointed, to attend at Vigils of the dead, who were members of the
said fraternity . . . whereby the said masters were very greatly ag-
grieved, and were injured through such absenting of themselves by
the journeymen, so leaving their labours and duties, against their
wish.

It is no great surprise to learn that the mayor and aldermen side with the
masters in this dispute, determining that in future the *yomen* "should
have no fraternity, meetings, or covins." It is evident that the masters
would wish their *yomen* and workers to have no social life at all beyond
the confines of the shop: every conversation could spell trouble for business. And yet the pleasures and privileges of political association and of
fraternity life are what every alderman, master, and master's wife lives for:

> It is ful fair to been ycleped "madame,"
> And goon to vigilies al bifore,
> And have a mantel roialliche ybore.
> (I.376-78)

Chaucer here momentarily adopts the viewpoint of the women who are
married to the five guildsmen in the *General Prologue*. Moments before he

had set out the ambitions of the guildsmen themselves; their qualifications for civic office are chiefly a matter of capital, property, and (to
venture a term that seems both anachronistic and apposite) image:

> Wel semed ech of hem a fair burgeys
> To sitten in a yeldehalle on a deys.
> Everich, for the wisdom that he kan,
> Was shaply for to be an alderman.
> For catel hadde they ynogh and rente.
>
> (I.369-73)

We have here not one associational form, but two: the "solempne and . . .
greet fraternitee" that employs the Cook and the corporation of mayor and
aldermen that this group dreams of becoming.[56] What, then, is the relationship of the Cook to these associational forms, real and imaginary?
The Cook as described in the *General Prologue* is absorbed by his office:
all lines but two are given over to boiling, tasting, roasting, simmering,
baking, and blancmange making—except, of course, for that couplet devoted to the "mormal" (I.386; "a species of dry scabbed ulcer, gangrenous
rather than cancerous")[57] he bears on his shin. This single sign of danger[58]
alerts us to further unsettling suggestions about the Cook's provenance
and personal habits in his own Prologue.[59] And yet, once he has launched
into his tale, we find him speaking lines worthy of a knight, alderman, or
mayor:[60] "Revel and trouthe, as in a lowe degree, / They been ful wrothe al
day, as men may see" (I.4397-98).

The lower classes are viewed here from the elevated perspective of the
General Prologue's guildhall dais (I.370). The argument is that the privileges and pleasures of association (i.s. *revel*) can only be entrusted to those
of proven virtue (dedicatees of *trouthe*, such as masters, aldermen, and
their wives). This is, of course, a circular argument, since if *trouthe* is to
have any social meaning it must be exercised as a public virtue; those forbidden any form of public association cannot, therefore, practice or em-
body *trouthe*. Since the lower classes cannot aspire to *trouthe*, what need
do they have of *revel*, or of any other form of association? Such logic (like
trouthe itself) pretends to impartiality, universality, and verifiability ("as
men may see"), but the state of angry enmity ("they been ful wrothe") between the lower orders and social order is there only because the City authorities say it is so. Hostility to public virtue is legislated into the lower
orders so that those of "lowe degree" can be legislated out of political existence.

Many critics have noted that the high-principled Cook of Fragment I
sorts ill with the Cook who, at the beginning of Fragment IX, has reached
the far side of revel and (the Host notes) is about to tumble:

> "Is ther no man, for preyere ne for hyre,
> That wole awake oure felawe al bihynde?
> A theef myghte hym ful lightly robbe and bynde.
> See how he nappeth! See how, for cokkes bones,
> That he wol falle fro his hors atones!
> Is that a cook of Londoun, with meschaunce?"
> (IX.6-11)

The fall of the Cook, when it finally comes, is strongly identified with the end of language. This end is presaged by the Cook's huge yawn that runs for six lines as the Manciple heaps abuse on him: the mouth is open, but emits no sound (35-40). The act of falling occupies the same narrative moment as the act of falling silent:

> And with this speche the Cook wax wrooth and wraw,
> And on the Manciple he gan nodde faste
> For lakke of speche, and doun the hors hym caste,
> Wher as he lay, til that men hym up took.
> (IX.46-48)

It is interesting that the notion of *wrothe* reappears at the moment of the Cook's falling: he too, it would seem, reveals himself to be a figure of "lowe degree" who, having revelled to excess, finds himself "ful wrothe" with *trouthe* (and also with language, the ground of *trouthe* as a social virtue). And the image of the drunken, voiceless Cook lying inert on the ground (thereby bringing the entire pilgrimage to a halt) seems to validate all the Letter Book arguments about the inability of the lower orders to function within an associative framework.

How, then, are we to reconcile this Cook of Fragment IX with the Cook of Fragment I? The first-Fragment Cook seems, in retrospect, a dummy of a character through which his masters ventriloquize the mores of craft masters and would-be aldermen. This makes him little better than the Summoner, who parrots terms learned from his masters in the law courts ("*Questio quid iuris*") without understanding them (I.637-46). But it is important to note that the Cook of Fragment IX does not remain on the ground; his fellow pilgrims pick him up and set him back on his horse. Nor does he remain in a state of enmity with the Manciple. He falls through drink, but through drink he rises or rides again: in taking the gourd from the Manciple and returning it to him, and in thanking him "in swich wise as he koude" (90-93), the Cook returns to some form of social consciousness. The Manciple's gesture of reconciliation is figured as an explicit rejection of *wrothe*: "I wol nat wratthen hym, also moot I thryve" (IX.80). The Host, having laughed "wonder loud" at this rapprochement, observes:

> . . . "I se wel it is necessarie,
> Where that we goon, good drynke with us carie;
> For that wol turne rancour and disese
> T'acord and love, and many a wrong apese."
> (IX.95-98)

This reference to "good drynke" might appear to suggest some reference to sacramental wine. But "good drynke" was also commonly associated with (employed as a facilitator of) "acord and love" in the meetings of craft and parish guilds:

> *Also ordeynd it is, yat eueriche nyth qwil drynkynd lastet3 at ye general time, yei shul haue ye preyeers for ye pees and ye state of holy chirche, and for ye pes and ya state of ye lond.*[61]

The association of communal drinking with the feast day of a guild's patron was sufficiently strong for this meeting to be referred to as the *potatio* or "ye drynkyng" or the "tyme of drynk."[62] Drinking on these occasions amounted to more than a symbolic gesture. The guild of Holy Cross, Hultoft, reckoned to get through thirty gallons of ale at its guild feast (the residue being given to the poor).[63] The alderman of the Guild of St. James, Lynn, was entitled to two gallons; every steward got a gallon, and "ye Clerk, a potel." Brothers or sisters of this guild who were absent through sickness "in tyme of drynkyng" were likewise entitled to "a potel."[64] Sick brothers and sisters of the guild of the Holy Cross, Bishop's Lynn, were entitled to a full gallon, as were "ony brother or sister . . . in pelgrimage."[65] Some guilds moved from the church to an inn for their guild-day meeting; some held their drynkyng at the house of a brother or sister.[66]

This emphasis on drinking no doubt accounts, in part, for the considerable space dedicated to group discipline in these guild regulations. No guild member shall call one of his brethren thief or "scurra"; nobody shall be "rebel of his tounge," or fall asleep "in tyme of drynke," or refuse to pass the cup.[67] There should be no "noyse or janglinge" at the meeting; any brother who resorts to physical violence at the *drynkyng* will be fined four pounds of wax.[68] One London guild states that "eny riotour, oþer contekour," shall be expelled from the guild until he amends his ways; all members "shul be helpynge aȝeins þe rebelle and unboxum." Brothers and sisters "ne schal noght debat with oþer." Those who do fall "in debat" shall reconcile their differences within the guild structure "and make bytwene hem a good acord": for the "fraternitee" was founded "for amendment of her lyues and of her soules, and to noriche more loue bytwene þe bretheren and sustren of þe bretherhede."[69] Another London guild specifies that every new brother and sister shall kiss each member of the fraternity "in tokenynge of loue, charite, and pes."[70] Conversation at such "dayes of spekyngges tokedere" shall be dedicated "to here comune profyte."[71]

The lexicon of misbehavior found in the 1389 guild returns is familiar enough to readers of *The Canterbury Tales*; so, too, is their concern to promise collective order and well-being. The associative ideal that the guild regulations record in such concrete detail is of particular importance for Chaucer's *compagnye*, a group that brings together a wide (not all-inclusive) range of backgrounds and professions. How, after all, could such a group hope to govern itself unless its members recognized some common parameters of collective behavior? Such behavior, I am suggesting, was learned in the guilds. The difference between a rich guild and its poor neighbor could, of course, be immense: the poor men's guild of St. Austin, Norwich, could hardly compete with the fraternity of Lincoln Cathedral that Philippa Chaucer joined in 1386 with Henry, earl of Derby, and other Lancastrian luminaries.[72] But within each guild, a comparable associative ethic was taught. Such is the schooling that has prepared each pilgrim for the associative project of Chaucer's *Canterbury Tales*.

Cooks and Canons: Chaucer's Londons

It is particularly interesting that Chaucer should choose the Cook and the Manciple to play out a reconciliation scene reminiscent of a guild-sponsored *drynkyng*, for both are men of "lowe degree," and both are Londoners (or "of Londoun"). Both men serve corporate organizations above their own station: Roger cooks for "a solempne and a greet fraternitee," and the Manciple purchases provisions for one of the London Inns of Court (I.567-86). The *Cook's Tale* and the mayoral Letter Books, we have noted, operate on the assumption that lower-class Londoners are incapable of peaceable association. The "acord and love" that breaks out between the Cook and Manciple (the last such reconciliation in *The Canterbury Tales*) would seem to discredit this assumption. Are we to conclude, then, that Chaucer begins his opus by endorsing the political outlook of London merchant capitalists and ends by celebrating the political capacities of the common man?

If Chaucer's opus were an organic and completed whole, like the *Commedia* or the *Decameron*, we might be tempted to look for an orderly progression in its politics. But *The Canterbury Tales* is an uncertain sequence of fragments, and the fragments featuring the Cook are plainly at odds with one another. The tale of Fragment I develops a strain of London discourse that we can associate with that of the Guildhall, but it comes to no conclusion, it breaks off incomplete. Fragment IX starts up as if the Cook had never spoken, or told a tale: perhaps, as Larry Benson suggests, this indicates that Chaucer intended to cancel the Cook's appearance in Fragment I.[73] Fragment I is itself, of course, ambivalent about the Cook: at one moment he suggests an ulcerated, low-life image and the next a figure who should sit at the Guildhall dais rather than wait on it. Each image found its illustrator: the Ellesmere Cook, with "his fleshhook, soiled apron, torn slippers, and bandaged shin" suggests—in V. A. Kolve's arresting phrase—"the livery . . . of labor and poverty and disease."[74] The Cambridge Cook (University Library MS Gg. iv. 27, fol. 193v) is a prosperous, fur-trimmed citizen holding a large, elaborate whip; his legs are covered.

These images might be reconciled by arguing that whereas the Ellesmere artist is guided by the *General Prologue* portrait of the Cook, the Cambridge illustrator is responding to the discursive level of the *Cook's Tale*. But the difficulty of sustaining such an argument might also suggest that the impulse to reconcile diverse aspects and embodiments of London on a single imaginative plane is altogether misguided: perhaps London can only be imagined as a discourse of fragments, discontinuities, and contradictions. But before committing ourselves to this conclusion we should consider, albeit briefly, one last narrative of London that suddenly and unexpectedly overtakes the pilgrimage in Fragment VIII. I am speaking, of course, of the *Canon's Yeoman's Tale* and specifically of its *pars secunda* in which a canon-alchemist swindles a London chantry priest to the tune of £40.

The key motif of this tale, and particularly its second part, is betrayal. The Canon is obviously intent on betraying the trust the London chantry priest puts in him as an alchemist. But the Canon, the Yeoman argues, is also betraying his own kind, canons; such a man is a Judas to his community (III.1007-9). And the narrator is himself, of course, engaged in a narrative of bad faith: he is betraying the professional secrets of the Canon he has served for seven years, the man he acknowledged at the outset as "my lord and my soverayn" (590). He may also be betraying the pilgrimage and the readership: the suspicion that the Canon of the first half of his tale is the Canon of the second is so strong that the Yeoman plucks it from the air—to deny it:

> This chanon was my lord, ye wolden weene?
> Sir hoost, in feith, and by the hevenes queene,
> It was another chanoun, and nat hee.
> (VIII.1088-90)

Earlier, as the duplicity of the first canon had begun to emerge, the Host was moved to ask a key question:

> "Where dwelle ye, if it to telle be?"
> "In the suburbes of a toun," quod he,
> "Lurkynge in hernes and in lanes blynde,
> Whereas thise robbours and thise theves by kynde
> Holden hir pryvee fereful residence,

> As they that dar nat shewen hir presence;
> So faren we, if I shal seye the sothe."
>
> (III.656-62)

By the beginning of *pars secunda* the disease that infects the canon-alchemist has been carried from the blind alleys of the suburbs, the criminalized margins of civic life, to the city itself:

> Ther is a chanoun of religioun
> Amonges us, wolde infecte al a toun,
> Thogh it as greet were as was Nynyvee,
> Rome, Alisaundre, Troye, and othere three.
>
> (VIII.972-75)

Nineveh was threatened with destruction; Troy was betrayed from within. What hope does London, New Troy, have of surviving this new threat in its midst? [75] The argument is made that the city may escape betrayal through language by more language: the Yeoman's alerts "us" (his word) to the second canon's duplicity so that "men may be war therby."[76] The discourse that saves us is, of course, the discourse of a *yoman* betraying his master. The form of the discourse adheres remarkably closely to depositions heard in the London Guildhall, and its tale of deception through magic or false science is no more fantastic than that of many Letter Book narratives. But the notion of a *yoman* proposing to save a city, or a pilgrim body, by betraying his master's secrets ("Thou . . . discoverest that thou sholdest hide," 695-96) turns the operative assumptions of the Guildhall on its head. It also raises the possibility that Chaucer's Yeoman may be a Sinon, a foreigner who betrays a community by joining it belatedly and pretending to save it from ruin. It is worth recalling that in the last *bolgia* of Dante's Hell we first encounter two Tuscan alchemists and then (after a passage lamenting the ruin of Thebes and Troy) two arch-deceivers: "false Sinon, the Greek of Troy" and Master Adam, falsifier of the gold florin.[77] London, as New Troy, knew that the threat of economic disaster posed by alchemy and false coinage was every bit as serious as the threat of political betrayal.

The discourses of London in Chaucer's *Canterbury Tales*, then, are freighted with suggestions of duplicity and bad faith: we have a Cook who sounds like two Cooks, one Yeoman, and two (perhaps one) canon-alchemists. Perhaps it is just an irony of history that the two most authoritative texts in *The Canterbury Tales'* manuscript tradition perpetuate and define such ambiguities: Ellesmere contains the *Canon's Yeoman's Tale,* and Hengwrt does not.[78]

The conclusion this essay seems bound for differs markedly from that offered (in advance, one might note) by D. W. Robertson's celebrated *Preface to Chaucer:* "To conclude, the medieval world was innocent of our profound concern for tension. . . . We project dynamic polarities on history as class struggles, balances of power, or as conflicts between economic realities and traditional ideals. . . . But the medieval world with its quiet hierarchies knew nothing of these things."[79] The most cursory reading of London history or of London legal documents makes such statements seem unintelligible: how on earth, one wonders, did Robertson manage to research and write a whole book on Chaucer's London without revising such opinions? The fact that Robertson did write such a book, prefaced by the strictures that preface A Preface to Chaucer,[80] only testifies to the determinant power of a certain mode of formalist reading and the nostalgic desire for a bygone epoch of "quiet hierarchies." David Aers, in his Community, Gender, and Individual Identity, suggests that in this passage Robertson is seeking to authorize his own critical agenda (and disguise its partiality) by presenting it as "seemingly . . . congruent with social models propagated by the medieval clerisy."[81] Aers is surely right here. At the same time we must concede that the notion of "community" (singular rather than plural) that figures so prominently in Aers's own agenda sometimes seems partial and archaic as it participates in the quest for "knowable community" associated with British socialists such as Raymond Williams. There is a nostalgia of the left as well as the right.[82]

My own reading of Chaucer and of London history is, of course, a partial one; an essay that sets out to read an absence cannot claim to be innocent of poststructuralist presuppositions. My account of the absence of a single, unified discourse that could be taken to represent the city as an organic and knowable entity seems suspiciously consonant with Gabrielle M. Spiegel's account of what happens to New Critical reading under deconstruction: "A text's coherent statement . . . is fractured into a series of discontinuous, heterogeneous, and contradictory codes which defy interpretive unification except at the level of allegorical recodification, itself suspect as the ideological imposition of a false coherence where none in truth exists."[83] I cannot claim to be thinking outside the terms of current critical thought. But I do claim that this essay does not deconstruct a "coherent statement" of city consciousness in Chaucer or in the archives for the simple reason that no such statement has been found. There is no idea of a city for all the inhabitants of a space called London to pay allegiance to; there are only conflicts of associational, hierarchical, and antiassociational discourses, acted out within and across the boundaries of a city wall or the fragments of a text called The Canterbury Tales.

The singularity of all this becomes more fully evident when we compare the absence of the city in Chaucer to the representation of Florence in Boccaccio. Boccaccio's tale of the friendship of a lowly baker and a powerful merchant-politician may well be read as "the ideological imposition of a false coherence." But it is important to note that such an ideological imposition, which romances the inhabitants of the city with the notion of unitas civium, is at least thought to be possible in Boccaccio's Florence.

No such attempt is made in Chaucer or in Chaucer's London because (as the *Cook's Tale* demonstrates so clearly) any discourse which begins with pretensions to all-inclusiveness soon reveals specific allegiances and hostilities. Not only is the city absent in Chaucer, then; the conditions for the possibility of a credible ideology of the city do not yet exist. One last trip to the Guildhall archive, specifically to an Anglo-Norman proclamation of 1391, makes this abundantly and painfully clear. Brembre, hanged for treason by the Lords Appellant, has been dead for three years; Northampton has not held political office since 1383. The chief threat to city independence in the 1390s is, of course, the king himself, the master mayor Adam Bamme must be seen to serve:

> *Whereas many dissensions, quarrels, and false reports have prevailed in the City of London, as between trade and trade, person and person, because of diverse controversies lately moved between Nicholas Brembre, Knight, and John Northamptone, of late Mayors of the said city, who were men of great power and estate, and had many friendships and friends within the same; to the great peril of the same city, and, maybe, of all the realm . . .*[84]

Here again, as in the *Cook's Tale*, we see that personal association of any kind is (to borrow an apposite Chaucerian term) *suspect*: no good can come of it; "destruction and annihilation to the said city may readily ensue."[85] In addressing the inhabitants of London the proclamation must find some associative terms suggestive of a common interest. But even as it deploys these unifying terms ("common profit"; "of one accord in good love") the Guildhall text once again points to divisions in the working world and so divides itself from the body politic it presumes to serve and govern. Its contradictory call for civic unity visualizes political association (beneath its own level of association) as a revel that leads to Newgate; its end, like that of the *Cook's Tale* in Fragment I and the Cook in Fragment IX, is silence:

> *[D]esiring to maintain the peace of our Lord the King . . . for the common profit, they [the mayor and the aldermen] have ordained and established, that no man, great or small, of whatsoever estate or condition he be, shall speak from henceforth, or agitate upon any of the opinions, as to either of them, the said Nicholas and John, or shall by sign, or in any other manner, shew that such person is of the one opinion or the other. But let the folks of the same city be of one accord in good love, without speaking, any person to another, on the said matter, in manner of reproof or of hatred; on pain, if any one shall speak or do against any of the points aforesaid, of imprisonment in Neugate for a year and a day, without redemption.*[86]

Notes

1. See Larry D. Benson, ed., *The Riverside Chaucer*, 3rd ed. (Boston, 1987), note to line 4422, p. 853. All references are to the Riverside edition. I argue later in the chapter that the *Canon's Yeoman's Tale, pars secunda*, may be read as a London fiction.

2. See V. A. Kolve, *Chaucer and the Imagery of Narrative: The First Five Canterbury Tales* (Stanford, Calif., 1984), p. 259; and Muriel A. Bowden, *A Commentary on the General Prologue to the Canterbury Tales* (New York, 1948), pp. 187-88. The first plea of debt is entered in 1377.

3. Martha Carlin, *The Urban Development of Southwark, c. 1200-1550* (Ph.D. diss., University of Toronto, 1983), p. 439.

4. Quoted in Carlin, *Southwark*, p. 467.

5. Ibid., p. 7.

6. See Chris Given-Wilson, *The Royal Household and the King's Affinity: Service, Politics, and Finance in England, 1360-1413* (New Haven, Conn., and London 1986), pp. 15, 22-23, 28-29, 34-35.

7. See Carlin, *Southwark*, pp. 550-53; Sylvia L. Thrupp, *The Merchant Class of Medieval London (1300-1500)* (Chicago and London, 1948), pp. 1-3; and H. T. Riley, ed. *Memorials of London and London Life in the XIIIth, XIVth and XVth Centuries, A.D. 1276-1419* (London, 1868), p. 492. Riley translates from the Latin of *Letter Book H*, fol. ccx, which records pleas held at the London Guildhall before Mayor Nicholas Extone in January 1387. The need for "good governance" in London is of paramount importance since "there is a greater resort, as well of lords and nobles, as of common people, to that city, than to any other places in the realm, as well on account of the Courts there of our said Lord the King, as for transacting business there" (p. 492).

8. *Letter Book H*, fol. ccx (1387), in *Memorials*, ed. Riley, p. 492.

9. Riley, ed., *Memorials*, p. 536.

10. Ibid., p. 465; *Letter Book H*, p. 184.

11. Riley, ed., *Memorials*, p. 444. Should this performance be counted as a dramatic record? On the problematics of such questions, see Teresa Coletti, "Reading REED: History and the Records of Early English Drama," in *Literary Practice and Social Change in Britain, 1380-1530*, ed. Lee Patterson (Berkeley, Calif., 1990), pp. 248-84, especially p. 268.

12. See David Aers, *Community, Gender, and Individual Identity: English Writing, 1360-1430* (London, 1988), pp. 20-35; and Miri Rubin, *Charity and Community in Medieval Cambridge* (Cambridge, Eng., 1987), pp. 291-93. Such discriminations were formulated and enforced as part of the reaction to the labor shortages occasioned by the Black Death. They mark the decline of a long-lived tradition of uncalculating almsgiving and the rise of a new work-oriented ethic.

13. Riley, ed., *Memorials*, pp. 490-94; *Letter Books*, pp. 295-96.

14. Riley, ed., *Memorials*, p. 520.

15. See ibid., pp. 536, 466.

16. See *Inferno* XVII. 52-78, in *Dante Alighieri: The Divine Comedy*, ed. and trans. C. S. Singleton, 6 vols. (Princeton, N.J., 1970-75). All references are to this edition. On the representation of commutative justice in Dante, see Anthony K. Cassell, *Dante's Fearful Art of Justice* (Toronto, 1984).

17. See *Decameron* II. 5, in *Tutte le opere di Giovanni Boccaccio*, ed. Vittore Branca, vol. 4 (Milan, 1976); David Wallace, *Giovanni Boccaccio: The Decameron* (Cambridge, Eng., 1991), pp. 39-41; and Riley, ed., *Memorials*, pp. 522-25.

18. See Riley, ed., *Memorials*, p. 435; *Letter Books*, pp. 132-33; the year is 1379. The same entry records the names of seven women who paid either 10s. or 6s. 8d. for the right to sell their wares near "Le Brokenecros" by the north door of St. Paul's. On the office of Common Hunt, see Thrupp, *Merchant Class*, pp. 241-42.

19. It is worth noting, however, that a good number of cases in the *Letter Books* record the participation of Ralph Strode as prosecutor or spokesman. Strode was an acquaintance of Chaucer's who was common serjeant of the City of London from 1373 to 1385. He is probably to be identified with the "philosophical Strode" to whom Chaucer commends his *Troilus and Criseyde*; see Stephen A. Barney's note to V.1856-59 in *Riverside Chaucer*, ed. Benson, p. 1058. Chaucer himself appears in *Letter Book G*, fol. cccxxi, on the occasion of his lease of the house above Aldgate in 1374 (see Riley, ed., *Memorials*, pp. 377-78; *CLR*, pp. 144-47).

20. This suggestion is scrutinized more closely later in the chapter. For now it is important to note the indefinite article: "*an* urban consciousness"; one, perhaps, of several.

21. See Louis Green, *Chronicle into History: An Essay on the Interpretation of History in Florentine Fourteenth-Century Chronicle*s (Cambridge, Eng., 1972); Christian Bec, "Il mito di Firenze da Dante al Ghiberti," in *Lorenzo Ghiberti nel suo tempo. Atti del Convegno Internazionale di Studi (Firenze, 18-21 Ottobre 1978)*, 2 vols. (Florence, 1980), 1:3-26; Donald Weinstein, "The Myth of Florence," in *Florentine Studies: Politics and Society in Renaissance Florence*, ed. Nicholai Rubenstein (London, 1968), pp. 15-44; and Charles T. Davis, "Il Buon Tempo Antico," in *Florentine Studies*, ed. Rubenstein, pp. 45-69.

22. See Luigi Pratesi, ed., *L' "Istoria di Firenze" di "Gregorio Dati: Dal 1380 al 1405* (Norcia, 1902), p. 74. Dati records that the citizens of Florence, in facing Gian Galeazzo Visconti in 1402, "sempre si confortavano con una speranza che pareva avere loro la cosa sicura in mano, cioé che il Comune non può morire e il Duca era uno solo uomo mortale, ché finito lui, finito lo stato suo" (cap. 97).

23. For a detailed discussion of this process, see my *Decameron*, pp. 39, 92-94; and David Wallace, "Chaucer's Body Politic: Social and Narrative Self-Regulation," *Exemplaria* 2.1 (1990), 221-40.

24. See Piero Boitani, "What Dante Meant to Chaucer," in *Chaucer and the Italian Trecento*, ed. Piero Boitani (Cambridge, Eng., 1983), pp. 115-39, especially p. 125.

25. See Antonia Gransden, *Historical Writing in England, II, c. 1307 to the Early Sixteenth Century* (Ithaca, N.Y., 1982), p. 61; and John Taylor, *English Historical Literature in the Fourteenth Century* (Oxford, 1987), pp. 14-16.

26. See Riley, ed., *Memorials*, pp. 448-51; and *Letter Books*, pp. 165-66.

27. These are the first six lines from the eighth stanza of a poem found in two MSS and printed in *Political Poems and Songs Composed during the Period from the Accession of Edward III to That of Richard III*, ed. Thomas Wright, 2 vols. (London, 1859-61), 1:250-52. The poem consists of eleven stanzas rhyming *ababbcbc*.

28. The first definition of *ideology* offered by *Webster's Ninth New Collegiate Dictionary* (Springfield, Mass., 1984) seems particularly apt for the novella we are about to consider: "visionary theorizing."

29. For a precise imaging of this process in Ambrogio Lorinzetti's famous Sienese fresco cycle (1337-40), see Quentin Skinner, "Ambrogio Lorinzetti: The Artist as Political Philosopher," *Proceedings of the British Academy* 72 (1986), 1-56, especially p. 34.

30. Translations follow Giovanni Boccaccio, *The Decameron*, trans. G. H. McWilliam (Harmondsworth, 1972). Quotations from the Italian text follow *Boccaccio*, ed. Branca, vol. 4 (Milan, 1976).

31. See Andrew Prescott, "London in the Peasants' Revolt: A Portrait Gallery," *London Journal* 7 (1981), 125-43, especially pp. 128-29. Trespass actions of John of Gaunt and John Butterwick list rebels from five counties. The group from Ware Hertfordshire is by far the largest (forty-three rebels); the next largest group is from Manningtree, Essex (seventeen).

32. Riley, ed., *Memorials*, p. 438; *Letter Books*, p. 139. This entry is in Anglo-Norman.

33. See Cotton Julius B II (in Kingsford): "And many fflemmynges loste hir heedes at that tyme, and namely they that koude nat say Breede and Chese, but Case and Brode"

(p. 15). This chronicle covers the years 1189-1432 and concludes with Lydgate's verses on the reception of Henry VI in London in 1432. Kingsford dates the manuscript 1435 (pp. viii-ix).

34. See E. J. Burford, *Bawds and Lodgings: A History of the London Bankside Brothels, c. 100-1675* (London, 1976), p. 78.

35. See Thrupp, *Merchant Class*, p. 17.

36. See Douglas Gray's note to I.4367 in *Riverside Chaucer*, ed. Benson, p. 853.

37. It is always worth reminding ourselves that the Knight, the Squire's father, is credited with having killed at least eighteen men (see I.43-78). It is interesting to note, too, that Chaucer makes the relationship of Knight to Squire a natural one (father to son), whereas the master-apprentice relationship exists only on paper.

38. See *The Oxford English Dictionary*, ed. James A. H. Murray et al. (Oxford, 1933), s. v. *menie*. The other fourteenth-century meaning noted is "4. The collection of pieces or 'men' used in a game of chess." *MED* records a comparable range of meaning under *meine*.

39. See *Boece* IV, prosa 1.41-42; *Nun's Priest's Tale*, VII.3394.

40. Apprentice contracts specify that an apprentice must not waste his master's goods on dice, dress, riot, etc.: see, for example, George Clune, *The Medieval Guild System* (Dublin, 1943), pp. 90-91.

41. See Riley, ed., *Memorials*, pp. 484-86; and *Letter Books*, pp. 271-72. For a more legitimate example of female apprenticeship, see *Letter Books*, pp. 185-86, where the daughter of a deceased "wolmongere" is first made a ward of John Munstede, draper, and then apprenticed as a "thredwomman" to John Appleby and his wife Johanna.

42. Riley, ed., *Memorials*, pp. 534-35.

43. Ibid., p. 480.

44. Ibid., p. 481 (same document).

45. See *Letter Books*, p. 226; and Ruth Bird, *The Turbulent London of Richard II* (London, 1949), pp. 63-85.

46. See A. F. Butcher, "English Urban Society and the Revolt of 1381," in *The English Rising of 1381*, ed. R. H. Hilton and T. H. Ashton (Cambridge, Eng., 1984), pp. 84-111, especially p. 101.

47. See *English Guilds*, ed. Toulmin Smith, EETS, OS 40 (London, 1870), pp. xxiv-xxv; and H. F. Westlake, *The Parish Gilds of Mediæval England* (New York, 1919), pp. 36-37.

48. See Caroline M. Barron, "The Parish Fraternities of Medieval London," in *Essays in Honour of F. R. H. Du Boulay*, ed. C. M. Barron and Christopher Harper-Bill (Woodbridge, 1985), pp. 13-37, especially pp. 20-21.

49. Westlake, *Parish Gilds*, p. 182.

50. See Riley, ed., *Memorials*, pp. 500-502; and *Letter Books*, p. 323.

51. See Riley, ed., *Memorials*, pp. 502-3.

52. For details of these episodes, see Given-Wilson, *Royal Household*, p. 52; Bird, *Turbulent London*, pp. 24-25, 86-101; and Caroline M. Barron, "The Quarrel of Richard II with London, 1392-7," in *The Reign of Richard II; Essays in Honour of May McKisack*, ed. F. R. H. Du Boulay and C. M. Barron (London, 1971), pp. 173-201.

53. Riley, ed., *Memorials*, p. 551; *Letter Books*, pp. 449-50. This Anglo-Norman document (fol. cccxxvii, 1399) apparently records an ordinance made during the mayoralty of Richard Whityngton (1398). This is the last numbered folio in *Letter Book H*, with the exception of fol. cccxxxi. Two of the three folios immediately preceding cccxxxi have been cut out; one half of the other, cut vertically, has been removed.

54. Riley, ed., *Memorials*, p. 496; *Letter Books*, pp. 311-12.

55. Riley, ed., *Memorials*, pp. 542-44 (especially p. 543); *Letter Books*, p. 431.

56. Britton J. Harwood rightly observes that these five guildsmen stood little chance of becoming aldermen of London: of the 260 aldermen elected in fourteenth-century Lon-

don, only nine were from the lesser companies these guildsmen represent. See "The 'Fraternitee' of Chaucer's Guildsmen," *Review of English Studies*, n.s. 39 (1988), 413-17.

57. Gray, note to I.386, in *Riverside Chaucer*, ed. Benson, p. 814.

58. Mormals were attributed, by some authorities, to generally intemperate or unclean habits. One critic argues that they were runny rather than dry; they were said to smell strongly (Gray in *Riverside Chaucer*, ed. Benson, p. 814). On the notion of "danger" as employed here, see Mary Douglas, *Purity and Danger: An Analysis of Concepts of Pollution and Taboo* (New York, 1966). The sign of danger confirms, of course, the need for social regulation and cleansing.

59. See pp. 70-71.

60. A good number of mayors and aldermen in Chaucer's London were, of course, knights; others refused to be knighted since they did not wish to be moved into a higher tax bracket.

61. *English Guilds*, ed. Toulmin Smith, pp. 71-72 (Guild of the Nativity of St. John the Baptist, Bishop's Lynn).

62. See respectively, Westlake, *Parish Gilds*, p. 168 (Guild of St. Anne, St. Peter's Parish in the Skin Market, Lincoln); *English Guilds*, ed. Toulmin Smith, p. 69 (Guild of St. James, Lynn); and *English Guilds*, ed. Toulmin Smith, p. 79 (Guild of St. John the Baptist, Bishop's Lynn).

63. Westlake, *Parish Gilds*, p. 166.

64. *English Guilds*, ed. Toulmin Smith, p. 70.

65. Ibid., p. 84.

66. See *English Guilds*, ed. Toulmin Smith, p. 30 (Guild of the Pelterers, Norwich); and Westlake, *Parish Gilds*, p. 166 (Corpus Christi, Hultoft).

67. See Westlake, *Parish Gilds*, p. 220 (Holy Trinity and Holy Cross, Daventry); and *English Guilds*, ed. Toulmin Smith, p. 84 (Guild of the Holy Cross, Bishop's Lynn). Barbara Hanawalt has pointed out to me that a payment or gift of drink was often employed to seal an arbitration or as a price for peace (see, for example, A. H. Thomas, ed., *Calendar of Early Mayor's Court Rolls Preserved among the Archives of the Corporation of the City of London at the Guildhall, A.D. 1298-1307* [Cambridge, Eng., 1924], pp. 16, 34).

68. *English Guilds*, ed. Toulmin Smith, p. 84 (Guild of the Holy Cross, Bishop's Lynn).

69. Ibid., pp. 3-5 (Guild of Garlickhith, London).

70. Ibid., p. 6 (Guild of St. Katherine, Aldersgate).

71. Ibid., p. 67 (Guild of St. Katherine, Lynn).

72. See *CLR*, pp. 91-93; Westlake, *Parish Gilds*, p. 202.

73. See *Riverside Chaucer*, ed. Benson, pp. 951-52.

74. Kolve, *Imagery of Narrative*, p. 264.

75. According to the Benedictine chronicler Walsingham, Nicholas Brembre, sometime mayor of London, had intended to massacre thousands of his fellow citizens, rename London "New Troy," and proclaim himself duke of the city. See Thomas Walsingham, *Historia Anglicana*, ed. Henry T. Riley, 2 vols., Rolls Series (London, 1863-64), 2:173-74.

76. "And," he adds as a curious afterthought, "for noon oother cause, trewely" (VIII. 1306-7).

77. See *Inferno* XXIX-XXX.

78. Norman Blake argues that the *Canon Yeoman's Prologue and Tale* are spurious and does not include them in his Hengwrt-based edition (see *The Canterbury Tales by Geoffrey Chaucer. Edited from the Hengwrt Manuscript* [London, 1980], pp. 6, 9). Critics generally agree that they were written late in the Canterbury period (see John Reidy's note in *Riverside Chaucer*, ed. Benson, p. 946). Their case is supported by Riley's observation that "this title [yoman] first appears in the City Books about this period"; Riley is commenting on an entry for 1396 (*Memorials*, p. 542). Riley speculates that the term may be "an abbreviation of the words 'yong man'" (*Memorials*, p. 542). But it

seems clear that the term refers to rank rather than age: a *yoman* is a nonliveried member of a company or trade.

79. D. W. Robertson, Jr., *Preface to Chaucer* (Princeton, N.J., 1962), p. 51.

80. D. W. Robertson, Jr., *Chaucer's London* (New York, 1968): "We should expect, then, to find in medieval London an hierarchical classless society" (p. 5).

81. Aers, *Community, Gender, and Individual Identity*, p. 7.

82. This point is well made, in a mean-spirited sort of way, by R. W. Johnson, "Moooovement," *London Review of Books* 12.3 (8 February 1990), 5-6.

83. "History, Historicism, and the Social Logic of the Text in the Middle Ages," *Speculum* 65 (1990), 59-86, especially p. 62. The phrase "in truth" is anomalous here since it is borrowed from the language of epistemological coherence that is itself the subject of suspicion.

84. *Letter Book H,* fol. cclix, in *Memorials,* ed. Riley, pp. 526-27, especially p. 526.

85. Riley, ed., *Memorials,* p. 526. For Chaucer's most intensive usage of the terms *suspect* and *suspecious,* see *Clerk's Tale,* IV.540-42.

86. Riley, ed., *Memorials,* pp. 526-27.

CHAPTER 5

William Langland
A London Poet
Caroline M. Barron

P iers Plowman is, in many ways, a baffling and teasing poem, particularly so for the historian, who is inclined to prefer source materials to be cut and dried. *Piers Plowman* exists in at least three
versions, none of which can be securely dated. The author (or authors) is
unknown, and although we may infer, from the internal evidence of the
poem, that his name was William Langland, it has so far proved impossible
to locate an appropriate man of that name in any of the surviving documentary sources for the later fourteenth century.[1] All we know of the author is derived from his poem: in Derek Pearsall's words, "The poem is, to
all intents and purposes, Langland's whole known existence and his whole
life's work."[2] The historian, when presented with a piece of historical evidence, likes to know who wrote it, where and when. *Piers Plowman* produces clear answers to none of these questions. Yet the historian must per-
severe, for the poet, whoever he was and wherever and whenever he wrote,
leads us along untrodden ways and shares experiences that are otherwise
inaccessible. The poet is the literate spokesman for a largely illiterate society.

The dating of the different versions of the poem is significant, if not of
primary importance. George Kane has recently summarized the current
thinking on this question: the A version originated in the period 1368-74,
the B version in the years 1377-81, and the C version in the period 1379/
81-circa 1385.[3] For many readers the exact dating of the different versions
of the poem, even if it were possible to ascertain this, would be comparatively unimportant. But it *can* be crucial. Anne Hudson has recently discussed the "Lollard" aspects of the poem, the ideological outlook of the author, and the impact that the poem may have had upon contemporaries.
Here the dating of the poem *is* important, since it must be read in tandem
with the events of Wyclif's life and the dissemination and condemnation
of his ideas.[4]

It would, obviously, help us to understand the poem and its social context if we could know more about the author. In 1965 Kane established
that all three versions of the poem were written by the same man, whom
he named as William Langland on the basis of the syllabic anagrams to be
found within the poem.[5] This is also the name given to the author of the
late-fourteenth-century ascription to be found in the Trinity College Dub-

lin manuscript of the poem.[6] But Kane, at the same time as he provided a single named author for all three versions of *Piers Plowman*, warned scholars against the "autobiographical fallacy," namely the attempt to extract from the dreamer's visions biographical material about the life of the poet.[7] His warning must be heeded, yet it may still be justifiable to attempt to locate the poet within his milieu and to assess the circumstances that shaped his visions.

There is no doubt that the author of *Piers Plowman* knew London well and probably lived there for a time. It is reasonable to suppose that he composed part of the poem in the city. M. L. Samuels's study of the dialect and grammar of the surviving texts of the poem has suggested that the B-text was predominantly copied in London workshops, often by scribes who were immigrants and retained their own dialectal individualism.[8] By contrast, a large number of the surviving copies of the later C-text appear to have been written in the area around the Malvern Hills (southwest Worcestershire, southeast Herefordshire, and northwest Gloucestershire). John Burrow demonstrated, over thirty years ago, that Langland's alliterative verse was modified, perhaps, for a more metropolitan audience. Whereas other alliterative poets wrote for known, regional audiences (particularly in the north and west), "Langland's poem was designed to be understood by a far-flung audience, centered particularly on London and the midlands."[9] He wrote "on the edge of the alliterative tradition, little concerned with producing its peculiar linguistic effects."[10] The evidence, therefore, of both the dialect and the verse style suggests that the author of *Piers Plowman* may have come to London, as so many others did in the fourteenth century, from the countryside, probably from the area around Malvern, and that he composed in part for the eclectic society that he found in the city. There his poem found a ready response and was copied in a variety of scribal workshops and in a variety of scribal dialects. The fact that the poet composed, and wrote, both in a West Midlands dialect and in modified alliterative verse seems in no way to have detracted from the popularity of the poem in a city full of immigrants, many of whom would, as A. I. Doyle has pointed out, "have been happy with what was familiar."[11] The poem seems to have enjoyed continued popularity until the mid-fifteenth century, but then the demand fell away. Caxton and other early printers seem not to have thought that the poem was worth printing: the "London" dialect, the verse style, and subject matter of Chaucer's poems won the day.[12] By the end of the fifteenth century *Piers Plowman* may indeed have seemed old-fashioned, but this had not been the case a hundred years earlier, and modern students of the poem have to beware of this anachronistic fallacy. In the 1370s when, we presume, the author of *Piers Plowman* was living and writing in London, his poetry would have appeared to be as relevant, stylish, and "modern" as that of Chaucer. Both were poets in London but, of the two, Langland is surely much more a London poet.

The influence of the city of London upon the author of *Piers Plowman* is striking and has only recently come to be acknowledged. The image of the poet of the Malvern Hills dies but a lingering death. It is true that the Malvern Hills are referred to three times in the poem, twice in the Prologue and once in Passus VII,[13] but these references barely justify the weight that has been placed upon them. The poet never suggests that he was born in that area or that he spent his childhood there, although it is true that the underlying authorial, as opposed to scribal, dialect of the poems certainly indicates that the author came from southwest Worcestershire or the Malvern area.[14] But even if the author did indeed, as is suggested by the dialect, come from Worcestershire, the content and the texture of the poem largely reflect an urban setting specifically, London. This is apparent in the topographical allusions. Apart from the references to the Malvern Hills, there are few place names from outside London and none from the west country. In the B-text there are references to the abbot of Abingdon,[15] the reeve of Rutland, the beadle of Buckinghamshire, the hound of Hertfordshire, and to the French "of Norfolk." All these topographical references seem to have a generic, or universal, quality and may well have been chosen to serve the needs of meter or alliteration. They do not suggest close or particular knowledge of the places named.[16] There is, however, a clutch of references to Hampshire that suggests a more specialized knowledge of the area. Langland refers to Wy (Weyhill near Andover),[17] which was the site of a famous fair, and to Winchester and the fair of St. Giles, which was held on a hill outside the town.[18] The poet is also aware of the dangers that merchants faced when they traveled through the Alton pass on their way to the Winchester fairs.[19] It seems unlikely that it was simply chance that led Langland to select these Hampshire references but, rather, some specific of local information. Well-known as the St. Giles fair at Winchester was, it was by no means the most famous fair in late-fourteenth-century England. Stourbridge fair, held near Cambridge, would have provided the poet with a more universal reference.

Apart from these Hampshire names, the most striking collection of topographical references centers on London. London itself is mentioned seven times, Westminster four times, and the river Thames (the only river mentioned by name in the poem) twice. The names of the suburban areas of Tyburn, Southwark, Stratford, and Shoreditch all occur, and, within the City, there are references to Cock Lane in Smithfield, Cheapside, Cornhill, and Garlickhythe. St. Paul's Cathedral is mentioned three times. These numerous topographical references demonstrate in a brief, if simplistic, way the extent to which *Piers Plowman* is a London poem.[20] It is, of course, much more than that, but it may be that because the poem is written in alliterative verse, which later became old-fashioned, and because the hero of the poem pursues a rural craft, the specifically London context of the poem has become obscured. Insofar as Langland's poem is rooted in time and place, it is rooted in the streets of London in the 1370s.

Recent studies of *Piers Plowman* have drawn attention to some of the London dimensions of the poem.[21] In chapter 6, "Need Men and Women Labor?," Lawrence Clopper convincingly interprets the famous autobiographical passage at the beginning of Passus V of the C-text in the light of the statutes dealing with the regulation of labor in London. In a similar vein James Simpson has interpreted the "Commonwealth of Crafts" passage in the penultimate Passus of the poem[22] in the context of London craft rivalries during the period. In this passage the poet uses the famous passage from I Corinthians 12.4, "there are varieties of gifts," as a model for a society that is no longer simply agricultural and hierarchical but increasingly egalitarian and that includes "urban occupations of commerce and artisanal practice."[23] This vision of a society in which there is harmonious interdependence of a wide variety of crafts, skilled and unskilled, clean and dirty, is, Simpson argues, in marked contrast to the factional fighting that dominated London politics in the 1370s and 1380s. Langland here proposes his own spiritual solution to the intercraft disputes that raged about him.

The London theme in *Piers Plowman* that I propose to examine here is that of government. In her 1981 book, *The Theme of Government in Piers Plowman*,[24] Anna Baldwin considers the important passage in the Prologue to the B-text in which Langland appears to put forward a "limited" or "democratic" view of royal government:

> Thanne kam ther a Kyng: Knyghthod hym ladde:
> Might of the communes made hym to regne.
> And thanne cam Kynde Wit and clerkes he made,
> For to counseillen the Kyng and the Commune save.[25]

But then, Baldwin observes, as Langland works on his poem and brings himself face to face with the problems posed by Lady Meed, he develops a more absolutist role for the king in which he can claim to be the head, guardian, and judge of everyone in his kingdom, with the right to take what is necessary both from the church and the commons.[26] Having, of necessity, arrived at this absolutist view of kingship by the time he finished composing the B-text, Langland then, Baldwin argues, adopts these absolutist views when working again on the C-text. Here the role of the commons is excised from the Prologue, and in the C-text the only restraints upon royal absolutism are reason and conscience, both qualities that must be innate within the king himself.

Baldwin accepts that Langland's solutions to the problems that faced his society were essentially moral, "but they are also political, and need to be understood in terms of contemporary political ideas, and Langland's own experience of law and government."[27] But, whereas it is possible that the poet had some understanding of law, there is very little evidence that he knew anything at all about government at the national level. He may well have hung around the law courts at Westminster,[28] but that would not have provided him with any clear idea of what took place in Parliament or how the king governed. It is for this reason that Langland's solutions to the evils of his day, to social instability, mercenary attitudes, wage and price inflation, lawlessness, heavy taxation, and so on, are so naive. When the poet writes of Parliament—and he seems to have only the haziest notions about it—he sees it as a supreme judicial court [29] and not a place in which debates about foreign policy or taxation took place. The absolutist king is an idealized figure: a simplistic solution to the problems of the realm. He is to have the support of the common people, to rule in justice, to uphold the laws, to reward his supporters, to defend the church, and to raise money to defend the realm. [30] Langland shared this simplistic view of what needed to be done to right the wrongs of the kingdom with the peasant rebels of 1381. The poet stood with them outside the political nation, and, with them, he saw the salvation of society to lie in the removal of traitors and Lady Meed and in the personal qualities of a monarch who, stripped of venal advisers and self-seekers, would rule his kingdom in justice and in peace. Such a vision grew naturally out of Langland's lack of any experience of government. It seems unlikely, moreover, that he had close contact with those who held sway in royal, or national, government.

But if we continue to pursue the theme of government in the poem, we can see that Langland does have some quite specific and well-understood things to say about the local government he had experienced at first hand, namely the government of the City of London. In the community within which Langland lived, it was the mayor, rather than the king, who really mattered and who exercised authority over the inhabitants of the city. About the duties of the mayor of London Langland is often quite specific. This elected civic dignitary is not given the idealized role that Langland has created for the more remote king.

Langland very precisely understands the duality, or ambiguity, of the mayor's role: he is elected by the citizens and yet answerable to the king. The role of the mayor is to act as a mediator between the king and the commons: "And a mene, as þe mayre is, bitwene þe kyng and þe comune." [31] Unlike the king, mayors are not accorded absolute powers. On the contrary, they are enjoined not to "overcarke" (overburden) the common people. [32] The wealth of the men who act as mayors and judges (the mayor of London acted as a judge in the mayor's court) will not, Langland warns them, serve to save them on the Day of Judgment, however many pardons and papal bulls they have purchased. [33] Indeed, Langland observes that a poor man is unlikely to be made a justice "to jugge men" nor a "mair above men" and so will be better able to achieve salvation. [34] The poet's view of the mayor's role is that it is hazardous, full of temptation, and dangerous to the soul. To this local ruler Langland does not willingly give the absolute powers that he elsewhere sees as the means to the salvation of contemporary society.

In marked contrast to the vague duties allocated to the king, the mayor is given quite specific instructions about his responsibilities. In a passage of considerable detail,[35] Langland enjoins the mayor to punish fraudulent brewers, bakers, butchers, and cooks so that they will be dissuaded from cheating the poor people who are forced to buy food from them piecemeal, in small quantities as they can afford it. Victualers like these, Langland observes, have grown rich through practicing "regratrie," that is, buying up food in one market and selling it at an enhanced price in another, which was forbidden by civic custom. These victualers have also grown rich through acting as landlords and letting out property to poor people at extortionate rents, while their ill-gotten gains have provided them with tall, grand timbered houses in which to live themselves. The mayor, instead of correcting these abuses and protecting the interests of the poor, takes bribes and turns a blind eye.[36] It is clear that Langland also understands the burden that inquest or jury service placed upon poor men who were compelled to serve, thereby not only losing a day's wages but also perhaps finding themselves in worse trouble. In the perfect world envisaged by Conscience, mayors would not summon such men to serve.[37] Langland is also critical of the free and easy way in which the mayor allowed men to purchase the freedom of the city, or citizenship. City custom allowed for the purchase of the freedom, although apprenticeship was the more usual route, but what Langland objects to is the mayor's failure to examine the credentials of prospective freemen, so that usurers and regrators (and other wrongdoers) are admitted into the privileged company of freemen.[38] It seems clear that the actions of the mayor had an immediate bearing on the lives of the inhabitants of London: he had the power to help the poor and to administer justice, and he often failed in these tasks. He was not a remote figure, but a man of flesh and blood who walked the city streets. Sometimes, Langland explains, a man like himself might be so witless, or absorbed in his "makings" that

> . . . thauh a mete with the mayre ameddes þe strete
> a reuerenseth hym ryht nauht, no rather then another.[39]

There is only one contemporary person who is mentioned by name in *Piers Plowman*, and then only in the B-text, and that is John Chichester, a goldsmith who was mayor of London in 1369–70 and who died in 1380.[40] It was customary for Londoners to date events by the mayoralty in which the occurred, and in this way Langland dates the drought that led to a scarcity of bread in the city. Perhaps he knew Chichester, or had received some hospitality at his house? We cannot know, but there is no doubt that the mayor of London was a real person, with real power, and a far cry from the idealized king who remains forever nameless.

There is not doubt that Langland knew well the varieties of tricks and deceits that were practiced by artisans, victualers, and merchants within urban communities. He knew how cloth was fulled and how weavers often cheated their piecework employees; he was aware of how brewers mixed good ale with poor and then sold it to those who were in no position to tell one from the other. He condemns the ubiquitous use of false weights.[41] All these deceits were widely practiced, widely condemned, and widely punished in fourteenth-century London, if we may judge from the cases brought before the mayor's court. But Langland knew that it was not only artisans and victualers who cheated their customers. Moneylenders lent out clipped coins and offered credit on terms so harsh that the borrowers had no hope of repaying, and as a result lost their lands and livelihood.[42] Drapers stretched out the cloth they had for sale to make it appear longer than it was, and other merchants used their apprentices to lure customers into their shops to buy their goods. To ensure a sale they would use blasphemous oaths and run down the goods offered by their rivals. They would even sell their goods on Holy Days.[43] It is the inhabitants of London who fill the field full of folk, who crowd into Lady Meed's train and provide the rich exempla of the seven deadly sins. But, on occasion, the poet moves outside the conventional vignettes and draws an individual picture.

His most revealing insight is, perhaps, into the true nature of grinding poverty, the desperate plight of men, women, and children who struggle for survival in a relentless environment.[44] It is hard not to believe that Langland, himself, had shared such poverty and could thus strip away the literary conventions so effectively. On other occasions the poet also seems able to get inside the skin of a rich merchant, and here, too, his observations have an inward quality. He notes that the high infant mortality rate in London, aggravated by the Plague, has led merchants to spoil their surviving children.[45] He knows and understands, but disapproves of, the obsessive anxiety of merchants who, while their agents are overseas carrying out their business in Bruges or Prussia,

> Mighte nevere me conforte in the mene tyme
> Neither masse ne matynes, ne none maner sightes;
> Ne nevere penaunce parfournede ne Paternoster seide
> That my mynde ne was moore on my good in a doute
> Than in the grace of God and hise grete helpes.[46]

Langland, we know, visited the houses of rich men and offered them spiritual counsel, doubtless reciting his poem. On occasion the merchant was unable to concentrate because of his anxiety about his goods ventured abroad. The poet knew well the weaknesses of the men whose hospitality he accepted, and he did not spare them. But he was not unremittingly critical of such men, and his portrait of their failings is devoid of the bitterness that characterizes his attacks on the friars.

Langland accepts that buying and selling of goods are not in themselves sinful activities, nor is wealth an automatic bar to salvation. There is hope for the wealthy man; indeed Charity

> Riche men he recomendeth, and of hir robes taketh
> That withouten wiles ledeth hir lyves.[47]

Anima tells the dreamer that Charity is to be found in many guises:

> For I have seyen hym in silk and som tyme in russet,
> Bothe in grey, and in grys, and in gilt harneis—
> And as gladliche he it gaf to gomes that it neded.[48]

Truth promises that merchants who use their winnings to help the poor and needy will be saved:

> Ac under his secret seel Truthe sente hem a lettre,
> And bad hem buggen boldely what hem best liked
> And sithenes selle it ayein and save the wynnyng,
> And amende mesondieux thermyd and myseise folk helpe;
> And wikkede weyes wightly amende,
> And do boote to brugges that tobroke were;
> Marien maydenes or maken hem nonnes;
> Povere peple and prisons fynden hem hir foode,
> And sette scolers to scole or to som othere craftes;
> Releve religion and renten hem bettre.[49]

If, in life, or at his death, the rich man carries out these acts of charity, then Truth will send the Archangel Michael to bring his soul in safety "to my Seintes in joye." A cursory glance through the wills of Londoners enrolled in the city's Husting Court reveals the extent to which the London merchants took advantage of the opportunities for salvation that Truth had thus presented to them. Langland seems to have experienced both poverty and wealth at first hand, and in both conditions he saw opportunities for salvation. With anima, he has found charity clothed both in russet and in silk.

If much of the poem is inspired by London experiences, then it may be reasonable to suppose that Langland wrote, in part at least, for a London audience, for those people whom he tells us that he visited once a month or so and by whom he was rewarded for his improving conversation (or recitation?) with hospitality. London households like these, at whatever point on the social scale, must have formed some part at least of Langland's audience. This we presume from the internal evidence of the poem. But what of the external evidence for Langland's audience?

Over thirty years ago John Burrow analyzed the possible composition of Langland's audience. He considered bequests of copies of the poem that were mentioned in wills, the references to *Piers Plowman* to be found in the "Peasant letters" that were copied into monastic chronicles at the time of the rising of 1381, and the ascriptions in the surviving manuscripts of the poem. On the basis of this evidence he concluded that *Piers Plowman* was read by "an old audience of clerks and a new one of prosperous literate laymen"; this view has not been seriously modified by scholars writing since.[50] Anne Middleton has, however, recently looked again at Langland's audience and has argued that these clerical and lay readers were not two separate audiences but, rather, one single audience made up from men who were involved in administration, whether ecclesiastical, royal, or civic. The text of the poem, she points out, is often found in collections that also contain historical narratives.[51] There is no doubt, however, that the appeal of *Piers Plowman* was very wide, perhaps even wider than has yet been suggested. Wills can, of course, provide a double insight: they tell us not only the name of the current owner of a copy of *Piers Plowman*, but also the names of those to whom copies were bequeathed. There is a presumption that the recipients will value such a book and, perhaps, even be able to read it.

So far we know of four wills, drawn up before 1440, in which the testators left copies of *Piers Plowman*. In 1396 Walter de Bruges, a canon of York, bequeathed his copy to Master John Wormyngton, a fellow clerk. Another Yorkshire clerk, John Wyndhill, who died in 1431, left his copy to John Kendale, whom, since he was married, we may presume to have been a layman.[52] Two other copies of the poem were in the possession of Londoners. William Palmere, who had been rector of the London parish church of St. Alphege since 1397, left "librum meum vocatum peres plowman" to a woman called Agnes Eggesfeld when he died in 1400.[53] Unfortunately we know little about Palmere and nothing at all about Agnes Eggesfeld. Palmere was by no means a wealthy cleric in the class of William de Bruges, and his will reveals signs of a man deliberately striving for simplicity: he calls himself simply "clerk," although he was the rector of the church, and he asked to be buried, not in the chancel, as was customary for rectors, but in the churchyard, where poor men were normally buried. The other Londoner who owned a copy of *Piers Plowman* was Thomas Roos, a wealthy mercer, who died at the end of 1433 and left "The Prick of Conscience" and "meum librum vocatum piers plowman," along with much else, to his son Guy.[54] The evidence of these testaments, meager as it is, does indeed suggest that it was an audience of prosperous clerics and laymen who appreciated Langland's poem.

The discovery of William Palmere's will takes us rather lower down the social scale into a class of owners and readers who were not, so far as we can tell, involved either in ecclesiastical politics or in royal or civic administration. William Palmere and Agnes Eggesfeld seem not to have been distinguished or wealthy, so Palmere's will provides an important link between the audience whom we know to have owned copies of Langland's poem and the "peasant" audience whom we perhaps may presume to have read the poem because of the references to "Peres the Plowman my brother" found in two of the six letters copied into their chronicles by Henry Knighton, a canon of St. Mary's Abbey in Leicester, and Thomas Walsingham of the Benedictine house at St. Albans.[55] Whether these letters were intentionally seditious or simply perceived to be so need not be discussed here, but the letters do suggest that a knowledge of *Piers Plowman* had penetrated this semiliterate class by 1381.[56] However, it is, of course, possible that Piers the Plowman was a well-known prototype employed both by the writers of the letters and by the author of the poem. The perception of Piers is, however, certainly the same in both the letters and in the poem: Piers is a good man who faithfully carries out the work to which he was called, which is to till the land so that it may produce the food whereby others may live. In the faithfulness of Piers lies both the hope and the means of salvation (although whether this salvation is to be political or spiritual remains ambiguous).

The evidence assembled thus far suggests that the poem of *Piers Plowman* was already quite widely known by 1381 and that copies of it were in the possession of rich and lowly clerics and and lay people in Yorkshire and in London by 1400. There remains the evidence that can be provided by the surviving manuscripts of the poem; this may enable us to enlarge the audience yet further. Very few of the manuscripts, however, reveal to whom they may have belonged. One manuscript of the version now known as the Z-text seems to have belonged to John Wells, a Benedictine monk from the Ramsey house who became a scholar of Gloucester College, Oxford. He died in 1388.[57] Finally there is the evidence provided by the well-known ascription in the manuscript at Trinity College, Dublin. This ascription, which has been added to the manuscript, declares that the book was made by William de Langland, the son of Eustace de Rokayle, who was born and bred at Shipton under Wychwood where he held land from Lord le Spenser.[58] This important ascription has, of course, been frequently discussed and used to help to identify the author of the poem. But this manuscript may also tell us something about the audience for the poem. The Trinity College copy of the C-text appears to have been written during the last quarter of the fourteenth century.[59] Very soon after it was written, a different hand added the Rokayle ascription, and this hand also added a series of memoranda "mainly concerned with events connected with the southern Welsh border."[60] The execution of Hugh le Spenser (or Despenser as he is more usually known) in 1326 is noted among this memoranda, and this may have been what "triggered" the scribe into writing the note about the authorship of the poem in which he associates the maker of the book called *Piers Plowman* with the le Spenser family. Brooks has suggested that this beautifully written, late-fourteenth-century manuscript of *Piers Plowman* may have been copied at the Benedictine Priory of Abergavenny. The dialect studies of M. L. Samuels seem to have corroborated this suggestion in that the scribal dialect of this manuscript has been identified as belonging to northwest Gloucestershire, close enough to Abergavenny for comfort.[61] Whoever wrote the ascription not only knew the poem, but claimed also to know something of the author. If the scribe came from the area around Gloucester and was a monk at Abergavenny, and if William Langland did indeed come from the area around Malvern (as later scholars have supposed and as dialect studies have tended to confirm)[62] then the Abergavenny monk may have been in a position to know something about the poet and his family. In fact, the Trinity College manuscript forms one of a considerable cluster of C-text versions of the poem that can be associated, on scribal grounds, with the area around Gloucester. It may be that this cluster suggests that late in life Langland returned to the area of the Malvern Hills and provided an "authorial presence" or it may simply mean "that the poet was well known in the area and had special connections with it."[63] Yet the fact that the Trinity manuscript can be traced to a Benedictine house in the area perhaps lends greater authority to the ascription. At the very least it suggests that Langland's work was valued, known, and copied in monastic houses and that monks, in spite of the criticisms in the poem, may have been among the friends and acquaintances of the poet.

Another manuscript, this time of the A-text, carries an ascription of a rather different kind. This is a mid-fifteenth-century manuscript (now Bodley Rawlinson Poetry 137) that contains a unique continuation to Passus XII of the A-text. In fact, this Passus survives in only three manuscripts: one provides 19 lines, one provides 88 lines, and the Rawlinson manuscript has 117 lines.[64] How much of the Passus is the work of the original poet and how much is the work of the continuator is hard to judge,[65] but it is certain that lines 99 onward must have been written by someone else. The writer of lines 99 to 117 tells us, in rather inferior verse, that Will, who wrote "that here is wryten, and other werkes bothe of Peres the Plowman and mechel puple also," had died and that others were now claiming his works as their own. The writer of this new "ende" reveals that his name was John But and that when he wrote, Richard was "king of this rewme."[66]

There is no reason not to believe that a man named John But, living during the reign of Richard II, actually knew the poet Will and knew of his death. His anxiety that Will should receive the credit for his work suggests that he was moved by friendship to make an end for Will's poem[67] and to solicit prayers for Will the poet, for But himself, and for King Richard. If we can find out more about this John But we will edge a little closer to the poet Will, for But claims to have known him. What manner of man was this friend of the poet of *Piers Plowman*?

As long ago as 1913 Edith Rickert identified John But as the royal messenger of that name.[68] She ascribed to John But lines 56 onward of the Passus and so argued that phrases such as "I am a mesager of deth" (line 83) and "a courrour of our house" (line 84) were deliberate allusions to But's profession. Rickert also found out quite a bit about John But the messenger, including the fact that he was probably dead by April 1387, when his office was granted to someone else.[69] If the John But who wrote the continuation to Passus A and tells of the death of Will was, himself, dead by 1387, then we at least have a terminus ante quem for the composition of the *Piers Plowman* poems. Rickert's identification of John But of the continuation with John But the royal messenger has not found universal acceptance.[70] Recently, however, Anne Middleton has been inclined to accept the identification, and there is further corroborative, although not conclusive, evidence that the John But who knew Will the poet and created an ending for his unfinished poem was the man of that name who was a royal messenger.

The will of John But survives, copied into the register of the commissary of London, and while it does not, alas, refer either to William Langland or to a "librum" called *Piers Plowman*, it does reveal rather more about the man who claimed to have known the author of *Piers Plowman*.[71] The will, in which John But describes himself as "messager," suggests that the testator came from Gloucester: he asks to be buried, depending on the place of his death, either in the abbey church at Gloucester, near the image of the Holy Trinity, or in the church of the Carmelite friars in London. But he makes no reference either to a parish church or to a parish priest, which suggests that he had no settled home but lived a peripatetic life. He left a silver girdle and a silver pyx decorated with the royal arms to the image of the Blessed Virgin at Kingswood, probably a statue in the Cistercian house at Kingswood, near Wotton-under-Edge, south of Gloucester. Twenty shillings was also provided for the upkeep of the steep road between Painswick and Gloucester, a matter perhaps of particular concern to a royal messenger. One of But's executors was to be John Rusby of Gloucester, a man who appears frequently as a witness to Gloucester deeds from 1372 onward and who became bailiff of the city in 1393. The But family is in evidence in Gloucester from 1200 onward, and between 1362 and 1385 a John But "corveyser" (or cordwainer) owned two shops lying between the two western bridges of the city.[72] A Robert But was steward of the city in 1391-92 and bailiff several times in the early fifteenth century.[73]

So John But, the royal messenger, appears to have come from a long-established and moderately prosperous artisan family in Gloucester. When did he become a royal messenger, and how? But first appears as a messenger attached to the household of the Black Prince in 1376-77.[74] It may be that when the Black Prince died in 1376 and his household was dispersed, But was taken on as a messenger in the royal household, for he is to be found acting in that capacity from 1377 until 1386.[75] In October 1378 But "messager" received the income from some lands at Barton on Humber in Lincolnshire that had been forfeited to the Crown and were expected to yield ten pounds per annum.[76] This income was augmented a year later by a pension from the house at St. Michael's Mount in Cornwall.[77]

Among his tasks But is to be found delivering writs to the sheriffs of five counties stretching from Berkshire to Herefordshire, summoning them to the Parliament that was to meet in Gloucester in 1378, together with letters of summons to the earls of Stafford, Warwick, and March to come to the King's Council.[78] His commissions seem to have been largely westward. In April 1386 he was sent with royal signet letters "to the west" for Matthew Gournay, Guy Brian, and other garter knights to inform them that the St. George's Day feast had been delayed.[79]

Royal messengers and "corsores"—or couriers—together numbered some twenty to thirty men, and they were members, albeit lowly ones, of the royal household. They lived at court, received their food and lodging there, and were paid their traveling expenses when they were sent about the country on royal business. They would probably have had rudimentary clerical skills (in But's case he would seem to have been sufficiently skilled to have written verse), and they were often drawn from landholding stock, probably from among the smaller free tenants of the royal demesne.[80] Earlier in the century some royal messengers had been drawn from Gloucestershire, but John But's urban background seems to have been comparatively unusual. There is no way of knowing how he came to be employed by the Black Prince. It is likely that he worked first in a noble household and from there was drawn into royal service.[81]

It was one of the perquisites of the messenger's office to receive gifts, either from the king or from those to whom the messenger had brought news, usually good news. But's will refers to a silver gilt girdle and to a silver pyx, both of which were decorated with the royal arms. He mentions also a silver girdle and a covered silver cup that he had been given by the wealthy and important London grocer and mayor, Sir John Philpot.[82] There were other Londoners mentioned in But's will, and he designates the White Friars' house in Fleet Street as one of his desired places for burial. He bequeathed 6s. 8d. to John Grene, a clerk who lived, But notes, in Carter Lane near St. Paul's, and John Maynard was given a silver girdle "cum campanis" (with bells?). Maynard was also named as an executor, and as it was he who proved the will in the commissary's court in July 1387, he is likely to have been a Londoner. There was a dyer of that name who lived in the parish of All Hallows in Thames Street and who died in 1407.[83] His will reveals no link with John But except that, like him, Maynard wished to be buried in the Carmelite church. It is possible that both men belonged to one of the fraternities that we know existed in the White Friars' church in the later fourteenth century. Such a fraternity would have provided a substitute "kin group" for a rootless traveler like John But.[84] The third executor of But's will was to be Master John Parker, described in the will as a chaplain living with the archbishop of Canterbury, at that time William Courtenay. The 1381 Poll Tax reveals two chaplains then living in London of that name, and in 1390 a John Parker was appointed to be rector of the London parish church of St. Pancras Soper Lane. Since this living was in the gift of the archbishop of Canterbury it is likely that it was given to a man who, in 1386, was described as living with the archbishop.[85]

John But had been married to Alice Glaysch, who was dead by 1384. She was the daughter of John Glaysch and may have come from Torrington in Devon, for she employed a bailiff to look after her lands there.[86] Before her death she drew up a testament, which was comparatively uncommon among married women, and bequeathed her goods and chattels to her husband and appointed him as one of her executors.[87] In his will But also mentions "Mathilda my servant, and William my son," who were jointly given the silver girdle and silver cup and cover that had been given to But by Philpot. It could be that Mathilda was the servant to whom the care of young William was entrusted, but the absence of any reference to William in the context of Alice Glaysch and her goods and the fact that he is paired together in a single bequest with "Mathilda my servant" suggests that "William my son" may have been the illegitimate offspring of an alliance between John But and his servant Mathilda. This was a not uncommon phenomenon in London households at the time.

There is no evidence that John But ever owned property in London or became a London citizen or, indeed, a parishioner. His duties in and around the royal household would have brought him to London, and he may well have lived there for short periods, but his will would suggest that his roots were still in Gloucester. There must have been glamorous and exciting aspects to the life of a royal messenger: the comings and goings of famous names in the royal household, the gifts given by the rich and noble, the feasts and meals in other aristocratic households, and the endless movement around the country, where a royal messenger would be considered as a person of some significance and importance. When John But came to draw up his will, however, on 20 February 1386, he was not a wealthy man; he had three silver girdles, two silver cups, 26s. 8d. in cash, and the goods and chattels that had been bequeathed to his wife by her father. But seems to have been dead by April 1387, when a new royal messenger was appointed in his place,[88] although his will was not proved until the following July. John But's life-style was unsettled and, to some extent, precarious. He did not share the urban prosperity or the settled security of "middle-class" Londoners.

The author of the *Piers Plowman* poem is presumed to have come from the Malvern area, not only because he mentions the Malvern Hills in his poems, but also because the authorial dialect of the poems can be located in the area lying to the northwest of Gloucester. But there can be no doubt that this west-country man traveled to London and lived there, if we may accept the autobiographical sections of the poem, in a "cot" on Cornhill with his wife and daughter. The poems are richly textured with London imagery and London knowledge, and much of the allegory, and the illustrative material, is derived from a perceptive understanding of the realities of life in London, of poverty, of artisan craftsmanship, and of the ebb and flow of mercantile wealth. It is possible that the poet returned at the end of his life to the Malvern area, and it is clear that he intended his poem to speak to people everywhere, yet the poem must have carried most meaning for those who knew London best. A great many Londoners were, like the poet himself, immigrants into the city from the countryside and smaller towns of England. One such immigrant Londoner was the royal messenger John But. He claimed to know Will, the author of *Piers Plowman*, and to know him well enough to care that others were claiming his work as their own. John But was dead by April 1387, and Will had died earlier. To most men But would appear to have been the more successful of the two since he had secured a post of some profit and panache in the royal household. He moved on the fringes of aristocratic society and dined in the great halls of great men. In his youth he had acquired some education, either in the town of Gloucester or, perhaps, at the Cistercian house at Kingswood, in any case sufficient to pen prosaic verse when under the influence of the greater poetry of his friend. William Langland also lived a peripatetic life, because in that way he could earn his daily bread by carrying out the tasks for which he felt himself to be best suited. Like John But he also ate many meals at other men's tables, and both men were drawn to London in search of fame, a job, an audience, and a milieu. But if they lived in London, they lived also "opelond," and like so many men and women in the late fourteenth century, they were endlessly on the move, jostling their way around the fair field of England, rubbing shoulders with all manner of men and women. For men who "wente wide in this world wondres to here," there was no denying the call of London.

Notes

I am very grateful to John Burrow, Rosalind Field, Barbara Hanawalt, James Simpson, Paul Strohm, and David Wallace, all of whom read an earlier draft of this essay and not only saved me from errors, but also made numerous illuminating suggestions.

1. For the most recent, but still unsuccessful, attempt to locate William Langland in the surviving archive material, see chapter 6, "Need Men and Women Labor?" by Lawrence Clopper.

2. Derek Pearsall, ed., *Piers Plowman by William Langland: An Edition of the C-Text* (London, 1978), p. 9.

3. George Kane, "The Text," in *A Companion to Piers Plowman*, ed. John A. Alford (Berkeley, Calif., 1988), pp. 175-200, esp. pp. 184-86. See also Pearsall, *Piers Plowman*, p. 9, where the suggested dates differ slightly. A "Z" version, possibly earlier than any other text, has been edited by A. G. Rigg and Charlotte Brewer: *William Langland, Piers Plowman: The Z Version* (Toronto, 1983).

4. Anne Hudson, *The Premature Reformation: Wycliffite Tracts and Lollard History* (Oxford, 1988), pp. 399-408.

5. George Kane, *Piers Plowman: The Evidence for Authorship* (London, 1965); see also Anne Middleton, "William Langland's 'Kynde Name,'" in *Literary Practice and Social Change in Britain, 1380-1530*, ed. Lee Patterson (Berkeley, Calif., 1990), pp. 15-82, esp. pp. 24-52.

6. Kane, *Piers Plowman*, pp. 26-32. See also E. St. John Brooks, "The *Piers Plowman* Manuscript in Trinity College Dublin," *Library* 6 (1951), 141-53. The ascription in this manuscript is now thought to be dated to c. 1400, i.e., quite close to the writing down of the poem itself (Brooks, p. 141).

7. George Kane, *The Autobiographical Fallacy in Chaucer and Langland Studies* (University College, London, 1965).

8. M. L. Samuels, "Dialect and Grammar," in *Companion to Piers Plowman*, ed. Alford, pp. 201-22, especially p. 206; see also Samuels's "Langland's Dialect," *Medium Aevum* 54 (1985), 232-47.

9. T. Turville-Petre, *The Alliterative Revival* (Cambridge, Eng., 1977), p. 46.

10. J. A. Burrow, "The Audience of *Piers Plowman*," reprinted in his *Essays on Medieval Literature* (Oxford, 1984), pp. 102-16.

11. A. I. Doyle, "Remarks on Surviving Manuscripts of *Piers Plowman*," in *Medieval English Religious and Ethical Literature: Essays in Honor of G. H. Russell*, ed. Gregory Kratzman and James Simpson (Woodbridge, 1986), pp. 35-48, esp. p. 40. For another alliterative poem, written in London in the 1390s in a northern dialect, see Ruth Kennedy, "A Bird in Bishopswood: Some Newly-Discovered Lines of Alliterative Verse from the Late Fourteenth Century," in *Medieval Literature and Antiquities: Studies in Honour of Basil Cottle*, ed. Myra Stokes and T. L. Burton (Woodbridge, 1987), pp. 71-87.

12. *Piers Plowman* was printed in 1550 by Robert Crowley, who appreciated its "Protestant leanings"; see Anne Hudson, "Epilogue: The Legacy of *Piers Plowman*," in *Companion to Piers Plowman*, ed. Alford, pp. 251-66.

13. Citations from the texts of *Piers Plowman* are from the following editions: A-text, *Piers Plowman: The A Version*, ed. George Kane (London 1960); B-text, *William Langland: The Vision of Piers Plowman*, ed. A. V. C. Schmidt (London, 1978); C-text, *Piers Plowman by William Langland*, ed. Pearsall. B Prol. 5 and 215; B. VII.142.

14. Samuels, "Langland's Dialect," p. 237.

15. B.X.323. This reference is generalized to "abbot of Engelonde" in C.V.176. It is possible that Langland chose to chastise the abbot of Abingdon because the abbot had recently (1368-72) been involved in a protracted dispute with his tenants in the town of Abingdon, a dispute that had come to the attention of Parliament in 1372 (see Gabrielle Lambrick, "The Impeachment of the Abbot of Abingdon in 1368," *EngHR* 82 [1976], 250-76).

16. B.II.110-11 and C.II.111; B.V.356; B.V.235. Pearsall, *Piers Plowman*, p. 60 n. 111, notes that "place names like this were probably not chosen for any particular satirical reason." He also notes that the change from "Bedel of Bokynghamshire" in the B-text to "bedel of Bannebury sokene" in the C-text is unlikely "to be significant." There are also two references to food from Essex: cheese (B.V.92) and the famous Dunmow flitch (B.IX.170).

17. B.V.201; see Pearsall, *Piers Plowman*, p. 118, n. 211.

18. C.VI.211; C.IV.51; see C.XIII.51.

19. B.XIV.301. The St. Giles Fair flourished at Winchester from the late twelfth century until the late thirteenth century, when it began to decline. Until 1398 the bishops, who reaped the profits from the fair, paid the cost of sending men to guard the Alton pass at the time of the fair so that merchants would not be deterred from coming by the dangers of the route (Derek Keene, *Survey of Medieval Winchester*, 2 vols. [Oxford, 1985], 2:1113-22).

20. References to London, B Prol. 85, 91, 160; B.II.135,156; B.V.128; B.XIII.263; references to Westminster, B.II.161; B.III.12, 285; B.XX.133; references to the Thames, B.XII.161; B.XV.338; reference to Tyburn, B.XII.190; reference to Southwark, B.XIII.339;

reference to Stratford, B.XIII.266; reference to Shoreditch, B.XIII.339; reference to Cock Lane in Smithfield, B.V.312; reference to Cheapside, B.V.315; reference to Cornhill, C.V.2; reference to Garlickhythe, B.V.317; reverences to St. Paul's Cathedral, B.X.46, 73; B.XIII.64. For a similar use of topographical and geographical references to locate the authorship of the different versions of the Arthur story, see Patricia Price, "Geographical Allusions in the Alliterative *Morte Arthure* and *Roman de Brut*, *Brut* and *Historia Regum Brittanniae*" (M.A. thesis, Northeast Louisiana University, 1982).

21. Middleton, "William Langland's 'Kynde Name,'" pp. 58-60.

22. B.XIX.200-263; C.XXI.199-261.

23. James B. Simpson, "Langland's Commonwealth of Crafts: Piers Plowman B.XIX.200-263," forthcoming.

24. Anna P. Baldwin, *The Theme of Government in Piers Plowman* (Woodbridge, 1981); see also John Taylor, *English Historical Literature in the Fourteenth Century* (Oxford, 1987), pp. 210, 248.

25. B Prol. 112-15.

26. Baldwin, *Theme of Government*, ch. 3.

27. Ibid., p. 2.

28. Anna Baldwin, "A Reference in *Piers Plowman* to the Westminster Sanctuary," *Notes and Queries* 227 (1982), 106-8.

29. C.IV.45.

30. B.IV and B.XIX. Recently James Simpson has interpreted B.IV in the context of the judicial activities of the King's Council, which Langland might well have observed at Westminster (*Piers Plowman: An Introduction to the B-Text* [New York, 1990], pp. 53-60).

31. C.I.156; see also B.III.76-77.

32. C.III.468; see also B.III.316.

33. B.VII.185-87; C.IX.337-39.

34. B.XIV.288; C.XIV.125.

35. B.III.76-92, which is considerably expanded in the later C.III.77-126.

36. B.III.76-92; see also C.III.77-89.

37. B.III.317; C.III.469.

38. C.III.108-14.

39. C.IX.122-23.

40. B.XIII.270. For details of Chichester's career, see T. F. Reddaway and Lorna E. M. Walker, *The Early History of the Goldsmiths' Company, 1327-1509* (London, 1975), pp. 289-92. I am grateful to Alistair Minnis, who has pointed out to me that the poet's claim to "jangle to this jurdan" may be a pun on *jordan* (chamber pot) and the name of the Dominican friar William Jordan (fl. 1351-68); see A. Gwynn, "The Date of the B-text of *Piers Plowman*," *Review of English Studies* 19 (1943), 1-24.

41. B.XV.450-53; B.XIX.399-403; B.V.225; B.XIV.292.

42. B.V.238-48.

43. B.V.205-10; B.II.213-15; B.V. 125-31.

44. C.IX.71-127.

45. B.V.34-40.

46. B.XIII.394-98.

47. B.III.257-58.

48. B.XV.220-22.

49. B.VII.223-32.

50. Burrow, "Audience."

51. Anne Middleton, "The Audience and Public of *Piers Plowman*," in *Middle English Alliterative Poetry and Its Literary Background*, ed. David Lawton (Woodbridge, 1982), pp. 101-23.

52. *Testamenta Eboracensia*, I Surtees Society 4 (London, 1836), pp. 207-10; *Testamenta Eboracensia*, II Surtees Society (London, 1855), pp. 32-35.

53. Robert A. Wood, "A Fourteenth-Century London Owner of *Piers Plowman*," *Medium Aevum* 53 (1984), 83-90.

54. Guildhall Library, MS. 9171/3 fol. 369r and v; Susan H. Cavanaugh, "A Study of Books Privately Owned in England: 1300-1450" (Ph.D. diss., University of Pennsylvania, 1980), 2:749-50.

55. Knighton, *Chronicon* 2:139; Thomas Walsingham, *Historia Anglicana*, ed. H. T. Riley, 2 vols., Rolls Series (London, 1864), 2:34. See also Hudson, *The Premature Reformation*, pp. 399-406.

56. See Middleton, "William Langland's 'Kynde Name,'" pp. 65-73, and chapters 9 and 10 by Richard Greene and Susan Crane in this volume.

57. Burrow, "Audience," p. 114. For John Wells, see A. B. Emden, *A Biographical Register of the University of Oxford to A. D. 1500*, 3 vols. (Oxford, 1959), 3:2008, who doubts that Wells owned the *Piers Plowman* manuscript, now Bodley MS. 851, but see *Piers Plowman: The Z Version*, ed. Rigg and Brewer, pp. 3-5. Another fifteenth-century MS (Oriel College Oxford MS. 79) is inscribed with the name of a fifteenth-century owner, William Rogger, who gave the manuscript to Roger Sambrook before John at Style, and other witnesses, 19 September 1438 (George Kane and E. Talbot Donaldson, eds., *Piers Plowman: The B Version* [London, 1975], pp. 11-12). These men cannot be traced in London records of the time, and the dialect of the manuscript is described by Samuels as "north Hertfordshire."

58. Trinity College Dublin MS. D.4.1. fol. 89v; see Kane, *Evidence for Authorship*, ch. 3. The Despenser family held Shipton under Wychwood from at least 1346; see *Feudal Aids, 1284-1431*, 5 vols. (1899-1908), 4:185.

59. Brooks, "The *Piers Plowman* Manuscript," p. 141.

60. Ibid., p. 146.

61. Samuels, "Dialect and Grammar," p. 206. It may be significant that a couple of miles away from Shipton under Wychwood lay the village of Bampton, which passed, on the death of Aymer de Valence, Earl of Pembroke, in 1324, to the Hastings family, who became earls of Pembroke and Lords of Abergavenny. I am most grateful to Nigel Saul for this information.

62. Samuels, "Langland's Dialect."

63. Samuels, "Dialect and Grammar," p. 208.

64. George Kane, ed., *Piers Plowman: The A Version*, pp. 8-9, 14, 16.

65. E. Rickert, "John But, Messenger and Maker," *Medieval Philology* 11 (1913-14), 107-16, especially p. 108; Kane, *Evidence for Authorship*, pp. 32-34; Anne Middleton, "Making a Good End: John But as a Reader of *Piers Plowman*," in *Medieval English Studies Presented to George Kane*, ed. Edward D. Kennedy, R. Waldron, and J. S. Wittig (Woodbridge, 1988), pp. 243-66, especially p. 246.

66. A.XII.101-2, 113.

67. Middleton, "Making a Good End," p. 246.

68. Rickert, "John But, Messenger and Maker."

69. 17 April 1387, *Calender of Patent Rolls, 1385-89*, p. 290 (hereafter cited as *CPR*).

70. Oscar Cargill, "The Langland Myth," *PMLA* 50 (1935), 35-56, where Cargill finds connections between Butts and Rokayles. Kane, *Evidence for Authorship*, p. 32 n. 3, is inclined to accept Cargill's arguments, although Middleton, "Making a Good End," favors Rickert's identification of John But of the poem with John But the messenger.

71. Guildhall Library MS. 9171/1 fol. 153v.

72. W. H. Stevenson, *Calendar of Records of the Corporation of Gloucester* (Gloucester, 1893). For John Rusby, see nos. 995, 1008, 1013-14, 1018, 1022-23, 1025-27, 1029, 1031, 1033; for the But family see nos. 978-79, 995, 1001, 1016, 1022, 1024, 1079.

73. Ibid., nos. 1025, 1028, 1041-42, 1053, 1067, 1073. But's links with Gloucester are, perhaps, confirmed by his prosecution of a London vintner, Philip Derneford, for trespass in Gloucestershire, 30 March 1381, *CPR 1377-81*, p. 615.

74. Public Record Office, E101/398/8 (hereafter cited as PRO). But may already have been in royal service by 1371, when he and two others were instructed to bring a prisoner from the Marshalsea to Castle Wallingford, *Calendar of Close Rolls, 1369-74*, p. 275 (hereafter cited as *CCR*).

75. PRO E101/317/40; E101/318/12; F. Devon, *Issues of the Exchequer* (London, 1837), p. 229. I am very grateful to Mary Hill for giving me these references.

76. *CPR 1377-81*, pp. 280-81; *CPR 1385-89*, p. 290.

77. *CCR 1378-81*, p. 343.

78. PRO E101/318/12, no. 11.

79. Devon, *Issues*, p. 229.

80. Mary C. Hill, *The King's Messengers, 1199-1377: A Contribution to the History of the Royal Household* (London, 1961), especially pp. 124-34.

81. Ibid., pp. 128-29.

82. For Philpot, see Sylvia Thrupp, *The Merchant Class of Medieval London* (Ann Arbor Reprint, Michigan, 1989), p. 360; and *The House of Commons, 1386-1422*, ed. J. S. Roskell (forthcoming).

83. Guildhall Library MS. 9051/1, part 2 fol. 181v.

84. We know of two fraternities in the late fourteenth century based on the Carmelite house: one dedicated to the Virgin and All Saints (see PRO C47/41/189), and the other, a fraternity of curriers dedicated to the Holy Trinity and the Virgin, (Bodleian Library, MS Rolls London 3). For the London fraternities, see Caroline M. Barron, "The Parish Fraternities of Medieval London," in *The Church in Pre-Reformation Society*, ed. Caroline M. Barron and Christopher Harper-Bill (Woodbridge, 1985), pp. 13-37.

85. A. K. McHardy, *The Church in London, 1375-92* (London, 1977), nos. 210, 212, 448, 487; George Hennessy, *Novum Repertorum Ecclesiasticum Parochiale Londinense* (London, 1989), p. 310.

86. *CPR 1381-85*, p. 369.

87. Ibid.; see also Guildhall Library MS. 9171/1 fol. 153v.

88. *CPR 1385-89*, p. 290.

CHAPTER 6

Need Men and Women Labor?
Langland's Wanderer and the Labor Ordinances

Lawrence M. Clopper

At the beginning of Passus V of the C version of *Piers Plowman*, Langland presents his Wanderer, Will, in a confrontation with two personifications, Reason and Conscience, who question him with regard to the major provisions of the Statute of Laborers. The curious element in their interrogation is that they do not charge him with a single infraction—for example, "did you take excess wages?" or "did you renege on the contract with your lord?"—instead, they query him on every article of the statute to see if he comes under it. It is as if they do not know who or what he is and so are trying to discover if he is in violation of any clause of the statute. But it is not clear why they do not know who or what he is. It should be fairly obvious if one is a laborer or a lord; however, Reason and Conscience even seem to be uncertain whether he is a layman or a cleric. The confrontration comes about because the Dreamer does not labor for his needs, yet has no clear justification for having given up his labor. By focusing the issue on the Dreamer—indeed, by having his own Reason and Conscience make the interrogation—the poet suggests that there is a complexity in answering the question whether men and women must labor for their needs. This issue is central to the poem, but especially to the scenes on Piers's half acre when the plowman defines the labors of the folk (B.VI.1-78) and seeks to establish guidelines for the treatment of idlers and beggars (VI.202-52).[1] It is also a crucial issue in the C-text additions to the gloss on Piers's pardon in which the poet makes a distinction between various kinds of legitimate poor and those who pose as beggars in order to live in idleness (IX.61-281). The Dreamer is implicated in this discussion because, though he claims to be a cleric and thus not under the statute, he also admits to being an idle beggar and wanderer, both of which contravene the law.

Because the confessional passage in C.V gives such a vivid and detailed representation of the Dreamer, it became, among early critics, the center of a discussion of the poet's life. They regarded the passage as the poet's autobiographical statement. In recent years scholars have emphasized the fictional character of medieval personae, and the poet has been dissociated from his persona. However, the discovery that part of the "autobiographical" passage directly invokes the Statute of Laborers offers an opportunity to use the scene to test whether there is an actual basis for the encounter, for, if the scene represents an event in the poet's life—no matter how he may have fictionalized the details—then we may find some trace of it in the historical record. Alternatively, an examination of why the poet had the Dreamer be asked such questions may enlighten us further about some of the poet's social concerns. Both endeavors require a search of the historical record in close conjunction with the literary text. As it happens, the test for a close relationship between persona and poet largely fails, but in the process of making the search, I found material that helped explain the significance of the Dreamer's interrogation and, as a consequence, something of the poet's personality.

In 1978 I set out on what now seems a naive search for documentary evidence of the poet William Langland based on the few details of his life in external records and the biography of his Dreamer-persona.[2] The poet is believed to have signed his name in the first Inner Dream when he falls into the "land of longing" (B.XI.7ff) and at XV.152: "I haue lyued in londe . . . my name is longe wille." The persona is represented as living in London on Cornhill with his wife, Kitte, and his daughter, Calote, but from the beginning of the poem he also describes himself as a wanderer and "mendinaunt." Although he is married, he claims to be a cleric who labors with his psalms, his *"pater-noster* and . . . prymer, *placebo* and *dirige"* (C.V.46); and he represents his wandering as a monthly itinerary on which he performs religious duties in "London and opelond bothe" (V.44, 49-51). He admits to being a beggar, which suggests he has no regular stipend; however, he claims that he begs "withoute bagge or botel but my wombe one" (V.52), which implies that he asks only for necessities. Donaldson concluded that the Dreamer had taken minor orders, his subsequent marriage precluding him from major ones, and that he remained a cleric by becoming a professional mourner or consoler.[3] The persona is also a maker of satirical poems (see B.XI.84-86 and C.V.3-5), and there is some question whether this is a legitimate occupation.[4] Therefore, the Dreamer both justifies his two occupations—being a cleric, being a maker—and confesses to his failings—his wandering and idleness, which he masks with his claim to clergy, and his uncharitable motive in accusing others of the very idleness, hypocrisy, and covetousness he exhibits himself.

The external evidence says that the poet was named William de Langlond, that he was the son of Stacy de Rokele (or Rokayle) who was a tenant of Lord Despenser in Shipton under Whychwood, Oxford. But several memoranda say that Langland's first name was *either* William *or* Robert, and some specify that he was born in Cleobury Mortimer near the Malvern Hills. The "authority" for his life eventually became the sixteenth-century bibliographer, John Bale, who had access to these fragmentary records and notes dating from the late fourteenth and early fifteenth centuries.[5] Bale embellished his account with the assertions that Langland was a priest and among the first of John Wyclif's disciples (a mixture of Reformation reception and interpretation of the text).[6]

This "historical record"—if these annalistic memoranda can be called "historical"—created confusion about the biography more than they resolved questions about the author.[7] Scholars pointed to several problems: Why is the poet's name given as Langland if his father's name was de Rokele? Does this suggest that he was illegitimate? And if he were a bastard, could he then have become a priest? Where is the Longlande which his name implies? If he were from Cleobury Mortimer, why then is his name not William de Cleobury Mortimer? Although in all versions of the poem and most manuscripts the persona is called Will, in the important manuscript F he identifies himself as Robert, but it remains unclear whether the two names in the memoranda, William and Robert, are the result of reading the poem or are historical in origin and reflected in the texts.[8] There were other issues that became involved, including the question of whether we were dealing with more than one poet; however, I think this précis should suffice to demonstrate that having a historical record did not resolve many of the issues we wished to have clarified. Indeed, there is some reason to believe that the examination of the historical record deterred people from reading the text or had the effect of distorting it.

It is clear—in Bale, for example—that the "historical record" had been confused—or fused—with the details of the literary text: the biography of the persona was the autobiography of the poet. In the twentieth century there has been increasing skepticism about the factual truth to be ascribed to literary personae. George Kane's elegant statement of the autobiographical fallacy in Chaucer and Langland, and his rigorous analysis of the external and internal evidence concerning Langland, suggested that there was little that we knew and little that we could expect to know. To counteract the unhistorical treatment of the persona, Kane separated it totally from the person of William Langland; we could not assume that the persona's life duplicated that of the poet.[9]

I agree that a medieval persona is not usually a factual portrait of an author; nevertheless, it occurred to me that the C-text biography offered a possibility for checking the accuracy of the external evidence. I did not think that the life of the Dreamer had to fit that of the poet in every detail or even in the order in which it was given, for there is ample evidence that medieval biographers and autobiographers reshape the events of lives to fit models they regard as appropriate. Einhard's biography of Charlemagne comes to mind. St. Francis "fictionalized" his life when he shaped it to fit Christ's, and his companions, especially Thomas of Celano, interpreted his life even more scripturally and eschatologically.

Although the details of the life of the Dreamer might not necessarily provide the facts of the poet's life, they do suggest certain areas to search. On the basis of the external and the internal evidence, I decided to examine records in Shropshire (where Cleobury Mortimer is located), ecclesiastical records for the diocese of Hereford (for the same reasons), Oxfordshire (because that was where Langland's father was a tenant), the

London records, especially those pertaining to the Cornhill area where Langland locates his persona, and ecclesiastical records of the bishops of London. Then, based on the admittedly uncertain years of Langland's activities, I estimated when during his life he might have been in each of these areas in order to narrow the number of records to be examined. And finally after examining somewhat randomly the kinds of records available, I decided to focus on those that had not been examined in the past and those new sources that were most likely to yield results. Since birth and parish records are largely absent for the period, and since other kinds of records—deeds, wills, and the like—had been fairly systematically searched, I came more and more to focus on two areas that had apparently not been examined: ecclesiastical records (e.g., bishops' registers, ecclesiastical courts) and civil court records. My points of concern gradually became reduced to three areas:

1. If Langland were a cleric, as some of the *internal* evidence implied, then he must have been anointed at some time and may have obtained a benefice; hence, it would be reasonable to look in bishops' registers and related documents.

2. But the *internal* evidence also suggested that if he had taken vows, he had abandoned them, and that the manner of life he had taken up was suspect enough that he was queried according to the provisions of the Labor Statute.

3. Therefore he might appear either in ecclesiastical records as a suspicious, possibly a heretical person, or in the civil records as a violator of the Labor Statutes. The statutes, then, that seemed especially appropriate were the Statutes of Labor and, possibly, the 1382 Statute against Itinerant Preachers (assuming that the last version of the poem was written in the mid-1380s).[10]

At the end of my search I concluded the following:

1. It is unlikely that Langland would have been called before an ecclesiastical court for the activities described in the poem, but, in any event, we have no pertinent records for the period.

2. It is possible that if Langland were openly preaching heresy—something like what became known as Lollardy—he might appear in one of the bishops' registers; however, he certainly is not recognizable in the continuous records of the diocese of Hereford or in the fragmentary ones of the bishops of London.

3. It is more likely that he would have been called before a justice of the peace as a violator of the Labor Statute, but there are no assize rolls or jail deliveries for London in the period he may have lived there and

there is no mention of him in the fragmentary records of the other geographical areas he can be linked with.

4. Further, Bertha Putnam and others indicate that cases under the Labor Statutes fell primarily under two provisions—contract and excess wages—rather than giving alms to able-bodied beggars, which may be the Dreamer's real crime.[11]

5. If he were an idle beggar, it is most likely that he would have been dealt with at the local London level, but there are no sheriffs' court records or other London records (except for Pleas in the Mayor's Court), and he does not appear in the Letter Books or Pleas, the latter of which, in any event, list only seven persons apprehended under the city ordinance against idle beggars.[12]

6. But since the Dreamer justifies his mendicant life on his clerical status, he would not be likely to appear in court records of labor infractions as long as he could prove his clerical calling.

But this last is the very issue raised by the Dreamer's encounter with Reason and Conscience: was he a layman or a cleric? Among all the records I searched, I found only three pieces of evidence, all of which are relevant to this point. According to his register, Thomas of Charlton, Bishop of Hereford, ordained a William de Clebury as subdeacon at Clun on 26 February 1327 and a William de Cleobury Mortimer as a priest at Wigmore on 24 December 1328.[13] One of the external pieces of evidence tells us that William Langland was said to be born at Cleobury Mortimer near the Malvern Hills. In addition, the register notes that on 28 May 1328 William le Longe (Tall William) was made acolyte. In the biographical prologue in the C-text the poet's persona tells us that he was "to long" to stoop, obviously some joke about his personal appearance, and in the signature at B.XV.152 the Dreamer says that his name is "longe wille." If these references are to our poet, then he not only took minor orders, as Donaldson had argued, but also major ones. We should keep in mind, however, that in the Inner Dream Will says that he abandoned "clergye"—or was dismissed from it—because he could not keep his vow of celibacy (XI.12-21). Those in minor orders do not vow celibacy.

The excitement occasioned by these discoveries soon dissipated. How would we know that this is our poet? Although I never found another "William de Cleobury" in any of the records I searched, the name "William" is relatively common, so a case that these records refer to our poet is difficult to sustain. Indeed, I found the search through documentary records an exquisitely frustrating experience. As I pursued each kind of evidence and narrowed it down to the crucial years that might yield something, I almost invariably found a gap or an absence in the record. I began to wonder if there were not some malicious muse of history sent on the sole mission to destroy those assize rolls, parish and court records, and other documents that might contain the references I sought. Perhaps Langland had intervened with some celestial plenipotentiary to hide the self that he had gone to so much trouble to hide from us. I express this in such extravagant terms in order to convey the obsessive quality of the search itself. I had set out to solve a puzzle—a safe kind of intellectual endeavor—only to find it becoming a personal involvement, sometimes an antagonistic one. Indeed, my search became very much like the Dreamer's pursuit of Piers Plowman. When the Dreamer first sees Piers, Piers is a simple plowman—a palpable Englishman who plows his half acre but who, mysteriously, is sapiential in his knowledge of Treuthe (both God and the way to God). But as the poem continues, Piers becomes more and more distant and less physically present. At the same time the Dreamer's desire—and need—to find him becomes more and more intense. In the final lines of the poem when the Dreamer and Conscience set off once again to find Piers, the plowman seems to have utterly disappeared, yet the need to find him is even greater because the world and Holy Church are about to be defeated by the Antichrist, and the now aged Dreamer, who is about to be awakened to eternal judgment, fears that he cannot be saved without the aid of Piers the Plowman.

I believe that my search for William Langland became so intense because of the personal nature of the poem itself. This poem is not a satire in which an authoritative voice points to and condemns the wickedness of others. It is a very passionate poem. It is a reckless poem—for the very act of writing it may endanger the poet's soul. That claim may sound extravagant, but it is one that is made in the poem itself.[14]

Whether Will's life matches that of William Langland or not, his anguished voice is no fiction. The Dreamer asks of himself the very questions he demands that others ask: Who am I? What was I called to do? How may I save my soul? These three questions are in fact but one question, for to know who you are is to know how to save your soul. Langland's rather pragmatic scheme of salvation depends as much on fulfilling the occupation to which one has been called as it does on Christian belief; in order to avoid spiritual indebtedness, a person must know precisely his calling because only by knowing his calling can he determine his obligations to others and therefore to God. The king, for example, may have great possessions because his need—and function—is greater than that of the plowman. A bishop also is permitted use of enormous amounts of goods because his need—and obligations to the poor—are greater than those of the parish priest. But there is a danger in superfluous goods or the misuse of possessions: if one takes more than one needs or if one does not use goods properly, they endanger the soul. The offices of kings and bishops—indeed the lives of all people—are risky because fulfilling one's function requires making decisions about what legitimately may be taken from others and what must be done in addition to care for those less fortunate than he.

115

Traditionally, all people are obligated, within their means and status, to perform works of charity—giving alms to the poor, feeding the hungry, visiting the sick and those in prison. But what is the beggar's obligation? If a beggar is so needy that he must beg, then he has no superfluities with which to perform charitable acts. Is the beggar, therefore, damned because he has nothing to give? To the contrary, the elevation of the poor above the rich in the gospels suggests that beggars like Lazarus will be saved whether they are able or unable to give to others; in Langland's words, Christ stands "borgh" (pledge) for those who beg rightfully (see B.VII.82 and XVII.320). However, the qualifier—"rightfully"—raises the issue of who the legitimate poor are. Are the "rightful" poor only those who are victims of misfortune or illness? What of the clergy who make themselves poor? May they take the alms of the faithful without imperiling their souls? Although Langland speaks to all estates in society—sometimes directly—the emblematic figure in his analysis of the world is the poor beggar. Langland's persona, Will, is himself a poor beggar. The poor are beggars of necessity. That is, their very poverty bespeaks their need. And they beg for their necessities by the outward signs of their poverty. But there are also beggars who beg by word of mouth. They claim to be poor and therefore in need. How does one distinguish a beggar from an idler? Piers says that need alone justifies begging, that the true beggar is one who is in dire need (B.VII.65-106).

Need, in fact, is the governing principle of Langland's society. [15] It is need alone that justifies possession and use of goods. It does not matter what one's rank in society is; for the good of society and the salvation of one's soul, need alone determines what one may have without incurring spiritual debt. Throughout the poem Langland focuses again and again on this reckless quality of human endeavor, for if one does not adhere closely to his calling, if one does not determine the needs of his status, if one recklessly disregards his function, then he is likely to be damned. To be saved, a person must know his calling, must know who and what he is so that he will know what he must do.

Therefore, a central question not only for society but for the individual as well is this: How does one come to the goods one needs? Must men and women labor for their needs? This is the question that the poem asks every man and woman to consider. King and plowman; bishop and parson. Beggar and poet.

The question whether men and women must labor for their needs is not a simple one. To be sure, no one in the Middle Ages, at least not the aristocracy, thought that nobles should soil their hands with labor. Nor did anyone, at least not the clergy, think that clerics should stain their vessels with sweat. It is true that the rules of Sts. Benedict and Augustine prescribed manual labor in order to deter idleness, the great sin of monks, but that provision was often set aside by aristocratic monks in favor of the *opus dei*. As one latter-day monk said,

> What sholde he studie and make hymselven wood,
> Upon a book in cloystre alwey to poure,
> Or swynken with his handes, and laboure,
> As Austyn bit? How shal the world be served?
> Lat Austyn have his swynk to hym reserved![16]

The requirement to labor with one's hands was put aside more than once because "it was old and somdel streit" (line 174), even though some orders managed to convince religious that it was good for their souls to suffer the shame of labor.[17] Nevertheless, most religious communities and most of the ecclesiastical hierarchy—those who plowed the vineyard with their tongues—did not perform manual labor for their needs. Only at the lowest level of the hierarchy might we find a sweat-stained Adam compounded in Christ, that is, the local parish priest plowing the worldly furrows of his glebe land.

Langland would seem to agree that the two ruling classes need not labor for their needs, that it was the function of the commons to provide for the needs of the community:

> Thanne kam þer a kyng; kny3thod hym ladde;
> Might of þe communes made hym to regne.
> And þanne cam kynde wit and clerkes he made
> For to counseillen þe kyng and þe communes saue.
> The kyng and kny3thod and clergie boþe
> Casten þat þe communes sholde [hire communes] *fynde.   *provide
> The communes contreued *of kynde wit craftes,   *by means of
> And for profit of al þe peple Plowmen ordeyned
> To *tilie and to trauaille as trewe lif askeþ   *till
> The kyng and þe commune and kynde wit þe þridde
> Shopen lawe and *leaute, ech [lif] to knowe his owene.   *justice
>   (B Prol. 112-22)

Although this image of the three orders has a certain riddling quality because of the mixing together of estates and mental faculties (e.g., "kynde wit"), it is basically traditional. The King, accompanied by his knights, is said to reign by the will of the commons; "kynde wit," apparently a name for the bishop since he makes clerks, provides the means to counsel the king and save the commons. The two ruling orders, "kyng and kny3thod" and "clergie," determine that the third order, "þe communes," should provide necessities for the nonlaboring classes and the commons as well. The three orders make laws so that each order will know its own function.

If we turn to the commons, those who were to labor to sustain the two ruling estates, the question of whether men and women should labor would seem simple, but is not. The key passage from the Labor Ordinance of 1349 and the articles on which Reason and Conscience interrogate the Dreamer are as follows:

> *Because a greate parte of the people and especially of workmen and*
> *seruauntes late dyed in pestilence many . . . wyl not serue onles they*
> *may receyue excessyue wages, & some rather wyllyng to beg in*
> *ydelnes than by labour to get theyr lyuyng: We . . . haue had de-*
> *liberacyon and treatie with the prelates and the nobles & wisemen*
> *assistyng vs, of whose mutuall counsell it is ordeyned that euery*
> *man and woman of oure realme of England of what condition he be*
> */ free or bond / able in body / and within the age of lx yeres / not*
> *lyuyng in marchaundise / nor exercysyng ony craft / nor hauyng of*
> *his own wherof he may lyue / nor propre land about whose tyllage*
> *he may hym selfe occupye / and not seruyng any other / yf he in co-*
> *nuenyent seruyce (his estate considered) be requyred to serue, he*
> *shalbe bound to serue hym whiche so shall hym requyre.*[18]

Those who do not labor—nobles and prelates—ordained that certain persons should labor: those under sixty, both men and women, who did not have income from lands, or their own lands to till, or who were not merchants or craftsmen. This legislation was primarily concerned with stabilizing wages, but there is one provision that sits in the background of our inquiry—it was a violation of the statute to give alms to the able-bodied poor:

> *Item bycause that many valyaunt beggars as long as they may lyue*
> *of beggyng do refuse to labour gyuyng them selfe to ydelnes and*
> *vyce & somtyme to theft and other abhomynacions: None vppon the*
> *sayde payne of ymprysonment shall vnder the colour of pitie or*
> *almes gyue ony thynge to suche whiche may labour or presume to*
> *fauour them towardes theyr desyres, so that thereby they may be*
> *compelled to labour for theyr necessary liuyng.*[19]

I have never found a record of anyone having been arrested for giving alms to an able-bodied beggar, but the matter was of such concern to no less a personage than Piers the Plowman that he asks an authority, Hunger, whether it is legitimate to give to idlers who ask for alms (B.VI.201-52). Hunger, rather profligately, tells him to give to whomever asks and leave the judgment to the Lord. Piers, perhaps more concerned with his proximate lord and the chief justice, expresses skepticism about Hunger's advice but finally allows that, if asked, he'll feed them sour bread.

When the justices who oversaw the Labor Laws were disbanded and the function was taken over by other courts, the City of London issued its own ordinance (c. 1359) to deal with the problem of idle vagrants:

> *Because many "hommes et femmes" who are able to labor for their*
> *needs come from diverse counties to London as "mendynauns pur*
> *avoir lour ese et repos" and deprive of their alms the legitimate poor,*

"leprouse, voegles, clochauntes" and others who are ill, we command, on behalf of the king, that all those "mendynauns" who are able to labor and do not, void the city between now and the following Monday. Those remaining are to be attached by the Constable and Beadle of each ward and put in the "seps sur Cornhull."[20]

Since the Dreamer is interrogated on Cornhill, which is where he also lives, I think it is legitimate to assume that Reason and Conscience are not only personifications of his own mental faculties but also of the two legal authorities, the Constable and Beadle, charged with enforcing the ordinance. Therefore, the question whether the Dreamer must labor for his needs becomes especially pertinent since he accuses himself and stands accused by the law. He confesses to being an able-bodied person with no visible means of support, so it would appear that he must be obligated to labor. But he has a very interesting explanation for why he should not. First, he confesses his idleness:

> For as y cam by Consience with Resoun y mette
> In an hot heruest whenne y hadde myn *hele   *health
> And lymes to labory with and louede wel fare
> And no dede to do but to drynke and to slepe.
> In hele and in *inwitt oen me apposede;   *mind
> Romynge in remembraunce, thus Resoun me *aratede.   *rebuked
> (C.V.6-11)

Then Reason and Conscience interrogate the Dreamer according to the provisions of the Labor Ordinance. They ask,

Are you a laborer or a cleric?

> "Can thow seruen . . . or syngen in a churche,
> Or *koke for my cockeres or to þe cart piche
> Mowen or *mywen or make bond to sheues?"   *cock hay
> (lines 12-13)   *stack

Are you a laborer or do you exercise a craft or live by merchandise?

> "Or *shap shon or cloth, or shep and kyne kepe   *make shoes
> *Heggen or harwen, or swyn or gees dryue,   *hedge or harrow
> Or eny other kynes craft þat to þe comune nedeth,
> *That þou betere therby þat byleue the fynden?" *That thereby you improve [the life] of those who provide you with food?
> (lines 18-21)

Do you have lands to live by?

"Thenne *hastow londes to lyue by . . . or lynage ryche   *hast thou
That fynde the thy fode?"
(lines 26-27)

Or are you legitimately disabled?

"Or thow art broke, so may be, in body or in membre
Or ymaymed thorw som myshap, whereby thow myhte be excused?"
(lines 33-34)

Halfway thru this interrogation, Will again admits that he's an idler (lines 22-25). He says he is too weak to work with sickle or with scythe and "to long [= tall] . . . lowe to stoupe."

Ultimately, he claims that he need not labor for his needs because his labor is wandering (lines 44-52). He does not admit this as blatantly as I have phrased it because wandering, as we know from elsewhere in the poem, is a disreputable "occupation": the poet condemns false hermits who wander off to Walsingham to see their wenches and "grete lobies and longe" who are idlers who clothe themselves as hermits (Prol. 51-55). Indeed the first—and the primary—division in the poem is between laboring and wandering: Will says he saw

A fair feld ful of folk . . .
Of alle manere men, þe mene and þe pore,
Worchyng and wandryng as þis world *ascuth.   *demands
(Prol. 19-21)

Pilgrimages the poet approves are those to Truth, which is a journey into the soul where Charity sits enthroned (VII.205-260), and Piers's initial pilgrimage, which entails staying at home to plow his half acre (VIII.56-65). Piers's is a pilgrimage of labor.

The Dreamer is a wanderer. When the poem opens we find him wandering through the world "wondres to here," but he also wanders when he is in residence in London because he does not labor for his needs. He tells us that he lived in Cornhill with Kitte, his wife, and Calote, their daughter, where he was little loved among the "lollares of Londone and lewede ermytes" (ignorant hermits), for, he says, "y made of tho men as resoun me tauhte" (V.1-5). The Dreamer's second disreputable "occupation" is writing poems. In the B-text (XII.16-19) his own Imaginatyf rebukes him for wasting time writing about Dowel, Dobet, and Dobest when there are plenty of friars who do it better. Writing poetry is "spilling of speche" (wasting of time), Imaginatyf charges (C.XIV.6-10); it is an intellectual form of wandering.

The Wanderer implicates himself further in unprincipled living when he reveals he resides on Cornhill "yclothed as a lollare" (V.3), that he is like the "lollares" he attacks.[21] In the long addition to the C-text gloss on Piers's pardon (IX.61-281), the poet distinguishes between "lollares and lewede ermytes" and the worthy poor, that is, between those who could labor and do not and the traditional poor, as well as those most abject poor who labor and still require assistance or those who ought not be required to labor. The "lewede ermytes" travel about in order to "lache men almesse" (seize men's alms), to eat and drink to their fill, and to return to their cotes at night and thereby live in idleness and ease on others' labors (lines 140-52). Such "ermytes" live by the highway and in cities; they beg in churches:

Al þat holy ermytes hatede and despisede,
As rychesses and reuerences and ryche menne almesse,
Thise lollares, *lache-draweres, lewede ermytes   *thieves
Coueyten þe contrarye, for as *coterelles they libbeth.   *cottagers
For hit ben but *boyes, *bollares at þe ale,   *rascals/drunkards
Noyther of lynage ne of *lettrure, ne lyf-holy as ermytes   *learning
That *wonede whilom in wodes with beres and lyons.   *dwelt
Summe hadde lyflode of his lynage and of no lyf elles
And summe lyuede by here lettrure and labour of here handes
And somme hadde *foreynes to frendes þat hem fode sente
                               *strangers
And briddes brouhte somme bred þat they by lyuede.
*Althey holy ermytes were of *heye kynne,   *Although/noble
Forsoken lond and lordschipe and alle lykynges of body.
             (lines 190-202)

Holy hermits renounced possessions and *dominium* to live in penance in the wilderness. The "lewede ermytes" live by the highways and in cities. They once labored but ceased when they saw friars living better from begging than they did by their craft:

    at the laste they aspyde
*That faytede in frere clothinge hadde fatte chekes.   *Those that begged
*Forthy lefte they here labour, this lewede knaues,   *Therefore
And clothed hem in copes, clerkes as hit were,
Or *oen of som ordre or elles a profete,   *one
*Aȝen þe lawe of Leuey, yf Latyn be trewe: *Against
Non licet uobis legem voluntati, set voluntatem coniungere legi.
             (lines 207-12)

These "lollares and lewede ermytes" do not perform the religious ob-
servances imposed on all men and women (lines 217-39); indeed, they remain in bed until noon when they swarm out dressed as religious in search
of alms:

> Ac aboute mydday at mele-tyme y mette with hem ofte,
> Come in his cope as he a clerk were;
> A bacheler or a *bew-pere beste hym bysemede,   *"good father"
> And for þe cloth þat *keuereth hym *ykald he is a frere, *covers/called
> Wascheth and wypeth and with þe furste sitteth.
> (lines 246-50)

Before this laborer became a "lollare and lewede ermyte," he acted more
humbly and lived a simple moral life:

> Ac while *a wrouhte in þe world and wan his mete with treuthe *he
> He sat at þe syde benche and at þe seconde table.
> Cam no wyn in his wombe thorw þe woke longe
> Ne no blanked on his bed ne whyte bred byfore hym.
> (lines 251-54)

These deceiving beggars defraud the legitimate poor who are the traditional recipients of charity: the aged who are helpless and needy, the blind
and bedridden, and the physically disabled (IX.175-77). To these, Langland
adds some categories that are not so traditional: "wymmen with childe þat
worche ne mowe" (cannot work; line 176), and "alle pore pacient," such as
lepers and poor mendicants, who are content with God's "sonde" (sending,
providence; lines 178-79). They are distinguished from the "lollares" by
the patient acceptance of their poverty; indeed, any who suffer misfortune
patiently, we are told, have pardon with Piers the Plowman be they prisoners, pilgrims, or victims of theft or misadventure (lines 180-86).

In one moving passage, the poet describes those legitimate poor, true
"cotiers," whom these "lollares and lewed ermytes" defraud: those

> Þat most neden aren oure neyhebores, *and we *nyme gode hede, *if/take
> As prisones in puttes and pore folk in cotes,
> Charged with childrene and chief lordes rente;
> Þat they with spynnyng may spare, spenen hit on hous-huyre,
> Bothe in mylke and in mele, to make with *papelotes   *porridges
> To *aglotye with here *gurles that *greden aftur fode.   *satiate/children/
>   cry out
>
> And hemsulue also soffre muche hunger,
> And wo in wynter-tymes, and wakynge on nyhtes
> To rise to þe reule to rokke þe cradel,

Bothe to carde and to *kembe, to *cloute and to wasche, *comb/patch
And to *rybbe and to *rele, *rusches to *pylie, *scrape/reel/rushes/peel
That reuthe is to rede or in ryme shewe
The wo of this wommen þat wonyeth in cotes;
And of monye oþer men þhat moche wo soffren,
Bothe *afyngred and afurste, to turne þe fayre outward, *hungry/thirsty
And ben abasched for to begge and wollen nat be aknowe
What hem nedeth at here neyhebores at noon and at eue.
(lines 71-87)

These "cotiers" are described mostly as wage-poor women who are engaged in the meanest paying jobs—preparing wool and, perhaps even less
rewarding, peeling rushes for rushlights.[22] Their lives are made hard by
high rents and the costs of caring for their children. What little money
they gain from spinning, they spend on meal and milk to make simple por-
ridges, but these prove insufficient and the children "greden" after more.
"Greden" means not only to cry out but to weep or lament, to cry out in
pain. "Aglotye" derives from Old French "gloutir," to swallow, and is used
here to mean "to fill to repletion."[23] But, of course, that is precisely what
these women *cannot* do. I believe Langland chose "aglotye" and "greden"
because they sound like "gluttony" and "greed," sounds that would in-
tensify the literal meanings of the words. The women attempt to slake the
hunger of their children who are greedy gluttons after more. These women
also suffer great hunger themselves and many other hardships, especially
in winter and at night when they "rise to þe reule to rokke þe cradel." In
these telling lines Langland sanctifies the lives of the poor by playing
theirs off against the monastic life of abstinence and prayer in which
monks, according to a rule, were to rise at night in order to labor at the al-
tar. The implication is that the hardships in the lives of these women are
greater—and therefore more deserving—than the self-imposed rituals of
monks who neither fast as they should nor live on simple fare (see Anima's remark at XV.315-17) nor perform manual labor for their needs. Further, unlike the clamorous beggars whom Langland condemns, these poor
men and women disguise their need ("turne þe fayre outward") because
they are ashamed to beg and do not wish it known that they are in need.
And yet, it is just such people as these that Will defrauds if he takes necessities that he could provide by his own manual labor.

 Ultimately, Will tries to justify his way of living by claiming that he was
called to clergy and is required to follow the admonition of St. Paul to remain in one's calling:

"When y ȝong was, many ȝer hennes,
My fader and my frendes *foende me to scole, *provided
Tyl y wyste witterly what holy writ menede
And what is beste for the body, as the boek telleth,

123

And *sykerost for þe soule, by so y wol contenue.   *most safe
And *foend y nere, in fayth, *seth my frendes deyede,   *found/since
Lyf þat me lykede but in this longe clothes.24
                    (lines 35-41)

Although his means of support have vanished, he feels that "clergie" is his calling since he had been sent to school. Therefore, if he is required to labor, he is obligated to remain in his calling:

And yf y be labour sholde lyuen and lyflode *deseruen,   *earn
That laboure þat y lerned beste þerwith lyuen y sholde.
    In eadem vocacione in qua vocati estis.
And so y leue yn London and opelond bothe;
The *lomes þat y labore with and lyflode deserue   *tools
Is *pater-noster* and my prymer, *placebo* and *dirige*,
And my *sauter som tyme and my seuene psalmes.   *psalter
This y *segge for here soules of suche as me helpeth,   *say
And tho þat fynden me my fode fouchen-saf, y trowe,
To be welcome when y come, *oþer-while in a monthe,
                                              *from time to time
Now with hym, now with here; on this wyse y begge
Withoute bagge or botel but my wombe one.
                    (lines 42-52)

He claims to have been called to clergy and thus must remain a cleric. He prays for those who give him alms. Sometimes he wanders in London. Sometimes he wanders upland. He begs, but with his belly alone—that is, according to need alone.

Having made his defense to Reason and Conscience, he turns to the offensive when he says that no one

    sholde constrayne no clerc to no knaues werkes,
For by þe lawe of *Levyticy* þat oure lord ordeynede,
Clerkes*ycrouned, of kynde vnderstondynge,   *tonsured
Sholde nother *swynke ne swete ne swerien at enquestes   *labor
Ne *fyhte in no *vawarde ne his foe *greue.   *fight/vanguard/harm
                    (lines 54-58)

His point is that clerics should neither do the manual labor of laborers nor the fighting that is the labor of knights.

But all this is clearly self-serving; it is intended to obfuscate the situation, for if it were apparent that Will were a cleric, then there would be no cause for the Constable and Beadle or his own Reason and Conscience to accost him. It is because he is not obviously a cleric that he is questioned.

And one of the reasons he is questioned is that he is married—which suggests that he is a layman. He claims to be clergy because he is a mendicant beggar, but he is an order unto himself since he is in no order and under no one's obedience (lines 89-91). He might well pay heed to the law of Levi quoted in the dream that follows: "It is not lawful for you to make the law conform to *your will*, but rather for you to conform *your will* to the law" (IX.212).

Later in the C-text a character named Rechelesnesse—a personification of absence of solicitude but also recklessness—defends "mendinauntes" from the provisions of the Labor Ordinance, the payment of tithes and other required religious services, and all other of man's laws *if* they have voluntarily given up all that they possessed in order to follow in the footsteps of Christ (XIII.32-97). Such people who have reduced themselves to need and are unsolicitous of their daily necessities need not labor for their needs. That is an argument that was recognized and accepted—by natural law, all men were permitted food, shelter, and drink—no matter how they come to get it, for *Necessitas non habet legem.* [25]

Will on Cornhill justifies his life of mendicant begging on the grounds that he takes no more than he needs: like the apostles, like the holy hermits who left lands and lordship, he begs without bag or bottle but by his belly alone. I want to emphasize that he *claims* to beg by his belly alone; he *claims* to take no more than he needs. If this is true, then he is justified. But it is clear—indeed, Will has confessed it—that he does not live by so stringent a standard.

Will also implies that his "making," the recording of his dreams, is his calling. But the legitimacy of this vocation remains in doubt as well because his motives for writing may be sinful. If the Wanderer "lacks" others out of envy, anger, and avarice, as he confesses at various points, then his uncharitable "makings" may damn him. Therefore, since writing *Piers Plowman* is part of the Wanderer's justification for his clerical status, the question stands: Need Will labor for his needs?

Langland provides only an outline of an answer, and that outline is as pertinent for his readers as it is for Will. Everyone must perform some kind of labor for the common good; if he does not, he differs little from the "lollares, lache-draweres, lewede ermytes," and deceiving beggars who ask for more than they need. Langland's general principle, therefore, does not provide an answer as much as it initiates a series of questions that can only be determined by the individual conscience: What is your calling? What are the obligations of that calling? What are the grounds for accepting the support of others? Since the "king and kny3thod" and "clergie" accept the "communes" of the commons, they differ from beggars only in status and function, not in essence. The commons, as producers, have a right to expect law and justice from the king and spiritual guidance from the clergy; they are not literally like beggars except that they are dependent upon their superiors for their physical and spiritual safety. These relations, divinely ordained and apparently simple, remain problematical because the layman must determine if he has been called to clergy or should remain a producer, the cleric must establish what his needs are so that he can expend his time and the goods placed at his disposal wisely, and the king and nobility must ensure that they take no more than is necessary to their protective and judicial functions.

I believe that Langland invoked the Statute of Laborers in the biographical passage because it focused succinctly so many major issues of the poem; further, it concentrated the questions posed about the persona's authority that we see even in the two earlier versions of the poem. In the case of the Wanderer, a kind of peripatetic Everyman, the question is whether a person who lives according to no rule, has no obediencer or spiritual adviser, and has no benefice or provision or lands to live by is legitimately exempt from the Statute of Laborers either in fact or morally. If one regards enacted law as a reflection of divine or natural law—and Langland seems to so regard it, as is evidenced in his image of the three estates and their functions—then the king's law would seem to be morally binding even when it is not legally so. The Wanderer cannot help but know how strait the way is. Reason and Conscience focus one set of requirements for him, but he cannot respond to these satisfactorily, so he stands, emblematically, where the roads diverge.

We may never find any meaningful records of William Langland's life, but, to my mind, when the poet chose to use the Statute of Laborers to interrogate his persona, when he had his Wanderer stand accused by his own Reason and Conscience on the matter of his labor, he spoke as directly and personally to us as he is ever likely to do.

Notes

1. Citations of the B-text will be from *Piers Plowman: The B Version*, ed. George Kane and E. Talbot Donaldson (London, 1975); those of the C-text from *Piers Plowman by William Langland*, ed. Derek Pearsall (Berkeley, Calif., and Los Angeles, 1979).

2. For analysis of the external and internal evidence of authorship, see George Kane, *"Piers Plowman": The Evidence for Authorship* (London, 1965). E. Talbot Donaldson provided the authoritative description of the poet/Dreamer's biography; John Bowers recently has given an extensive analysis of the passage as part of a rebuttal to Donaldson's reading and in order to show that the poem is a spiritual, not a factual, autobiography. I do not find the readings incompatible. See E. Talbot Donaldson, *"Piers Plowman": The C-Text and Its Poet*, Yale Studies in English 113 (New Haven, Conn., 1949), pp. 199-226; and John Bowers, *The Crisis of Will in "Piers Plowman"* (Washington, D.C., 1986), pp. 165-89.

3. A. K. McHardy has recently shown that the number of unbeneficed clergy outnumbered those having benefices and that the unbeneficed tended to settle in cities, especially in areas where there were laymen with enough disposable income to pay for prayers and other services (McHardy, "Ecclesiastics and Economics: Poor Priests, Prosperous Laymen, and Proud Prelates in the Reign of Richard II," in *Church and Wealth*, ed. W. Shields and Diane Woods, Studies in Church History 24 [Oxford, 1987], pp. 129-37.

4. The passages on the Dreamer's "makings," alluded to below, are discussed in more detail in my essay, "The Life of the Dreamer, the Dreams of the Wanderer in *Piers Plowman*," *Studies in Philology* 86 (1989), 261-85. In the discussion that follows I have borrowed a few passages from this essay.

5. *Scriptorvm Illustrium maioris Brytannie quam nunc Angliam & Scotiam uocant* . . . (Basel, 1557?), p. 474.

6. In the 1548 edition of his work Bale had ascribed *Petrum Argricolam* to Wyclif himself; see *Illvstrium maioris Britanniae scriptorvm* (Wesel: Theodoric Plataenus), fol. 157r. For the Reformation reception of *Piers*, see J. N. King, "Robert Crowley's Editions of *Piers Plowman*: A Tudor Apocalypse," *Modern Philology* 73 (1976), 342-52.

7. W. W. Skeat summarized the discussion to his day in his edition, *The Vision of William Concerning Piers the Plowman in Three Parallel Texts*, 2 vols. (Oxford, 1886), 2:xxvii-xxxviii. Biographical studies and discussions of authorship are conveniently gathered and annotated in A. J. Colaianne, *Piers Plowman: An Annotated Bibliography of Editions and Criticism, 1550-1977* (New York, 1978), pp. 1-22.

8. The important discussion is R. W. Chambers's "Robert or William Longland?" *London Mediaeval Studies* 1 (1937-39), 430-62.

9. George Kane, *The Autobiographical Fallacy in Chaucer and Langland*, Chambers Memorial Lecture (London, 1965); reprinted in Kane, *Chaucer and Langland: Historical and Textual Approaches* (Berkeley, Calif., 1989), pp. 1-14. Recently, Mary Riach, J. A. Burrow, and George Economou have taken issue with Kane's argument and have tried to reassert that, at least in limited ways, the passages about the Dreamer are autobiographical. See Mary Riach, "Langland's Dreamer and the Transformation of the Third Vision," *Essays in Criticism* 19 (1969), 6-18; J. A. Burrow, "Langland *Nel Mezzo Del Cammin*," in *Medieval Studies for J. A. W. Bennett*, ed. P. L. Heyworth (Oxford, 1981), pp. 21-41; and George Economou, "Self-Consciousness of Poetic Activity in Dante and Langland," in *Vernacular Poetics in the Middle Ages*, ed. Lois Ebin, Studies in Medieval Culture 16 (Kalamazoo, Mich., 1984), pp. 177-98. A. V. C. Schmidt does not claim to reconstruct the facts of the poet's life but nevertheless argues that the conflict in the poem between being a cleric and a maker is true for the poet as well; see Schmidt, *The Clerkly Maker: Langland's Poetic Art*, Piers Plowman Studies 4 (Cambridge, Eng., 1987), pp. 1-20.

10. George Kane has summarized the evidence for the circulation of the three versions; he places the C tradition at 1379/81-c. 1385; see Kane, "The Text," in *A Companion to "Piers Plowman,"* ed. John A. Alford (Berkeley, Calif., 1988), pp. 185-86.

11. Bertha Putnam, *The Enforcement of the Statute of Labourers during the First Decade after the Black Death, 1349-1359*, Columbia University Studies in History, Economics, and Public Law 32 (New York, 1908), pp. 157, 179-81.

12. All seven of these beggars were arrested at the same time in May 1381, shortly before the Peasants' Revolt. Langland, if that is his name, is not among them. See Corporation of London Records Office, *Letter Book G*, fol. 78; the essential details of the London ordinance are given in *Letter Book G*, fol. 111. The ordinance, or a variant, was reissued in 1367, 1372, 1378, and 1381. The attachment of the beggars is entered in the Corporation of London Records Office, Memoranda Rolls, A24, mb. 7, and A25, mb. 3; the essential details are given in the *Calendar of Pleas and Memoranda Rolls . . . of the City of London*, ed. Arthur H. Thomas et al., 6 vols. (London, 1926-61), 2:286; 3:5-6. Both the ordinance and other evidence suggest that the justices, sheriffs, manorial lords, constables, and beadles were encouraged to attach and even imprison able-bodied vagrants without recourse to justice, so it is probable that most arrests were never registered.

13. *Registrum Thome de Charlton, Episcopi Herefordensis, A.D. MCCCXXVII-MCCCXLIV*, ed. William W. Capes, Canterbury and York Society 9 (London, 1913), pp. 95, 103; the third entry is on p. 98. The notation at the end of the line indicates the ordination to the priesthood was by private patrimony.

14. Clopper, "Life of the Dreamer," pp. 269-71.

15. Robertson and Huppé, Bloomfield, and Lawlor have argued that need ìs the controlling principle of Langland's society; see D. W. Robertson, Jr., and Bernard Huppé, *Piers Plowman and Scriptural Tradition* (Princeton, N.J. 1951), p. 227; Morton Bloomfield, *"Piers Plowman" as a Fourteenth-Century Apocalypse* (New Brunswick, N.J., 1961), pp. 135-36; and John Lawlor, *Piers Plowman: An Essay in Criticism* (London 1962), pp. 178-79.

16. Geoffrey Chaucer, *The Canterbury Tales, General Prologue*, lines 184-88; *The Riverside Chaucer*, ed. Larry D. Benson (Oxford, 1988).

17. Elizabeth Kirk has described the idealization of labor, especially among Cistercians and Franciscans, that developed in the later Middle Ages; see Kirk, "Langland's Plowman and the Recreation of Fourteenth-Century Religious Metaphor," *The Yearbook of Langland Studies* 2 (1988), 1-21.

18. *The great boke of statutes* . . . (London, 1524-33; STC 9286), E.vi-F.iv.

19. Ibid.

20. Corporation of London Records Office, *Letter Book G*, fol. 78; my translation. The "seps" are the stocks.

21. Langland's use of "lollare" has been a matter of debate, but scholars are almost unanimous in agreeing that Langland was not a Lollard or Wycliffite. The most recent and detailed discussions are Pamela Gradon, "Langland and the Ideology of Dissent," *Proceedings of the British Academy* 66 (1980), 179-205; and Christina von Nolcken, *"Piers Plowman*, the Wycliffites, and *Pierce the Plowman's Creed,"* Yearbook of Langland Studies* 2 (1988), 71-102. In his edition Pearsall argues that Langland made this addition to the C-text in order to distinguish his position from that of the Lollards (= "lollares"; pp. 15-16, and his note to 5.2, p. 97). Langland derives "lollares" from the "Engelisch of oure elders" (line 214) rather than from continental usage where the word means heretic or a person who exhibits hypocritical piety (see Dietrich Kurze, "Die festlandischen Lollarden," *Archiv fur Kulturgeschichte* 47 [1965], 48-76). Wendy Scase has argued that Langland coined "lollares" to refer to idlers but that this usage was overwhelmed by later usage as a term for heretics and Wycliffites; see Scase, *"Piers Plowman" and the New Anticlericalism*, Cambridge Studies in Medieval Literature 4 (Cambridge, Eng., 1989), pp. 120-37, 150-207. Standard commentaries on the meaning of "Lollard" in English texts are Skeat, *Parallel Texts* 2:60-61, and Margaret Deansley, *The Lollard Bible* (Cambridge, Eng., 1920), pp. 70 n. 1, 273-74. On the relation of "Lollard" to "Wycliffite," see the revisionist theory of Anne Hudson in *The Premature Reformation: Wycliffite Texts and Lollard History* (Oxford, 1988), pp. 2-4.

22. Derek Pearsall has emphasized how unusual these passages on the urban wage-poor are in literature before the industrial age; see Pearsall, "Poverty and Poor People in *Piers Plowman*," in *Medieval Studies Presented to George Kane*, ed. Edward D. Kennedy, Ronald Waldron, and Joseph S. Wittig (Woodbridge, 1988), pp. 167-85. Langland's attitude toward the poor runs counter to that described by Mollat and his collaborators; they discern in the late Middle Ages a growing antagonism toward the poor, especially in cities, and the labeling of poverty as a consequence of sin and hence a reason for *not* providing for the destitute. See Michel Mollat, *The Poor in the Middle Ages: An Essay in Social History*, trans. Arthur Goldhammer (New Haven, Conn., 1986); and *Études sur l'histoire de la pauvreté*, ed. Michel Mollat, 2 vols. (Paris, 1974). Other studies of Langland's views are Geoffrey Shepherd, "Poverty in *Piers Plowman*," in *Social Relations and Ideas: Essays in Honour of R. H. Hilton*, ed. T. H. Aston et al. (Cambridge, Eng., 1983), pp. 169-89; and David Aers, *"Piers Plowman* and Problems in the Perception of Poverty: A Culture in Transition," *Leeds Studies in English* 14 (1983), 5-25.

23. The *MED* cites this line as the only instance in Middle English of "aglotye."

24. The "longe clothes" to which he refers are his "lollares" garb, which is gray russet, a cheap woolen cloth worn by plowmen, hermits, the abjectly poor—and the Fran-

ciscans. The Wanderer refers to his robe as russet at B.VIII.1; Anima indicates "russet" is gray at XV.167.

25. Rechelesnesse quotes the maxim in his parable at C.XIII.43, as does Friar Nede in the waking moment before the last vision (XXII.10). The principle is well attested, e.g., in Gregory IX, *Decretals*, Book 5, tit. 41, cap. 4 (*Corpus iuris canonici*, ed. Aemelius Friedberg [Graz, 1955], 2.927).

PART III

✛

Literature of the Countryside

CHAPTER 7

Medieval Hunting
Fact and Fancy
Nicholas Orme

Medieval Hunters

There is a passion for hunting something, deeply implanted in the human breast," wrote Dickens in *Oliver Twist*. Surely, the passion has seldom been stronger than it was in medieval England, when hunting occupied the minds and bodies of people across the whole of society.[1] Its spell extended from the king to the lowest commoner. Hunting was a royal sport, part of the training and upbringing of princes from their childhood. Henry V had a hunting treatise written for him between 1406 and 1413 while he was a young man; Henry VI hunted hares and foxes at Bury St. Edmunds in 1434 when he was thirteen, and Edward V, who died at age twelve in 1483, is said to have been devoted to horses and dogs?[2] Kings went on hunting in their adulthood, staying in palaces like Clarendon, Windsor, and Woodstock close to royal forests and hunting parks, where royal forest laws preserved the deer for their sport.[3] Servants, horses, and hounds were kept to assist them. Henry IV's establishment in 1407 included a master of the harthounds, forty hounds and four yeomen berners in charge of them, twelve greyhounds handled by two yeomen fewterers, and three tracking dogs or limers.[4] The sport entered into the imagery and ceremony of kingship. Richard II chose a beast of the chase as his emblem (the white hart), as did Richard III (the boar), and when Henry VI was crowned at Paris in 1431, a stag was hunted through an artificial forest in his presence and presented to him as a gift.[5]

It was a sport that cemented relations between the king and his nobility and gentry. Sharing his passion for it, they could be entertained and wooed on hunting expeditions, or rewarded with the privilege to hunt. Henry III's "Charter of the Forest" (1217) allowed earls and barons to take a beast or two whenever they traversed the royal forests, provided they took them openly, and records show this happening in practice.[6] Richard, earl of Cornwall, the king's brother; the earl of Gloucester, Richard de Clare; the earl of Derby, Robert de Ferrieres; and the count of Aumale, William de Forz—all appear hunting in the king's woods in Northamptonshire in 1248-55.[7] They could be experts too, like Edward, duke of York (d. 1415), who was both master of Henry IV's harthounds and author of the hunting treatise for Henry V.[8] The lesser aristocracy were equally avid for the sport: knights, esquires, and those known by the fifteenth century as gentlemen. They hunted in the king's forests and in the private chases and parks of the nobility, sometimes legally and sometimes not. The Northamptonshire records of the mid-thirteenth century mention such knights as Geoffrey de Langley, John de Lessington, Henry de Montfort, John du Plessis, Elias de Rabayn, and Guy de Rochefort, taking the venison with harthounds or greyhounds.[9] In 1382 John of Gaunt allowed Sir Bernard Brocas to hunt in all his warrens in Norfolk while Brocas was traveling on pilgrimage to Walsingham, [10] and Chaucer may have envisaged his Knight doing so on the way to Canterbury, else why did he provide him with a yeoman forester equipped with bow and arrows?[11] During the fourteenth and fifteenth centuries the lesser aristocracy acquired their own private parks for deer hunting and warrens for pursuing hares and rabbits. In Cornwall the Carminow family had a park at Polsode in 1357 and another at Boconnoc in 1435; by 1500 they had been joined by the Arundells at Lanherne, the Bassets at Carn Brea, the Peverells at Egloshayle, and the Trevansons at Carhays. There were at least fifteen such gentry parks in the county by the beginning of the sixteenth century.[12]

The privilege of hunting in the king's forests was extended, by Henry III's charter, to the bishops, and accordingly we find them also mentioned in the Northamptonshire records. In 1249 the bishop of Carlisle dispatched a buck, the bishop of Lincoln (the great Robert Grosseteste) a hind and a roe, and the abbot of Westminster a buck and a buck's pricket.[13] Prelates like these were also aristocratic in status and life-style, so it is not surprising that they practiced hunting, especially Grosseteste, who was known even among lay noblemen as a master of courteous behavior. Such a man, surrounded by a retinue of lay servants, entertaining earls and knights and sometimes bringing up their sons in his household, could not avoid becoming involved in the favorite sport of the laity. True, there was an ancient tradition in the church that disapproved of hunting by the clergy, and some church leaders issued laws forbidding it. The so-called Canons of Edgar (1005-8) ordered clerks who hunted to abstain from meat for a year, priests for three years, and bishops for five, as a penance.[14] St. Richard, bishop of Chichester (1245-53), prohibited his clergy from hunting altogether, and Bishop Quinil of Exeter in 1287 forbade them to keep any hunting birds or dogs.[15] But not many bishops seem to have issued such regulations, and in practice hunting was widely practiced by the secular clergy: cathedral canons and parochial rectors, vicars and chaplains. The Huntingdonshire and Northamptonshire forest records mention accusations of poaching in 1255 against Simon of Overton, rector of Old; Robert le Noble, chaplain of Sudborough; the chaplain of Wotton; and no less than seven unidentified clerks.[16] At Cambridge in 1286, scholars of the university itself were indicted for poaching in the warren near the town, including Alan le Fraunceis, a wealthy Durham clerk, and Thomas of Middleton, who was also archdeacon of Norwich.[17] In the 1250s the arrest of

clerks for forest-law offences was frequent enough to become an issue between the church and the lay power, causing the former to threaten ex-
communication against lay officers who held suspected clerics and did not
hand them over to their bishops.[18]

There were stricter rules for the monastic clergy.[19] Cistercian monks
were forbidden to keep sporting dogs or birds in 1283, and the Council of
Vienne in 1311-12 extended this ban to all monks and regular canons, specifically instructing them to abstain from hunting or hawking.[20] The papal
statutes for the Augustinian canons in 1339 permitted hunting and hawking on their lands (presumably by guests and servants), but not by the canons themselves.[21] Visitations of religious houses often prohibited the keeping of dogs and birds on the premises and the practice of hunting by the
brethren. Nevertheless the rules were sometimes broken. Thomas Blytone,
guestmaster of Kyme Priory (Lincolnshire), kept hounds and went hunting
in 1440; John Godefrey of Dunstable (Bedfordshire) was accused of for-
saking the choir to hunt in 1442-43; and Thomas Ewelme of Notley (Buckinghamshire) was charged in 1447 with spending a whole night out, hunting with bows and arrows and drinking in a tavern.[22] Exceptions were also
made for heads of houses, who spent much of their time in manor houses
on their estates or supervised (like Chaucer's Monk) a small dependent
cell. These men often hunted to entertain guests, please their retinues, or
enjoy themselves. Abbot William Clowne of Leicester (1345-78) was so famous for his skill in pursuing hares that Edward III, the Black Prince, and
other lords hunted with him, though the abbot told his canons that he did
so not for pleasure but to forward business with important men.[23] In 1408
Archbishop Arundel, prohibiting hunting at Glastonbury, allowed the abbot to keep a reasonable number of hounds for his parks and warrens, and
at Bruton (Somerset) in 1452 Bishop Beckington of Bath and Wells (a con-
scientious diocesan) permitted even the ordinary canons to hunt for recreation if they had the leave of the prior or his deputy and did so in their
presence.[24] Hunting was never successfully excluded from the religious
life.

As the sport bridged the division between lay noblemen and the clergy,
so it did that between noblemen and merchants. The citizens of London
had ancient hunting rights; a royal charter of 1131 confirmed that they
should have their "grounds for hunting as their ancestors best and most
fully had them, in the Chilterns and Middlesex and Surrey." Similar privileges were granted to Canterbury, Colchester, and Swansea in the second
half of the twelfth century.[25] The practice continued in London during the
later Middle Ages. By the fifteenth century the city corporation kept horses, a pack of hounds, and an officer called "the common hunt" to supervise
the city's hunting and fishing rights, with a salary of £10 a year. London
merchants individually acquired the right to hunt in royal parks or to establish parks and warrens of their own.[26] The "Cely Letters" show a merchant family varying their commercial business in London, Calais, and the

Cotswolds with gentlemanly sports in their country house at Butts Plac near Aveley (Essex). In 1478 Richard Cely the younger wrote to his brother George that he had had the vicar and chaplain of Aveley and another priest staying with him for three nights, "good shooters and mannerly fellows all three"; three great harts had appeared in the wheat at noon, and the litter of hunting whelps was doing well. "Hector is a fine hound, and a fat; his sore is whole." But the Celys' hunting got them into trouble. In 1481 they were maliciously accused of shooting a hart and two hind calves from the royal forest and had to pay a good deal of money to get the charge dismissed. Soon afterward, the head of the family, Richard the elder, decided to get rid of the hunting greyhounds and to confine himself to the safer sport of hawking with spaniels.[27]

We think of hunting as an elite sport, but the majority of hunters may well have been members of the lower orders. Aristocratic hunting required the help of officers and servants: foresters and parkers to protect the game preserves and huntsmen to prepare and assist with the chase. The author of *Sir Gawain and the Green Knight* (late fourteenth century) imagined a great lord hunting with a hundred men, and Edward, duke of York, in the treatise he wrote shortly afterward, envisaged a big royal deer shoot involving the king's twelve or so professional huntsmen, his foresters, and other men and dogs drafted in by the local sheriff.[28] Foresters often hunted lawfully in the sense of shooting game for their masters' tables, and they also did so unlawfully. Alan the forester, John the parker, Simon the woodward, and the hunter of the abbot of Ramsey all appear on charges of poaching in thirteenth-century forest records.[29] While hunting was controlled in royal forests and private parks and warrens, there was at first no law against it being practiced outside such areas. King John, when disafforesting a district in Essex, gave freedom to its inhabitants to "take and have all manner of game that they may take within the aforesaid bounds."[30] It was not until 1390 that the Commons in Parliament (members of the social elite) got the Crown to agree to a general restriction on hunting. Artificers and laborers without lands or tenements worth 40*s.* a year, and clergy with benefices worth less than £10, were forbidden to keep greyhounds or other dogs unless bound or led, hobbled or lawed, on the grounds that hunting was "the sport of the gentle."[31] This was the first of a series of game laws restricting the right to hunt, but like the earlier forest laws they were often disregarded by ordinary people. Going back to the forest records of the thirteenth century, we find proceedings for poaching against such men as Gilbert, the doorkeeper of Rockingham Castle; Henry son of Gervais, the fisher of Islip; Richard, cook of the earl of Gloucester; Robert, submaster of Huntingdon school; William the miller; and Roger Grim, reaper of the abbot of Peterborough.[32]

Children and women are found hunting too. We hear in the forest records of a justice's boy servant with a horn and seven arrows, a page bearing weapons for his master, and another page on horseback implicated in poaching offences.[33] They also hunted lawfully, like the royal princes or John, the son of the Suffolk gentleman John Hopton, who spent two days at Wissett in 1463-64 while a schoolboy, killing deer with the vicar of Covehithe.[34] Schoolmasters used hunting in lessons as a means of interesting boys in learning Latin. Ælfric introduced a hunter and his activities into his late-tenth-century *Colloquy*, and an Oxford collection of translation passages from about 1500 mentions hunting the hare with greyhounds and chasing a wild boar with curs, mastiffs, and spaniels.[35] There is even a fifteenth-century poem in which a schoolboy imagines his master turned into a hare, himself into a hunter, and the master's books into hounds:

I wold my master were an hare
And all his bokes howndes were,
And I myself a joly hontere;
To blow my horn I wold not spare,
For if he were dede I wold not care.[36]

Much less is said about girls and women, but some of the aristocracy certainly followed the sport. Queen Eleanor of Provence is mentioned as taking venison in Rockingham Forest (Northamptonshire) in 1251, and Edward of York expected the queen to be present at deer shoots with her ladies in waiting and to kill deer with her bow, for he discusses the disposal of her winnings.[37] Margaret, daughter of Henry VII, shot a buck at Alnwick Park in 1503 when she was fourteen, on her journey north to marry the king of Scotland.[38] One popular late-medieval hunting treatise professes to be the advice of a mother to her son on all the techniques of the sport, which ought to imply that a gentlewoman could possess such knowledge.[39] Women of lower rank were not needed as hunting assistants and probably did not poach, but a fifteenth-century poet talks of village wives seizing a stick to hit a hare who is eating their cabbages, or setting their dogs on him, and Chaucer describes a chase of women after a predatory fox in the *Nun's Priest's Tale*.[40] All women must have been in touch with hunting through hearing about it and helping to dress the spoils.

Hunting in Practice

How did one hunt? The earliest evidence of how it was done is mainly to be found in narrative literature such as the Welsh *Mabinogion* and the Anglo-French chansons de geste and romances of the twelfth century. One or two early didactic works, notably Ælfric's *Colloquy* and John of Salisbury's *Policraticus* (1159) also contain some valuable details, and documentary records provide a further important source by the twelfth century, especially records of the royal forests, which throw light both on formal hunting and on covert, illegal poaching. Specialized treatises on the sport were written in classical times, but they do not seem to have circulated in medieval England.[41] Instead, treatises appear to have been invented afresh, beginning in the early fourteenth century. The oldest text is the *Art de Venerie* by William Twiti, huntsman to King Edward II; it is a short prose tract in French, in question-and-answer form, containing discrete pieces of advice on hunting the hart, boar, and hare. It is not comprehensive, but explains such matters as the technical terms for animals of different ages, the way to call the hounds when out in the field, and the proper method of blowing horn signals. Two manuscripts survive of the French text, and two of an English translation made in the early fifteenth century.[42] Twiti's treatise influenced a second work, perhaps two works: the so-called *Tristram*, an English poem of the late fourteenth or early fifteenth century, in which a mother explains a selection of terms and techniques of hunting for the benefit of her "son," "sons," "child," or "children." Sandwiched within this work is a text, apparently of separate origin and also in verse, in which a master huntsman and his man discuss the physical characteristics of harts and hares and the methods of disembowelling harts and boars— material that was presumably felt to supplement the information in the mother's poem.[43] *Tristram* also survives in only two manuscripts, but it must have circulated quite widely by the middle of the fifteenth century, since Sir Thomas Malory refers to it in his translation of *Tristram de Lyones*, evidently assuming his readers would know it.[44] In contrast, *The Tretyse off Huntyng*, a similar diffuse kind of work of the same period, is confined to a single manuscript.[45]

These rather chaotic texts containing disparate topics in a free unstudied order are typical of a newly emerging genre of literature that has not yet achieved coherent form. They expect that their readers will have gained a good deal of knowledge orally and practically, and aim to correct and improve this in certain respects. The next treatise to appear, *The Master of Game* by Edward, duke of York (1406-13), came from a different tradition and is better designed, being a prose translation of *Le Livre du Chasse* by Gaston, count of Foix, written in 1389-91.[46] Edward's work is more orderly in method and detailed in treatment. Its thirty-six chapters survey all the animals normally hunted; hounds, their varieties and their management; horns and horn calls; and how to organize a hunt of harts. The duke inserted various small glosses into the text, pointing out where the usage of England differed from that of France, and he added three chapters at the end describing how a hart should be hunted "in strength" with horses and dogs, how to hunt the hare, and how to hunt deer with bows and greyhounds. The work is not complete, saying little about the hunting of boars or foxes and lacking a precise account of the seasons when hunting is done, but it survives in several manuscripts and might have been expected to become the standard work. Oddly enough it did not, perhaps because of its foreign character, and the more disorderly *Tristram* achieved eventual dominance. It was the first hunting work to be printed in the so-called *Book of St. Albans* (1486),[47] along with treatises on hawking and heraldry, and in this form it had a wide circulation, for the *Book* was reissued in more than twenty editions throughout the sixteenth century and well into the seventeenth.

The treatment of hunting in narrative literature, up to the fourteenth century, tends to be simple and lacking in technical detail. The hunters—kings or noblemen—usually go out on horseback, sometimes with attendants on foot. They track or pursue their prey with bows, arrows, swords, and dogs, greyhounds being sometimes specified. Their objects are preeminently deer, boars, and hares. Béroul's *Tristran*, dating from the late twelfth century, differs in taking poaching as its theme when Tristran flees with Yseut to the Morrois forest and feeds them both by stealing the local deer. He achieves this by using archery, inventing a spring bow that the deer trigger as they pass, and teaching his dog to follow and retrieve game without barking—practices no doubt akin to those of poachers.[48] But the shortage of detail in these early narratives probably arises from the authors' interests lying elsewhere, rather than in accurately reflecting how hunting was done. In contrast, John of Salisbury, in an extended essay on the subject in the *Policraticus*, shows that it was already a complex business by the mid-twelfth century. He talks of the use of special terminology and the observance of special rituals. When animals are killed, there is applause and the blowing of horns, the carcasses are carefully butchered, and the heads of the victims are borne home in triumph.[49] Documentary sources from the twelfth and thirteenth centuries support this view, revealing the existence of numerous technical terms. There were words for animals of different ages (brocket, hogster, pricket, and sore) and for different kinds of hounds (berners, kenets, and limers). The place where the hunter awaited his prey was the "tryst." Seasons for hunting were also recognized: the "time of grease" when harts and bucks were fattest (from May to September) and the "fermison" when hinds and does were taken (September to February).[50]

The evidence about terms and procedures grows when we reach the fourteenth and fifteenth centuries. The hunting treatises are precise, indeed pedantic, about the words to use in describing the ages of beasts, their movements, tracks, cries, and names of groups. Advice is given on when and when not to hunt, the method of tracking animals, the organization of the hunt, the correct blowing of horns to signify what is happening, and the butchering of the carcasses, including the distribution of shares to the hounds and hunters. In turn, this technicality makes its way into narrative literature, which becomes more detailed than before about the way that hunting is done. Whether this reflects the fact that hunting was becoming more formalized or whether it is the result of narrative authors becoming more realistic is hard to say, but the change is evident. In Chaucer's *Knight's Tale* (c. 1380s), for example, we are made more aware of the organization of a hunt: it starts at dawn, trackers locate the hart and lead the hunters there, and the ladies present wear a special color, green.[51] His earlier *Book of the Duchess* (c. 1369) has even more details. The poet, waking up from a dream, joins in the hunting of a hart "with strength," a technical term. The hunt begins with the master huntsman blowing three "motes" on his horn to announce the commencement, the hounds are uncoupled, and there are limers to track the prey. When a hart is found it is pursued with shouts, and when it is lost the huntsman blows a "forloin" to signify the fact.[52] Chaucer expects that his audience will recognize these details and appreciate them.

This interest in technicality is taken further in two other poems of Chaucer's time. *The Parlement of the Thre Ages* (c. 1350-90) is primarily a work about the three ages of man, but uses hunting (or rather poaching) as a means of setting the scene for the main topic. The narrator tells of rising early one May morning to take a hart or hind, evidently illegally. He brings along a dog on a leash and a crossbow, and conceals himself under leaves to await the deer. A hart comes by with "royals" and "surroyals" of six and five, descriptive terms that appear in the treatises. He stalks it carefully, and the poet conveys the stealth, quiet, small sounds and movements involved in the process, until the hunter releases the crossbow and shoots the hart, which flees. The dog is loosed and finds the beast dead in a cave, after which the hunter proceeds to butcher the carcass in the customary elaborate manner. He cuts out the tongue and opens the bowels, on which the dog is fed. He probes the carcass for the "assay" to estimate its fatness and finds it to be two fingers deep in the flesh. The hunter slits it from jaw to tail and removes in turn the stomach, legs, and shoulders. A piece of gristle at the end of the sternum, called the "corbyn's bone," is thrown away as an offering to the crows. At last, the butchered joints of meat are concealed in one hole and the stomach and intestines in another, hidden with fern; the horns and head are put in a hollow tree. The poacher then sits down to watch the place in case wild boars smell out the meat, till sunset comes and he can safely take it away.[53]

The range of information in *The Parlement* is surpassed by the author of *Sir Gawain and the Green Knight,* who depicts not one but three hunts, each of them a distinct episode with a good deal of technical detail, yet deftly integrated into the whole story. The hunts are set in the Cheshire region during the last three days of December, in cold sunny weather. They are lawful, public events, presided over by the wealthy lord of a splendid castle, with a large supporting force of hunters and followers. Each day he rises before dawn, hears mass, has breakfast, and sets off. The first hunt is a planned event to shoot hinds and does with bows and arrows. Three motes are blown at the start, and the hounds are brought out by their "catchers." The lord and his men take up their positions at trysts, and the deer are driven past by beaters to be shot at and brought down by greyhounds. At the end the carcasses are collected and assayed for fatness. The dogs are given part of the intestines with bread soaked in blood, the crows are thrown their "fee," and each man gets his customary share. The hunters go home, blowing their horns.[54] On the second day the hunt is not planned. Dogs are uncoupled and discover a boar, which is chased on horseback with bows, arrows, and loud cries. This is a dangerous business; the boar is fierce and strong, and wounds the men and hounds that get too near. When at last it turns to bay, the lord dismounts and kills it with his sword. Horns are blown again and the dogs are made to bark. The boar is "unlaced" (a special term for its dismemberment), the hounds are again fed on bread, blood, and intestines (the last-mentioned cooked), and the company goes home carrying the boar's head on a stake with the carcass behind.[55] On the last day the hounds put up a fox who twists and doubles about, making the hunt a battle of wits to keep him in sight. This hunt lacks formality. The hounds rush in a "rabble," the hunters on horseback shout and threaten the fox, calling him "thief," and when he is finally caught (by the lord throwing a sword at him and the hounds leaping onto him), there is a wild outburst of cries which the poet likens to a funeral dirge—reiterating the mocking, parodic tone of the whole fox hunt.[56]

So much is said about hunting in these last two works that they approach in form the chapters of a treatise. Like Chaucer's work they show how much interest there must have been in procedure and terminology by 1400. Why did hunting become so formalized? One reason must have been the parallel growth of formality in aristocratic life indoors, illustrated in the conventions of courtly love, table etiquette, and polite speaking, which provided the material for a large number of courtesy books from the twelfth century onward.[57] The emphasis of hunters on correct language and correct butchering brought this indoor culture to the most popular sport of the out-of-doors. Another reason must have been that formalized hunting, like formalized etiquette, had a social utility. It provided a freemasonry that linked the aristocracy together and distinguished them from lesser people. Hawking, heraldry, and the use of titles all did the same, and all (as well as hunting) were being written about and emphasized in the later Middle Ages. The social point is spelled out by Malory in his translation of *Tristram de Lyones*:

Wherefore, as me semyth, all jantyllmen that beryth olde armys ought of ryght to honoure sir Tristrams for the goodly tearmys that jantylmen have and use and shall do unto the Day of Dome, that thereby in a maner all men of worshyp may discover a jantylman frome a yoman and a yoman frome a vylane. For he that jantyll is woll draw him to jantyll tacchis and to folow the noble customys of jantylmen.[58]

It followed that hunting, being associated with the aristocracy, could arouse feelings of envy among lesser people. Their views were rarely recorded, but one chronicler claims that the rebels of the Peasants' Revolt of 1381 demanded that all forests, parks, and warrens should become free for hunting by poor as well as rich.[59] Poaching, too, may have involved an element of social discontent, besides the simple desire for food and adventure.

The growth of hunting into a highly formal activity was paralleled in the later Middle Ages by the development of the tournament. It grew from being an informal training for war into a stylized activity of its own, with only an indirect military application.[60] In the history of sport, hunting and the tournament can be seen as the first amusements since classical times to develop the distinctive characteristics of modern sports. Like sports today, they were fueled by moneyed patronage, enabling them to develop sophisticated equipment. They were practiced in special places: one in the tiltyard and the other in the enclosed park, examples of which proliferated among the late medieval gentry. Both sports acquired special equipment: in the case of hunting, distinctive horns, particular types of dogs, and various weapons. Most of all, these two sports came to possess standardized national rules that had to be followed and treatises embodying the rules for consultation and study. It only remained for Sir Thomas Elyot in 1530 to suggest that hunting could be adjudicated to see who achieved the most and that prizes could be given to the best performers.[61]

Hunting Observed

There was no single attitude toward hunting in the Middle Ages; a variety of views, for and against the sport, coexisted in society at the same time. The dominant opinion was probably one of approval of hunting and those who pursued it. Asser praised Alfred for doing so, Froissart described with relish the hunting of Edward III, and writers of fiction were especially fond of presenting their heroes as skilled in the art.[62] The princes of Welsh literature like Arthur, Culhwch, and Pwyll of Dyfed are shown as hunters, and so are the knights of Anglo-French romances: Guy of Warwick, Horn, Ipomedon, and most especially Tristan.[63] Chaucer and the Gawain poet, as we have seen, continued this tradition into the later Middle Ages. Writers approved of hunting by noble women too, like Emilye and Hippolyta in the *Knight's Tale* or the rather more fanciful ladies of Amazonian type in some Arthurian stories. [64] The sport was even used to suggest the glamour of nonaristocratic heroes such as Robin Hood and William Cloudesly in the fifteenth- and sixteenth-century outlaw ballads. [65] Literary writers liked hunting for its splendor of clothes, horses, and dogs and for the strength, skill, and success of those who hunted. In the outlaw ballads, hunting is also associated with freedom. It is a pleasure in defiance of the law, and like all hunters the outlaws have the attractiveness of not belonging to the humdrum world of everyday life.

Other writers, while approving of hunting, analyzed its functions more deliberately and sought to establish its ethical and social values. Langland tried to do this in respect of the aristocracy. In the first or A-text of *Piers Plowman*, written in the 1360s, and again in the later B and C versions, the godly plowman advises his master the knight,

> And go þou hunte hardily to hares and to foxes,
> To beores and to bockes þat breketh menne hegges,
> And fecche þe hom faucuns þe foules to quelle,
> For þei comen into my croft and croppen my whete.[66]

Hunting is credited here with benefiting peasants and laborers and keeping the knight aware of his duties toward them. The view that hunting made the aristocracy better men was shared by Edward of York, who said, translating Gaston, that its practitioners were more alert and enterprising, better acquainted with routes and terrain, and more involved with good customs and manners (the point that Malory was later to make, as well).[67] In the fifteenth and sixteenth centuries, hunting was often praised as educational for children, as a means of training them physically and psychologically for war and battle.[68] John Hardyng, in a proposed curriculum for noble boys in 1457, suggests that after learning reading, dancing, and singing in childhood,

> At fourtene yere they shall to felde i-sure,
> At hunte the dere and catch an hardynesse,
> For dere to hunte and sla[y] and se thaym blede,
> Ane hardyment gyffith to his corage,
> And also in his wytte he takyth hede,
> Ymagynynge to take theym at avantage.

Military training was then to follow at the age of sixteen.[69] Similar views were expressed by educational writers in Tudor and early Stuart England like Sir Thomas Elyot, John Cleland, and Henry Peacham, despite a contrary humanist belief that hunting distracted gentlemen from literary studies and impaired their fitness for public duties.[70]

But not all writers about hunting were so complimentary. The chase was also used by storytellers as a means of getting characters away from home and into an adventure, sometimes with alarming and unpleasant results. In Ovid's *Metamorphoses* the stories of Actaeon and Diana, Adonis and Venus, Meleager and Althaea, and Narcissus and Echo all commence in some kind of hunting context and end with fatal results for the hunter concerned.[71] In early Christian legend, St. Eustace was out hunting when he saw a stag bearing a cross between its horns and heard Christ speaking—a surprise that led to his becoming a Christian.[72] In Anglo-Saxon tradition, Eadric Wild was hunting when he met the fairy bride whom he afterward lost, and Pwyll of Dyfed was doing the same in *The Mabinogion* when he encountered the king of the underworld.[73] There are similar happenings in Arthurian literature. In *The Wedding of Sir Gawain*, King Arthur pursues a stag into the forest and is caught by a knight who propounds him a difficult riddle; in *Sir Gawain and the Carl of Carlisle,* Gawain and his companions lose their way while chasing a reindeer and take refuge in the strange house of the Carl.[74] In many of these stories there is, perhaps, an implicit warning for those who hunt. Men who start out with pride and confidence have the tables turned on them; the hunters become the hunted, at least for a time.

This point was made more forcibly in the later Middle Ages through the influence of the legend of "The Three Dead and the Three Living," which first appears in European literature in the second half of the twelfth century.[75] It tells how three men meet three decomposing corpses who warn them that they will meet a similar fate and must take care to live good Christian lives. The story made its way all over western Europe in art and literature and duly reached England, where a visiting Italian count bought tablets showing it in 1303 and where one of the early French poems on the topic survives in Anglo-Norman copies.[76] In principle, the story is an attack on pride in general, but it soon came to have associations with field sports, no doubt because they were such obvious manifestations of human strength and glory. Pictures of the story usually show a hawk being held by one of the three living, and an early mural in Ditchingham church (Norfolk) depicted the encounter with the dead taking place in a forest setting.[77]

By the early fifteenth century a specific link had developed between the story and hunting. *The Awntyrs off Arthure* (c. 1400-1430), a northern poem, tells a similar but not identical story of how Arthur, Guinevere, and their knights set out from Carlisle to hunt in the neighborhood of Tarn Wadling in Cumberland. They wore beautiful clothes and observed all the proper hunting rituals of the day. Guinevere and Gawain went into a hunting shelter made of branches near the Tarn, but suddenly the day grew dark as midnight, and a specter came out of the water and approached them. It resembled a corpse, bedaubed with clay and foul with toads and serpents. Gawain adjured the ghost in the name of Christ to explain itself, and the ghost revealed that it was once a queen. Guinevere, it warned, would come to the same end herself, so let her have pity on the poor and arrange thirty trentals of masses on behalf of the ghost to bring its soul to bliss. Guinevere promised a million masses, and she later got all the religious people in the West to "read and sing" to this effect.[78] At about the same time as the *Awntyrs*, John Audelay wrote the poem *De Tribus Re-*

gibus Mortuis (c. 1430), which is a reworking of the original legend. The narrator tells how he watched a boar being brought to bay by hounds and how three kings appeared, bearing themselves as if they were lords of the woods and wastes. Again the weather turns misty and dark, and they call on God to deliver them. Out of a wood come three men in the shape of decaying bodies:

> Schokyn out of a schawe, þre schalkys at ene,
> Schadows vnshene were chapid to chow,
> With lymes long and lene and leggys ful lew,
> Hadyn lost þelyp and þelyuer seþyn þai were layd loue.

They reveal themselves as "your fathers" and recall how they used to have worship and wives, were mirthful and jested at others; now nobody bows to them. The kings will share their fate unless they live by Christ and turn from fleshly things. After this warning the ghosts go back to their graves and the sun reappears. The kings amend their lives and build a minster where masses are celebrated; the story is recorded on a wall.[79]

It is not surprising that a moral story aimed against human pride should come to be associated with hunting, for there was a tradition of religious hostility toward the sport that went back to the early Christian centuries. St. Jerome in his *Tractate on Psalm 90* observed that "Esau was a hunter, therefore he was a sinner, and indeed we do not find in holy scripture any virtuous hunter." St. Augustine said of another Old Testament hunter, "Nimrod was a hunter against the Lord. For what does this word 'hunter' mean but the deceiver, oppressor and destroyer of earthborn creatures?"[80] This view was endorsed in twelfth-century England by John of Salisbury and Alexander Neckham, especially by the former, who criticized hunting at length in the *Policraticus*.[81] It was, he declared, "an activity characterized by self-indulgence and vice," and he quoted numerous condemnations of it from classical and Christian writers. It was displeasing to God; "divine wrath by many authentic miracles has smitten leaders while engaged in the hunt." It was bad for the individual, causing him to become brutalized and unsuitable for public service. It was also bad for society. Hunting led to wild animals, gifts of nature, being appropriated by a few men and to harsh forest laws. Peasants were hampered by legal restrictions from getting their livelihood and were exploited by hunters demanding food and gifts as they passed. In the fourteenth century an English preacher similarly complains how

> the rich man goes hunting with his dogs and falcons and catches the hare or the bird, and tramples down the poor man's corn while the latter gets no share in the booty,[82]

and Chaucer refers to the "text" "that seith that hunters ben nat hooly men." [83] The criticisms remained significant enough for both Gaston of Foix and his translator Edward of York to feel the need to refute them. Noting that hunting is said to lead to idleness, sin, and ungodliness, they urge that, on the contrary, it brings health, knowledge, and employment. The hunter rises early, eats and drinks more moderately, and has no time for evil thoughts. "He that fleeth the seven deadly sins, as we believe, he shall be saved; therefore a good hunter shall be saved."[84]

Hostility by clerics toward hunting also manifested itself strongly against their fellow clerics who followed the sport. William of Pagula in the mid-fourteenth century accused them of being readier to track a hare than to be in church, swifter to acquire dogs than to look after the poor. A generation later Thomas Wimbledon complained of the misuse by clergy of the profits of their benefices to buy hawks and hounds.[85] Langland adopted this view, despite his tolerance of hunting by the lay aristocracy. "Religion," he avers, meaning the religious orders collectively, is nowadays

A priker on a palfray fro manere to manere,
An heep of houndes at his ers, as he a lorde were.[86]

Nor are the secular clergy any better. In his portrait of Sloth, which brings together slothful attributes of various kinds of people, the slothful priest confesses that he knows more about hunting than he does of the psalms:

I haue be prest and parsoun passynge þretti wynter,
ʒete can I neither solfe ne synge, ne seyntes lyues rede,
But I can fynde in a felde or in a fourlonge an hare,
Better than in *beatus vir* or in *beati omnes*
Construe oon clause wel and kenne it to my parochienes.[87]

In an ideal world, believes Langland, such men should lose their livelihood. Chaucer alludes to similar views in his portrait of the Monk, though he does not express them as strongly. His Monk, like Langland's, is the kind of dignitary who rides about the countryside with the privilege or opportunity to hunt, and like Langland's priest he is expert at hunting hares. Chaucer, however, avoids a direct condemnation. He prefers to juxtapose references to the rules of St. Augustine and St. Benedict and to the text about unholy hunters. This raises the question of whether hunting is compatible with the monastic life, rather than insisting that it is not.[88]

By our standards, medieval critics of hunting did not give much attention to its victims: the animals. There is some endorsement of kindness to hunted animals in certain lives of the saints. St. Godric of Finchale (Durham) gave sanctuary to them in his hermit's cell, and St. Petrock of Cornwall saved a deer from the servants of a local nobleman. When the latter attempted to take revenge, he lost the use of his limbs until the saint prayed for his recovery.[89] Such stories, however, are not developed into deliberate teaching or preaching about cruelty to animals. Even the appearance of Christ between the stag's horns in the legend of St. Eustace seems primarily intended to call a disciple, not to condemn a hunter. Relatively few scholars, like Augustine and John of Salisbury, stated or implied their dislike of hunting on the grounds of its cruelty. In the fifteenth century two poems were written that purported to give the animals' point of view. "The Hunted Hare" is a lament by the hare for the life he leads, subject to ceaseless pursuit. Hunters start out early, not staying even for mass; dogs run in every furrow, and their masters follow on horseback; the first to see the hare cries "so howe!" In the snow they search for his tracks. Only a gentleman gives the hare an acre's start before his hounds are loosed, "for dred of lossynge of his name" (for not acting in a gentlemanly way). When caught by the greyhounds, the hare's bowels are thrown away, and he is borne home on a stave and hung up.[90] "Will Bucke his Testament" tells how an archer shoots a buck in a park and follows him for an hour until he is brought to bay. The buck asks for grace to make his will and dictates a testament: his body he bequeaths to the cellar, his skin to the bowbearer, his throat to the hounds, and so on, reflecting the careful dissection of carcasses and the allocation of shares to different people.[91] But neither poem, by our standards, is truly sympathetic to animal suffering. They are whimsical pieces, by authors who are complacent about the fate of hunted beasts, or at best only slightly concerned about what it involves.

Conclusion

Hunting was remarkably diverse in its topography, the beasts pursued, the types of hounds, the age, gender, and ranks of the hunters, and the culture of customs, artifacts, art, and literature to which it gave rise. Broadly speaking, it bridged two extremes. One was male, violent, and aggressive.[92] Laymen dominated the sport in its most ambitious forms: hunting deer, boars, or wolves "in strength" with horses and hounds. Women, clerics, and younger children seem to have spent more time on hare coursing or deer shooting. Men hunted to such an extent, believed John of Salisbury, that they became brutalized by the sport, forfeiting their humanity and turning "from levity to lewdness, from lewdness to lust," and finally "into every type of infamy and lawlessness."[93] Some evidence exists to support his belief, especially where poachers were concerned. Forest records mention them going armed and with violence, sometimes masked and sometimes openly and impudently. In the summer of 1255, a gang of fifteen men or more, who had spent the day poaching in Rockingham Forest and had killed several deer, engaged in mocking the authorities in the following way. They cut off a buck's head, impaled it on a stake so that the mouth gaped toward the sun, and placed a spindle in the mouth, "in great contempt of the lord king and his foresters"—a gesture certainly insolent and perhaps, as Barbara Hanawalt has suggested, obscene.[94] Some poachers wounded foresters or killed them—acts that stimulated relish and approval from other people. The fifteenth-century ballad "Robyn and Gandelyn" tells how two young men go into the forest where Robyn kills a deer, only to be shot in turn by another youth, Wrennok of Donne—whether forester or rival poacher is not clear. Gandelyn avenges Robyn's death, and the ballad ends with his exultation over his fallen enemy—

> Now shalt thu never yelpe, Wrennok,
> At ale ne at wyn,
> That thou hast slawe goode Robyn
> And his knave Gandelyn

—a sentiment that the listener is expected to share.[95] The authors of the Robin Hood ballads similarly approve of their heroes' violence. In "Robin Hood and the Monk," not only is the monk killed near the forest, but his little page "ffor ferd lest he wold tell," and in "Robin Hood and Guy of Gisborne," Robin, after slaying Guy in the woods, disfigures his face with a knife.[96]

The other extreme of hunting was the civilized one. The sport in its formal dress was organized, mannered, and pedantic, affected by conventions of courtesy through the presence of women, the careful carving of the carcasses, and the complicated disposal of "fees" to those taking part. By the late fourteenth century it was being emphasized as the sport of gentle people, and (as "The Hare's Lament" reveals) a gentleman hunter might be expected to be more sportsmanlike than a lesser man. Despite the hostility of some clerics, there was a close relationship between hunting and religion. In a well-regulated household, mass could form the prologue to hunting, as it did in *Sir Gawain and the Green Knight.* The chase could be followed, as Sir Bernard de Brocas meant to do, while on pilgrimage. The forest or park where you hunted might contain a hermitage, like those in the forests of Charnwood, Inglewood, and Wychwood, or a chapel like those in the parks of Liskeard and Restormel in Cornwall.[97] Nor was the church so hostile to hunting as to forgo the chance of taking tithes from the proceeds. Two sets of English ecclesiastical statutes in the late thirteenth century order tithes to be paid from hunting, and as late as 1515 the parker of Framlingham (Suffolk) delivered a buck a year to the local rector for tithes.[98] "Will Bucke his Testament" refers to a quasi-Jewish Levitical practice of giving the priest the deer's right shoulder, a custom that may go back to the thirteenth century.[99]

Hunting permeated church life indoors too, its beasts and equipment furnishing trophies and emblems. The present Salisbury Cathedral, according to a fourteenth-century legend, was built where a stricken deer lay down and died, slain by an arrow.[100] At Durham Cathedral, in the thirteenth century, the Nevill family offered a dead stag every year at St. Cuthbert's shrine on the day of the saint's translation (4 September), until Ralph de Nevill fell out with the prior in 1290 and withheld the offering.[101] York Minster kept in its treasury Ulf's horn, an ivory hunting horn of the early eleventh century, which still survives and has long been shown to visitors.[102] At Exeter, the cathedral vestments in 1506 included a green cope decorated with stags and griffins of gold, and a cope with blue orphreys bearing golden lions and hinds; the coat of arms of the cathedral dean was a stag's head with a cross between the horns.[103] At St. Paul's Cathedral (London), hunting even entered the liturgy. In 1275 Sir William Baud of Corringham (Essex) granted the cathedral a doe in winter and a buck in summer forever, in return for permission to enclose twenty-two acres of its land in his deerpark. Thereafter, every year

> on the feast day of the commemoration of St. Paul [30 June], the bucke being brought up to the steps of the high altar in Powls church at the hour of procession, the dean and chapter being apparrelled in coapes and vestments, with garlands of roses on their heades, they sent the body of the buck to baking and had the head fixed on a powle, borne before the crosse in their procession, untill they issued out of the west dore, where the keeper that brought it blowed the death of the bucke, and then the horners that were about the cittie presently aunswered him in like manner.[104]

The ceremony lasted until the Reformation and was briefly revived under Mary Tudor. John Stow, the London historian, witnessed it, probably on one of the last occasions it happened, in 1557-58.[105]

Nor must we forget that hunting appealed to people's aesthetic sense as well as to their savage instincts. It was portrayed in art as beautiful: on tapestries, in book illuminations, and on other artifacts—a large body of evidence that there has not been space to consider. Its equipment was lovingly described by Chaucer in his portrait of the Yeoman, and its sounds and movements by the author of *Sir Gawain and the Green Knight*. He, perhaps better than anyone, conveys its attractive side, depicting it on sunny winter days, now among trees, now among rocks and streams. At one point he evokes the silence of a quest or a struggle, at another the noise of barking dogs and horns, and says that he found them uplifting—"list upon lif" to hear.[106] It was an affirmation that, two hundred years later, Shakespeare would also put into the mouths of Theseus and Hippolyta in *A Midsummer Night's Dream*.[107]

Notes

1. The present article deals with hunting (not hawking), chiefly between 1200 and 1500. For introductions to the topic, see J. Strutt, *The Sports and Pastimes of the People*

of England, ed. W. Hone (London, 1833), pp. 1-23; and C. Petit-Dutaillis, "The Forest," in *Studies and Notes Supplementary to Stubbs' Constitutional History*, 3 vols. (Manchester, 1911-29), 2:147-251. Recent works include N. Orme, *From Childhood to Chivalry: The Education of the English Kings and Aristocracy, 1100-1530* (London and New York, 1984), pp. 191-98; J. Cummins, *The Hound and the Hawk* (London, 1988); and Barbara A. Hanawalt, "Men's Games, King's Deer: Poaching in Medieval England," *Journal of Medieval and Renaissance Studies* 18 (1988), 175-93.

2. Orme, *From Childhood to Chivalry*, pp. 191-98.

3. H. M. Colvin, *The History of the King's Works*, vol. 2, *The Middle Ages* (London, 1963), pp. 895-1021.

4. Edward, duke of York, *The Master of Game*, ed. W. A. and F. Baillie-Grohman (London, 1904), pp. 169-70. Subsequent references are taken from the more accessible 2nd ed. (London, 1909).

5. B. P. Wolffe, *Henry VI* (London, 1981), p. 61.

6. W. Stubbs, *Select Charters . . . of English Constitutional History*, 9th ed. (Oxford, 1913), p. 347, sect. 11.

7. *Select Pleas of the Forest*, ed. G. J. Turner, Selden Society 13 (London, 1901), pp. 34, 40, 93, 104.

8. Edward, duke of York, *The Master of Game*, ed. Baillie-Grohman, pp. 1-2.

9. *Select Pleas*, ed. Turner, pp. 92, 98.

10. *John of Gaunt's Register, 1379-1383*, ed. Eleanor C. Lodge and R. Somerville, Royal Historical Society, Camden 3rd ser., 56 (London, 1937), 1:210.

11. Geoffrey Chaucer, *The Canterbury Tales, General Prologue*, in *The Riverside Chaucer*, ed. Larry D. Benson (Oxford, 1988), I (A). 101-17.

12. C. Henderson, *Essays in Cornish History* (Oxford, 1935), pp. 157-63.

13. *Select Pleas*, ed. Turner, pp. 92-93.

14. *Councils and Synods I: A.D. 871-1204*, ed. Dorothy Whitelock, M. Brett, and C. N. L. Brooke, 2 vols. (Oxford, 1981), 1:335.

15. *Councils and Synods II: A.D. 1205-1313*, ed. F. M. Powicke and C. R. Cheney, 2 vols. (Oxford, 1964), 1:465, 2:1013.

16. *Select Pleas*, ed. Turner, pp. 14, 31-33, 38, 94.

17. Ibid., pp. 129-30.

18. *Councils and Synods II*, ed. Powicke and Cheney, 1:508, 577, 677-78.

19. On hunting by the regular clergy in general, see J. R. H. Moorman, *Church Life in England in the Thirteenth Century* (Cambridge, Eng., 1945), pp. 343-44; and David Knowles, *The Religious Orders in England*, 3 vols. (Cambridge, Eng., 1948-59), 2:246-47.

20. *Statuta Capitulorum Generalium Ordinis Cisterciensis, 1116-1786*, ed. J. M. Canivez, 8 vols. (Louvain, 1933-41), 3:229; *Corpus Iuris Canonici*, ed. E. Friedberg, 2 vols. (Leipzig, 1879-81), 2:1167.

21. *The Triennial Chapters of the Augustinian Canons*, ed. H. E. Salter, Oxford Historical Society 74 (Oxford, 1920), pp. 214-67.

22. *Visitations of Religious Houses in the Diocese of Lincoln, 1436-1449*, ed. A. Hamilton Thompson, 2 vols., Lincoln Record Society 14 and 21 (Lincoln, 1918 and 1929), 1:85, 169; 2:257.

23. Knighton, *Chronicon* 2:127.

24. *The Register of Thomas Bekynton, Bishop of Bath and Wells*, ed. H. C. Maxwell-Lyte and M. C. B. Dawes, 2 vols., Somerset Record Society 49-50 ([Cheddar], 1934-35), 1:181, 2:556.

25. A. Ballard, *British Borough Charters, 1042-1216* (Cambridge, Eng., 1913), p. 83.

26. Sylvia Thrupp, *The Merchant Class of Medieval London* (Chicago, 1948), pp. 145-46.

27. *The Cely Letters, 1472-1488*, ed. Alison Hanham, EETS, OS 273 (London, 1975), pp. 17-18, 72, 115, 124-26, 179.

28. *Sir Gawain and the Green Knight*, ed. J. R. R. Tolkien, E. V. Gordon, and N. Davis, 2nd ed. (Oxford, 1967), line 1144; Edward, duke of York, *The Master of Game*, ed. Baillie-Grohman, p. 188.

29. *Select Pleas*, ed. Turner, pp. 16-19, 36, 56, 58.

30. *Select Pleas*, ed. Turner, p. cxxiii; Petit-Dutaillis, "The Forest," p. 155.

31. *The Statutes of the Realm*, 10 vols. (London, Record Commission, 1810-24), 2:65, ch. 13.

32. *Select Pleas*, ed. Turner, pp. 1-2, 6, 13, 21, 30, 35.

33. Ibid., pp. 14, 95, 115.

34. C. Richmond, *John Hopton: A Fifteenth Century Suffolk Gentleman* (Cambridge, Eng., 1981), p. 133.

35. Ælfric, *Colloquy*, ed. G. N. Garmonsway, 2nd ed. (Exeter, 1978), pp. 23-26; *A Fifteenth Century School Book*, ed. W. Nelson (Oxford, 1956), pp. 24-25.

36. *A Selection of English Carols*, ed. R. L. Greene (Oxford, 1962), pp. 145-46, 241-42.

37. *Select Pleas*, ed. Turner, p. 113; Edward, duke of York, *The Master of Game*, ed. Baillie-Grohman, pp. 190, 194, 196.

38. J. Leland, *Collectanea*, ed. T. Hearne, 2nd ed., 6 vols. (London, 1770), 4:278.

39. See p. 138.

40. R. H. Robbins, *Secular Lyrics of the XIVth and XVth Centuries*, 2nd ed. (Oxford 1955), pp. 107-10; Chaucer, *The Nun's Priest's Tale*, VII.3375-3401 (B^2 4565-91).

41. J. K. Anderson, *Hunting in the Ancient World* (Berkeley, Calif., and London, 1985), pp. 17-19, 107-21, 129-35.

42. William Twiti, *La Vénerie de Twiti*, ed. G. Tilander, Cynegetica 2 (Uppsala, 1956); *The Art of Hunting*, ed. B. Danielsson, Stockholm Studies in English 37 (Stockholm, 1977).

43. Rachel Hands, *English Hunting and Hawking in "The Boke of St Albans"* (London, 1975), pp. 57-79.

44. See p. 141.

45. The *Tretyse off Huntyng*, ed. Anne Rooney (Brussels, 1988).

46. Edward, duke of York, *The Master of Game*, ed. Baillie-Grohman, p. 12.

47. *The Boke of St. Albans*, ed. W. Blades (London, 1905).

48. Béroul, *Tristran*, ed. A. Ewert (Oxford, 1939), vol. 1, lines 1279-84, 1573-1636, 1751-66.

49. John of Salisbury, *Policraticus*, ed. C. C. J. Webb, 2 vols. (Oxford, 1909), bk. 1, ch. 4, translated as *Frivolities of Courtiers* by J. B. Pike (Minneapolis, 1938), pp. 13-26.

50. On the evidence for these terms, see R. E. Latham, *A Revised Medieval Latin Word-List Based on British and Irish Sources* (London, 1965); the glossary in *Select Pleas*, ed. Turner, pp. 133-53; and *The Oxford English Dictionary*, ed. J. A. Simpson and E. S. C. Weiner, 2nd ed., 20 vols. (Oxford, 1989).

51. Chaucer, *The Knight's Tale*, I.1673-95 (A).

52. Chaucer, "The Book of the Duchess," lines 344-86.

53. The *Parlement of the Thre Ages*, ed. M. Y. Offord, EETS, OS 246 (London, 1959), lines 1-99, 655-59.

54. *Sir Gawain and the Green Knight*, ed. Tolkien et al., lines 1133-77, 1319-71.

55. Ibid., lines 1412-67, 1561-1618.

56. Ibid., lines 1690-1730, 1894-1923.

57. On this topic, see Orme, *From Childhood to Chivalry*, pp. 136-40; and J. W. Nicholls, *The Matter of Courtesy* (Woodbridge, 1985).

58. Malory, *Works* 1:375, 3:1445.

59. Knighton, *Chronicon*, 2:137.

60. On the tournament, see R. Barber and Juliet Barker, *Tournaments: Jousts, Chivalry and Pageantry in the Middle Ages* (Woodbridge, 1989).

61. Sir Thomas Elyot, *The Book Named the Governor*, ed. S. E. Lehmberg (London, 1962), pp. 67-68 (bk. 1, ch. 18).

62. *Asser's Life of King Alfred*, ed. W. H. Stevenson (Oxford, 1904), p. 20; Jean Froissart, *Chroniques*, ed. S. Luce and G. Raynaud, 11 vols. (Paris, 1869-99), 5:225.

63. *The Mabinogion*, trans. G. Jones and T. Jones (London, 1949), pp. 3-9, 69, 79, 117-19, 131-35; Orme, *From Childhood to Chivalry*, pp. 83-84.

64. Orme, *From Childhood to Chivalry*, pp. 200-202.

65. *Rymes*, ed. Dobson and Taylor, passim.

66. William Langland, *Piers Plowman*, ed. W. W. Skeat, 2 vols. (London, 1886), A.VII. 32-35, B.VI. 30-3, C.IX. 28-31; cf. C.X. 223-27.

67. Edward, duke of York, *The Master of Game*, ed. Baillie-Grohman, pp. 4-13.

68. John of Salisbury (*Policraticus*, trans. Pike, p. 18) also knew of this concept, but disapproved of it.

69. Hardyng, *Chronicle*, pp. i-ii.

70. N. Orme, "Hunting and Education in England, 1100-1600," *Proceedings of the XIth HISPA International Congress*, ed. J. A. Mangan (Jordanhill, Glasgow, 1987), pp. 74-76.

71. Ovid, *Metamorphoses*, bks. 3, 7, 8, 10, 14.

72. D. H. Farmer, *The Oxford Dictionary of Saints* (Oxford, 1978), p. 144; William Caxton, *The Golden Legend*, 7 vols. (London, 1900), 6:83-86. The same incident was incorporated (by the fourteenth century) into the life of St. Hubert (Farmer, *Oxford Dictionary of Saints*, p. 198).

73. Walter Map, *De Nugis Curialium*, ed. M. R. James, 2nd ed. (Oxford, 1983), pp. 154-59; *The Mabinogion*, trans. Jones and Jones, pp. 3-4; cf. p. 79.

74. *Middle English Verse Romances*, ed. D. B. Sands (New York, 1966), pp. 326-27 (lines 15-60), 355 (lines 115-44).

75. W. Rotzler, *Die Begegnung der drei Lebenden und der drei Toten* (Winterhur, 1961); *Dictionnaire des lettres françaises: Le Moyen Age*, ed. R. Bossuet, L. Pichard, and G. Raynaud de Laye (Paris, 1964), pp. 721-22.

76. *Les cinq poèmes des trois morts et des trois vifs*, ed. S. Glixelli (Paris, 1914), especially pp. 10, 37-38, 41-42, 87 (line 74).

77. "Archaeological Intelligence," *Archaeological Review* 5 (1848), pp. 69-70, and plate.

78. *The Awntyrs off Arthure*, ed. R. Hanna (Manchester, 1974), passim.

79. *The Poems of John Audelay*, ed. Ella K. Whiting, EETS, OS 184 (London, 1931), pp. xiv, 217-23.

80. *The Riverside Chaucer*, ed. Benson, p. 807.

81. John of Salisbury, *Policraticus*, trans. Pike, pp. 13-26; Alexander Neckham, *De Naturis Rerum*, ed. T. Wright, RS (London, 1863), pp. 216-17.

82. G. R. Owst, *Literature and Pulpit in Medieval England*, 2nd ed. (Oxford, 1966), p. 329.

83. Chaucer, *General Prologue*, I.177-78 (A).

84. Edward, duke of York, *The Master of Game*, ed. Baillie-Grohman, pp. 4-13.

85. Owst, *Literature and Pulpit*, p. 279.

86. Langland, *Piers Plowman*, ed. Skeat, B.X. 306-9.

87. Ibid., B.V. 422-26, C.VIII. 30-34; B.III. 309-12, C.IV. 467-70.

88. Chaucer, *General Prologue*, I.175-91 (A).

89. *Nova Legenda Anglie*, ed. C. Horstman, 2 vols. (Oxford, 1901), 1:481, 2:319.

90. Robbins, *Secular Lyrics*, pp. 107-10.

91. F. M. Padelford and A. R. Benham, "The Songs of Rawlinson MS C. 813," *Anglia* 31 (1908), 350-52.

92. For a perceptive analysis of this aspect, see Hanawalt, "Men's Games, King's Deer," pp. 175-93.

93. John of Salisbury, *Policraticus*, trans. Pike, p. 18.

94. *Select Pleas*, ed. Turner, p. 38; Hanawalt, "Men's Games, King's Deer," pp. 190-91.

95. *Rymes*, ed. Dobson and Taylor, pp. 256-57.

96. Ibid., pp. 119, 144.

97. Rotha M. Clay, *The Hermits and Anchorites of England* (London, 1914), pp. 17-31; Henderson, *Essays in Cornish History*, p. 161.

98. *Councils and Synods II*, ed. Powicke and Cheney, 2:1053, 1391; E. P. Shirley, *Some Account of English Games Parks* (London, 1869), pp. 29-33.

99. Padelford and Benham, "The Songs of Rawlinson MS C. 813," p. 350; Leviticus 7.32-33; *Select Pleas*, ed. Turner, p. 37.

100. R. Spring, *Salisbury Cathedral* (London, 1987), p. 10.

101. *Historiae Dunelmensis Scriptores Tres*, ed. J. Raine, Surtees Society 9 (1839), pp. 73-74.

102. G.E. Aylmer and R. Cant, *A History of York Minster* (Oxford, 1977), p. 39.

103. G. Oliver, *Lives of the Bishops of Exeter and a History of the Cathedral* (Exeter, 1861), pp. 336-38.

104. J. Stow, *A Survey of London*, ed. C. L. Kingsford, 2 vols. (Oxford, 1908).

105. Ibid., 1:333-35, 348.

106. *Sir Gawain and the Green Knight*, ed. Tolkien et al., especially lines 1420-33, 1694-1720.

107. William Shakespeare, *A Midsummer Night's Dream*, act 4, scene 1, lines 111-32.

CHAPTER 8

Ballads and Bandits
Fourteenth-Century Outlaws and the Robin Hood Poems

Barbara A. Hanawalt

obin Hood, the courteous outlaw, the rebel against authority, and the friend of the poor husbandman, was a popular subject for ballads in late medieval England and has lost little of his universal appeal today. It is safe to assume that the ballads were recited frequently in villages, towns, and castles of late medieval England, for around 1377 a passing reference to them appears in *Piers Plowman*, when Sloth confesses that he can recite the popular rhymes of Robin Hood but cannot recite the paternoster.[1] We can readily appreciate Robin Hood's appeal for medieval audiences. His prowess in weaponry, courtly behavior toward women, and enjoyment of hunting appealed to the nobility; his concern for the plight of a knight about to default on a mortgage won over knights and gentry; and his explicit concern for the villagers assured him a ready audience with them.

> But loke ye do no husbonde no harme
> That tylleth with his ploughe
> No more ye shall no gode yeman
> That walketh by grene wode shawe.
>
> Ne no knyght ne no squyer
> That wol be a gode felawe.[2]

He was a hero who could defy the law, right wrongs done by corrupt officials, fleece the church, and be rewarded by the king for his actions.

Robin Hood has been no less appealing to historians and collectors of ballads. Recent scholarship has focused on the social class of a possible historical personage, the origins of the ballad tradition, and the audience to whom the legend appealed.[3] In the hands of a modern historian, E. J. Hobsbawm, Robin Hood has become a primitive rebel for peasant resistence and thus has been made to serve as an anachronistic folk hero for modern political ideology.[4]

It is not my purpose here to look for a historical Robin Hood (the evidence is insufficient), nor are the origins of the ballads necessary for this article. It suffices that the ballads were part of the general oral tradition of

England, widely known and recited in the later Middle Ages. If they provided any ideology for peasant revolt in 1381, no historical evidence exists. Indeed, Richard Firth Green's essay in this volume indicates that the rebels explicitly wanted Hobbe the Robber to be chastised. My essay *will* have something to say about the audience for the poems in that those who wrote, recited, and listened to them knew a great deal about organized crime in late medieval England and had an ambigious feeling about it. In their unease, late medieval English audiences were very much like modern ones who enjoy the numerous films about the Mafia, but nonetheless feel that such criminals must ultimately be brought to justice.

The purpose of this essay is twofold: to compare contemporary banditry with the medieval poems of the Robin Hood tradition and to examine the alterations in Robin Hood's character that could make *him* a hero when ordinary bandits were regarded with mixed feelings. The surviving Robin Hood poems and ballads are fine examples of the universal qualities that turn ordinary criminals into mythical bandit heroes. Late medieval England had reason to know all too well the experience of having bands of robbers roaming their land. Armies for the Hundred Years' War and the war with Scotland recruited soldiers from among the outlaws of England and then released them back into the countryside during periods of peace. Pillaging gangs were not only well known, they received encouragement and support from local magnates who used them for their own fights.[5] We would expect, then, that the crafters of the legend would incorporate something of the organization, tactics, patrons, and personnel that could be met with in bands roaming the countryside. But since we will also find that these strong-armed robbers were ultimately more feared than liked, we must analyze how the heroic Robin Hood differed from real bandits.

Sources

The sources for our study are derived from both criminal court records and literary remains. In order to eliminate modern influences on the tradition, I have used only those poems that Dobson and Taylor in *The Rymes of Robyn Hood* positively identified as belonging to the medieval tradition. *A Gest of Robyn Hode* provides the fundamental story of the cycle and exists in a fifteenth-century manuscript. It is an epic poem apparently pieced together from various ballads current at the time and probably represents the conflation of at least two different cycles. The other poems and balladry in the cycle that have medieval roots are *Robin Hood and Guy of Guisborne, Robin Hood's Death, Robin Hood and the Potter,* and *Robin Hood and the Monk.*[6] Dobson and Taylor have expressed reservations that the surviving ballads bring us into "intimate and undistorted contact with the thoughts and attitudes of the mass of English population."[7] I am less concerned about the thinking of the medieval English audience here than in the ways that the poems reflect their experience with real organized crime. Although the *Gest* is put into a complex, literary form, the tales are based on popular versions and are rooted in a context that was generally familiar to their audiences.[8]

I will compare the material from the poems to the activities of real bandits as reflected in the jail delivery rolls.[9] These are the records of the fourteenth-century circuit justices who were sent out two to three times a year to try criminal cases. Criminal associations appeared routinely in these records because the justices made an effort to try all people associated in the commission of a crime at one time. When indictments were made, indicting juries presented the names of all members of a group suspected of having committed a crime together. Suspects were held in jail for trial until the other suspects could be arrested.

Crimes committed by two or more people were common in jail delivery, constituting 55 percent of all cases tried.[10] Isolating bandits from other, less formal, criminal associations that appear in the records will be aided by defining "banditry." Criminologists have distinguished between formal and informal criminal associations on the basis of the amount of rationality, cohesiveness, and division of labor involved in the associations' organization. By far the most common type of criminal association in both medieval and modern crime patterns is the informal one in which the people involved come together for the commission of one or two crimes and then disband. They have little organization and do not make a living through crime. Formal criminal associations, on the other hand, have a hierarchy of command similar to that found in bureaucracies or corporations: defined roles, limited membership, rigid rules of conduct, and appropriate punishments for members breaking them.[11] Such associations did not exist in medieval England, but were just beginning to appear in Sicily in what has become known as the Mafia. Bandits fall between the informal and formal associations. They have defined leadership and, perhaps, a chain of command, but their organization lacks the longevity of the more formal associations.

In order to separate bandit associations from the more informal ones, I used what modern detectives call the modus operandi employed in various criminal acts. Robbery is traditionally the crime of the bandit and highwayman, involving stealth, violence, and two or more criminal associates. In the jail delivery records, 78 percent of all robberies involved groups of two or more people and all met the other criteria. Burglary cases involving personal violence as opposed to simple breaking and entering were similar to robbery in their techniques: cover of darkness and criminal associates. Arson, an uncommon crime in the record, was committed by two or more people in 72 percent of the cases. All of these crimes were more frequently committed by strangers to the community and hence were more likely to be the work of outlaws. Although somewhat crude as a device for identifying bandit groups, it is the most feasible one. A more refined method of detection of outlaw bands would be to trace the bandits through their re-appearances in court records, but such a search is prohibitive because of problems in detecting crimes, gang mobility, use of aliases, and variant name spellings such as Hood, Hode, and Hobbe. [12]

A more intimate view of banditry sometimes appears in approvers' testimony that the coroners recorded. Approvers, confessed felons who turned state's evidence, revealed the names and crimes of their associates in an effort to prolong their lives. They would be kept in jail until the suspects were arrested and tried. Eventually, they would be hanged for their confessed crimes. Their confessions give a wealth of detail that would not otherwise be available on series of crimes, shifting membership of gangs, and their relationship with the local community. While one might question the veracity of such confessions, it must be remembered that they had to repeat these charges word for word again at the trial and their narratives had to be believable at the time they confessed. [13]

Real Bandits and Ballad Bandits

On the whole, in membership, rewards, and techniques of banditry, real bandits encountered in court records closely resembled the ballad bandits. The divergence between the two occurs with the victims of banditry in fact and fiction.

In the Robin Hood poems, most of the action involved only the central characters: Robin Hood, Little John, Much the Miller, and William Scarlett. These formed the core of their band. Robin Hood laid plans for one of his robberies thus:

> "Take thy gode bowe in they hand,"
> sayde Robyn,
> "Late Much wende with the,
> And so shal Willyam Scarloke
> An no man abyde with me."[14]

In many of the adventures, Robin Hood sets out only with Little John. [15] An analysis of the bands appearing in the criminal courts also shows that they were small, flexible units capable of highway robbery. Two member bands predominated (41 percent), followed by gangs of three (22 percent) and four (12 percent).

When Robin Hood needed a larger group, he could blow his horn and call up seven score men from the greenwood to aid him.

> Robyn toke a full grete horne,
> And loude he gan blowe;

> Seven score of wyght younge men
> Came redy on a rowe.[16]

Likewise, depending on the crime to be committed, real bandits might use five to twenty or more members (25 percent of the gangs). Robbery of a well-guarded person or taking over a market required a small army of bandits.

The poetic tradition aptly speaks of "Robin Hood and his merry *men*." Maid Marian was a sixteenth-century addition to the poems.[17] In jail delivery courts, women were tried with 12 percent of the gangs, but their part of the total personnel of bandits was only 5 percent. Their role in the criminal associations is not spelled out, but perhaps they acted as decoys to stop travelers. Hugh of Nuttle and Lucia, his concubine, formed one such association, which held the pass at Emethrop Rye in Yorkshire and robbed various people there. [18]

The Robin Hood band does not include a set of brothers or other kin, although such kin pairing is common in adventure literature and was a very common occurrence in real banditry. [19] The family unit was a natural one for criminal associations, since it already contained the basic division of labor and commitment to working together so necessary for successful crime. [20]

Millers, yeomen, potters, and peasants all appeared in the poems, as they did among the real bandits. Although occupation was not consistently given in court records, we have enough evidence to know that indicted bandits were not the dregs of society, but rather at least middling peasants or yeomen. [21] At only 1 percent, knights were not common in these bands and certainly no nobility were ever indicted in jail delivery for banditry.

Remarkably absent among the merry band around the medieval, fictional Robin Hood was a clergyman. Friar Tuck, like Maid Marian, was a sixteenth-century addition. The monks that do appear are all figures of corruption and, therefore, apt victims. Clergy played a dominant role in real banditry. The clergy in jail delivery evidence were readily identifiable because they could claim benefit of clergy when they were tried. That is, on presenting evidence in the form of their ecclesiastical habit, their ability to read, or a bishop's record that they had taken orders, they could move their case to the bishop's court where hanging was not a punishment. Clergy were members of 13 percent of the bandit gangs and comprised 7 percent of the bandits' personnel (in ordinary crime they comprised only 4 percent). In general, clerics' abnormally high participation in violent crime leads one to speculate that shrewd criminals planning a career in crime took the lower orders of clergy or learned to read in order to claim benefit of clergy and thus avoid hanging. A late fourteenth-century gang of Sir John de Colesby and Sir William Bussy involved thirty-eight men who committed a series of crimes in Yorkshire netting £3,000. All were convicted, but many were able to prove that they were members of the clergy.[22]

The ballads do not say how far Robin Hood's band traveled to join ranks with such a notorious felon. With a reputation such as his, a real bandit could draw members from a wide region. Informal criminal associations drew their membership from their family and from fellow villagers.[23] At the most their members came from an area of an easy walking distance from the village. The bandits, however, found associates farther afield.[24] Bandits were, therefore, a more geographically heterogeneous group than were informal criminal associations.

A few examples of bandit groups from approvers' confessions make both the membership and the functioning of the bands clearer. Richard Randolf of Sharneforth in Cambridgeshire appealed John Paulyn from Leicestershire and John son of John from Sharneforth of helping him steal six oxen worth 60s. and driving them to Paulyn's home. In February 1345 he claimed that John de Flanmyll, Sr., and the previous John, his son, helped him steal a horse in Warwickshire. The chaplain kept the horse. Finally, he formed a group that included another fellow villager, the chaplain and his son, and John de Flanmyll and his son. They took a horse worth 5 marks and £40 in silver coins in September 1343 from a member of the clergy.[25]

While Richard Randolf worked with both local and distant partners and traveled great distances to commit his crimes, Elliot Avenel worked with men of the surrounding villages in Cambridgeshire and selected particular, well-known local targets. The first burglary he confessed to was the home of Henry Avenel, a kin of his. He, along with seven men and one woman, entered into the house and stole cloth worth 100s. in August 1342. On Christmas Day 1344 he and seven others, including a man and woman from Essex, broke into the home of John le Cheseman in Illeford, killed John, and stole a horse, linen and woolen cloth, and money. With four other men he crossed into Essex in 1345 and broke into the home of John Bakere, stealing cloth worth 100s. and money worth 100s. He was with the same group for another robbery in Essex in December 1345 when they stole five oxen worth 100s.[26]

The high profits in these cases explain why recruitment to banditry held attractions. The average robbery netted £4, considerably greater profits than could be made following the plow. The excitement and romance of banditry were additional attractions. One can imagine that even ordinary people felt the lure of banditry, as did the legendary hero. According to the *Gest*, Robin Hood, after finding a comfortable position within the law as a yeoman of the king, missed the old excitement of the greenwood and eventually deserted his post as many of his band had done before him.

> By than the yere was all agone
> He had no man but twayne,

> Lytell Johan and good Scathelocke
> With hym all for to gone.
> "Alas!" then sayd good Robyn,
>
> "Alas and well a woo.
> Yf I dwele lenger with the kynge,
> Sorrowe wyll me sloo."

He lived as an outlaw for twenty-two more years, even though he dreaded the wrath of the king: "For all drede of Edwarde our kynge, / Agayne wolde he not goo."[27] Bandits' success depended upon their organization: defined leadership, trustworthy members, rules of conduct, and cooperation with other bands of outlaws. All of these characteristics appear in the Robin Hood ballads. The crucial element for the outlaw band was an outstanding leader—a Robin Hood. He commanded respect because he was the strongest or the best shot or was a natural leader or had the highest social status in the group.

The ballads are not explicit about Hood's qualifications for leadership. Our only hint comes in the many archery contests and the disputes to which they give rise. In entertaining the king disguised as a monk, Robin Hood sets up an archery contest in which the loser gets buffeted on the head. Robin finally misses a shot, but only the guest (i.e., the king) is allowed to buffet him. The force of the blow identifies the king. The king and Robin subsequently square off to a shooting match.

> And many a Buffet our kynge wan,
> Of Robyn Hode that day;
> And nothynge spared good Robyn
> Our kynge in his pay.[28]

That Robin Hood should be on equal footing with the king is fitting because Robin Hood is in his own domain and the king has already accepted Robin Hood's livery of Lincoln green. The king has become his man but must retain his dignity in the larger social hierachy. The ballads stop short of a world turned upside down.

When Little John wins the informal contests in the woods, a crisis of leadership always occurs, leading to a split between Robin and John and ultimately a situation in which Little John must prove his loyalty to Robin. Thus in *Robin Hood and the Monk*, John wins five shillings from Robin, but gets paid in a blow. John draws his sword and says:

> "Were thou not my maister," seid Litull John,
> "Thou shuldid by hit ful sore;
> Get the a man wher thou wil[t],
> For thou getis me no more."[29]

Robin also fights with William Scarlett in *Robin Hood's Death,* so that the crisis in confidence about leadership again portends bad luck.[30] Unlike the contests of skill with the king, these are struggles for dominance and leadership.

A dominant leader was necessary not only for disciplining group behavior and providing direction in criminal activities, but also because the society naturally turned to the model of an overlord as the normal form of social organization. Outlaws may have escaped the conventional relationships of man to lord by seeking refuge in the greenwood, but their social thinking made it natural for them to model their organization along the lines of feudal government.

In choosing their leaders, real bandits honored the traditional social hierarchy. If the band included a knight, he was the leader. In addition to Sir John de Colesby and Sir William de Bussy, one may add Sir Thomas de Heslarton, who was *capitalis de societate* of a gang of his relatives, servants, neighbors, and outlaws.[31] Clergy provided leadership for 8 percent of the bands in criminal court. Where families were the core of the gang, the father or oldest brother became the leader. Associations may have had other standards than social status for picking their leaders, but they are hard to identify in the court records.

A *capitalis de societate* held a position very similar to that of Robin Hood of the ballads, and the general substructure followed the pattern of the poems. Members of Hood's band addressed him as "master," and he delegated some of his responsibilities to his lieutenants: Little John, Much the Miller, and William Scarlett. Such an organizational hierarchy has a historical echo in a letter from a northern outlaw who even adopted a royal style of address: "Lionel, king of the rout of raveners salutes, but with little love, his false and disloyal Richard de Snaweshill. We command you, on pain to lose all that can stand forfeit against our laws, that you immediately remove from his office him whom you maintain in the vicarage of Burton Agnes, and that you suffer that the Abbot of St. Mary's have his rights in this matter." Lionel was in the pay of the Abbot of St. Mary's and was handling a problem of an ecclesiastical living for him. He promised grave property damage and bodily harm if the Abbot did not get his way. The operation was to be undertaken by "our lieutenant in the North," a parallel to Little John. He closed his letter again in the royal style: "Given in our Castle of the North Wind, in the Green Tower, in the first year of our reign."[32]

The parallels between both the real and fictional robber bands to royal and magnate households indicate that the bandits used these legitimate institutions as models. Like the liveried followers of magnates, Robin Hood's band wore his color of Lincoln green. As we have seen, even the king wore Hood's livery when he was in the greenwood. Indeed, the king even expressed some envy at the respect Hood commanded over his followers:

> "Here is a wonder semely syght
> Me thynketh, by Goddes pyne,
> His men are more at his byddynge
> Than my men be at myne."[33]

Since real bandits occasionally served as hired thugs in noble households, as Lionel was doing, they were very familiar with their hierarchical nature.

A further exposure to the royal power structure came through service in the army. The fictional Robin Hood's year of service as a king's yeoman is similar to the experiences of real-life bandits. Like those of real bandits, his band was semimilitary in that Little John was his second in command. Outlaws could gain pardon for their crimes by serving a year or more in the royal armies, and during the fourteenth century they composed as much as 2 to 12 percent of the troops.[34] Some of these unsavory veterans returned to civilian life as bandits, organizing their bands along military lines and even adopting royal language in their communications. Trailbaston and peace commissions speak of criminals writing "as if in a royal style to knights, widows, abbots, priors . . . and others whom they deem wealthy . . . [demanding] stated sums of money by grievous menaces."[35] A typical gang was that of Walter Osborn of Holcham, John Bryd, John le Speller of Holcham, and John de Bylneye of Holcham, who were accused of piracy in 1327, but produced pardons stating that they had been of service to the king against the Lancastrian rebels and the Scots.[36]

Along with a leader and a semimilitary organization, the bandits had other rules of behavior that one would expect of an organized gang: division of spoils, cooperation in criminal acts, and keeping the names of members secret.

The division of spoils appears in criminal records and in ballads. In the *Gest* Robin Hood divided £40 he took from the king into equal parts, giving half to his men and returning his half to the victim.[37] The principles of division are less clear in actual cases. In a large gang robbery in 1302, the members retired to a place of safety and there shared "among the aforesaid mercery and spicery each according to his degree," implying status in the gang. John Drestes, a gang member who turned approver, testified that he and nine other men robbed Robin Wyot, a fisherman in Walsham (Norfolk), of cloth and money valued at 50s. John got 17s. for his part. But one man told the justices that in a three-way split of 18s., he got only 1s. 6d.[38] The amount awarded could depend on the risk taken as well as on the status of the felon.

Although secrecy about gang membership was a rule, many of the men who became approvers alleged at their trial that they had been tortured into confessions. The coroner invariably testified that they made their confessions freely. Since 96 percent of the approvers withdrew their appeals at the trial, perhaps it was considered adequate for the maintenance of honor to declare innocent all those gang members they had accused under duress. One man claimed that he was insane at the time he turned approver, and three men appealed people who were already dead and thereby protected accomplices. [39]

In both fiction and real life, bandits needed places of refuge other than the greenwood and so they cultivated local lords and villagers. When Little John was shot in the knee in a skirmish with the Sheriff of Nottingham, Robin Hood and Much the Miller carried him to Sir Richard at the Lee's castle and remained there until John was healed.[40] Sir Richard certainly owed Robin a favor for giving him money to pay off his mortgage to the Abbot of St. Mary's, but sheltering a known outlaw was a felony. Receiving known felons was the most common charge against the nobility in court records. When royal justices came to Somerset in 1305 to make special inquiries into criminal activities, they found that Sir Simon Montagu, Sir Robert Fitz Payn, Lady Juliana la Brett, and Sir Robert de Brent were all suspected of receiving felons, as were the high churchmen of the county. Lord Simon's trusty felon was named John le Little.[41]

Although Robin Hood does not seek shelter with peasants, he relied on the good will of the local people. Peasant householders might willingly shelter felons because they almost always received some of the stolen goods. The approvers' appeals give rich information on the pattern of receiving. Robert Redynge worked with four men in a series of robberies. Matilda, wife of Walter le Bond, received them in the home of her mother, and he paid her in grain. In another rampage in which they robbed and murdered a victim, they retreated to the home of Alice Robyn of Buckeby where they gave her part of the clothing from the robbery.[42] Not all peasants entertained these dangerous men of their free will. One woman claimed that her husband came home with fellow members of his gang and forced her to receive them, but they were now "outlaws in Gloucestershire." Another woman said she knew that she was sheltering a notorious outlaw, but that he had terrified her into letting him enter the house when her husband was away.[43]

If all means of avoiding arrest, stopping indictments and trials, or procuring a pardon failed and a gang member was to be hanged, it behooved the other members to go to the rescue. In the dramatic climax of *Robin Hood and the Monk*, Little John rescued Robin Hood from the sheriff's dungeon. [44] Adam Bell, another outlaw hero, rescued his fellow outlaw, William Cloudesly, from the gallows.[45] Real life was as dramatic as fiction. In 1318 a group of unknown persons entered Norwich castle jail and released Richard Phelip. In a more desperate rescue, Nicholas Tailor of Garsington, Elliot son of Eve de Lynton, Adam Thresshefeld, and Henry of Plumpton cut down from the gallows Nicholas's brother, Henry, who was being hanged for burglary. They took him to a church where he abjured the realm. When one gang arrived at the gallows too late, its members took revenge by killing the hangman.[46]

Victims: Real and Imagined

Organizing for criminal activity was only part of the problem facing bandits; they also had to provide for their daily bread. All of the ballads take place in the "greenwood" in May and June, not in winter.

> In somer, when the shawes be sheyne
> And leves be large and long,
> Hit is full mery in feyre forests
> To here the folys song.[47]

A fifteenth-century love poem, "The Nut Brown Maiden," gives a more accurate picture of the outlaw's life.

> Yet take good hede, for ever I drede,
> That ye coulde not sustain .
> The thoorney ways, the depe valeis,
> The snow, the frost, the reyne,
> the cold, the hete; for drye or wete
> We must lodge on the plan;
> And, us above non other roue,
> But a break, bussh, or twayne.[48]

Life in the deciduous forest could be bleak, and outlaw bands needed blankets, cooking utensils, clothing, and other amenities. Furthermore, a diet of the king's deer alone was unpredictable and hardly balanced. Bandits needed beer, bread, wine, and perhaps some vegetables and fruit. These were items they could not produce themselves and would have to buy or steal.

Such basic needs raise the question of who the victims were. In this respect, the poems and reality diverge. Robin Hood lives on venison, red wine, dark ale, and good white bread, but the poems never tell the reader where he got the latter three items. The criminal cases *do* say what goods are stolen and who the victims are. More often than not, victims were peasants.

In the famous passage at the beginning of the *Gest*, Robin Hood lists who will and will not be his victims. Yeomen, husbandmen, women, good knights and squires were to be left alone, but

> "These bisshoppes and these archebishoppes,
> Ye shall them bete and bynde,"[49]

as well as the sheriff of Nottingham. As the stories unfold, however, innocent bystanders lose their lives to Robin Hood's band. In the desperate and bloody rescue of Hood from the sheriff's prison, Little John and Much the Miller beheaded a monk and killed a little page accompanying him for fear the child would tell who murdered his master, and porters at gates and other innocent servants of authorities were killed.[50] Servants in the Middle Ages were extensions of the authorities they served and were not exempt from the wrath of real or fictional bandits.

Robin Hood also exempted women from his potential victims, but not so the real bandits.

> Robyn loved Oure dere Lady;
> For dout of didly synne
> Woulde he never no compani harme
> That any woman was in.[51]

A study of thirteenth-century homicide showed that 37 percent of the victims of criminal bands were women, compared with 18 percent in the ordinary homicide pattern. Children were also more likely to be victims of bandits (4 percent) than of ordinary homicide (2 percent).[52] One reason is that women and children were present in houses where bandits committed burglaries with violence.

In the poems, Robin Hood and his band confined their thefts to the high value, glamour items such as money, fine horses, and valuable plate and cloth. Real-life bandits also stole these items, but they stole more low-value household goods, clothing, and food than did ordinary thieves. Their need for this sort of daily provision was greater than the ordinary, peasant thief who already had a house and food.[53] Bandits had no higher social conscience than the ordinary thieves who stole primarily from fellow villagers.

The low-valued, everyday goods bandits stole from husbandmen, village craftsmen, and shepherds violate the credo of Robin Hood and other "social bandits." But real bandits knew that bread, beer, blankets, and cooking implements were more readily accessible in peasant houses than in the well-guarded and fortified dwellings of the sheriff, abbot, or lord. A Wakefield manor (the territory of the legendary Robin Hood) indictment demonstrates the problems outlaw bands caused ordinary people.

> *Richard del Wyndhill taken as a suspected thief because he came with a message from several thieves to the wife of the late William de Stodley (begging!) victuals for the said thieves and because he threatened the woman to burn her unless she sent food and money by him, and fled when the Earl's foresters tried to attach him for this. He shot at the foresters.*[54]

Here we have a delightful case of role reversal in which the foresters save the unfortunate widow from the putative Robin Hood.

Bandits did not confine their attacks to the peasantry, of course, because the greatest wealth came from traveling merchants, clergy, nobility, and government officials, the preferred victims of Robin Hood. Bandits stole from clergy and churches more frequently than did ordinary suspects appearing in jail delivery. In Norfolk a band of thieves, led by a clerk, entered the priory church at Thetford, killed the prior's nephew, and stole vases, the prior's seal, goods, and horses.[55] Clergy on the road were also vulnerable. In one notorious case, nineteen men were accused of holding up the bishop-elect of Norwich on his way to his ordination.[56] Robin Hood's attacks on the Abbot of St. Mary's are not the stuff of romance alone; real bandits could be even more audacious.

Attacks on merchants were common among real bandits, but it was the attacks on ports, market towns, and fairs that terrified people. John of Allerston and John Scot of Whitby and their gang were charged with holding the port of Whitby, robbing two men, stopping ships and sailors, and generally endangering the lives and property of people in the port. Armed robbers held Scarborough twice in the fourteenth century, fortifying the town and robbing the citizens.[57]

The balladeer reflected well the terror of the Nottingham citizens when the disguised king and his men, dressed in Lincoln green, entered the city along with Robin Hood's band. They were convinced that the king had been killed and the bandits were going to take over the town and kill them all.

> Full hastly they began to fle,
> Both yeman and knaves,
> And olde wyves that myght evyll goo,
> They hypped on theyr staves.[58]

For the people of Nottingham being either a yeoman or a woman did not assuage their fear of Robin Hood's band. When, in *Robin Hood and the Monk*, the sheriff asks them to turn out and capture Robin Hood in the church, "many was the moder son / To the kyrk with hym can fare" carrying staves and other arms.[59]

Like Robin Hood, bandits also occasionally attacked authorities who were charged with bringing them to justice. While a number of these attacks were purely for the wealth these men transported with them, sometimes they were specifically called "insurrection against the king." Two men who resisted arrest and maltreated a man sent to arrest them were accused of insurrection. A Norfolk band under the leadership of John son of John Emmes abducted the king's assize justice, Stephen de Hales, and his fellow justices.[60] The most famous case of attacks on justices was the murder of Sir Roger Bellers by the Folville and the Coterel gangs.[61]

Altruistic Outlaws or Strong-Armed Robbers?

Did real outlaws rob from the rich and give to the poor? Did the legendary Robin Hood of the fourteenth century engage in such altruistic behavior?

The poems cite no specific aid to the poor. The only person receiving a charitable loan was the knight, Sir Richard at the Lee, and that money was given with payment expected and received. The potter was the only good yeoman to receive a reward for cooperation, but other townsmen clearly feared Robin Hood. At the close of the *Gest* come the only lines that hint at the tradition:

> Fore he was a good outlawe,
> And dyde pore men moch god.[62]

The first literary reference to any relationship between Robin Hood and the poor comes in 1632 in Martin Parker's *True Tale of Robin Hood*, in which he portrays the hero as the Earl of Huntingdon.[63] His model is perhaps closer to noblesse oblige than social banditry.

Medieval people did not have a romantic expectation about the liberality of bandits. Bandits could sometimes benefit them, but they could also be a scourge. They were useful to peasant communities in that they provided an opportunity for some illegal acquisition of movable property. Peasants joined with bands temporarily; they received bandits and their stolen goods in payment for sheltering them; and they bought their stolen goods at prices much below market value because such goods were hard to dispose of. As we have seen, however, bandits could also be a dreadful menace—killing and robbing the local population, demanding shelter, and interrupting routine trade.

Until 1521, the literary image of the outlaw, and Robin Hood in particular, was negative.[64] The first extant reference in *Piers Plowman* implies that Sloth had frivolous knowledge in the rhymes. Robert the Robber was also condemned in that work. John Ball wrote in a letter, "Chatise wel Hobbe the Robbere." In 1439 a petition in Parliament about a gang that went around terrorizing "and, in manere of Insurrection, went into the wodes and in that Contre, like as it hadde be Robynhode and his meyne."[65] Only in the sixteenth century, when the real problems of bandits were curtailed, did Hood become a hero.[66] Even in *A Gest of Robyn Hode* Sir Richard at the Lee is afraid of appearing before Robin Hood, although he protests that he has heard much good about him, and the king, too, has qualms when Robin Hood calls his men in from the forest.[67]

The jurors' response to robbers and burglars confirms the general fear and distaste felt for people engaging in these criminal activities. While normally only 23 percent of the indicted were convicted, 31 percent of robbers and burglars were. The jurors could tolerate homicide (12 percent convictions) because it was more often the result of direct fights between people who knew each other well and were defending their honor. But robbery and burglary were committed by strangers to the community, in stealth and often at night, and in criminal associations. Thus the crimes in which bandits engaged were among the most feared and hated.[68]

Bandits, however, did not have an entirely evil reputation among the public. As we have seen, they had something of a symbiotic relationship with everyone from peasants through aristocrats. Furthermore, bandits did sometimes attack common oppressors of the populace, and these acts brought public approval. Forty to fifty years after the Folvilles participated in the murder of Justice Bellers and the ransoming of Justice Willoughby, they had sufficient reputation to appear as heroes in *Piers Plowman*. Grace foretells the coming of the Antichrist and the weapons God's creatures will use against him. One of these is "Foleuyles laws": "duty of restoring by force ill-gotten gains to the defenceless or unfortunate."[69]

The Appeal of the Myth

If the attitude toward the real bandits was ambiguous and, on the whole, negative, medieval audiences completely enjoyed the poems and ballads. The historian J. C. Holt identified the following characteristics as the basis for their appeal to medieval audiences: "a roughly enforced and crudely conceived idea of justice and morality; a code of honesty; a good fight, and adventurous chase; the joke of trickery by disguise, the king *incognito*."[70]

The continued popularity of Robin Hood suggests a greater universality of appeal that goes beyond medieval audiences and suggests that the poems' themes have deep roots in our culture. For instance, the poems provide scenes of vicarious violence in fights and mutilations,[71] a common theme in medieval chronicles and poetry that is duplicated in modern popular culture. It is significant that the major poem in the cycle is called a "gest," for it resembles the earlier medieval gest literature, such as the *Song of Roland*, in its descriptions of personal combat, chivalric ideals, and the absence of female characters.

A second fantasy-fulfilling aspect is that Robin Hood can attack authority figures and be rewarded for it by the king. The officials he confronts are those who are perennially disliked and feared: corrupt judges, brutal law enforcement officials (the sheriff), hypocrites (monks who take vows of poverty but live in ostentatious wealth), and harsh creditors (the Abbot's treatment of Sir Richard at the Lee).[72] We now have other folk heroes who uncover these villains for us, such as investigative reporters, public advocates, and the occasional district attorney. We also have altered the occupations of the villains, although their roles remain the same: industrialists and bankers have replaced the abbot and politicians have replaced hypocritical clergy.

Hood, however, is not an omnipotent force that knows no limits or controls. While he mercilessly attacks corrupt local authority figures, he has a remarkable reverence for royal authority. One might say, in Freudian terms, that he takes on siblings but not the father. But even this reverence is ambiguous. He continually professes his respect and fear of the king and shows extreme loyalty to the king's seal.

> "I love no man in all the worlde
> So well as I do my kynge;
> Welcome is my lordes seale."

And yet in the same passages he has admitted to killing the king's deer and feasting the disguised king with his own venison. When Little John and Much the Miller kill the monk and page and take the message of Hood's capture to the king, they get away with their ruse and dupe the king's sheriff into letting them into the prison to get Hood. Needless to say, most men would be fined or hanged for poaching, and duping the king might easily result in the exaggerated punishment of drawing and quartering, which was reserved for treason. The king rather weakly acquiesces:

> "Speke no more of this mater," seid oure kyng.
> "But John has begyled us alle."[73]

Thus even the king is more a first to an equal than an absolute authority. Hood will serve him, but only for a year. Thereafter he will not serve, but he will continue to fear him.

Thus another universal element in Robin Hood's appeal is that he represents freedom writ large. Not only does he have no lord in the greenwood (important to the medieval audience), he has no parents, no wife, and no children, not even hunting dogs, much less pets. He considers himself loyal to his king on his own terms, the Virgin Mary (he does not even recognize the existence of a vengeful God), and his companions. Even when romance is added in the sixteenth century, it is in the form of a pretty mistress, Marian, rather than a wife. This addition has clung to the outlaw mystique and reappears with the gangster's moll and Bonnie and Clyde.

The myth presents a hero who, because of his athletic prowess and skill, manages to win lucrative games of skill and chance and narrowly escape danger. On all occasions when it is possible to introduce an archery contest, the balladeers do so. After banquets in the forest, wands are set up for the outlaws to shoot at. When Robin Hood meets Guy of Guisborne, they set up targets. As Robin Hood and Little John wander through the forest, they pass the time by shooting at targets. All of these are in addition to the official archery contests in Nottingham. While Robin Hood usually wins, anyone who is equally skilled, such as the potter, is admired and becomes an ally.

The theme of raw masculinity also appears in Robin Hood's knowledge of woodcraft and his excellence in hunting, quintessential to medieval definitions of manhood.[74] When Hood leaves the king's service, his act of defiance and reassertion of his domination of the greenwood is the killing of a famous hart.

> Robyn slewe a full grete harte;
> His horne than gan he blow,
> That all the outlawes of that forest
> That horne coud they knowe.[75]

He had mastered the wilds, shown contempt for the dreaded forest laws, and his reward is to eat daily from a prestigious form of protein to which even the nobility did not have unlimited access.

In order to mediate his pervasive violence and prowess in deadly sport, Robin Hood must have the qualities of courtesy and generosity, otherwise the hero would be too threatening and would become a villain. If even the king cannot control him, he must be able to temper his own wrath. The ordinary people in the audience must be exempt from acts of violence. Thus the yeoman and husbandman must come to no harm and their wives and daughters must not be violated; the balladeers explicitly exclude these groups from among the victims. While courtesy and generosity are qualities that dominate the romances of medieval nobility, their appeal was more general and became an integral part of the Robin Hood myth.

A final appealing characteristic of the Robin Hood ballads perhaps is less important to us now than it was in preindustrial Europe and America—the feasts. The whole of the *Gest* revolves around Robin Hood refusing to sit down to a meal until he has a guest. The meals that he hosts are very lavish for a preindustrial population: venison and other game (forbidden to the general population), dark beer and red wine (a luxury in England), and, best of all, plenty of good white bread.

> Anone before our kynge was set
> The fatte venyson,
> The good whyte brede, the good rede wyne,
> And thereto the fyne ale and brown.[76]

White bread is a universal theme found in hagiography, chronicles, poems, plays, and stories. It was the ultimate luxury to a society in which all ordinary bread was rye, oat, whole wheat, or a mixture of them. We have achieved the ultimate preindustrial fantasy about bread in our white, manufactured loaves. It is one of the great achievements of our industrialization.

The poems that survive about Robin Hood from the Middle Ages are realistic in many aspects of their portrayal of organized crime. The structure of the gang, with small units committing most of the crimes and the large band reserved for major encounters, is true to life, as are the techniques of crime and the internal organization of the gangs. For the most part, fictional and real bandits mirror the hierarchical model of society as a whole, selecting their leaders according to social rank and imitating noble and royal authority. The greatest divergence between the two is in their choice of victims. Hood insisted that he left the lower and middle ranks alone, but real bandits robbed from the peasants as well as the nobles and clergy because the ordinary people were better targets for daily necessities such as beer and bread. Nor were the bandits altruistic in sharing their loot.

Perhaps it would be better if a historic Robin Hood were never found, for in all probability he would be closer to the real bandits surveyed in this paper. As Bruce Rosenberg concluded from his research on Custer and the epic of defeat, the true historical character at the base of the myth is inevitably disappointing. He points not only to Custer, but also to such heroes as Lord Cardigan. The myth goes far beyond reality and takes on its own life in fulfilling the hopes and aspirations of its audience.[77] In the case of Robin Hood, the myth is an extremely powerful and appealing one.

Notes

I would like to thank the Newberry Library for its generous support while I worked on versions of this essay. I would also like to thank the community of scholars collected there who provided useful suggestions.

1. Quoted in *Rymes*, ed. R. B. Dobson and J. Taylor, pp. 1-6.

2. Ibid., p. 80.

3. Hope of finding a historical character has dominated the research of historians. Dobson and Taylor feel that there must have been a real person at the base of the tale. J. G. Bellamy, *Robin Hood: An Historical Enquiry* (Bloomington, Ind., 1985) has looked at the possibility of discovering a historical basis for the other characters. Folklorists, however, seem to take a more reasonable approach. W. E. Simeone, "Still More about Robin Hood," *Journal of American Folklore* 65 (1952), 420, concludes, "A historical figure may be at the matrix, and he may wear the tatters of a god, but certainly the legend has been built, ballad by ballad, overwhelmingly if not exclusively, by the ballad maker." See also his "Robin Hood and Some Other Outlaws," *Journal of American Folklore* 71 (1958), 28-31. M. J. C. Hodgart in *The Ballads* (New York, 1962), pp. 66-70, points out not only that a historical Robin Hood is hard to find, but also that only a very few of the ballads that purport to tell history can be tied to actual historical events and figures. On the audience for medieval ballads, see J. C. Holt, "The Origins and Audience of the Ballads of Robin Hood," *Past and Present* 18 (1969), 89-110; and more recently, idem., *Robin Hood: People's Hero or Lawless Marauder?* (London, 1982); and P. R. Coss, "Aspects of Cultural Diffusion in Medieval England," *Past and Present* 108 (1985), 70-77. See also R. H. Hilton, "The Origins of Robin Hood," *Past and Present* 14 (1958), 30-44; Maurice Keen, "Robin Hood—Peasant or Gentleman?" *Past and Present* 19 (1961), 7-15; idem, *The Outlaws of Medieval Legend* (London 1961); and J. C. Holt, "Robin Hood: Some Comments," *Past and Present* 19 (1961), 16-18. For a summary of the arguments of these various historians on the dating of the origins of the legend, see J. R. Maddicott, "The Birth and Setting of the Ballads of Robin Hood," *EngHR* 93 (1978), 276-99.

4. E. J. Hobsbawm, *Primitive Rebels* (Manchester, 1959), and idem., *Bandits* (London, 1969).

5. Barbara A. Hanawalt, *Crime and Conflict in English Communities, 1300-1348* (Cambridge, Mass., 1979), ch. 7. The crime statistics for the first half of the fourteenth century show that in periods of truce in the Hundred Years' War the number of cases increased. In Yorkshire, where continued war with the Scots caused unrest, the level of violent criminal indictments remained high. The Commons was well aware of the problem and complained about the returning veteran-felons in Parliament. For magnates in organized crime see my "Fur-Collar Crime: The Pattern of Crime among the Fourteenth-Century English Nobility," *Journal of Social History* 8 (1976), 1-18.

6. *Rymes*, ed. Dobson and Taylor, p. 7.

7. Ibid.

8. David C. Fowler, *A Literary History of the Popular Ballad* (Durham, N.C., 1968), has a discussion of popular minstrelsy, including a chapter on Robin Hood.

9. The jail delivery rolls are preserved in the Public Record Office in London under the classification of Justice Itinerant 3. They will be referred to in this text as Just. 3. The records used for this study are those from Norfolk, Northamptonshire, and Yorkshire for the years 1300-1400.

10. Hanawalt, *Crime and Conflict*, pp. 4-18.

11. For a more complete discussion, see Donald R. Cressy, *Criminal Organization: Its Elementary Forms* (London, 1972); and Marshall B. Clinard and Richard Quinney, *Criminal Behavior Systems* (New York, 1967).

12. Hanawalt, *Crime and Conflict*, pp. 188-90. In this study I used the simpler device of calling gangs of two, informal ones and gangs of three, formal ones. The present method is more sophisticated, since it is based on an analysis of criminal behavior (see ch. 3 of the same book for techniques of crime). In a study of recidivism, pp. 216-21, it was impossible to detect the presence of bandits.

13. The confessions of approvers are recorded in the coroners' rolls. These are preserved in the Public Record Office in London under the classification of Justice Itinerant 2. They will be referred to in this text as Just. 2. The series that I used for this study are those from Northamptonshire.

14. *A Gest of Robyn Hode*, verse 17, in *Rymes*, ed. Dobson and Taylor, p. 80.

15. *Rymes*, ed. Dobson and Taylor, p. 116. In *Robin Hood and the Monk*, verse 9, Robin Hood says that of all his men "I wil none have, / But Litull John shall beyre my bow." Likewise in the versions of *Robin Hood's Death* (pp. 134, 137), Little John is the sole companion.

16. *Gest*, in *Rymes*, ed. Dobson and Taylor, p. 107, verse 389.

17. When Robin Hood became fused in the May Day plays, both Maid Marian and Friar Tuck were added (*Rymes*, ed. Dobson and Taylor, p. 41).

18. Just. 3/78 m. 46. In another case (Just. 3/125 m. 9d.), Isabel, daughter of Stacie of Rudham, was accused, along with her husband and four other men, of holding Hertford bridge in Norfolk and committing robberies there. In general, women accounted for 10 percent of the indictments, so their role in banditry was half that of their ordinary record.

19. Of all gangs, 21 percent had a kin group within them. Brothers dominated the kinship groupings with 47 percent and spouses were next with 33 percent. Fathers and sons accounted for 17 percent and brothers and sisters for only 3 percent.

20. Barbara Hanawalt Westman, "The Peasant Family and Crime in Fourteenth-Century England," *Journal of British Studies* 13 (1974), 1-18. In informal associations only 19 percent had kin groups, and in these husband and wife and father and son combinations dominated.

21. James B. Given, *Society and Homicide in Thirteenth-Century England* (Palo Alto, Calif., 1977), p. 121, found that the accused had a mean value of chattels worth over 8s. He interprets the evidence to indicate that they were at the bottom of society, but failed to realize that that figure represents the movable goods rather than the rents and properties. Since 10s. in chattels (movable goods) was the cutoff for taxation, these people would have been at least in the middling group. In a record linkage project I found that most of the people indicted in jail delivery were from the well-established, prosperous village families (Barbara A. Hanawalt, "Community Conflict and Social Control: Crime in the Ramsey Abbey Villages," *Medieval Studies* 39 [1977], 402-23).

22. On clergy in crime, see Hanawalt, *Crime and Conflict*, pp. 136-38. A thirty-seven-member gang with a similar composition worked around Knaresborough (Just. 3/74/4 ms. 1-2).

23. Hanawalt, *Crime and Conflict*, pp. 196-97.

24. Only 28 percent committed crimes with fellow villagers or family; 26 percent chose their associates from one to ten miles away, 33 percent from ten to fifteen miles, and 13 percent from fifteen or more.

25. Just. 2/18 m. 35.

26. Ibid.

27. *Gest,* verses 434-50, in *Rymes,* ed. Dobson and Taylor, pp. 110-11.

28. *Gest,* verses 397-408, 424-26, in *Rymes,* ed. Dobson and Taylor, pp. 107-10.

29. Verse 15, in *Rymes,* ed. Dobson and Taylor, pp. 115-22. In the end John rescues Robin Hood from the Sheriff's prison through a ruse and a number of homicides.

30. Verses 2-4, in *Rymes,* ed. Dobson and Taylor, pp. 134-35.

31. Just. 3/79/1 ms. 5-9. See also Just. 374/4 ms. 1-2; KB 27/248 m. 10; Just. 3/78 m. 44; King's Bench 27/334 m. 29; Just. 3/49/2 m. 4. R. H. Hilton, *A Medieval Society: The West Midlands at the End of the Thirteenth Century* (London, 1966), pp. 256-58, identifies Sir Malcom Musard as a leader of a band. He could trace his lineage back to the times of William the Conqueror.

32. E. L. G. Stones, "The Folvilles of Ashby-Folville, Leicestershire, and Their Associates in Crime, 1326-41," *TRHS,* 5th ser., 7 (1957), 134-35; original in KB 27/307 m. 27.

33. *Gest,* verse 391, in *Rymes,* ed. Dobson and Taylor, p. 107.

34. H. T. Hewitt, *The Organization of War under Edward III* (Oxford, 1975), pp. 173-75.

35. Stones, "Folvilles," p. 134.

36. Just. 3/119. Other examples are Just. 3/78 ms. 13, 20, 22, 48. The public of the day was very concerned about the problems of returning veteran-felons. In a petition to the king in 1327, the Commons complained that homicides and robberies increased because of the abuse of granting pardons. The king had responded to the problem through repeated statutes but had not stopped the practice. The king and the Commons were right to be worried about the problem of veterans, because homicide had increased in the 1340s and so, too, had crime in general. Pardoned felons did appear in the records increasingly in the 1340s, particularly in Yorkshire, where many were discharged from the armies formed to fight the Scots. Hanawalt, *Crime and Conflict,* pp. 236-38.

37. *Gest,* Third Fytte, in *Rymes,* ed. Dobson and Taylor, pp. 89- 93.

38. J. J. Jusserand, *English Wayfaring Life in the Middle Ages,* trans. L. T. Smith (London, 1961), p. 37; Just. 3/49/1 m. 43d.; Just. 3/51/3 m. 2. The usual arguments occurred over division of spoils and appeared in coroners' inquests (R. F. Hunnisett, "Pleas of the Crown and the Coroner," *BIHR* 32 [1949], 117-37).

39. For a discussion of torture of approvers, see Hanawalt, *Crime and Conflict,* pp. 36-37; Just. 3/48 m. 11; Just. 3/49/1 m. 27.

40. *Gest,* verses 298-316, in *Rymes,* ed. Dobson and Taylor, pp. 101-2.

41. Just. 1/764 ms. 2d., 3. This was a commission of trailbaston.

42. Just. 2/110 m. 4.

43. Just. 3/99 m. 1; *Bedfordshire Coroners' Rolls,* trans. R. F. Hunnisett, Bedfordshire Historical Society 41 (1960), pp. 20-21. In this last case the sheriff's posse was following and eventually beheaded the felon.

44. Verses 67-72, in *Rymes,* ed. Dobson and Taylor, p. 119.

45. Francis J. Child, *The English and Scottish Popular Ballads* (Boston, 1882), 3:25-26.

46. Just. 3/49/1 m. 30. See also Just. 1/632 m. 96; Just. 3/75 ms. 13-16; Just. 3/49/1 m. 44d. *Bedfordshire Coroners' Rolls,* p. 109.

47. *Robin Hood and the Monk,* verse 1, in *Rymes,* ed. Dobson and Taylor, p. 120.

48. *Early English Lyrics: Amorous, Divine, Moral and Trivial,* ed. E. K. Chambers and F. Sidgwick (London, 1966), p. 41.

49. *Gest,* verses 14, 15, in *Rymes,* ed. Dobson and Taylor, p. 79.

50. *Robin and the Monk*, verses 41, 52, in *Rymes*, ed. Dobson and Taylor, pp. 119, 121.

51. *Gest*, verse 10, in *Rymes*, ed. Dobson and Taylor, p. 79.

52. Given, *Society and Homicide*, p. 117.

53. See Hanawalt, *Crime and Conflict*, pp. 65-90, 190-91, for comparative figures.

54. *Court Rolls of the Manor of Wakefield*, ed. and trans. W. P. Baildon, John Lister, and J. W. Walker, The Yorkshire Archaeological Society Record Series 47 (1917), p. 148.

55. Just. 3/99 m. 1. See also Just. 3/48, 3/18 m. 3, 3/164 m. 37.

56. Just. 3/81/2 m. 16.

57. Just. 3/79/1 m. 19; Just. 3/81/2 m. 55. Henry de Roston of Scarborough and six men of the city were tried in one instance, and in 1391 William March of Scarborough and his band were accused of the same (Just. 3/176 m. 122). William of Coventry, a famous outlaw, and his band took over Foxele market (Just. 2/111 m. 16).

58. *Gest*, verses 428-29, in *Rymes*, ed. Dobson and Taylor, p. 110.

59. Verses 24, 25, in *Rymes*, ed. Dobson and Taylor, p. 117.

60. Just. 3/182 m. 1, 3/164 m. 37.

61. Stones, "Folvilles"; J. G. Bellamy, "The Coterel Gang: An Anatomy of a Band of Fourteenth-Century Criminals," *EngHR* 79 (1964), 698-717.

62. Verse 456, in *Rymes*, ed. Dobson and Taylor, p. 112.

63. Holt, "Ballads of Robin Hood," p. 91.

64. Maddicott, "Ballads of Robin Hood," p. 294, points out that Henry Knighton expressed some reluctant admiration for the Folvilles' participation in the murder of Sir Roger Bellers. The first really strong expression of approval of Robin Hood comes from the chronicler John Major in *Historia Majoris Britaniae* (1521), in which he described him as a historical personage who was generally better than his usual sort: "The robberies of this man I condemn, but of all robbers he was the most humane and the chief." Major is quoted in *Rymes*, ed. Dobson and Taylor, p. 5. Holt, "Ballads of Robin Hood," p. 92, shows that even in the seventeenth-century traditions he is sometimes shown as generous to the poor and sometimes not.

65. Holt, "Ballads of Robin Hood," p. 93.

66. *Rymes*, ed. Dobson and Taylor, pp. 1-3.

67. *Gest*, verses 28 and 396, in *Rymes*, ed. Dobson and Taylor, pp. 81, 107. Peter Burke, *Popular Culture in Early Modern Europe* (New York, 1978), p. 167, also notes this about the Robin Hood stereotype.

68. Hanawalt, *Crime and Conflict*, pp. 55-62, explains the factors in convictions.

69. R. H. Bowers, "Foleuyles Lawes" (*Piers Plowman*, C.XXII. 247), *Notes and Queries*, n.s. 8 (1961), 327. Jacques Mesrine, France's recent "Robin Hood," gained his reputation by acting out some of the classics from the myth: prison break, successful kidnapping of an industrialist and a chief judge of a Paris appeals court, disguises, and finally the betrayal of his hideout and the final shoot-out. He added a modern touch to the old stereotype by giving interviews with a leftist flavor criticizing French justice and society.

70. Holt, "Ballads of Robin Hood," p. 101.

71. *Robin Hood and Guy of Guisborne*, in *Rymes*, ed. Dobson and Taylor, pp. 141-45, is perhaps the most gruesome of the combat scenes.

72. Burke, *Popular Culture*, p. 166, sees legends as allowing ordinary people to dream of revenge on these authority figures. Not all of the clergy were bad in the Robin Hood ballads. The prior of the monastery begged for mercy in Sir Richard's case, saying that it would be a pity to disinherit a knight in the way the abbot planned (*Gest*, verses 88-90, in *Rymes*, ed. Dobson and Taylor, p. 85). The Robin Hood poems are not anticlerical or antichurch; they are against corrupt clergy, a common theme at the time.

73. *Gest*, verses 385, 386, and *Robin Hood and the Monk*, verse 122, in *Rymes*, ed. Dobson and Taylor, pp. 107-9, 115-25.

74. Barbara A. Hanawalt, "Men's Games, King's Deer: Poaching in Medieval England," *Journal of Medieval and Renaissance Studies* 18 (1988), 175-93, explores the importance of hunting in male identity and the games that poachers and foresters played. The *Gest* portrays one of these games. The disguised king and Hood hunt the king's deer together. While they consume the venison, Hood boasts to the king that he frequently poaches.

75. *Gest*, verse 447, in *Rymes*, ed. Dobson and Taylor, p. 111.

76. *Gest*, verse 393, in *Rymes*, ed. Dobson and Taylor, p. 107. See Hanawalt, "Men's Games, King's Deer," for a discussion of the prestige of venison as a food for feasts.

77. Bruce Rosenberg, *Custer and the Epic of Defeat* (University Park, Pa., 1974).

CHAPTER 9

John Ball's Letters
Literary History and Historical Literature
Richard Firth Green

P ierce the Ploughman's Crede (c. 1394) is hardly one of the more frequently read Middle English poems, but it contains one particularly
striking passage, a description of the life of a fourteenth-century
plowman. This is how that description is characterized by one commentator:

> [The] lines enshrine a moment of truth caught with vivid intensity
> and in the cruel details—the ragged ploughman guiding his ex-
> hausted, half-starved oxen, the patient bare-foot wife marking the
> snow with her blood-stained footprints, the little child weeping in
> its "crumb-bowl" at the end of the furrow—we are spared nothing of
> the hopeless distress suffered by a tiller of the soil. [1]

Such a passage could, in my judgment, have been written by either a historian or a literary scholar (even if the elegance of its prose might lead one
to suppose the former). In fact, though it appears in a festschrift for a distinguished historian, it is the work of an English professor, Beatrice White,
and thus offers a useful vantage point for surveying the borderland between the two disciplines. It is not difficult to imagine how such a march-
er castle built between the domains of literary scholar and historian might
be vulnerable to attack from either side.

   Let us begin with the undisciplined ranks of the literary critics. *Pierce
the Ploughman's Crede*, they will say, is first and foremost a literary artifact whose relationship with real life is at best highly problematical. The
more disorderly battalions in this army will insist that such an artifact has
no existence outside the reader's mind, that it must be remade at each re-
reading, and that no reading can lay claim to objective reference because
authorial intention, rhetorical conventions, and even historical context are
quite as much subjective constructs as the work itself; since, moreover,
the construing subject is inevitably heterogeneous and fragmented, critical
reading can never do more than scoop contingent meaning from the Her-
aclitean flux, and then sit back to watch it trickle between the fingers.
Such battalions have, to be sure, won few recruits among medievalists, but
even some of our more grizzled critical campaigners might agree that authorial intention is a tricky concept, and that White is rash to claim un-
equivocally that "the author of *Pierce the Ploughman's Crede . . .* was

deeply resentful of the bitter misery endured by the poor."[2] As Jill Mann's study of the far better known portraits in the *General Prologue* to *The Canterbury Tales* has taught us,[3] the proportion of rhetorical convention in such a depiction is likely to be high, its author turning more readily to literary stereotype than first-hand observation for his authenticating details, and having in any case no reason to conceive of dispassionate mimesis as a nobler artistic goal than affective moralization. Read in context, moreover, the passage White quotes is certainly open to other interpretations.

The poem, which reveals clear Wycliffite sympathies, is mainly concerned to expose the abuses of the mendicant orders, and its detailed depiction of patient poverty appears to owe far more to rhetorical contrast than to meticulous realism. Thus, the central character in what George Kane has called this "ghastly vignette"[4] must be formally opposed to the Dominican friar with his "face as fat as a full bledder, . . . Þat all wagged his flesh as a quyk myre,"[5] while even such lifelike details as the plowman's patched and knobbly shoes from which his toes stick out or his wife's bloody stumbling, "barfote on Þe bare iis" (line 436), serve primarily to remind us that

> Frances bad his breÞeren barfote to wenden;
> Nou han Þei bucled shon for bleynynge of her heles,
> And hosen in harde weder y-hamled by Þe ancle.
> (lines 298-300)

Antifraternal satire often mocks the friars' concern for their dress, and we may wonder whether we are any safer under such conditions in taking a Lollard's plowman at face value than in regarding its contrary, a Dominican's depiction of Jack Upland in *Friar Daw's Reply*, as a realistic portrayal of a typical smallholder:

> What meeneÞ Þi tipet, Iakke, as longe as a stremer,
> Þat hangiÞ longe bihinde and kepiÞ Þee not hoot?
> An hool cloiÞ of scarlet may not make [Þee] a gowne
> And Þe cloiÞ of oo man my3te hele half a doseyne.
> Whi is Þi gowne, Iakke, widder Þan Þi cote,
> And Þi cloke al aboue as round as a belle,
> SiÞ lasse my3te serue to kepe Þee from coold?[6]

White's gaunt figure of the plowman, then, seems to stand less as a memorial to feudal oppression of the poor than, in Kane's words, "for a life in whole accord with spiritual values by contrast with that of self-indulgence exemplified by the friars."[7]

If even the conservative ranks of literary scholarship might be expected to tilt at White's faith in the historical realism of such a passage, the social historian's forces will be apt to show it equal hostility. The quanto-historians in particular, to borrow Gertrude Himmelfarb's term, will oppose any attempt to privilege its evidentiary status, complaining not only that it is partial and particular, but that its very imaginative power is likely to distort conclusions based on more trustworthy, if less seductive, witnesses. To cite Peter Laslett's well-known example, "anyone who supposes that English women married in their early teens in Shakespeare's day and gives as the reason the marriage of Juliet in *Romeo and Juliet* at the age of thirteen is making a mistake so serious that he can be said to have mis-under-stood the whole of the familial system of our country at the time, since that time and before that time."[8] No doubt, then, Laslett would have been equally incensed at the idea of anyone drawing similar conclusions about family life in Chaucer's day from the Wife of Bath's claim that her first marriage, "at chirche dore," occurred when she was twelve.[9] Of course the bride's age in these two examples is a particularly exact and therefore falsifiable detail, and it is hard to imagine how the plowman's portrait in *Pierce the Ploughman's Crede* might be similarly misapplied; one does not have to be a professional historian to recognize that the description of his three squalling children is somewhat weaker evidence for, say, the typical size of peasant families than is the testimony of wills or manorial court rolls. For the quanto-historians, "the historical value of literature," as Keith Thomas has recently put it, "is thus reduced merely to illustrating what is known already."[10] Denied the status of hard evidence, our plowman's portrait merely provides a bit of local color to set alongside the miniatures from the Luttrell Psalter or the Duc de Berri's *Très Riches Heures* in an attempt to breathe some vicarious life back into the world we have lost.

From what I have said, we might suppose that the main bone of contention between historian and literary scholar is simply a matter of the treatment of evidence. "You historians are so literal-minded," complains the literary critic; "You literary people are so impressionistic," responds the historian. In fact this difference is largely illusory. John Fleming has charged David Knowles with obtuseness for not recognizing that when, on the eve of the reformation, the abbot of Fountains wrote to the head of his order at Citeaux that he was sending him a shipment of roses and lilies, he was "simply using the elementary literary technique of allegory."[11] Such a slip (if indeed it is one—the abbot of Fountains would not have been the first to make token acknowledgment of an obligation, whether with flowers or peppercorns) is not, however, fundamental. Fleming and Knowles may bring different kinds of experience to bear on the incident, but it should, in principle at least, be possible to arbitrate between them; such differences are not irreconcilable. Nor is the picking of textual locks a skill peculiar to literary scholars. Anyone who has looked at all carefully at legal records from late medieval England will know how creatively they represent the truth, and most historians are far more adept at recognizing such fiction in the archives than are their literary colleagues. Few literary critics, for instance, on learning that Sir Thomas Malory "feloniously broke out of [Colchester] jail with force and arms, to wit swords, pikes and daggers,"[12] stop to ask themselves what might have happened to any jailer foolish enough to report that his charge had walked out of the front gate. Though even an experienced researcher can sometimes be caught out taking a witness at his word,[13] historians by and large will treat their sources with every bit as much circumspection as good literary scholars.

One might argue that in some ways the gap between the two disciplines has been narrowing in recent years. Where at least it is not being used to justify textual "appropriation" or "subversion" or "transgression" (all too often euphemisms for self-promotion), the insistence in modern critical circles upon the absolute contingency of literary value carries with it the implication that any interpretative enterprise, however approximate and provisional, must acknowledge the primacy of social context in the re-creation of meaning; in the case of older literature this cannot but legitimate attempts to read it in its historical setting. To be sure, this strategy will hardly seem novel to most medievalists, who are constantly reminded by the archaic language of the poems they study of their status as historical artifacts. Unimpressed in the past by the self-deceptive ahistoricism of the more extreme new critics, they may be excused for deprecating the novelty of the "new historicism" and "new philology" as so much reinventing of wheels. A second characteristic of recent critical theorizing, an insistence on the textual basis of all intellectual experience, has tended to break down the discrete categories into which literary critics and historians have been accustomed to sort their primary materials. No longer can we safely distinguish chronicle from romance on the assumption that one relates fact and and the other fiction. We may recognize how far such thinking has penetrated academic discourse when we discover that the bald assertion that "there is no fundamental difference between a 'literary' source and a 'non-literary' source" is made, not by Paul de Man, but by Keith Thomas.[14] This perception has led to considerable cross-border raiding, and it is surely a sign of the times that last year witnessed a historian citing Langland's portrait of Lady Meed in support of his theory of bastard feudalism[15] and a previous editor of Langland using the work of Walsingham to exemplify the power of interpretative models.[16]

If historian and literary scholar cannot be easily separated on the basis of the way they interpret evidence, or even on grounds of the evidence they choose to interpret, there is, I believe, a fundamental distinction to be found in the priority each would assign to text and context. The difference is perhaps largely temperamental. As Natalie Zemon Davis has written, "What I have noticed in past exchange with critic/scholars of literature is that at its end we want to explain something different. The critic will return to his or her literary text, its author, relations around the text, or the nature of a genre; I to a set of events, to cultural, economic, or political connections, or to an actor in one of these settings."[17] To put it another way, for the literary scholar the work under investigation will be the primary focus and everything unearthed in the course of research will relate back to it; for the historian, on the other hand, the work itself, even if it is a work as intriguing as the record of Martin Guerre's trial, is only a means to understanding something else. This helps to explain why, while literary scholars fuss obsessively over their primary texts, editing and reediting the works of major authors every few years, historians are apparently unruffled by the hoary antiquity of some of their major sources (like the *Rotuli Parliamentorum* or the *Statutes of the Realm*) and will at a pinch refer to authorities, like Hearne or Dugdale, who make even the early volumes in the Rolls Series look up-to-date.

Which brings me to the main texts I wish to consider here. Two fourteenth-century chroniclers published in the Rolls Series, Henry Knighton and Thomas Walsingham, preserve letters that purport to have been written by John Ball at the time of the Peasants' Revolt. These letters, so intimately associated with one of the most dramatic events of the late Middle Ages, have traditionally been the preserve of the historian, but since two of them make reference to *Piers Plowman* and all but one contain scraps of verse, they have occasionally caught the attention of literary commentators as well. They thus occupy a significant position in the ever-widening no-man's-land between the two disciplines. For historians they offer precious clues to the aims of one of the revolt's most important leaders. For literary scholars they offer dramatic examples of a minor literary genre, variously categorized as estates satire, complaint literature, or the literature of popular protest. In simple terms, discussion of such literature has generally been restricted to the question of whether it should be seen as expressing a potentially explosive reaction to genuine social injustice or as conventional and essentially conservative moralization. Perhaps the best spokesman for the first point of view is the late Rossell Hope Robbins: "In Ball's poem, a typical complaint, which could be found in the books or on the lips of any orthodox cleric or layman, was turned into a call for action"; [18] and for the second, George Kane: "For Robbins that prayer is 'a summons to man the barricades'; more accurately it is a commonplace of apocalyptic thinking. It would be sounder not to romanticize John Ball."[19] We shall be returning to this debate later, but for the moment I should like to approach John Ball's letters as the narrowest of literary scholars, focusing on them for their own sake, to see what they may be able to tell us about themselves.

Let us begin with the comparatively simple questions of authenticity and authorship. After what I have said of the greater persnicketiness of literary scholars about textual matters, it is somewhat chastening to have to admit that a careless slip in the Brown-Robbins *Index of Middle English Verse* has introduced an unnecessary complication into the question of textual authority. The identification of the source for the verses in the

John Ball letters as Stow's *Annales*[20] has led even a normally scrupulous scholar like Siegfried Wenzel to write, "Whether John Ball ever spoke or wrote these lines is of course anybody's guess, given the late date of the records that have preserved them."[21] Though the Robbins-Cutler supplement to the *Index* partially corrects this error, it still leaves Stow at the head of the list of authorities and even adds to the confusion by suggesting that both the earlier chronicles give all the letters: "text preserved in early chronicles, such as Walsingham and Knighton, and followed in most later chronicles."[22]

To set the record straight then, one letter attributed to Ball is preserved in Thomas Walsingham's *Historia Anglicana,* and five others, two of which appear under Ball's name and the remainder under transparent pseudonyms, are preserved in Henry Knighton's *Chronicon.*[23] Both Walsingham and Knighton were eyewitnesses of the revolt, and both their accounts are preserved by unimpeachable witnesses: the first in British Library, MS Royal 13 E. IX, written around 1400 at Walsingham's own abbey of St. Albans,[24] and the second in British Library, MS Cotton Tiberius C. VII, written in the late fourteenth century and owned by Knighton's house at Leicester.[25] Among major fourteenth-century literary works, only John Gower's is represented by manuscripts of comparable authenticity. While there is a reliable transcription of the Walsingham letter in Kenneth Sisam's anthology, *Fourteenth-Century Verse and Prose,*[26] for the Knighton letters we have been forced to rely on Joseph Lumby's edition, published by the Rolls Series in 1895; this edition does not inspire much confidence and thankfully is soon to be superseded.[27] For the purpose of this chapter I have provided transcripts of all six letters in an appendix.

The question of Ball's authorship of the letters remains, of course, a more open one—though still hardly "anybody's guess." The strongest evidence in favor of it is its corroboration by two independent contemporary witnesses.[28] There is no reason to suspect collaboration between Walsingham and Knighton, yet both claim that Ball wrote letters, and the specimens they offer exhibit extensive parallels. Many of the phrases in the Walsingham piece find echoes in one or another of the Knighton letters: both chroniclers give versions of the couplet "Iohan þe Mullere haþ ygrounde smal, smal, smal; / þe Kynges sone of heuene schal paye for al"; both mention not only Piers the Plowman, but also the character Hobbe the Robber and the injunction to "do wel and bettre," details that may well have been taken from Langland's poem; the names John (or Jack) Miller, Carter, and Trueman appear in both; finally, Walsingham's statement that Ball sent the commons of Essex a certain letter, "ad hortandum eos ut incepta perficerent," is echoed by the exhortation, "þat 3e make a gode ende of þat 3e haue begunnen" in Knighton's second and fourth letters.[29] Of course, Knighton appears to regard Jack Miller, Jack Carter, and Jack Trueman as real, rather than pseudonymous, leaders of the revolt and presents their words as speeches, apparently made at Smithfield, rather than actual letters: "Jakke Mylner alloquitur socios sic . . ." He does, on the other hand, identify Ball's two letters as such ("Exemplar epistole Johannis Balle" and "Prima epistola Johannis Balle"). To be set against this is Walsingham's clear implication that Ball adopted pseudonyms, since his own "Littera Johannis Balle" begins "Iohon Schep [i.e., "shepherd," or "pastor"] . . . greteth wel . . ." Some mysteries still remain. How did a canon of Leicester, by no means a major center of sedition, get his hands on copies of five of Ball's letters, when a monk of St. Albans, the town where Ball was executed, acquired only one? And why are there traces of northern dialect in a number of the letters?[30] Against the supposition that they might be forgeries put about for propaganda purposes, however, is the very obscurity of their contents; one might imagine that forged letters would be closer in tone and import to the sermons that Walsingham and Froissart put into Ball's mouth. In sum, the balance of probability does seem to favor Dobson's conclusion that all six letters were written by one man, and that that man was John Ball.[31]

In turning from the circumstances surrounding the preservation of these letters to the letters themselves, we enter a far murkier world. Walsingham describes his example as "aenigmatibus plenam" (full of riddles), and what a contemporary found obscure is unlikely to appear crystal clear to a commentator five hundred years later. As Dobson argues, attempts to read them as political allegory (Hobbe the Robber standing, for instance, for the treasurer Robert Hales) are unconvincing.[32] On the other hand, Norman Cohn's millenarian interpretation, evoking a final great battle between the poor and their oppressors, does not seem to me to be much more firmly rooted in the actual texts.[33] I believe these letters do in fact contain substantial clues to the way they should be read, certainly enough to justify the explication de texte I am about to attempt.

Let us begin with the last of them, Knighton's fifth letter. Some time ago Rossell Hope Robbins pointed out that a perfectly orthodox version of the rhyme in this letter occurs in Bodley, MS Rawlinson D. 893, fol. 75r, where the verses simply cite the ubiquity of the seven deadly sins as evidence that God will soon destroy the world.[34] Ball's version differs in reversing the order of Sloth and Envy and omitting, perhaps for obvious reasons, Wrath altogether; it also drops the final millenarian couplet and, in Robbins's view, turns criticism into subversion by adding the line "God do bote, for nowe is tyme." Macray's catalogue suggests that this copy is from the late fourteenth century, but it certainly preserves a rhyme that in some form predates the Peasants' Revolt, since a third version, in which the sins are given their Latin names, the attributes of lechery and gluttony are reversed, the order is completely changed (pride and covetousness are numbers six and seven), and the final couplet is missing, appears in a manuscript that can be firmly dated to before 1372.[35] Yet a fourth version, headed "Ðe Prophecia," and beginning "When pryde is moste in prys," mentions only the first three sins (to which it adds theft) and concludes "þenne schall englonde mys-chewe";[36] it is preserved in two British Library manuscripts (Royal 17 B. XVII, fol. 2v and Addit. 8151, fol. 200v).[37] The original poem to which these four versions bear witness has evidently suffered a certain amount of corruption, in part no doubt because it circulated orally and in part because those who quote it are adapting it to their own particular purposes. The purpose for which at least one of its copyists wanted it is quite clear: the manuscript made before 1372 contains the preaching notes of a Franciscan friar called John of Grimestone, and the rhyme is one of 246 such verse items in his collection.[38] The Bodleian version is on a single leaf, perhaps once a flyleaf, bound in a collection of miscellanea, so that its provenance cannot be established with certainty; however it seems likely to have come from either a preacher's handbook or a manual of private devotions.[39] Both British Library manuscripts contain devotional material.[40]

We shall be returning to the phrase, "nowe is tyme," but for the moment the only other point to make about this fifth letter is that its emphasis on "trewthe" ("stonde manlyche togedyr in trewthe, and helpez trewthe, and trewthe schal helpe owe") is echoed in the *Anonimalle Chronicle's* story that the rebels took as their "wache worde" the phrase "Wyth kynge Richarde and wyth the trew communes."[41] A similar parallel between Ball's exhortations and chronicle accounts of the revolt can be found in his injunction (appearing in both Knighton's second letter and the Walsingham letter) "þat Hobbe Robbyoure be wele chastysed for lesyng of 3oure grace." Knighton himself tells how the mob burning down Gaunt's palace of the Savoy threw a looter into the flames, "saying they were worshippers of truth and justice, not robbers and thieves" (*dicentes Zelatores veritatis et justitiae, non fures aut latrones,* 2:135).

Another of the letters that lays emphasis on the quality of truth is Knighton's third. Here too the verse, in this case ascribed to Jakke Trewman, is not original with Ball; the quatrain, though with its first two lines reversed, occurs in two other manuscripts. The version closest to Ball's is found along with several other similar verses in B.L., MS Harley 2316, fol. 26v, a fourteenth-century collection of miracles and moral exempla, compiled, possibly by a Dominican, for preaching purposes.

> Now goot falshed in eueri flok
> And trewthe is sperd vnder a lok;
> Now no man may comen 3er to,
> But yef he singge *si dedero.*[42]

A second version appears in a manuscript we have already met, B.L., MS Royal 17 B. XVII, fol. 99r. [43] The first two lines of yet another poem are closely related to these two:

> Now is loue and lewte shet vndir lok,
> Falshode and flateryng berith the bell in euery flok.[44]

The main item in the manuscript is an English treatise called the *Memoriale credentium* (fols. 7r-106v), but the immediate context of this poem resembles that of the verses in the Rawlinson fragment (lists of the ten commandments, five wits, etc.). The phrase "to sing *si dedero*" is widespread,[45] occurring in the early-fourteenth-century poem, the *Simonie* (48), in Gower's *Vox Clamantis* (3.4.234), in Lydgate's *Isopes Fabules* (327), in *Peter Idley's Instructions to His Son* (560), and in the morality plays the *Castle of Perseverance* (879) and *Mankind* (456).[46] It is worth noting that the context for a number of these citations is legal venality and that a marginal gloss on the Harley version of the verses appropriated by Ball reads "contra falsos iudices." Lawyers were, after all, a particularly prominent target of the Peasants' Revolt.[47]

I have not found quite as precise a parallel for the second verse in Knighton's third letter, but the phrase "Trew love is away" has echoes in a number of verses. One might, for instance, compare the following couplet from the *Fasciculus Morum*, an early-fourteenth-century preaching manual, apparently of Franciscan origin:

> Trewe loue in herbers spryngeth in may,
> Bote trewe loue of herte went is away;[48]

or these lines, apparently translating a Latin original:

> Symonie is aboue,
> & awey is trwloue;[49]

or these dating from about 1360, from B.L., MS Harley 7322, fols. 145r-146v, a fourteenth-century collection of "moralized tales and expository discourses evidently intended for the use of preachers":[50]

> Loue is out of lond iwent;
> Defaute of loue þis lond haþ shent.[51]

I shall come back to John of Bath and his "Speke, spende and spede," but for now let us turn to the verses in the Walsingham letter.

I know of no close parallel for the first couplet (on John the Miller),[52] but the next three and a half lines are a variant on a well-known set of proverbs.[53] The nearest in both form and date to Ball's verses appear in two sources we have already met: in Friar John of Grimestone's preaching notes of 1372[54] and in the preaching miscellany that contains the *si dedero* quatrain.[55] Of these, the Harley version is the closer:

> He is wys 3at kan be war or him be wo;
> He is wys 3at lovet his frend and ek his fo;
> He is wys 3at havet i-now and kan seyn, "ho!"
> He is wys 3at kan don wel, and doeth al so.[56]

Grimestone differs significantly only in his last line, "He is wis þat dot3 ay
wel an seit ay so," a variant found also in a fifteenth-century version in
B.L., MS Harley 116, fol. 170v,[57] which in other ways, such as line order, is
rather more distant. Here, more clearly than in the parallel adduced by
Robbins, we can see how Ball adapted stock material. His is the only version that reads "do wel and bettre" (confirmation, if any were needed, that
this is a conscious Langlandian allusion), and he seems, moreover, to have
deliberately changed, for rather obvious reasons, the pacific injunction to
love both friend and foe (the later version has "þer yeue betwene frend and
foo") into the more menacing "Knoweth 3our freende fro 3our foo." Ball's
version is also the only one with the line "sekeþ pees, and hold 3ou ce-
rinne," which Kane (glossing "seek peace, keep yourselves in peace") cites
as an example of the unrevolutionary nature of the letters;[58] it seems to
me, however, quite possible to give the first phrase a slightly different emphasis, "Strive for peace" (see *MED sechen* v. 6[a]), and to see it as a quite
conventional expression of one of the fundamental principles of the just
war.[59]

One other phrase in the Walsingham letter looks like an echo of some
kind: the injunction to "bee war of gyle in borugh." Although I have found
no specific parallel, one might compare the following lines from a carol
preserved in a fifteenth-century manuscript from Bury St. Edmunds (MS
Sloane 2593, fol. 5b):

> Coweytise in herte is lent;
> Ryght and resoun awey is went;
> Man, bewar thou be not schent;
> Gyle wil thi herte slo.
> Now haght gyle get hym gre,
> Bothe in town and in cete;
> Gyle goth with gret mene,
> With men of lawe and othere mo.[60]

Once again we might note the attack on the venality of lawyers, though
this is at best only implicit in Ball's phrase.

Of all the scraps of verse in these letters the most elusive is that in
Knighton's first letter (with its reprise, evidently somewhat corrupted, in
the fourth). The introductory reference to the mill with its four sails and
its post standing in steadfastness suggests that these lines may echo a lost
poem in which the sails of a windmill were allegorized as the four qualities of Might, Right, Will, and Skill. Be that as it may, the rhyming of
"might" and "right" is prominent in a poem called the "Sayings of the
Four Philosophers," which was, according to Wenzel, "of great popularity
with medieval preachers, writers, and audiences."[61] As recounted by the
Speculum Christiani (c.1400),[62] a king having enquired of four philosoph-

ers, "be what cause tho myshaps fellen [more] in the peple in his tyme than in tymes of predescessours," is given rhymed answers by each one in turn; the first philosopher replies that "Myght es ryght . . . Light es nyght . . . Fyght es flight."[63] A slightly different version in the Auchinleck manuscript offers these gnomic tercets as a reason "[Whi] Engelond is brouht adoun," and glosses the first line, "For miht is riht, the lond is laweles" (clxxxvi). [64] Slightly closer to the Ball verses (in that it adds "will" to "might" and "right") is a quatrain appearing in a manuscript from Durham (B.L., MS Harley 4894, fol. 78r), containing the sermons of Master Robert Ripon (c. 1400):

> When myght and will and ryght wer ane,
> Þen was welthe in ilk a wane.
> Bot sen myght want will and ryght.
> hase ben sorow day and nyght.[65]

Finally, the rhyme "skill" and "will" is found in some lines, possibly proverbial,[66] in a poem of religious provenance on abuses of the law:

> werk not after wil for 3e know wel be skil
> þt þe on side haþ truþe and þt o[þ]er tresoun
> & þer for ground 3ow vp on good feyth & not after wil
> for wil is no skil wiþ owt good resoun.[67]

The mention of a proverbial expression brings us to a final element that is very prominent in these letters.

Among several proverbs that appear there, [68] two seem particularly worth singling out: "Now is time," which appears three times (Knighton 2, 3, and 5), and the cryptic saying attributed to John of Bathon in the third of Knighton's letters. Although Ball's letters have sometimes been categorized as apocalyptic (Kane) or millenarian (Cohn),[69] we have already noticed that when he quoted the "Now pride is in pris" verses, Ball showed no interest in its final chiliastic couplet (always assuming, that is, that the version known to him contained it):

> Now haþ god enchesyn
> To dystrie þys worle by reson.

Cohn takes the line "God do bote, for nowe is tyme" as one instance of the millenarianism of these letters,[70] but it seems to me to be an obvious reference to one of the best-known passages of proverbial wisdom in the Bible, the passage that begins "to every thing there is a season" and includes "a time to keep silence and a time to speak; a time to love and a time to hate; a time of war and a time of peace" (Eccles. 3.7-8). Ball's phrase occurs in a verse translating Ecclesiastes from a sermon in the popular Franciscan preaching manual, the *Fasciculus Morum*:

> Now ys tyme to sle and tyme to hele
> Tyme to geder and tyme to dele.[71]

Although the context here is one of private penance, as it is in another sermon verse that uses the phrase,

> Quo sabet [i.e., *whoso haveth*] longe ligge in sinne,
> nu is tyme þat e blinne,[72]

it is not hard to see how these words might be turned into a rallying cry. In Knighton's second letter, the variant, "nowe is tyme to be ware," echoes a couplet from yet a third sermon verse:

> 3if þou be bigylet so,
> ano3er time beth iwar;[73]

and though the context for this is a discussion of the sin of despair, the emphasis is placed on active self-help:

> 3if þou be icast adoun
> aris vp and tak þe beth.

While I have quite failed to come up with an appropriate John of Bath for Knighton's third letter, the gnomic saying attributed to him, "speak, spend, and speed," seems clearly to belong in the same sententious tradition. In addition to the biblical "a time to keep silence and a time to speak" (Eccles. 3.7), one might cite from Whiting's collection of Middle-English proverbs, "Tyme is to spende tyme is to spare,"[74] which loosely renders Ecclesiastes 3.6 (*Tempus acquirendi, et tempus perdendi*), "He that never spendeth but alway spareth, Comonlye oft the worsse he ffareth," [75] and, from the early sixteenth century, "who first speake first spede."[76] "Speak, spend, and speed," in other words, appears to be a modification of sentences of the Ecclesiastes type, first to something like "he that never speaks (or spends) never speeds," then to "speak (or spend) and speed," with a final amalgamation in "speak, spend, and speed."

I trust I have by now done enough to establish a firm social context for John Ball's six letters. As we might have guessed, they reflect the world of the popular preacher, their proverbs and scraps of vernacular verse turning up in sermons, sermon notes, and preaching manuals throughout the fourteenth century. So all this fussing over the literary text seems to have taught us little more than we knew already. Froissart and Walsingham both imply that Ball was a charismatic preacher, and both suggest that he had been delivering incendiary sermons for many years before the Revolt, a suggestion confirmed by independent evidence.[77] Scholars have often assumed that Ball's letters reflect the tradition of the popular sermon: Richard Kaeuper, for instance, notes that "the uncompromising scriptural passages and the powerful *exempla* of the preachers . . . provide links with the 'dark sayings' embodied in the obscure vernacular letters which circulated at the time of the rising."[78] Walsingham draws attention to Ball's taking a rhymed proverb ("Whan Adam dalf, and Eve span, / Wo was thanne a gentilman?") as the text of his sermon at Blackheath (2:32), and, as Owst noted long ago, this verse too turns up in homiletic material earlier in the century.[79] That the tradition of the popular sermon should bear marks of affinity with complaint literature is equally unsurprising; John Peter's general characterization of "the free and continuous osmosis that went on between [pulpit] oratory and verse"[80] has been considerably refined in recent years by the work of Siegfried Wenzel. Maurice Keen has even characterized the very verses we have been discussing as "snatches culled largely from contemporary pulpit literature."[81]

On the other hand, this dusty assembling of analogues may be able to carry us a little further than unsupported intuition. There are, I think, three questions that a fuller knowledge of the tradition underlying Ball's letters can help us answer. The first, a largely literary matter, concerns how we should assess Ball's individual contribution to the actual texts; the second, mainly a matter of literary history, how closely we should identify the themes of these letters with the events of 1381; and the third, a historical question, how these letters might affect our interpretation of the Peasants' Revolt itself.

The complaint tradition of a world upside down, of the appointed divisions of society breaking down, is of great antiquity. Its ultimate medieval ancestor, the *De duodecim abusivis*, has been traced back to seventh-century Ireland,[82] and the first rendering of these "Twelve Abuses of the Age" in English is to be found in the late-tenth-century sermons of Ælfric.[83] The antiquity of this tradition, the repetitiveness of its major themes, the consistency of its moral standpoint, and the anonymity of many of its expositors have all tended to direct attention to the timeless quality of its conventions. Peter, who sees complaint literature as deliberately eschewing "the specific, the provocatively direct,"[84] believes that from the thirteenth century until the mid-sixteenth "the whole genre virtually stands still";[85] though conceding that one may sometimes be conscious "of a personal attitude masquerading as a broad moral judgement," he stresses that this is the exception rather than the rule.[86] His is the position adopted by George Kane when he warns against romanticizing John Ball, yet to dismiss Ball's letters as mere homelitic commonplaces, as Kane would have us do, seems to me unduly reductive. The better acquainted we are with the tradition, the more possible it becomes to distinguish from the commonplace what Dobson imagines might be Ball's "own note of personal hysteria."[87] I have endeavored to point out a number of places where Ball's text is subtly at variance with known analogues (by omitting wrath from some conventional verses on the seven deadly sins, for instance, or by turning an injunction to act as peacemaker into a call to recognize one's enemies); we might, moreover, learn to hear Ball's personal voice still more clearly by contrasting it with the voices of contemporaries. John Gower in the *Vox Clamantis*, for instance, has a long passage deeply indebted to the "twelve abuses,"[88] but the way in which *he* exploits the tradition is quite different: Gower's "Sic modus est pompa" (Thus ostentation is called restraint)[89] and Ball's "Now regnith pride in pris" may be equally conventional, but in context they sound quite distinct notes.

What Maddicott has called "the historian's usual problem when he draws on literary sources: how to distinguish the conventions of literature from the conditions of real life,"[90] has an obvious relevance for my second question: how closely should we identify the themes of Ball's letters with the events of 1381? Kane, following Peter, equates convention with timelessness, but even if we could show that every single line in the letters could be paralleled somewhere in the complaint tradition, we would still not be justified in arguing that they have no specific relevance for the Peasants' Revolt. There is after all the possibility that Ball's letters are indeed entirely conventional, but that for some reason their very conventions, however pacific in origin, had become inflammatory by 1381. Traditional complaint literature may well have been as profoundly conservative in outlook as Kane claims, but if at the same time it helped articulate and focus popular discontent, as Robbins suggests, perhaps this was because those who rallied to its call were also conservative—because they were trying to prevent a new age, not usher one in; reactionaries, not revolutionaries; Luddites, not Bolsheviks. Ambrose Raftis has insisted that reaction to profound economic, social, and legal changes, to a traumatic loosening of the ties that bound, lay at the very heart of the uprising, so perhaps it is hardly surprising that "the oft-quoted language of the Revolt" should, as he puts it, have "been familiar to fourteenth-century folklore for generations and did not signify some new consciousness."[91] In these terms, Robbins and Kane may not be quite as far apart as they first seem.

There may, however, be more specific details in Ball's letters to link them with the 1381 uprising. Even the general exhortation to "stonde manlyche togedyr in trewþe, and helpez trewþe, and trewþe schal helpe 3owe" places rhetorical emphasis on a term that, however common in complaint literature, was developing important new senses in the 1360s and 1370s, as Kane himself has shown,[92] and was something of a keyword for both Chaucer and Langland. Similarly, attacks on the venality of lawyers certainly formed a conventional element in complaint literature,[93] but it is difficult to believe that there is no connection between the veiled allusions to judicial corruption in Ball's letters and the widespread violence shown to judges, lawyers, and jurymen (not to mention the destruction of legal archives) during the course of the revolt. Finally, as I have suggested, the references to "Hobbe þe Robbere" (far less easily dismissed as conventional) seem to be paralleled by the rebels' firm treatment of any looters found in their ranks; apart from Knighton's testimony, quoted above, we have the comments of the "monk of Westminster" on the sacking of the Savoy that "if anyone had been caught in an act of theft he would have been taken off for execution without trial or verdict" (*si quis in aliquo furto fuerat deprehensus sine processu sine judicio ad mortem rapiebatur decapitandus*),[94] and of the continuator of the *Eulogium Historiarum* who says that those who threw the valuables from the Savoy into the Thames did so to avoid the accusation of looting (*dicentes, "Nolumus esse fures"*).[95] Even Walsingham agrees that in forbidding looting, the rebel leaders were being careful to preclude any suspicion of material self-interest: "ut patesceret totius regni communitati eos non respectu avaritiae quicquam facere" (1:457).

My third question (how might a reading of Ball's letters affect our interpretation of the Peasants' Revolt itself?) really comes down to the question of the role played by men like Ball in directing, or at least inspiring, the rebellion. Was the Peasants' Revolt a spontaneous popular uprising that threw up its own catch-as-catch-can leaders as it gathered momentum, or were Ball and his fellows genuine instigators of armed resistance? Was, in other words, the social criticism to be found in vernacular sermons merely a reflection of a widespread malaise, or did it provide a real focus for peasant discontent? Maddicott's suggestion that Ball's letters contain links with some kind of "floating manifestation of commonly held grievances, given a memorable shape in verse, usually transmitted orally, and serving to satisfy the perennial pleasure of the shared grumble"[96] seems to me in need of qualification. Siegfried Wenzel's work shows that the kind of verses appropriated by Ball are at least as likely to have been composed or translated by the preachers who disseminated them as to have floated up from the demotic miasma. We need not, on the other hand, go quite so far as Owst, who, noting the resemblances between Froissart's version of Ball's sermon and the extant sermons of less notorious preachers, proclaims, "We have at last a measure of the extent to which the preaching not merely of friars but of other orthodox churchmen of the day was ultimately responsible for the outbreak of the Peasants' Revolt."[97] This is a large claim and most of us would certainly wish to look further afield for final causes. Nevertheless, however timeless and universal the moral lessons of the homilists, their illustrations were often deliberately topical, and it is not difficult to imagine how a preacher who sought to illustrate the torments of hell by taking as his example "þise false questmongers þat for a litill money or els for a good dyner wil saue a theffe and dampne a trewe man"[98] might provoke in his listeners as much animus against legal corruption as fear for their own souls. At the very least, the tradition of popular preaching and the complaint literature associated with it may be said to have helped inflame deeply banked resentments in 1381.

This raises one final question. The old claim of Walsingham, Knighton, and the *Fasciculi Zizaniorum* that Wyclif and his followers were behind the uprising has been cautiously revivified recently by R. B. Dobson and Anne Hudson,[99] but if John Ball's letters are any indication, this claim should still be treated with some skepticism. In one particular, Ball shows himself anything but a typical Lollard, for, compared with the tradition of the popular preacher that he exemplifies, Lollard preaching was austerity itself. "No Lollard sermon contains any story material from outside the Bible—no classical anecdote, no pious saint's life story, no moral exemplum," writes Hudson; indeed, Lollard opposition to the use of "croniclis wiþ poyses and dremyngis and manye oþir helples talis" in preaching was, as she says, "vociferous and constant," and interestingly, "the friars were held to be the worst offenders." The friars, alleges one polemical piece, preach "lesyngus and japes, docken Goddis word and tateren it biþer rimes."[100]

We have seen that the kind of material Ball drew on for his letters is prominent in mendicant preaching manuals like B.L., MS Harley 2316, Grimestone's notebook, or the *Fasciculus Morum*; if we must look for scapegoats, the friars would at first glance seem to offer a better prospect than the Lollards. It is true that there is no evidence for the clerical leaders of the uprising, men like William Grindecobbe, John Wrawe, and of course John Ball himself, having had any mendicant affiliations, and at least one friar, the minorite physician William of Appleton, was a victim of the revolt (though no doubt the fact that he was a servant of John of Gaunt made him a more conspicuous target than his grey habit). Of the major chronicle sources, only Walsingham openly implicates the friars; not only does he single out the mendicant orders for special attention in his survey of general degeneracy on the eve of the revolt (even if "encouraging the errors of the mob" [*commune vulgus in errore foventes*] is only one item in a familiar list of charges [2:13]), but he also includes in Jack Strawe's scaffold confession the admission that when all churchmen had been killed, "the mendicants alone were to have lived in the land, which would have left sufficient for celebrating the sacraments" (*soli mendicantes vixissent super terram, qui suffecissent pro sacris celebrandis*, 2:10). This might be easier to dismiss as a malicious fabrication were it not for a curious detail from the continuator of the *Eulogium Historiarum*: after breaking into prisons and releasing the prisoners, the chronicler tells us, the mob offered up "the iron chains of Newgate in the church of the Friars Minor" (*vincula ferrea de Nova Porta obtulerunt in ecclesiam Fratrum Minorum*, 3:353).

Perhaps it was a fear of being themselves implicated in the rising that made the friars so eager to tar Lollards with the same brush. As early as February 1382 the four mendicant orders at Oxford addressed a letter to John of Gaunt complaining that Wyclif "had attempted, through 'the tongues of a number of pseudo-doctors,' to pin the blame for the rebellion on them," [101] and we might note that the alleged confession of John Ball with its suspiciously neat incrimination of Wyclif shows every indication of being a Carmelite forgery. Moreover, the number of early anti-Lollard polemicists drawn from the mendicant orders is striking—William Woodford, a Franciscan; Roger Dymmock, a Dominican; and the Carmelite, Thomas Netter, are only the best known.[102] One should of course be careful not to assume that differences between Lollard and friar were as clearly drawn at the time of the Peasants' Revolt as they were later to become. After all, before 1378 Wyclif had found several friends and supporters among the mendicants.[103] Moreover, as Thompson has pointed out, the Lollard movement itself was unlikely to have been doctrinally homogeneous in the 1380s, when there must in any case have been much "common ground between acceptable and condemned forms of piety."[104] For the devotee of popular preaching there may at times have been little to choose between the newly inspired Wycliffites and the more demogogic representatives of the traditional orders.[105] Nevertheless, there seems to be some reason for believing that mutual recriminations in the wake of the revolt helped sharpen the differences between the two, and were perhaps a precondition for the "hardening of the lines between orthodoxy and heresy" that Thompson would place somewhat later.[106]

The bitter and enduring hostility between Wycliffite and mendicant goes deeper than this, however. One point upon which both Kane and Robbins agree is that if a revolutionary spirit is to be found anywhere in the late Middle Ages, we should look for it among the Lollards.[107] Where estates satire had generally lamented the failure of men and women to accept the station to which God had appointed them, Wycliffite doctrine sought to undermine the very authority of the estates themselves.[108] In light of the strong vein of conservatism within the tradition of popular preaching that the mendicants did so much to foster, they must have found such an attitude shocking; hostility between Lollard and friar, we might anachronistically argue, reflects the mutual antipathy of radical and reactionary. On this still inchoate political spectrum we would have to place the leaders of the Peasants' Revolt firmly to the right, and for signs of true revolutionary zeal turn, not to John Ball's letters, but to the bloody battle between the Pelican and the Gryphon that concludes the Wycliffite *Ploughman's Tale.*

Which brings us back to *Pierce the Ploughman's Crede.* From what I have said, we might now be in a position to detect a strain of genuine radicalism in the poem—not certainly a direct summons to man the barricades, nor even an impassioned expression of solidarity with the oppressed, but at least an "unconscious formulation," as Robbins might have put it, of a "basically dissident position." [109] At first sight, the central figure of the *Crede* seems no readier to question the exercise of secular power than his counterpart in Langland's far greater poem, and indeed both appear to share the same distaste for those who would rise above their station:

> And lordes sones lowly to þo losells aloute,
> Knytes croukeþ hem to, and crucheþ full lowe;
> And his syre a soutere y-suled in grees,
> His teeþ wiþ toylinge of leþer tatered as a sawe.
>
> (lines 750-53)

If we look no further than the poem and its literary relations, we can easily file it away with other estates satires after stamping it with the conservatism so typical of its genre, but if we turn from text to context, we may find in it signs of a discontent with the source of cultural authority more profound than anything in John Ball's letters. A poem that shows the simple seeker after truth being forced to turn for instruction in the basic tenets of his faith to a poor plowman suggests a skepticism about the efficacy of traditional institutions that would serve ultimately to put the entire system in jeopardy. In William Tyndale's later struggle to ensure that "a boy that drivest the plough [should] know more of the scriptures" than the prelates he saw about him, we can perhaps recognize the destabilizing potential of such skepticism.

Appendix

Knighton
B.L., MS Cotton Tiberius C. VII, fols. 174r-174v [T] (compared with B.L., MS Cotton Claudius E. III, fol. 269v [C])

> [1] Jakke Mylner *alloquitur socios sic:*
> Iakke Mylner asket help to turne hys mylne aright.
> He hath grounden smal, smal;
> Þe kinges sone of heven he schal pay for alle.
> Loke þi mylne go ary3t wiþ þe foure sayles, and þe post stande in stedefastnesse.
> Wiþ ry3t & wiþ my3t,
> Wiþ skyl and wiþ wylle,
> Lat my3t helpe ry3t;
> And skyl go before wille
> And ry3t before my3t,
> Þan goth oure mylne aryght.
> And if my3t go before ryght
> And wylle before skylle
> Þan is oure mylne mys ady3t.

[2] Jak Carter:
> *Jakke Carter prayes* 3owe alle þat 3e make a gode ende of þat 3e haue begunnen, and doþ wele and ay bettur and bettur, for at þe euen men heryth the day. ffor if þe ende be wele, þen is alle wele. Lat Peres þe Plowman my broþer duelle at home and dy3t vs corne, and I wil go wiþ 3owe and helpe þat y may to dy3te 3oure*

mete and 3oure drynke þat 3e none fayle. Lokke þat Hobbe Robbyoure be wele chastysed for lesyng of 3oure grace, for 3e haue gret nede to take God wiþ 3owe in alle 3oure dedes. ffor nowe is tyme to be war.

*C: prayeth

[3] Jakke Trewman:
Jakke Trewman doþ yow to vnderstande þat falsnes and gyle haviþ regned to longe,

& trewþe hat bene sette vnder a lokke,
And fal[s]nes* regneþ in euerylk† flokke;
No man may come trewþe to,
But he syng si dedero.
Speke, spende and spede, quoþ Ion of Bathon; ‡ and þerfore,
Synne fareth as wylde flode
Trew loue is away þat was so gode,
And clerkus for welthe worche hem wo.

God do bote, for [fol. 174v] nowye is tyme.

*falnet (t *corrected to* s) and (*expunged and followed by a caret*) †C:euery. ‡Bathon *has a suspension over the* a

[4] Exemplar epistole Iohannis Balle:
Ion Balle gretyþ 3ow wele alle, & doþ 3owe to vnderstande he hath rungen 3oure belle.

Nowe ry3t & my3t,
Wylle and skylle,
God spede [euerydele].*

Nowe is tyme, Lady helpe to Ihesu þi sone, and þi sone to his fadur, to mak a gode ende, in þe name of þe Trinite, of þat is begunne. Amen, amen, pur charite, amen.

*euery ydele; C:euery dele

[5] Prima epistola Iohannis Balle:
Iohn Balle, Seynte Marye prist, gretez wele alle maner men, & byddes† hem in þe name of þe Trinite, Fadur, and Sone, and Holy Gost, stonde manlyche togedyr in trewþe, and helpez‡ trewþe, and trewþe schal helpe 3owe.*

Now regneþ pride in pris,
and couetys is hold wys,
and leccherye wiþ[outen schame],§
and glotonye wiþouten blame;
Enuye regniþ wiþ tresone,
and slouthe is take in grete sesone.

God do bote, for nowe is tyme. Amen.

*C:greteth †C:biddeth ‡C:helpes §-outen schame o*mitted in both MSS (though T has a caret)*

Walsingham
B.L., MS Royal 13 E. IX, fol. 287r

Iohon Schep, som tyme Seynte Marie prest of ʒork, and now of Colchestre, gret-eth wel Iohan Nameles, & Iohan þe Mullere, and Iohon Cartere, and biddeþ hem þat þei bee war of gyle in borugh, and stondeth togidre* in Godes name, and biddeþ Peres Plouʒman go to his werk, and chastise wel Hobbe þe Robbere, and taketh wiþ ʒow Iohan Trewman, and alle hiis† felawes, and no mo, and loke schappe ʒou to on heued, and no mo.

<blockquote>

Iohan þe Mullere haþ ygrounde smal, smal, smal;
Þe Kynges sone of heuene schal paye for al.
Be war or [ʒ]e‡ be wo;
Knoweth ʒour freende fro ʒour foo;
Haueth ynow, & seith "Hoo";
And do wel and bettre, and fleth synne,
And sekeþ pees, and hold ʒou þerinne;

</blockquote>

and so biddeth Iohan Trewaman and alle his felawes.

*togidedre †followed by and (expunged) ‡þe

Notes

I should like to express here my gratitude to the John Simon Guggenheim Memorial Foundation, whose generous support afforded me the time to complete this essay.

1. Beatrice White, "Poet and Peasant," in *The Reign of Richard II: Essays in Honour of May McKisack*, ed. F. R. H. Du Boulay and Caroline M. Barron (London, 1971), p. 70.
2. Ibid.
3. Jill Mann, *Chaucer and Medieval Estates Satire* (Cambridge, Eng., 1973).
4. George Kane, "Some Fourteenth-Century 'Political' Poems," in *Medieval English Religious and Ethical Literature: Essays in Honour of G. H. Russell*, ed. Gregory Kratzmann and James Simpson (Cambridge, Eng., 1986), p. 85.
5. *Pierce the Ploughman's Crede*, ed. W. W. Skeat (Oxford, 1906), lines 222-26. All subsequent references are to this edition and appear parenthetically in the text.
6. In *Jack Upland, Friar Daw's Reply, and Upland's Rejoinder*, ed. P. L. Heyworth (London, 1968), lines 360-66. All subsequent references to *Friar Daw's Reply* are to this edition and appear parenthetically in the text.
7. Kane, "'Political' Poems," p. 89.
8. Peter Laslett, "The Wrong Way through the Telescope: A Note on Literary Evidence in Sociology and in Historical Sociology," *British Journal of Sociology* 27 (1976), 333.
9. Geoffrey Chaucer, *The Wife of Bath's Tale*, line 4.
10. Keith Thomas, *History and Literature: The Ernest Hughes Memorial Lecture* (Swansea, 1988), p. 4; I should like to thank Ian Maclean for bringing this paper to my attention.
11. John V. Fleming, "Historians and the Evidence of Literature," *Journal of Interdisciplinary History* 4 (1973), 104.
12. Malory, *Works* 1:xxiv n. 4.

13. Thomas, *History and Literature*, p. 10.

14. Ibid.

15. P. R. Coss, "Bastard Feudalism Revised," *Past and Present* 125 (1989), 60.

16. Derek Pearsall, "Interpretative Models for the Peasants' Revolt," in *Hermeneutics and Medieval Culture*, ed. Patrick J. Gallacher and Helen Damico (Albany, N.Y., 1989), pp. 63-70.

17. Natalie Zemon Davis, "A Renaissance Text to the Historian's Eye: The Gifts of Montaigne," *Journal of Medieval and Renaissance Studies* 15 (1985), 47.

18. Rossell Hope Robbins, "Middle English Poems of Protest," *Anglia* 78 (1960), 201.

19. Kane, "'Political' Poems," p. 91.

20. Carleton Brown and R. H. Robbins, *Index of Middle English Verse*, Index Society (New York, 1943) (hereafter cited as *IMEV*), nos. 1654, 1655, 1791, and 1976. The error apparently goes back to a nineteenth-century edition of the letters by Charles Mackay, which he took "from Stowe's Annals"; *A Collection of Songs and Ballads Relative to the London Prentices and Trades*, ed. Charles Mackay, Percy Society, 1, pt. 2 (London, 1841), pp. 1-4.

21. Siegfried Wenzel, *Preachers, Poets, and the Early English Lyric* (Princeton, N.J., 1986), p. 198.

22. Rossell Hope Robbins and J. L. Cutler, *Supplement to the Index of Middle English Verse* (Lexington, Ky., 1965), nos. as in *IMEV*, plus 1790.8 (hereafter cited as *IMEV Supp.*).

23. Thomas Walsingham, *Historia Anglicana*, ed. H. T. Riley, 2 vols., Rolls Series (London, 1864), 2:33-341; Knighton, *Chronicon* 2:138-40 (hereafter cited as Walsingham and Knighton, respectively).

24. N. R. Ker, *Medieval Libraries of Great Britain: A List of Surviving Books*, 2nd ed. (London, 1964), p. 167; John Taylor, *English Historical Liteature in the Fourteenth Century* (Oxford, 1987), p. 66.

25. Ker, *Medieval Libraries*, p. 113; M. V. Clarke, *Fourteenth Century Studies*, ed. L. S. Sutherland and M. McKisack (Oxford, 1937), p. 294.

26. Kenneth Sisam, ed., *Fourteenth-Century Verse and Prose* (1921; Oxford, 1975), pp. 160-61.

27. G. H. Martin is completing an edition of Knighton's *Chronicon* for the Clarendon Press. I should like to express my gratitude to him for his help and advice on Knighton's text of the Ball letters.

28. This independence has been questioned by H. M. Hansen, "The Peasants' Revolt of 1381 and the Chronicles," *Journal of Medieval History* 6 (1980), 393-415. Any two accounts of the same event will inevitably contain similarities, and the question of whether such similarities are conditioned by the event itself or by reports of it will be a contentious one. As Susan Crane points out to me, Hansen's paper and Dobson's brusque dismissal of it—"chronicles . . . do after all convey genuine news about real events" (Dobson, ed., *The Peasants' Revolt of 1381*, 2nd ed. [London, 1983], p. xxxii n. 2)—offer a nice paradigm of the distinction I have been trying to elaborate between literary and historical approaches. Even by the canons of textual criticism, however, it seems to me that Hansen's case is a weak one, and it would not be difficult, from a textual analysis of the letters alone, to turn her claim that "Knighton is secondary to Walsingham" (p. 405) on its head (in other words, Walsingham might conceivably have produced a précis or digest from Knighton's five letters, but Knighton seems very unlikely to have manufactured five separate pieces from Walsingham's solitary example). In this particular instance, however, it seems safer to continue to regard each as an independent witness.

29. Other parallels between Walsingham's text and Knighton's are "Iohon Schep, som tyme Seynte Marie prest" (Walsingham) and "Iohn Balle, Seynte Marye prist" (Knighton 5); "biddeþ hem þat þei bee war of gyle" (Walsingham) and "falsnes and gyle haviþ regned to longe" (Knighton 3); "Be war or [3]e be wo" (Walsingham) and "nowe is tyme to be war" (Knighton 2).

30. E.g. *prayes* (Knighton 2), *euerylk* (Knighton 3), and *gretez, byddes*, and *helpez* (Knighton 5); interestingly, a slightly later copy of the *Chronicon* (B.L., MS Cotton Claudius E. III, fol. 269v) normalizes all but the last of these.

31. Dobson, ed., *The Peasants' Revolt*, p. 379.

32. Ibid.

33. Norman Cohn, *The Pursuit of the Millenium: Revolutionary Millenarians and Mystical Anarchists of the Middle Ages* (1957; reprint, London, 1970), p. 203.

34. Rossell Hope Robbins, ed., *Historical Poems of the XIVth and XVth Centuries* (New York, 1959), p. xlii.

35. Edward Wilson, *A Descriptive Index of the English Lyrics in John of Grimestone's Preaching Book*, Society for the Study of Medieval Languages and Literature (Oxford, 1973), p. 58, no. 219.

36. For the larger family of complaint poems to which these four belong and whose "genetic makeup" they share, see Wenzel, *Preachers*, pp. 193-203; Wenzel believes this family to be native to England, with its origins in the late thirteenth century. It is interesting to note that earlier versions tend to conform to a "when . . . then" structure, whereas later ones, including Ball's, are of the "now . . . now" type. A similar development is noted by Peter: "the poets [tend] more and more to substitute for 'the world' more precise designations like 'þis lond' or even 'Yngland'" (John Peter, *Complaint and Satire in Early English Literature* [Oxford, 1956], p. 67).

37. F. J. Furnivall, ed., *Queene Elizabethes Achademy, A Book of Precedence, &c.*, EETS, ES 8 (London, 1869), p. 85. In both, the verses are immediately followed by two couplets beginning "þat I hete & þat I drynke þat may I haue" (*IMEV* 3274), a quatrain beginning "all hyt is fantome þt we wiþ fare" (*IMEV* 190), and a popular poem on the abuses of the age beginning "Gyfte is domusmane" (*IMEV* 906); these four poems are copied without a break, and the two versions are textually very close.

38. Wilson, *John of Grimestone*, pp. ix-xvi.

39. It shares the leaf with some proverbial verses (*IMEV* 836); a list (in Latin) of the six virtues of holy water; mnemonic lines on the ten commandments, the five senses, the seven deadly sins, and the seven works of mercy; and a thirty-line poem, incl. "Nil valet ille locus ubi nil patet utilitas."

40. B.L., MS Royal 17 B. XVII is a late-fourteenth-century collection containing the *Lay Folk's Mass Book* and treatises by Richard Rolle and his followers (C. Horstman, ed., *Yorkshire Writers: Richard Rolle of Hampole and His Followers* [London, 1896], 2:1-71), though the verses in question have been copied into it later. B.L., MS Addit. 8151 contains William of Nassington's *Mirrour of Lyfe*, a translation of a work by the Augustinian friar John Waldeby (fols. 1v-199r), and, immediately before the verses, a poem on prayer (199v-200v).

41. *The Anonimalle Chronicle, 1333-1381*, ed. V. H. Galbraith (Manchester, 1970), p. 139. All subsequent references are to this edition and appear parenthetically in the text.

42. *Reliquiae Antiquae*, ed. Thomas Wright and J. O. Halliwell, 2 vols. (London, 1841-43), 2:121. For a partial description of the contents of this MS, see J. A. Herbert, *A Catalogue of Romances in the Department of Manuscripts in the British Museum*, 3 vols. (London, 1883-1910), 3:573-81, also 2:307-9 and 677; there are Dominican references in i.2, i.31, and ii.62.

43. Horstman, ed., *Yorkshire Writers*, 2:65.

44. Bodley, MS Tanner 201, fol. 2r. Robbins regards these lines as part of *IMEV* 2500, but Wenzel points out that they belong to a quite separate quatrain (Wenzel, *Preachers*, p. 184 n. 32).

45. See *The Macro Plays*, ed. M. Eccles, EETS 262 (London, 1969), p. 190 n. 879.

46. The *Simonie*, also known as *A Satire of Edward II's England*, is edited (under the latter title) by T. W. Ross, Colorado College Studies 8 (Colorado Springs, 1966); John Gower's *Vox Clamantis* is in *The Latin Works*, vol. 4 of *The Complete Works of John*

Gower, ed. G. C. Macaulay (Oxford, 1902); *Isopes Fabules* are in the *Minor Poems of John Lydgate*, ed. H. N. MacCracken, 2 vols., EETS, ES 107 and OS 192 (London, 1911 and 1934), 2:566-99; *Peter Idley's Instructions to His Son* is edited by C. D'Evelyn (Boston, 1935); the *Castle of Perseverance* and *Mankind* are both in the *Macro Plays* (ed. Eccles). For further instances of the phrase from Latin proverbial material, see Hans Walther, *Proverbia, Sententiaeque Latinitatis Medii Aevi*, 6 vols. (Göttingen, 1963-69), 4:865 (nos. 28415-19).

47. A Harding, "The Revolt against the Justices," in *The English Rising of 1381*, ed. R. H. Hilton and T. H. Aston (Cambridge, Eng., 1984), pp. 165-93; Andrew Prescott, "London in the Peasants' Revolt: A Portrait Gallery," *London Journal* 7 (1981), 125-43.

48. Siegfried Wenzel, *Verses in Sermons: The Fasciculus Morum and Its Middle English Poems* (Cambridge, Mass., 1978), p. 160, no. 25.

49. Robbins, *Historical Poems*, p. 144, no. 55; part of a poem incorrectly printed as continuous with "The Twelve Abuses" by Robbins. (See Wenzel, *Preachers*, p. 189.) It is preserved in Cambridge, MS St. John's 37, fol. 56v, a fifteenth-century collection of medical receipts and devotional pieces.

50. Herbert, *Catalogue of Romances* 3:166.

51. F. J. Furnivall, *Political, Religious, and Love Poems*, EETS, OS 15 (London, 1866), p. 228.

52. Derek Pearsall suggests to me that it may owe something to the ancient proverb, best known to English readers from Longfellow, "The mills of God grind slowly, yet they grind exceeding small." Though its earliest English appearance seems to be in George Herbert's *Jacula Prudentum* (1640), this proverb was certainly known in the Middles Ages: "Sera deum mola sed tenues molit undique partes." Walther, *Proverbia* 4:805 (no. 28057); cf. 4:815 (no. 28109) and 5:551-52 (nos. 32568a/b).

53. B. J. Whiting, *Proverbs, Sentences, and Proverbial Phrases from English Writings Mainly before 1500* (Cambridge, Mass., 1968), p. 626 (W45).

54. Wilson, *John of Grimestone*, p. 61, no. 230.

55. B.L., MS Harley 2316, fol. 26r.

56. Wright, *Reliquiae Antiquae* 2:1-20.

57. R. L. Greene, ed., *The Early English Carols*, 2nd ed. (Oxford, 1977), p. 437.

58. Kane, "'Political' Poems," p. 91.

59. The Augustinian argument that "war was an instrument of peace and should only be waged to secure peace of some sort" (F. H. Russell, *The Just War in the Middle Ages* [Cambridge, Eng., 1975], p. 16) formed the basis for the *bella pacata* defended by medieval canonists (p. 61) and theologians alike (p. 262).

60. Greene, ed., *The Early English Carols*, p. 227, no. 383.

61. Wenzel, *Preachers*, p. 185.

62. For the date of the *Speculum Christiani*, see Vincent Gillespie, "The Evolution of the *Speculum Christiani*," in *Latin and Vernacular Studies in Late-Medieval Texts and Manuscripts*, ed. A. J. Minnis (Cambridge, Eng., 1989), p. 54 n. 40. The "Might is Right" verses, however, are certainly older, since they also occur in the Auchinleck manuscript (1330-40).

63. *Speculum Christiani: A Middle English Religious Treatise of the Fourteenth Century*, ed. G. Holmstedt, EETS, OS 182 (London, 1933), p. 124.

64. For other sermon verses exploiting the rhyme "might" and "right," see Wenzel, *Verses*, p. 194, no. 52, and Wenzel, *Preachers*, p. 183.

65. Siegfried Wenzel, "Unrecorded Middle English Verses," *Anglia* 92 (1974), 76, no. 86.

66. Whiting, *Proverbs, Sentences, and Proverbial Phrases*, W273.

67. R. H. Bowers, "A Middle English Poem on Lovedays," *Modern Language Review* 47 (1952), 375.

68. I. e., Whiting, *Proverbs, Sentences, and Proverbial Phrases*, B233, E158, E83.

69. See notes 4 and 33 above.

70. Cohn, *Millenium*, p. 203.

71. Wenzel, *Verses*, p. 200, no. 58.

72. Wenzel, "Unrecorded Middle English Verses," p. 77, no. 92; Cambridge, MS Pembroke 100, fol. 114v (this is a collection of sermon materials, mostly thirteenth-century, from Bury).

73. P. C. Erb, "Vernacular Material for Preaching in MS Cambridge University Library Ii. III. 8," *Mediaeval Studies* 33 (1971), 79.

74. Whiting, *Proverbs, Sentences, and Proverbial Phrases*, T316.

75. Ibid., S626.

76. B. J. Whiting, *Proverbs in the Earlier English Drama*, Harvard Studies in Comparative Literature 14 (Cambridge, Mass., 1938), p. 98.

77. David Wilkins, ed., *Concilia Magnae Britanniae*, 4 vols. (1737; reprint, Brussels, 1963), 3:64-65.

78. Richard W. Kaeuper, *War, Justice, and Public Order: England and France in the Later Middle Ages* (Oxford, 1988), p. 374.

79. G. R. Owst, *Literature and the Pulpit in Medieval England*, 2nd ed. (Oxford, 1966), p. 291.

80. Peter, *Complaint and Satire*, p. 46.

81. Maurice Keen, *The Outlaws of Medieval Legend*, rev. ed. (London, 1977), p. 166.

82. Wenzel, *Preachers*, pp. 176-77.

83. Carleton Brown, "The 'Pride of Life' and the 'Twelve Abuses,'" *Archiv* 128 (1912), 73.

84. Peter, *Complaint and Satire*, p. 36.

85. Ibid., p. 58.

86. Ibid., p. 48.

87. Dobson, ed., *The Peasants' Revolt*, pp. 15-16.

88. John Gower, *Latin Works* 7.4.217 ff.

89. Ibid., 7.4.241.

90. J. R. Maddicott, "Poems of Social Protest in Early Fourteenth-Century England," in *England in the Fourteenth Century: Proceedings of the 1985 Harlaxton Symposium*, ed. W. M. Ormrod (Cambridge, Eng., 1986), p. 140.

91. J. A. Raftis, "Interpretations of the Peasants' Revolt," in *Social Unrest in the Late Middle Ages*, ed. F. X. Newman, Medieval and Renaissance Texts and Studies (Binghamton, N.Y., 1986) p. 17.

92. George Kane, *The Liberating Truth: The Concept of Integrity in Chaucer's Writings*, John Coffin Memorial Lecture, 1979 (London, 1980), pp. 9-10.

93. Peter, *Complaint and Satire*, p. 84.

94. *Polychronicon Randulphi Higden monachi Cestrensis*, ed. J. R. Lumby, 9 vols., RS (London, 1865-86), 9:2.

95. *Eulogium* 3:352.

96. Maddicott, "Poems of Social Protest," p. 139.

97. Owst, *Literature and the Pulpit*, p. 304.

98. Woodburn O. Ross, ed., *Middle English Sermons*, EETS, OS 209 (London, 1960), p. 174.

99. Dobson, ed., *The Peasants' Revolt*, pp. xxxvii-xxxviii; Anne Hudson, *The Premature Reformation: Wycliffite Texts and Lollard History* (Oxford, 1988), pp. 66-69.

100. Hudson, *Premature Reformation*, p. 270 and n. 214.

101. Joseph H. Dahmus, *The Prosecution of John Wyclyf* (New Haven, Conn., 1952), p. 84.

102. Hudson, *Premature Reformation*, pp. 45-55.

103. David Knowles, *The Religious Orders in England*, 3 vols. (Cambridge, Eng., 1948-1959), 2:70.

104. J. A. F. Thompson, "Orthodox Religion and the Origins of Lollardy," *History* 74 (1989), 51.

105. The fifteenth-century Carmelite Thomas Scrope offers a good illustration of such a representative; see R. M. Clay, *The Hermits and Anchorites of England* (London, 1914), pp. 163-64. I am grateful to my colleague Nicholas Watson for this reference.

106. Thompson, "Orthodox Religion," p. 53.

107. Kane, "'Political' Poems," p. 90; Rossell Hope Robbins, "Dissent in Middle English Literature: The Spirit of (Thirteen) Seventy-Six," *Medievalia et Humanistica*, n.s. 9 (1979), 34-36.

108. Robbins, "Dissent," p. 35.

109. Ibid., p. 28.

CHAPTER 10

✛

The Writing Lesson of 1381

Susan Crane

At the beginning of his 1789 tract *What Is the Third Estate?* Emmanuel Sieyes summarizes that estate's prerevolutionary history in two questions and responses: "What has [the third estate] been until now in the political order? Nothing. What does it seek? To become something."[1] The conceptual space between that nothing and that desired something is the concern of this paper. One of the many fields that constitute "the third estate" as a historical category is writing. We know the rebels of England's 1381 rising through chronicles, court records, charters, poems, and so on. Yet the rebels remain outside representation in that they do not represent themselves for the written record. They are reimagined by those who write. Maintaining a largely oral culture alongside an increasingly literate higher culture, England's lower strata appear in written records as incoherent and irrational creatures or as models of submission and faith, variously constructed by various writers' own positions and preoccupations.

The distortion of records does not render them useless. Historians have striven to recover the rebels' actions and motives by reading chronicle accounts against one another, searching court rolls for proceedings earlier brought on behalf of villeins against lords, interrogating the records of perhaps spurious accusations and confessions subsequent to the revolt, and recognizing in other ways that all histories are interpretive and incomplete accounts. From my own partial position—partial, that is, in being both disposed toward literary analysis and limited by a professional training in literature—I would like to examine the written absences that historians work to overcome and to propose that absence is an important feature of the rebels' cultural status.

One privilege of my literary perspective on this question is that I am not primarily concerned with the accuracy of the record to the events. Recently Derek Pearsall has elegantly expressed the irrecoverability of events in a short article on the rising of 1381, using as an example the old chair on which a knight climbs to read King Richard's pardon to the rebels in the *Anonimalle Chronicle*: "This has the air of something seen, not invented: the arbitrariness of the old chair carries authenticity. Yet is it entirely arbitrary? Does not the old chair carry some impression of impropriety and indignity which enhances the image of the reversal of order?"[2] Granted that events and written accounts are tenuously connected, my concern is with how writers imagine the rebels and interpret the actions they impute to the rebels, rather than with the more difficult problems of whether and when writing can represent events.

I will begin to consider the relation of the 1381 rebels to writing by treating their illiteracy as a context for their destruction of documents, their demands for new documents, and their superiors' responses to these acts. Limitations in the literate/illiterate dichotomy will then lead me to consider ways in which fourteenth-century writing represents the rebels as altogether outside articulation, relegated to the nothingness of Sieyes's formula. This holds true for narrative accounts of the rising as well as for responses to it in works of William Langland and Geoffrey Chaucer. Whether hostile or sympathetic in tone, writers attribute inarticulateness to the rebels and impute political inefficacy to that inarticulateness. Excluded as a group, if not in every individual case, from participation in literate culture, the rebels of 1381 appear in our records as the "nothing" in contrast to which "something" else exists.

Modern historians note that the participants in the rising of 1381 were of diverse social origins, despite the chroniclers' tendency to use categorical terms such as *servi, rustici,* and *comunes.* With regard to writing, the disparate groups involved in the rising had perhaps more in common than with regard to occupations and degrees of bondedness. Yet R. B. Dobson has recently reemphasized the common interests and interconnected situations of different rebel groups, particularly of the rural peasantry and the townspeople of York, Beverley, and Scarborough, "themselves so often first- or second-generation immigrants from the surrounding countryside."[3] Resisting "a false dichotomy between town and countryside" in studies of the rising, A. F. Butcher argues that in Canterbury "the so-called alliance between townsmen and villagers in 1381 was not . . . a temporary phenomenon but a natural expression of a regional social structure in which town and countryside were inextricably entwined."[4] More relevant than the difference in status between villein, sokeman, artisan, and apprentice was the common position of the rebels outside the circles of power. Rodney Hilton summarizes the groups involved in the rising as "below the ranks of those who exercised lordship in the countryside and established authority in the towns."[5] This common position "below" also characterizes the rebels' relation to literate structures, despite the frequently noted difference between literacy levels in town and country.[6]

The groups rebelling in 1381 were by some measures perhaps partly literate. Estimates of the ability to read or to sign vary for the whole population of the period from 15 percent to 5 or 10 percent. Jo Ann Hoeppner Moran concludes that in the later Middle Ages literacy "was not altogether absent even among the very poor," yet for 1500 she estimates a literacy rate in northern England of only 15 percent. David Cressy's more conservative estimates for 1500 are 90 percent illiteracy for men and 99 percent for women.[7] Since education was almost entirely restricted in the fourteenth century to those of gentle and clerical status, neither Moran's nor Cressy's estimates for the total population allow for a significantly literate commons.[8] M. T. Clanchy's argument that the possession of a seal counts as participation in written culture makes the most positive case possible for the relation between literate culture and the commons. Noting that "the statute of Exeter of 1285 actually required 'bondsmen' to have seals to authenticate their written evidence, when they served on inquests for which there were insufficient freemen," Clanchy comments that "the possessor of a seal was necessarily a person familiar with documents and entitled to participate in their use."[9]

But the place in literate culture that the seal conferred, like the place in law conferred by bonded status, functioned broadly to restrict rather than to liberate the illiterate individual. The institutional use of texts was in the fourteenth century no longer a new phenomenon, but the distinctions this use perpetuated between "literate" and "illiterate" and between "learned" and "popular"—distinctions, Brian Stock has shown, that "were themselves the byproducts of literate sensibilities"—continued to reinforce social stratification.[10] Particularly for considering the role of texts in the 1381 rising, it is significant that literacy in medieval culture disadvantaged the illiterate as well as serving them. Literate culture did not develop in a vacuum but interacted with and contested a prior, nonliterate culture now labeled deficient. Supplementing the church's increasing emphasis on clerical education and the instruction of the laity through canonical texts, the Inquisition and other branches of the church strove to eradicate popular beliefs. It is a curious irony that the records of the Inquisition provide historians today with much of their information about suppressed popular culture. One such record, the interrogation of a sixteenth-century miller whose beliefs about the cosmos are the subject of Carlo Ginzburg's *The Cheese and the Worms*, attests to the popular awareness that institutions deploy literacy to the disadvantage of the unlettered: the miller begins his testimony by objecting to the use of Latin in the courts, "a betrayal of the poor because in lawsuits the poor do not know what is being said and are crushed; and if they want to say four words they need a lawyer."[11] Despite the ways traced by Stock and Clanchy in which the unlettered were able to participate in literate culture, stratification was not thereby eradicated. Indeed, literacy provided a further measure of social differentiation and a new site of friction between social groups.

In the seignorial courts of the fourteenth century, the lord's authority is overwhelmingly perpetuated against the claims of subordinates. Legislation, custom, and court cases forbid or restrict suits by villeins against lords and impose taxes, fines, and amercements arbitrarily in addition to the familiar merchet, death duty, and similar levies. Where the lower orders have legal contact with writing, it is not evident that the contact works to their advantage. Regulations stipulating that vagrants carry documents testifying to their trustworthiness and that warrants of lawful purchase accompany sales of livestock seem designed to facilitate seignorial control rather than to protect the parties concerned. The Peterborough *Cartae Nativorum,* copies of charters conveying small amounts of land or property, reflect, according to Clanchy, not the right of peasants to legal instruments but the abbey's seizure of documents to which its serfs have no right. [12] The remarkable series of forty attempts by villages in 1377 to prove freedom from customary services on the basis of exemplifications from Domesday Book meets with a parliamentary statute from lords and commons condemning "their malicious interpretation" of Domesday and ordering that the landlords concerned may themselves receive exemplifications demonstrating their rights, "letters patent under the Great Seal, as many and such as they may need, if they wish to ask for them."[13] Even the rudimentally symbolic tally stick was so often a means of fleecing peasants in the lord's name rather than striking an agreement with them that its coercive use becomes a literary commonplace.[14] If it can be said that the lower orders are acting within literate structures in cases such as these, their slight participation in literacy may have operated on their consciousness as historians argue their slightly increasing prosperity operated—to make the exclusions and restrictions that characterized their condition more visible than previously, and less tolerable.

This possibility is sustained by the role writing plays in the revolt of 1381. Although records note that rebel actions differ by region, George M. Trevelyan concluded long ago that the burning of charters, court rolls, and other documents was "the most universal feature of the Rising."[15] Christopher Dyer has identified 107 separate instances of destruction of documents, "including the burning of central estate archives such as those of the archbishopric of Canterbury, Stratford Abbey and Waltham Abbey that affected the records of many manors."[16] So salient was this feature of the rising to Thomas Walsingham that he subsumed the murder of various officials under the broader hostility to writing: "They strove to burn all old records; and they butchered anyone who might know or be able to commit to memory the contents of old or new documents. It was dangerous enough to be known as a clerk, but especially dangerous if an ink-pot should be found at one's elbow: such men scarcely or ever escaped from the hands of the rebels."[17] Walsingham's perception that the rebels were hostile primarily to documents and only derivatively to the writers of documents might illuminate why relatively few landlords, and relatively more lawyers and clerks, were killed in the 1381 rising.

The *Anonimalle Chronicle* similarly attributes violence against writers to animosity against writing in its account of Richard's attempt to disperse the rebels by having a pardon read aloud to them by the knight who stood on the old chair: Richard tries to disperse the rebels by having "a clerk write a bill in their presence" that he then seals in their presence, pardoning them "all manner of trespasses and misprisions and felonies done up to this hour" and requesting that everyone go home and "put his grievances in writing, and have them sent to him." Hilton quite reasonably attributes the commons' rejection of the bill to its status as a pardon rather than a manumission such as those provided the following day at Mile End. Yet the chronicler emphasizes writing so persistently, in the clerk called to inscribe, the knight to read aloud, and the commons to reply in writing, that some connection between the commons' anger and the emphasis on literate exchange is implied. Indeed, the chronicler proposes a cause-and-effect relation between this episode and the next that can only be understood as predicated on the commons' hostility to literate exchange: "And when the commons had heard the bill, they said it was nothing but a trifle and a mockery. Therefore [*purceo*] they returned to London and had it cried around the city that all lawyers, all the men of the Chancery and the Exchequer and everyone who could write a writ or a letter should be beheaded, wherever they could be found."[18] As in the passage cited above from Thomas Walsingham, the *Anonimalle Chronicle* here subsumes violence against writers under a generalized hostility to documents.

How might we read these attacks on writing? They contribute to historians' analyses of popular attitudes toward judicial institutions, corruption, or tenure of land. From a more generalized perspective, the rebels' attacks on writing together with their demand for new charters perceive writing to be an instrument of control. Claude Lévi-Strauss concludes in his "Writing Lesson" that control of others is the dominant function of writing in a culture where some are literate and others are not. When Lévi-Strauss gives pencils and paper to the illiterate Nambikwara of Brazil, they imitate the writing he does to record data by making wavy lines; soon thereafter the leader of the group uses such a piece of "writing" at a gift exchange with an unfriendly group "to amaze his companions and persuade them that his intermediacy was responsible for the exchanges" by "enhancing the prestige and authority of one individual—or one function—at the expense of the rest of the party."[19] At first angry at the ignorant misuse of a skill designed to promote understanding, remembering, and knowing, the anthropologist proposes on reflection that from the earliest to modern times, the appearance of writing in cultures correlates not with an increase in knowledge but with the development of complex social hierarchies. "If my hypothesis is correct, the primary function of writing, as a means of communication, is to facilitate the enslavement of other human beings." [20] The Nambikwara leader, Lévi-Strauss concludes, has in fact apprehended the essence of writing in using his imitation document to establish control over the distribution of gifts.

Several features of Lévi-Strauss's account find echoes in the events of 1381. The widespread burning of documents suggests that to the rebels writing appeared innately to be an instrument of oppression. Manorial and court rolls having to do directly with rebel grievances were not the only targets of the revolt. Miscellaneous papers and books were also seized and burned at manor houses, as well as papers belonging to small households.

The rebels who sacked Edmund de la Mare's manor impaled a bundle of Admiralty papers on a pitchfork to carry before them when they marched on to London.[21] Various private animosities and local hostilities could account for the range of papers destroyed in 1381, but only if the rebels had already a global perception of the power of writing that would channel particular animosities into this most characteristic act of the rising.

A second parallel between the rebels and the Nambikwara of Lévi-Strauss's "Writing Lesson" is their attempt to appropriate writing as a means of control. To the Nambikwara leader's paper marked with his own wavy lines we might compare the rebels' new charters dictated to their own specifications. According to the *Anonimalle Chronicle*, King Richard's clerks spent a full day writing out "chartres et patentes et protectiones" to the rebels' requirements. Walsingham reports that in Bury St. Edmunds the rebels exacted a promise from the monks that they would seal a charter to be drawn up by the rebels themselves, and that in St. Albans the charter the abbot was compelled to write proved inadequate to the rebels' wishes, so that a clerk was called forth to attempt to take down the words of the assembled crowd.[22] Both chroniclers and modern historians have called the faith of the rebels in their new charters naive: Jean Froissart describes those who are pleased with Richard's charters at Mile End as "the simple, ignorant, plain men who had come there without knowing what they wanted."[23] But insofar as they have at least imitated the act of writing as an act of control, the rebels have grasped the functional authority of writing in their culture.

Like the Nambikwara leader's piece of paper, however, the rebels' charters do not carry authority with the literate. Lévi-Strauss's initial outrage at having his superior function of writer usurped by those he believes ignorant of that function stresses again the hierarchizing potential of literacy and the low esteem in which those who are comparatively unlettered can easily come to be held. "So the Nambikwara had learnt what it meant to write!" Lévi-Strauss exclaims to himself, "But not at all, as one might have supposed, as the result of a laborious apprenticeship." The anthropologist is at first angered that the tribal leader can use spurious writing to signify falsely that "he had allied himself with the white man, as equal with equal, and could now share in his secrets."[24] If the usurpation of writing by the Nambikwara can so raise the specter of race prejudice within anthropological discourse, it is hardly surprising that the forces of order in 1381 responded with dismissive scorn to the rebels' new documents. In Ospringe as in other towns, according to Froissart, the king and council held inquiries and executed rebel leaders, "and the letters that had been given and accorded to them were requested, and they were brought and surrendered to the king's men, who tore them and cast them to the ground in the presence of all the people." Henry Knighton writes that charters of manumission were "broken, annulled, and judged void and invalid" by the Westminster Parliament of 1381. Burned rentals, titles, and other documents were gradually recreated and assigned the value of the originals.[25] In Walsingham's version, the particular imagery of Richard's repudiation of the liberties given at Mile End substitutes for the rebels' written charters the text of their bodies, on which will be inscribed the dangers of rebellion: "Rustics you were and rustics you remain. . . . For as long as we live . . . we will strive to trample on you so that your slavery may be an example to posterity, and so that those like you may now and in future have always before their eyes as if in a book *[tanquam pro speculo]* your misery and reasons for cursing you and for fearing to do such things as you have done."[26] The rebellious rustics are made an instructive *speculum* for rustics; they are not themselves writers but the ground on which Richard and his magnates will record the necessity of servitude for all to read.

The substitution of the rebels' bodies for their charters raises a limitation in Lévi-Strauss's model, suggestive as it is for the relation of the rebels to documents in 1381. By making instructive texts of his subjects, Richard illustrates that conventional writing is not the only means of authoritative articulation: speeches, gestures, and punishments are further communications that can carry authority. Thus the validity of Lévi-Strauss's distinction between literacy and illiteracy is called into question in Jacques Derrida's response to "A Writing Lesson," and a revision is proposed that can, I believe, better describe the situation of the rebels in relation to writing and to their larger culture.

Derrida accepts as evident the association between literacy and stratification. "It has long been known that the power of writing in the hands of a small number, caste, or class, is always contemporaneous with hierarchization," he agrees, although he questions whether hierarchization must always imply domination.[27] For Derrida a particular weakness of Lévi-Strauss's formulation lies in the claim that writing—"linear and phonetic notation"—can be considered separately from speaking. Writing and speech are both symbolic systems based on the perception of differences between symbols, sounds, and concepts that represent rather than reproduce the world. If writing and speech are understood as two aspects of a global "arche-writing," then "it should be possible to say that all societies capable of . . . bringing classificatory difference into play, practice writing in general. No reality or concept would therefore correspond to the expression 'society without writing.'"[28] The Nambikwara can "write" in this larger sense, as can their anthropologist, as can England's peasants, lords, and clerics alike, in knowing the world through systems of classificatory difference.

This analysis leads me to consider the speaking as well as the writing situation of the rebels. What does it matter if they are unlettered, so long as they can practice arche-writing? The link between speech and writing provided by the Derridean concept of arche-writing critiques the hierarchical social distinction between literacy and illiteracy, but it does not better the representational status of the rebels in their own time. Rather, the spuriousness of the distinction between speaking and writing clarifies the degree to which literate culture silences the lower social strata in medieval texts generally. As I noted at the outset, the rebels of 1381 are beyond our apprehension insofar as they do not represent themselves for the written record. To that extent, they are beyond the apprehension of their contemporaries as well. The lower social strata become for those who write an alien, incoherent Other in contradistinction to whom writers can lay claim to reasoned articulation and discursive meaningfulness. I believe this familiar point calls for only brief discussion, after which I will move on to qualify the point by looking to some writing that seems outside its limits: the letters said to have been written by the rebels themselves and passages in works of Langland and Chaucer that may respond to the revolt. My conclusion will be that inarticulateness remains a defining characteristic of the lower orders even in writing that recognizes their sorry condition and the mechanisms of suppression that silence them.

That the chronicles of 1381 relegate the rebels to the status of beasts, monstrosities, or misguided fools is a well-known function of the writers' attempts to condemn the revolt and make good sense of its repression. Noting how oddly the chroniclers' narration of acts that illustrate planning and self-discipline among the rebels collides with assertions that those same rebels are mindless and bestial, Paul Strohm concludes that the "total strategy" of the chronicles is "to discredit the social standing, judgment, and objectives of the rebels at every level of representation."[29] In his penetrating analysis Strohm retrieves some indications of rebel ideology and demands from the chronicles' distortions. For my focus on the chronicles' overt strategies of silencing, it is particularly relevant that those who write about the rising tend to discount the rebel demands they report and to emphasize the raw vocalization of rebels. John Gower's experience of the revolt becomes a dream-vision in which the rebels' moral corruption is made evident in their transformations into wild animals. A "jackdaw well-trained in the art of speaking" addresses the crowd, "O miserable servile race, whom the world has subjected for a long time by its law, now behold, the day has come when the serfs will triumph and force the free men to leave their lands. May all honor cease, may justice perish, and may no virtue that existed heretofore persist any longer on earth." This morally twisted speech is an exception to the utter wordlessness characteristic of the mob: "They cried over and over in the great voices of monsters and in various ways made a variety of noises."[30] For Froissart and Knighton, too, the rebels' cries express most tellingly the error of their cause: on first seeing King Richard the crowd "gave such a huge cry that it truly seemed as if all the devils of hell were among them"; once inside London, "neither fearing God nor revering the honour of mother church, they pursued and executed all those against whom they raised their noisy cry."[31] Walsingham also represents the rebels' desires through his conviction of their irrationality: they "hoped to subject all things to their own stupidity"; when

committing violence "words could not be heard among their horrible
shrieks but rather their throats sounded with the bleating of sheep, or, to
be more accurate, with the devilish voices of peacocks."[32] Noise replaces
speech. The chroniclers guarantee the lucidity of their own accounts in
part by repudiating the rebels' senseless racket. The rebels of the chronicles have nothing meaningful to communicate; the meaning of the revolt
lies beyond their agency, whether in God's decision to punish the world's
sins or in faults within the administration of government.

Despite conceiving the rebels as an inarticulate mob, the chroniclers occasionally note a leader's eloquence and two even reproduce letters supposedly written by the rebels. These English letters invade the authoritative
Latin of the narrative account with words as close as we can come to those
of the rebels, yet the message of the letters is obscure. One way to understand (but not illuminate) their obscurity is to propose that they deliberately veil references to contemporary events. Dobson believes the letters may be coded: "these 'dark sayings' . . . have created more problems
than they have solved. On this occasion we are confronted with evidence
that is intentionally obscure"; Nick Ronan concludes that "these letters
are anti-allegories, since their purpose is not to provide enlightenment, but
disguise." [33] A contrary way to make sense of the letters is to align them
with orthodox poetic topoi of their period. R. H. Robbins notes a particularly close similarity between Knighton's "prima epistola Johannis
Balle" and conventional "abuses of the age" poetry:

John Balle seynte Marye prist gretes wele alle maner men and
byddes hem in the name of the Trinite, Fadur, and Sone and Holy
Gost stonde manlyche togedyr in trewthe, and helpez trewthe, and
trewthe schal helpe 3owe. Now regneth pride in pris, and covetys is
hold wys, and leccherye withouten shame and glotonye withouten
blame. Envye regniþ with tresone, and slouthe is take in grete se-
sone. God do bote, for nowe is tyme amen.[34]

> Now pride ys yn pris,
> Now couetyse ys wyse,
> Now lechery ys schameles,
> Now gloteny ys lawles,
> Now slewþe ys yn seson,
> In envie & wreþe ys treson;
> Now haþ god enchesyn
> to dystrie þys worle by reson.[35]

Other rebel letters are similarly conventional in images and diction, as
Richard Firth Green's essay in this volume amply demonstrates. If we are
to read sedition in the letters, we must catch at a few words such as the
closing "nowe is tyme" of Ball's first letter, echoed in other letters, the ex-

hortations to "stonde manlyche togedyr" and "be war," and the repeated emphasis on "trewthe" pointed out by Green. Even these sentiments would, however, be innocent in other contexts.[36]

Context indeed provides the surest argument that the letters mean more than their words can convey, and the appeal to context originates with the chronicles themselves. Walsingham declares the letter he quotes to be "full of enigmas" but provides his own meaning by bracketing his citation of the letter with its discovery in the tunic of a hanged man and its role in the hanging of John Ball: however obscure, these are words deserving death.[37] Alternatively, Green proposes that the letters may be innocent of seditious intent but that in 1381 they came to be understood as veiled invitations to revolt. I believe it is possible that the letters meant more to the rebels as documents per se than as meaningful messages: whatever the writing said or failed to say, the letters would have provided those normally beyond the pale of literate culture with documents of their own to pass from hand to hand.

As to the content of the letters, my point is that whether the words are intentionally obscure or simply unstable in ways that permit contradictory interpretation, their meaning is lost to us. Are the chroniclers reimagining rebel letters they saw or heard at an earlier time, using the topoi of clerical poetry familiar to them? Or is written expression so fully the province of the privileged that the letters, even if genuine, say less about popular culture than about culture imposed on the populace from above? Whether, with Ronan, we attribute the letters' obscurity to a "shared masonic code of addresser and addressee" or, with John Scattergood, to an unfamiliarity with writing that gave the rebels "no more appropriate way of speaking in verse," the letters do not communicate to us successfully.[38] They illustrate again that the rebels are effectively voiceless within literate discourse. By including letters attributed to the rebels and yet asserting the rebels' inarticulateness, the chronicles further illustrate that to be accorded a voice within a dominant culture, it is not enough for a suppressed group to practice "arche-writing." Recognizing a voice is a political gesture. When the French revolutionary Sieyes elaborates his brief answer to what the third estate wants, "to become something" involves speaking, being heard, and achieving representation: the government should respond not to writers on human rights but to the many petitions of municipalities; the state should elect not defenders of the third estate's interests but members of the third estate itself.[39] From his position outside the third estate, Sieyes is engaged in the very advocacy he argues must be surpassed, but he moves beyond medieval chroniclers in his willingness to find meaning in the vocalizations of the commons.[40] In the fourteenth century the lower social strata are legally and ideologically inferior to such a degree that in the circles of power their own speech and writing cannot successfully represent them. They must be spoken for by other social groups rather than speaking for themselves.

Some writing treats the voicelessness of exploited groups not simply as a feature of their low status but as a constructed situation that might be questioned. Two passages from Langland and Chaucer can illustrate briefly how we might look to literary works for reactions to the rising of 1381.

The rebel letters invoke *Piers Plowman*, current in the B-text version before 1381, in urging that "Peres the Plowman my brother duelle at home and dy3t us corne" and that followers "doþ wele and ay bettur and bettur," referring to the visions of Dowel and Dobet; Hobbe the Robber, unless a proverbial name, may echo Langland's Robert the Robber. The *Dieulacres Abbey Chronicle* records names of the rebel leaders John B, Jack Straw, and Per Plowman, suggesting a wider currency for Piers's name than in the letters alone.[41] Yet Langland's work does not advocate manumission or radical changes in existing social and political structures. Although Langland's sympathy for the oppressed is obvious, like many contemporaries he attributes oppression to wrongful distortions of fundamentally valid institutions. Moreover, Langland is not so much a political analyst as a religious thinker. His ideas and his audience are in many respects removed from the ferocious confrontations of 1381.[42] In figuring Piers as their ally in rebellion, the authors (or author) of the letters were misappropriating a work they perhaps knew only slightly and imperfectly.

Some of Langland's revisions in the C-text of *Piers* seem to react against that misappropriation. In relation to the widespread destruction of documents in 1381, it is suggestive that Piers's angry tearing of the written pardon in the B-text is deleted from the C-text.[43] Langland's positions are sufficiently nuanced, however, that revisions apparently conservative and even hostile to the 1381 rebels bear close attention. The revision to the Prologue's account of the ideal state is a case in point:

> Thanne come there a kyng; kny3thode hym ladde;
> Mi3t of the comunes made hym to regne.
> And thanne cam kynde wytte, and clerkes he made
> For to conseille the kyng and the comune saue.
> The kyng and kny3thode and clergye bothe
> Casten that the comune shulde hem-self fynde.
> The comune contreued of kynde witte craftes,
> And for profit of alle the poeple, plowmen ordeygned,
> To tilie and trauaile as trewe lyf asketh.
> The kynge and the comune and kynde witte the thridde
> Shope lawe and lewte, eche man to knowe his owne.
> (B 112-22)[44]

> Thenne cam ther a kyng, knyghthede hym ladde,
> Myght of tho men made hym to regne.
> And thenne cam Kynde Wytt and clerkus he made
> And Conscience and Kynde Wit and knyghthed togedres

211

> Caste þat þe comunes sholde here comunes fynde.
> Kynde Wytt and þe comune contreued alle craftes
> And for most profitable a plogh gonne þei make,
> With lele labour to lyue while lif on londe lasteth.
>
> (C 139-46)[45]

The changes recorded in these lines invite us to consider the relevance of the 1381 rising that intervenes between them. E. Talbot Donaldson and others have associated the rising to the shift from the B-text's "mi3t of the comunes made hym to regne" to the C-text's "myght of tho men [i.e., the "knighthede" of the preceding line] made hym to regne." According to Donaldson, Langland intended by "mi3t of the comunes" to indicate the whole commonwealth, which in constitutional theory is the source of the power to rule, but after the events of 1381 he subsumed the common-wealth into the might of the second estate so as to correct the misapprehension that by "comunes" he meant the third estate alone, the commons. Donaldson concludes that Langland's revision is still in line with current constitutional theory and avoids the potential misapprehension that the common people determine who rules: "The C-revision, though made at a certain sacrifice in breadth of conception, is unequivocal."[46]

I am not convinced that the historical author's attempt to avoid mis-understanding can describe the range of revisions in this passage. Once the term "comunes" is removed and "knyghthede" substituted, it does not matter whether "comunes" referred to the whole commonwealth or just to the common people: in either case, commoners have been excluded from establishing the ideal state. Further revisions in the passage contribute to suppressing the agency of commoners. The B-text evokes the trifunctional model in which each estate's role contributes importantly to the general good: knights, clerics, and commoners have separate functions connected with rule, counsel, and production of food, respectively; each has an area of initiative in working "for profit of alle the poeple." The C-text effaces the trifunctional ideal by deleting roles for clerics in counseling the king and saving the commons, and by revising or deleting those passages where two estates cooperate (B 112-13, 116-17, 121-22). The shift from "for profit of alle the poeple" to "for most profitable" also shies away from the social ideal of estates that work separately to sustain one another. Further, the C-text's alterations attribute an inertness to the commons that contrasts with the B-text's images: a plow metonymically replaces plowmen, re-ducing the peasant's significance to that of an implement; a pun on "com-mons" and "food" similarly identifies the estate with its product only; and the closing ideal of "lele labour" replaces the B-text's closing emphasis on the active shaping of society by its members.

Although I am arguing that Langland's revisions suppress and enmargin-ate the common people more decisively than Donaldson, Bloomfield, and others would suggest, it does not necessarily follow that Langland's text censures the rebels of 1381. The same revisions that, in ideological terms, restrict the commons also betray, in the very act of revision, that ideal systems are constructed rather than fixed truths. While the direction of the revisions validates suppression, the text's mobility simultaneously asserts the temporal contingency of the revised model under which the plowman is as silent and without agency as the plow.

Thus Langland's revisions can be read as a reconsideration of the conventional estates model in relation to the rising of 1381. The B-text passage is strikingly orthodox in its version of the separate functions of the interdependent estates. A contemporary account of Richard II's coronation presents the roles of the estates similarly. According to the *Anonimalle Chronicle*, the lords of the realm lead Richard to Westminster Abbey for coronation. A host of clergy participate in the consecration; at a certain point the Archbishop of Canterbury "asked the commons [*communes*] if they wanted to assent and to take Prince Richard as their king." The question is clearly addressed to the common people attending the ceremony, not to representatives of the Parliamentary Commons or to all in attendance without respect to estate. The *Anonimalle Chronicle* uses the term "poeple" to refer to undifferentiated groups of people—for example, the archbishop demands "before the people in a loud voice" if Richard will maintain the laws and customs of England—and uses "communes" to refer earlier to the lesser citizens in the streets of London, later to the rebels of 1381, and thus here to the common people at the coronation. The archaic and primarily theoretical model of the three estates is thus acted out ceremonially: the second estate presents Richard for coronation ("kny3thode hym ladde"), the first estate annoints the king, and "mi3t of the comunes made hym to regne": in the *Anonimalle Chronicle* ceremony "they answered with a great cry and noise: 'Yes, we want it.'"[47]

The revised estates passage in Langland's C-text makes sense as an ideologically grounded repudiation of the rebels' actions and their citations of *Piers Plowman*, yet the passage also makes contrary sense as an acknowledgment of the gap between ideology and event that was made evident in both the rising of 1381 and its suppression. The passage cited above from the C-text, in constricting the role of the common people and reducing the interdependence of estates, tallies with the relations among estates as they appeared after the rising. From that perspective, the "yes" of the coronation ceremony, suggestively joined to the "great cry and noise" of the mob, does not appear to be a meaningful assent. Rather, it is a predetermined response that has been scripted for commoners: it would not be possible for them to answer "no." Spoken to and spoken for, the commons do not speak on their own terms.

Chaucer's works also express the limitations on the commons in terms of speaking and writing. Many instances are worthy of discussion, such as the comparison in the *Nun's Priest's Tale* between the noisy fox chase and the "shoutes half so shrille" of Jack Straw and his followers (VII.3395), the

Plowman's positioning as the only major figure from the *General Prologue* who is not assigned a tale to tell, the lower birds in the *Parliament of Fowls* crying "Kek kek! kokkow! quek quek!" so loudly "that thourgh myne eres the noyse wente tho" (lines 499-500), and the Miller interrupting the Host's ordered plan for the *Canterbury Tales* with drunken insistence that he may "mysspeke" (I.3139).[48] Each instance of the commons' racket, silence, or misspeaking remanipulates incoherence as a touchstone of low status. Critics have treated each in terms of Chaucer's depiction of social hierarchy and political tensions. For my focus on the rebels' relation to writing in 1381, the closing encounter of the *Wife of Bath's Prologue* is the most intriguing passage in Chaucer's work. Here the physical destruction of Jankyn's book consummates a resistance to authority in which texts are persistently in evidence as constraints on behavior and identity.

In an important article on the historical situation of Chaucer's ideological allegiances, Lee Patterson argues that the *Miller's Tale* articulates a peasant consciousness that is opposed to "the tyrannical embrace of dominant ideology" in its parodic inversions of the *Knight's Tale*, its celebration of the natural world, and its narrator's wit and eloquence, which prove "that the peasant is not the inarticulate and brutal figure that hostile representations had depicted."[49] But, according to Patterson, "this embrace of peasant self-confidence is immediately registered as threatening, and the subsequent development of the *Tales* serves to contain this threat—a containment that is accomplished first by the Wife of Bath." For although she (as a clothmaker) and the Miller are both representatives of "the aggressive rural economy that was threatening seigneurial/mercantile dominance," the Wife claims a "socially undetermined subjectivity that stands apart from *all* forms of class consciousness," in contrast to the Miller whose "challenge is class-determined." For Patterson, the Wife of Bath sustains dominant ideology against "political or social change" by conceiving herself as a private subjectivity outside of social construction, internalizing class-based oppositions to the private realm of marriage and socially undetermined selfhood.[50]

Patterson's argument is far more subtle than this summary can indicate, but with regard only to the Wife's ideological positioning I would argue that she is so visibly and powerfully constructed by estates ideology and clerical antifeminism that we cannot understand her as a private subjectivity, nor does she so understand herself. Patterson justly notes that, subsequent to her identification as a clothmaker in her *General Prologue* portrait, Alison of Bath expresses no consciousness of class identity or resistance to feudal institutions. Clothmaking is not, in fact, how she lives; rather, she wins money by marrying repeatedly and cajoling, browbeating, or outliving her husbands. But the suppression of her trade in favor of her identity as a wife does not at all entail that she perceive herself to have no place in social structures and no interests or antagonisms that are in-

stitutionally determined. She consistently speaks through and against clerical antifeminist literature, which assigns women social identity according
to their relations with men and determines those relations to be always
deleterious. As wives, despite their apparent differences in age and temperament, women will always make their husbands suffer:

> . . . right as wormes shende a tree
> Right so a wyf destroyeth hire housbonde;
> This knowe they that been to wyves bonde.
> (III.376-78)

Constructed herself from these literary antecedents, the Wife turns on
them to attempt an argument against the position of inferiority they posit
for women.

In so doing she identifies herself as the voice of a maligned group, a
group outside literate culture and thus disadvantaged at countering literate
culture's authority. To assert with Patterson that the Wife, in arguing for
the worth of female sovereignty, does not want "political or social change"
is to exile gender and gender relations to the realm of the depoliticized
"self" as if they had no political or social implications. The *Wife of Bath's
Prologue* resists this move by persistently referring Alison's identity, gestures, and voice to those of wives generally as they are represented in writings of the first estate. Alison presents herself as a "wys wif" among many
whose confidantes resemble her: a gossip with her own name of Alison,
"another worthy wyf" (III.536), her niece, and her mother. Her adversaries
she also identifies as a social group—clerics, specifically in their capacity
as writers. Their authoritative texts, she argues, are subjectively shaped by
their peculiar way of life, and could be answered by women's texts if wom-
en could write (III.688-710). Although Chaucer's performance is highly literary, even a literary insiders' joke in that it invites the wife created by
antifeminist writing to argue for her worthiness in the teeth of her constructed unworthiness, still the analogies between the *Wife of Bath's Prologue* and the rising of 1381 are so striking as to deserve commentary. Alison shares with the rebels inferior status, exclusion from literate circles, a
sense of undervaluation by the powerful, and a consequent hostility to
writing as the instrument of these interrelated oppressions.

An account of the 1381 rising in MS Arundel 350 describes a scene particularly reminiscent of Alison's and Jankyn's final confrontation. In Cambridge, as in St. Albans and Bury St. Edmunds, the rebels' dispute with the
powerful was inextricably bound up with anticlerical sentiment. The Cambridge scholars' extensive privileges and immunities were attacked in sei-
zures of documents and books alike and in one large bonfire in the market
square where "a certain old woman named Margaret Starre scattered the
heap of ashes to the wind, crying 'Away with the knowledge of clerks,
away with it.'"[51] This account encapsulates several aspects of Alison's nar-

rative: a woman of low status is the site for conflating resistance to clerical authority with a wider hostility to clerical learning; the woman's words equate a concrete instance of book burning with the extinction of learned perspectives in general. Indeed, Alison even presents burning her clerical husband's book as part of their reconciliation, a mutual step toward a new order rather than an act of destruction:

> And whan I saugh he wolde nevere fyne
> To reden on this cursed book al nyght,
> Al sodeynly thre leves have I plyght
> Out of his book, right as he radde. . . .
> . . . .
> But atte laste, with muchel care and wo,
> We fille acorded by us selven two.
> He yaf me al the bridel in myn hond,
> To han the governance of hous and lond,
> And of his tonge, and of his hond also;
> And made hym brenne his book anon right tho.
> (III.788-91, 811-16)

The two women's claims are radical, yet also suspect, in celebrating destruction and in suggesting that fundamental changes can arise from limited acts of destruction. The Wife of Bath and Margaret Starre are characteristically feminine by clerical antifeminist standards in their hostility to learning as well as to writing and in their irrational conviction that clerical learning can simply be done away with. In the wider narrative plan of the chronicles, such claims exemplify the outrageous unreason of the rebels and justify the punishments later meted out to them. In Arundel 350, Margaret Starre's act is the ultimate example of misbehavior before the concluding observation that "the aforesaid malefactors suffered a fitting punishment for their execrable wickedness."[52] Chaucer's narrative is more complex. Alison's closing hyperboles communicate both the appeal of her vision and its status as romantic fantasy:

> After that day we hadden never debaat.
> God helpe me so, I was to hym as kynde
> As any wyf from Denmark unto Ynde,
> And also trewe, and so was he to me.
> (III.822-25)

The otherworldly perfection of this vision contributes to its beauty while expressing its impossibility. It is not to be taken seriously as reportage, but as an expression of desire that takes no real shape. If the *Wife of Bath's Prologue* can be said to evoke the rising of 1381, the text's admixture of violence, illogic, and longing constitutes the most substantial response to the rising in Chaucer's works.

A final feature of Margaret Starre's and Alison of Bath's losing battle is that neither moves beyond condemnation to an articulated alternative. Alison's resort to the language of romance in the closing lines of her *Prologue* is one of many inadequate efforts to describe or defend a worthy female sovereignty. Her destruction of Jankyn's book expresses her opposition to clerical writing about women, but also expresses her inability to communicate to Jankyn, as to her pilgrim audience, a coherent argument in defense of women's authority over men. She is a notoriously self-contradictory and unreliable speaker, misusing her sources, lying to her husbands, and shifting her versions of what she wants throughout her prologue.[53] Her attempts at self-justification illustrate the clerical claim that women are by nature unreasonable yet verbose: as Chaucer's own Clerk puts it, "Ay clappeth as a mille, I yow consaille. . . . The arwes of thy crabbed eloquence / Shal perce his brest" (IV.1200, 1203-4). The topos of woman's incoherence, which R. Howard Bloch has recently termed "woman as riot," again resonates with literary representations of the rebels as self-contradictory, irrational, and noisy—which is to say effectively voiceless.[54]

Yet Alison does not simply reiterate antifeminist topoi in her own contradictions as in her chosen citations. Incoherence itself bears a message in the *Wife of Bath's Prologue*. Here again I differ from Patterson's analysis of the *Miller's Tale* in relation to the rising of 1381 and the Wife of Bath. It is true that there is nothing "crabbed" about the Miller's eloquence: his is a virtuoso performance. But it is a performance within a recognized genre familiar in court literature, the fabliau of bumbling peasants and small-town manipulators who amuse the more sophisticated audience with their simple wit. The Miller respeaks a form already established in literary culture, albeit so brilliantly that some endorsement of lower-class capability may well be implicit in his narration. The Wife of Bath attempts to speak against an established discourse, and in so doing moves beyond cultural paradigms toward positions unprecedented in medieval literature. In staging the impossibility of speaking beyond literate paradigms, Chaucer makes the voicelessness of suppressed groups a subject rather than an unconsidered condition of his writing. He returns us to Sieyes's revolutionary formulation of what the third estate has been, "nothing," and what it wants, "to become something." Insubstantial as that expression of desire may be—desire for a "something" as yet unexperienced and unarticulated—its inscription in writing is a first recognition that those outside literate culture may indeed have something to say.

Notes

I am very grateful to Ed Cohen, Lisa DiCaprio, Susan Gal, and Maryanne Kowaleski for particular suggestions in the early stages of this project, and to Caroline Barron, Barbara Hanawalt, Maryanne Kowaleski, and Paul Strohm for their thoughtful comments on the project as a whole.

1. Emmanuel Sieyes, *Qu'est-ce que le Tiers état?* ed. Roberto Zapperi (Geneva, 1970), p. 119.

2. Derek Pearsall, "Interpretative Models for the Peasants' Revolt," in *Hermeneutics and Medieval Culture,* ed. Patrick J. Gallacher and Helen Damico (Albany, N.Y., 1989), p. 67. Examples of historical essays that attend particularly to the problems of bias and influence are Andrew Prescott, "London in the Peasants' Revolt: A Portrait Gallery," *London Journal* 7 (1981), 125-43; and V. H. Galbraith, "Thoughts about the Peasants' Revolt," in *The Reign of Richard II: Essays in Honour of May McKisack,* ed. F. R. H. Du Boulay and Caroline Barron (London, 1971), pp. 46-57.

3. R. B. Dobson, "The Risings in York, Beverley and Scarborough, 1380-81," in *The English Rising of 1381,* ed. R. H. Hilton and T. H. Aston (Cambridge, Eng., 1984), p. 141.

4. A. F. Butcher, "English Urban Society and the Revolt of 1381," in *The English Rising,* ed. Hilton and Aston, pp. 85, 110.

5. Rodney Hilton, *Bond Men Made Free: Medieval Peasant Movements and the English Rising of 1381* (London, 1973), p. 184.

6. Accounts of the disturbances in Bury St. Edmunds and St. Albans suggest that some rebels in those towns were literate; these are for Hilton exceptions to the generally lower social level of the rebels in other areas (*Bond Men,* p. 198). According to Thomas Walsingham, the rebelling tenants of Bury St. Edmunds asked the townspeople to verify the contents of documents the monks had surrendered (Walsingham, *Historia Anglicana,* ed. H. T. Riley, Rolls Series No. 28, pt. 1, 2 vols. [London, 1863, 1864], 2:4).

7. Jo Ann Hoeppner Moran, *The Growth of English Schooling, 1340-1548: Learning, Literacy, and Laicization in Pre-Reformation York Diocese* (Princeton, N.J., 1985), pp. 178, 181; David Cressy, *Literacy and the Social Order: Reading and Writing in Tudor and Stuart England* (Cambridge, Eng., 1980), p. 176. Cressy's percentages are for inability to sign; he comments that "writing skills were the preserve of a very small minority, although probably a somewhat greater proportion could read" (p. 176).

8. Moran notes that "sons of the poor had traditionally been denied access to a clerical education. Despite this, there are notices scattered throughout fourteenth-century memorial rolls of serfs paying fines for licenses to enable their sons to attend school and occasional examples of serfs refusing to pay at all" (*English Schooling,* p. 175). But these sons are receiving schooling by shifting from common to clerical status, whereas the rebels of 1381 were by and large commoners rather than clerics. In towns, some schooling seems to have been compatible with maintaining artisan status in the fourteenth century (p. 177).

9. M. T. Clanchy, *From Memory to Written Record: England, 1066-1307* (Cambridge, Mass., 1979), pp. 34-35; this enfranchisement is for Clanchy not dependent on the ability to read or write: "Neither the medieval seal nor the modern sign manual on a document indicates that the signatory has anything more than a minimal competence in the skills of literacy" (p. 184).

10. Brian Stock, *The Implications of Literacy: Written Language and Models of Interpretation in the Eleventh and Twelfth Centuries* (Princeton, N.J., 1983), p. 529.

11. Carlo Ginzburg, *The Cheese and the Worms: The Cosmos of a Sixteenth-Century Miller,* trans. John and Anne Tedeschi (Baltimore, Md., 1980), p. 9.

12. Clanchy, *From Memory to Written Record,* pp. 32-38; see also Christopher Dyer, "The Social and Economic Background to the Rural Revolt of 1381," in *The English Rising,* ed. Hilton and Aston, pp. 9-42.

13. *Statutes of the Realm,* vol. 2 (1816; reprint, London, 1963), pp. 2-3; Rosamond Faith, "The 'Great Rumour' of 1377 and Peasant Ideology," in *The English Rising,* ed. Hilton and Aston, pp. 43-73; J. H. Tillotson, "Peasant Unrest in the England of Richard II: Some Evidence from Royal Records," *Historical Studies* 16 (1974), 1-16. Of the twenty exemplifications requested in 1377, Tillotson finds one to have been successful (pp. 2-3).

14. E. g. John Wyclif, *The English Works of Wyclif*, ed. F. D. Matthew, EETS, OS 74 (London, 1880), pp. 233-34: "also lordis many tymes don wrongis to pore men . . . & taken pore mennus goodis & paien not þerfore but white stickis, & dispisen hem & manassen hem & sumtyme beten hem whanne þei axen here peye." See also William Langland, *Piers Plowman: The B Version*, ed. George Kane and E. Talbot Donaldson, rev. ed. (London, 1988), Passus IV, lines 57-58. Janet Coleman notes the importance of literacy to control in the fourteenth century: the middle strata grow in influence "by money and by the professions that required their practitioners to possess the skills of literacy that, in effect, made them England's legislators: in Parliament, in the market place, in the law courts" (*Medieval Readers and Writers, 1350-1400* [New York, 1981], p. 14).

15. G. M. Trevelyan, *England in the Age of Wycliffe* (London, 1909), p. 218.

16. Dyer, "Social and Economic Background," p. 12.

17. Walsingham, *Historia* 2:9; trans. R. B. Dobson, ed., *The Peasants' Revolt of 1381*, 2nd ed. (London, 1983), p. 364. For this essay I have used extensively Dobson's admirable collection of materials on the rising.

18. *Anonimalle*, pp. 143-44; trans. Dobson, ed., *Peasants' Revolt*, pp. 159-60. For Hilton's analysis, see *Bond Men*, pp. 223-24.

19. Claude Lévi-Strauss, *Tristes Tropiques*, trans. John Russell (London, 1961), pp. 289-90.

20. Lévi-Strauss, *Tristes Tropiques*, p. 292; the passage continues, "The use of writing for disinterested ends, and with a view to satisfactions of the mind in the fields either of science or the arts, is a secondary result of its invention—and may even be no more than a way of reinforcing, justifying, or dissimulating its primary function."

21. Charles Petit-Dutaillis, in André Réville, *Le soulévement des travailleurs d'Angleterre en 1381* (Paris, 1898), p. lxxii.

22. *Anonimalle*, p. 146; Walsingham, *Historia* 2:3-4, 1:474-77. Barbara Harvey describes a document apparently drafted as part of a petition for manumission: "Draft Letters Patent of Manumission and Pardon for the Men of Somerset in 1381," *EngHR* 80 (1965), 89-91.

23. Jean Froissart, *Chroniques*, vol. 10, ed. Gaston Raynaud (Paris, 1897), p. 113.

24. Lévi-Strauss, *Tristes Tropiques*, pp. 289-90.

25. Froissart, *Chroniques*, 10:131; Knighton, *Chronicon* 2:133-34; on the repudiation of extorted documents and recreation of destroyed ones, see *Rotuli Parliamentorum*, 6 vols. (n.c., n.d. [London, 1767-77]), 3:99-100, 114, 116; *Statutes of the Realm*, 2:21, 27; and J. A. Tuck, "Nobles, Commons and the Great Revolt of 1381," in *The English Rising*, ed. Hilton and Aston, pp. 200-202.

26. Walsingham, *Historia* 2:18. I believe *speculum* has in this passage its metaphoric sense of an instructive text, since the terrible punishments are to distinguish the rebels from the onlooking *rustici*, who thus see in the rebels' suffering not their own reflection but a cautionary lesson on the dangers of revolt.

27. Jacques Derrida, *Of Grammatology*, trans. Gayatri Chakravorty Spivak (Baltimore, Md., 1976), pp. 130-31.

28. Derrida, *Grammatology*, p. 109. I have drawn on only one aspect of Derrida's critique, which reads *Tristes Tropiques* against Lévi-Strauss's dissertation and other works and treats the relation of writing to morality ("The Violence of the Letter: From Lévi-Strauss to Rousseau," pp. 101-40). Anthropologists have also argued for the "inextricability of speaking and writing in even those modes of discourse that seem most exclusively a matter of writing and reading" (Wallace Chafe and Deborah Tannen, "The Relation between Written and Spoken Language," *Annual Review of Anthropology* 16 [1987], 383-407 [quotation at p. 398]).

29. Paul Strohm, "'A Revelle!': The Chronicles and Rebel Ideology in 1381," in *Huchon's Arrow: The Social Imagination of Fourteenth-Century Texts* (Princeton, N.J., forthcoming, 1992). Galbraith argues for the *Anonimalle Chronicle*'s lesser prejudice

against the rebels, though he notes the author shares with other chroniclers "the normal upper-class prejudices of his time" ("Thoughts about the Peasants' Revolt," p. 52).

30. John Gower, *Vox Clamantis*, in *The Latin Works* [vol. 4 of *The Complete Works of John Gower*], ed. G. C. Macaulay (Oxford, 1902), pp. 41, 44.

31. Froissart, *Chroniques* 10:106; cf. 10:109 ("chils mescheans peuples huoit si hault que il sambloit que tout li diable d'infer fuissent entre iaulx"); Knighton, *Chronicon*, 2:136; trans. Dobson, ed., *Peasants' Revolt*, p. 185.

32. Walsingham, *Historia* 1:454, 460; trans. Dobson, ed., *Peasants' Revolt*, pp. 132, 173.

33. Dobson, ed., *Peasants' Revolt*, p. 379; Nick Ronan, "1381: Writing in Revolt: Signs of Confederacy in the Chronicle Accounts of the English Rising," *Forum for Modern Language Studies* 25 (1989), 307.

34. Knighton, *Chronicon* 2:140; see also the transcriptions of the letters in R. F. Green's appendix to chapter 9, "John Ball's Letters: Literary History and Historical Literature," in this volume.

35. *Historical Poems of the XIVth and XVth Centuries*, ed. Rossell Hope Robbins (New York, 1959), p. xlii.

36. Caroline Barron has pointed out to me that "be war" and "nowe is tyme" are among the phrases cast on church bells in this period; an introduction to bell inscriptions is H. B. Walters, *Church Bells of England* (London, 1912), pp. 315-27.

37. Walsingham, *Historia* 2:33-34.

38. Ronan, "1381," p. 306; John Scattergood, *Politics and Poetry in the Fifteenth Century* (London, 1971), p. 355. Ronan concludes, despite their "uninterpretable word-play" (p. 313), that the letters are subversive because their indeterminate meaning is "in dialogic opposition" to the discursive meaning of official writing such as that of the chronicles (p. 311). I am not convinced that the allegorical technique of the letters attributed to the rebels differs significantly from that of conventional fourteenth-century allegory that is not seditious in content.

39. Sieyes, *Qu'est-ce que le Tiers état?*, pp. 134, 156.

40. On the limitations of the abbé Sieyes's sympathy for the third estate, see William H. Sewell, Jr., "Le Citoyen/la Citoyenne: Activity, Passivity, and the Revolutionary Concept of Citizenship," in *The Political Culture of the French Revolution* [vol. 2 of *The French Revolution and the Creation of Modern Political Culture*], ed. Colin Lucas (New York, 1987), pp. 105-23.

41. Knighton, *Chronicon* 2:139; Walsingham, *Historia* 2:34; on these and further examples see Anne Hudson, "The Legacy of *Piers Plowman*," in *A Companion to "Piers Plowman*," ed. John A. Alford (Berkeley, Calif., and Los Angeles, 1988), pp. 251-66.

42. For examples from the broad critical consensus summarized here, see Morton W. Bloomfield, *Piers Plowman as a Fourteenth-Century Apocalypse* (New Brunswick, N.J., n.d. [1962]); John Burrow, "The Audience of *Piers Plowman*," *Anglia* 75 (1957), 373-84; and A. C. Spearing, *Criticism and Medieval Poetry* (London, 1964), pp. 107-34.

43. *Piers Plowman: The B Version*, Passus VII, 1. 119.

44. *The Vision of William Concerning Piers the Plowman*, ed. Walter W. Skeat, 2 vols. (1886; corr. ed. London, 1924), Prologue, B-text. I quote from Skeat's edition rather than Kane and Donaldson's because the latter revise line 117 to read "Casten þat þe commune sholde [hire communes] fynde." The editors explain that the emendation produces a "normatively alliterative line" and reintroduces the C-text's pun, perhaps omitted by copyists (pp. 92, 135-40); I argue that the unemended line as it stands in almost all B manuscripts is consistent in content with the rest of B's version of the political order, and that the C-text's pun is consistent with its other revisions of the B-text.

45. *Piers Plowman by William Langland: An Edition of the C-text*, ed. Derek Pearsall (Berkeley, Calif., and Los Angeles, 1978), Prologue; on the date of the C-text see pp. 9-10.

46. E. Talbot Donaldson, *Piers Plowman: The C-Text and Its Poet*, Yale Studies in En-

glish 113 (New Haven, Conn., 1949), p. 108. Anna Baldwin provides further background in political philosophy for the C revisions, which she relates to Langland's preference for absolutism [*The Theme of Government in Piers Plowman* [Cambridge, Eng., 1981], pp. 12-23).

47. *Anonimalle*, quotations at pp. 109-10; for contrasting uses of the terms "poeple" and "communes," see also pp. 107, 114, 136-38.

48. All quotations of Chaucer's works are from *The Riverside Chaucer*, 3rd ed., ed. Larry D. Benson et al. (Boston, 1987). On the Plowman as the pilgrim without a tale, Paul Strohm comments that "the complicated exclusions that render Chaucer's mixed commonwealth possible are epitomized in the silence of the Plowman, the single peasant participating in the pilgrimage" (*Social Chaucer* [Cambridge, Mass., 1989], p. 173).

49. Lee Patterson, "'No Man His Reson Herde': Peasant Consciousness, Chaucer's Miller, and the Structure of the *Canterbury Tales*," in *Literary Practice and Social Change in Britain, 1380-1530*, ed. Lee Patterson (Berkeley, Calif., and Los Angeles, 1990), pp. 113-55 (quotations at pp. 137, 148-49). Patterson notes that millers are in some respects outside the peasantry; the 1381 rising, which encompassed other social groups along with peasants, included millers both as participants and as allegorical figures in Walsingham's and Knighton's rebel letters (pp. 125-29).

50. Patterson, "Peasant Consciousness," pp. 123-24, 150 (italics his).

51. London, British Library, MS Arundel 350, fols. 15v-17v (an account of the rising in Cambridge): "Et vetula quedam nomine Margareta Starre cineres collectos in ventum sparsit clamando abcedat clericorum pericia abcedat" (fol. 17v). The bonfire in the Cambridge market is also recounted in the *Rotuli Parliamentorum* 3:108.

52. Arundel 350, fol. 17v: "sed malefactores predicti penam suis nephandis sceleribus dignam subierunt. . . ."

53. I argue this point more fully in "Alison's Incapacity and Poetic Instability in the Wife of Bath's Tale," *PMLA* 102 (1987), 20-28.

54. Bloch, "Medieval Misogyny," *Representations*, no. 20 (Fall 1987), 1-24.

Contributors

⁂

Caroline M. Barron is reader in the history of London in the University of London (Royal Holloway and Bedford New College). She has edited the *Reign of Richard II* (1971) and *The Church in Pre-Reformation Society* (1987), has written *The Medieval Guildhall of London* (1986), and is working on a major study of London in the period 1200-1485.

Michael J. Bennett is reader in history at the University of Tasmania. His *Community, Class, and Careerism: Cheshire and Lancashire in the Age of "Sir Gawain and the Green Knight"* (1983) is a study of the regional society that produced the finest works of the alliterative revival.

Lawrence M. Clopper is a professor of English at Indiana University in Bloomington. He has edited the dramatic records of Chester for *Records of Early English Drama* and has published numerous essays on medieval drama. His contributions on *Piers Plowman* have appeared in *Modern Language Quarterly, Modern Philology, Studies in Philology, Chaucer Review*, and other journals. He is currently completing a book on *Piers Plowman* and is working on the poems of the *Pearl* manuscript.

Susan Crane is an associate professor of English at Rutgers University. She is working on a book that argues for the importance of gender to the genre of romance in Chaucer's *Canterbury Tales*. Her publications include *Insular Romance: Politics, Faith, and Culture in Anglo-Norman and Middle English Literature* and articles in *PMLA, Studies in the Age of Chaucer*, and *The Chaucer Review*.

Richard Firth Green is an associate professor of English at the University of Western Ontario. His *Poets and Prince Pleasers: Literature and the English Court in the Late Middle Ages* (1980) was one of the early books on literature in historical context. He is currently writing a book on law and literature.

Barbara A. Hanawalt is a professor of history at the University of Minnesota and is the author of *Crime and Conflict in English Communities, 1300-1348* (1979) and *The Ties That Bound: Peasant Families in Medieval*

England (1986), and is editor of *Women and Work in Preindustrial Europe* (1986).

Nicholas Orme has written widely on educational, religious, and cultural history including *From Childhood to Chivalry* (1984) and *Education and Society in Medieval and Renaissance England* (1989). He is a professor of history at Exeter University.

Nigel Saul is a reader in Medieval History at Royal Holloway and Bedford New College, University of London, England. The author of two books on English gentry, *Knights and Esquires: The Gloucestershire Gentry in the Fourteenth Century* (1981) and *Scenes from Provincial Life: Knightly Families in Sussex, 1280-1400* (1986), he is currently working on a reissue of Smyth's *Lives of the Berkeleys* and a biography of King Richard II.

Paul Strohm teaches English at Indiana University in Bloomington. He is the author of *Social Chaucer* (1989) and *Huchon's Arrow: The Social Imagination of Medieval Texts* (in press).

David Wallace has taught at St. Edmund's College, Cambridge, and the University of Texas at Austin and is currently Paul W. Frenzel Chair in Medieval Studies and professor of English, University of Minnesota. His publications include *Chaucer and the Early Writings of Boccaccio* (1985) and *Giovanni Boccaccio: Decameron* (1991).

Index

✠

abbeys, 204; Benedictine, at St. Albans, 181; Benedictine priory at Abergavenny, 100; Cistercian, 105; Haughmond, 4; Kingswood, 102; Kyme priory, 135; Waltham, 204; Westminster, 16, 48, 213.
abbots. *See* clergy
Abergavenny, 100
Abingdon, 93
Absolon (character), 71
Adam (Biblical personage), 43, 117
Adam, Master (character), falsifier of the gold florin, 83
Admiralty papers, 206
aequitas, Ciceronian, 67
Aers, David, 48, 84
agents, mercantile, 97
alchemy, 41, 82-83
Aldgate, 48
ale-taker, 61, 63
Alfred, king of England, 142
aliens, 60, 64, 76
Alison (character), 71
All Hallows, parish of, 103
alliterative tradition, 3, 16, 92
alms, xvii, 118, 121-22; almsgiving, xvi, 116
Alnwick Park, 137
amercements, 203
Andreuccio of Perugia (character), 64
Anglesey, 14
Anglo-Norman: language, 62; poems, 144; proclamation of 1391, 85
Anima (character), 98, 123
Annales (Stow), 181
Annales Ricardi Secundi, Regis Angliae (Anon.), 24, 27, 29-30
Anne of Bohemia, queen of England, 10
Anonimalle Chronicle (Anon.), 183, 201, 204-6, 213
Antichrist, 115, 168
antifeminism: clerical, 214-17; literature, 215
apostles, 125
apprentices, xv, xvii, 61, 71-74, 77, 97, 202; female, 73
apprenticeship, 96, 206
approvers (state's evidence), 162-63
arbitration, xv

Archangel Michael (character), 98
archbishops. *See* clergy
archery, 134-41, 147, 160, 169
arche-writing (concept), 207, 210
archives, xi, 179; central estate, 204; Guildhall, 85; legal, destruction of, 190
aristocracy. *See* nobility
army, 68, 72, 162
arson. *See* crime
Art de Venerie (Anon.), 138
Arthur, King (character), 142, 144; literature about, 142, 144
artisans, 67, 96-97, 102, 118, 136, 202; barbers, 63; clothmakers, 96, 214; cordwainers, 76, 102; crafts, 71, 75, 79, 121; craftsmanship, 105; drapers, 76, 97; dyers, 103; embroidery, 73; millers, 158, 203; potters, 158, 167; printers, 92; saddlers, 76; village crafts, 165; weavers, 96
Arundel, 32, 33
Arundel, Archbishop, 135
Arveragus (character), 47
Asser, Bishop, 142
associations, criminal, xx, 155-59, 161-67, 183; Coterels, 166; families as, 158, 161; Folvilles, xix, 166, 168; formal, 156; informal, 156; jail escapes, xviii; leadership, 160-61; membership, xvii, 162-63; military nature of, 162; mobility, 155, 157; organization, 160-62, 170; rules of conduct, xviii; victims (women and children), 165. *See also* bandits, criminals
astrology, 9
Auchinleck MS, 186
audiences, xii, 4-5, 154-56; courtly, 7; of literary works, xxi; medieval, xiv, xvi, 155, 168-69, 185; poets, xiii; primary, 6, 13, 16; secondary, 6; women, xiii
Audley, John, 4-5
Audley, Nicholas, 13
Aurelius (character), 47
authority, city, 73, 78; crown, 75; legal, 119; religious, 62; royal, 170; secular, 62
Aveley, 136
Awntyrs off Arthure, The (Anon.), 144